The Rosenwald Schools of the American South

New Perspectives on the History of the South

UNIVERSITY PRESS OF FLORIDA

Florida A&M University, Tallahassee
Florida Atlantic University, Boca Raton
Florida Gulf Coast University, Ft. Myers
Florida International University, Miami
Florida State University, Tallahassee
University of Central Florida, Orlando
University of Florida, Gainesville
University of North Florida, Jacksonville
University of South Florida, Tampa
University of West Florida, Pensacola

New Perspectives on the History of the South
Edited by John David Smith

The Rosenwald Schools
of the American South

MARY S. HOFFSCHWELLE

Foreword by John David Smith

University Press of Florida
Gainesville/Tallahassee/Tampa/Boca Raton
Pensacola/Orlando/Miami/Jacksonville/Ft. Myers

11 10 09 08 07 06   6 5 4 3 2 1

Library of Congress Cataloging-in-Publication Data
Hoffschwelle, Mary S., 1955–
The Rosenwald Schools of the American South / Mary S. Hoffschwelle;
foreword by John David Smith.
p. cm.—(New perspectives on the history of the South)
Contets: Contents: pt. 1. The Rosenwald school-building program—
pt. 2. Rosenwald schools and public education in southern states.
ISBN 0-8130-2957-0 (alk. paper)
1. African Americans—Education—Southern States—History—
20th century. 2. School buildings—Southern States—History 20th century.
3. Julius Rosenwald Fund—Buildings—Southern States. I. Title. II. Series.
LC2802.S9H64 2006
379.2'630975965   2005058564

The University Press of Florida is the scholarly publishing agency
for the State University System of Florida, comprising Florida A&M
University, Florida Atlantic University, Florida Gulf Coast University,
Florida International University, Florida State University, University
of Central Florida, University of Florida, University of North Florida,
University of South Florida, and University of West Florida.

University Press of Florida
15 Northwest 15th Street
Gainesville, FL 32611–2079
http://www.upf.com

For Van

Contents

Illustrations

Foreword

Historians and writers from Ulrich Bonnell Phillips, C. Vann Woodward, and Howard Zinn to Wilbur J. Cash, William Faulkner, and Lee Smith have underscored the South's distinctiveness. For many persons, the South signifies more than a region. For them, it represents an idea, an abstraction, even an ideology. For some, the South has become an obsession. Since the colonial period, the South has been both connected to and distanced from the rest of North America. Its settlement pattern, its crops, and, most significantly, its commitment to racial slavery earmarked the Old South as different from the rest of the nation. As Woodward noted in 1960, the South has many "burdens." Its defeat in the Civil War and its experiences during and after Reconstruction left an indelible blot on the fabric of southern history. Yet in the twenty-first century, the South seems very much "American"—more like the rest of the country, not some mythic land apart.

Dating back to the 1880s, historians and critics have defined and redefined southern history in innumerable ways. The nationalist historians, the Dunning School, the Agrarians, the revisionists, the postrevisionists, the Marxists, and, today, all manner of postmodernists have tried to squeeze some contemporary meaning from southern history. Historians and others regularly interpret the region's history and culture in such varied journals and magazines as the *Journal of Southern History, Southern Review, Southern Humanities Review, Southern Living, Southern Exposure*, and *Southern Cultures*. In 1979, the *Encyclopedia of Southern History* appeared, followed ten years later by the *Encyclopedia of Southern Culture*. Both within and beyond the region, there seems to be an insatiable appetite for information on the South and its people.

In fact, no other region in America, including New England and the West, has received as much in-depth analysis and reflection as has the American South. Insiders (native southerners) and outsiders (nonsoutherners, including an unusually large number of northern and European specialists on the South) agree that the Southland has a particular Weltanschauung, one loaded with irony, pathos, paradox, and racial and class conflict. Southern history long has reigned as a major research specialty in some universities, which confer doctorates in the field. Many academic publishers consider "southern studies" a strong part of their list. Books about the South sell on both sides of the Mason-Dixon

Line and overseas. Associations and institutions sponsor regular symposia and conferences regionally, nationally, and internationally on the South's past.

In the last century, when the South ranked as "the nation's economic problem No. 1," sociologists dissected the region's pathologies, especially its historic race problem and poverty. Today, social scientists and economists marvel at the "Sun Belt"—its thriving and alluring prosperity built atop long-standing anti-union sentiment, its daunting skyscrapers, its rapid transit systems, its social and racial progress. Atlanta, the region's bourgeois Mecca, has numerous lesser rivals throughout the former Confederacy—Dallas, New Orleans, Miami, Nashville, Charlotte, Raleigh, and Richmond. Cable television, chain restaurants, New York City department stores, malls, and their accompanying outlet shops—even the *New York Times'* "national edition" (printed in several southern cities and delivered to the doorsteps of thousands of southerners)—dot the southern landscape like the proverbial cotton plants of old.

An appreciation of the South's distinctiveness and its diversity lies at the heart of the University Press of Florida's New Perspectives on the History of the South series. This broadly based series publishes the highest-quality new scholarship on the history of the American South. The books cover all aspects and periods of the southern past, with special emphasis on the region's cultural, economic, intellectual, and social history.

Mary S. Hoffschwelle's *The Rosenwald Schools of the American South*, the latest volume in the series, is a deeply researched and highly analytical history of the early twentieth-century rural southern school-building program initiated by Chicago philanthropist Julius Rosenwald and Alabama black leader Booker T. Washington. Between 1913 and 1932, Rosenwald, in tandem with matching grants from state and local school systems and local initiative, constructed 5,358 school buildings for African American students in fifteen states and in virtually every county in the South. These schools introduced modern education to twentieth-century black southerners. They accounted for more than half of the increased value of the region's public school facilities between 1920 and 1930 and contributed significantly to increased school attendance and literacy among black southerners.

Rosenwald envisioned the schools as tangible, lasting structures for African American uplift that would promote black citizenship. According to Hoffschwelle, the schools helped to define twentieth-century African American educational practice and contributed significantly to African American community life. Her history of the Rosenwald schools' conceptualization, funding, and construction illumines competing theories of black education, reveals tensions between philanthropy and paternalism, and illustrates the evolution and broad cultural meaning of public school architecture from the age of Jim Crow to the Great Depression.

While Hoffschwelle underscores the importance of the Rosenwald school-building program to the history of African American education in the South, she contextualizes it within Progressive-era understandings of racial reform— understandings that circumscribed Rosenwald and Washington from the start. Their school-building program never "offered a direct challenge to the discrimi-natory legal system of Jim Crow education that made such a program neces-sary." The Rosenwald schools alone could topple neither decades of insufficient funding for black schools in the post–Civil War South nor centuries of white racism. "That the people involved in building Rosenwald schools," Hoffschwelle writes, "did not solve all of the problems of Jim Crow education is not a failure so much as an indictment of the forces of racism and indifference and the grim determination of black southerners to hammer away at those forces."

As Hoffschwelle explains in her gracefully crafted and beautifully illustrated book, the combination of Rosenwald's philanthropy, funding from state and local sources, and local grassroots activism empowered African Americans and their communities. They viewed their Rosenwald schools with deep pride and a sense of achievement. "Their cooperative efforts secured new spaces for a his-toric African American tradition, new places invested with their cultural capi-tal, that correlated education with community advancement." This was no small factor in the evolution of today's decidedly distinctive and diverse South.

John David Smith
Series Editor

Acknowledgments

Rosenwald schools are the tangible legacy of partnerships forged by thousands of people in the American South. Their creators were people of different backgrounds, experiences, and expectations who sought to transform the landscape of the South. A book about Rosenwald schools is also the result of many partnerships, and I owe many thanks to all the people who have made it possible with their support, knowledge, and wisdom.

Middle Tennessee State University has been very supportive of this project over its long gestation. The Department of History provided release time for research at several crucial points, and the university provided support through faculty research and creative activity grants and a noninstructional assignment. My research benefited from the help of the Walker Library staff in the interlibrary loan office and the microtext division. I must give special thanks to the staff of the Center for Historic Preservation for including me in some of their Rosenwald school projects, especially Caneta Skelley Hankins, who organized the university's 1995 conference on Rosenwald schools. My departmental colleagues in the Women's Work Group have been sympathetic listeners and sound critics over the years, and I owe them much for their encouragement. Special thanks go to Kristine McCusker for reading the manuscript at critcal times in its development.

Additional support for the research dates back over a decade to my graduate student days, when a grant from the Rockefeller Archives Center and a Spencer Dissertation Fellowship started me down the road to Rosenwald schools. More recently, the John Hope Franklin Collection of African and African-American Documentation supported research at Duke University.

My research travels have taken me into many libraries across the South, and I thank the staff members who patiently helped me through their collections. In particular, I am grateful to the staff members at the Alabama State University Library's Special Collections and Archives; the Hill Memorial Library at Louisiana State University; Duke University's Rare Book, Manuscript, and Special Collections Library, especially Elizabeth Dunn; the Tulane University Library Special Collections; the Amistad Research Center; the Historical Collection at South Carolina State University; the South Carolina State Library; the South Caroliniana Library at the University of South Carolina; and the University of

Chicago Library's Special Collections Research Center, especially Jay Satterfield, Debra Levine, and Barbara Gilbert.

I owe much to the archivists who have joined me in searching for Rosenwald school-building program records, especially the staffs of the Alabama Department of Archives and History; the Arkansas History Commission; the Atlanta University Center Archives; the Florida Agricultural and Mechanical University's Southeastern Regional Black Archives Research Center and Museum, especially E. Murrell Dawson; the Florida State Archives; the Georgia Department of Archives and History, in particular Dale L. Couch and Greg Jarrell; the Kentucky Department of Libraries and Archives; the Louisiana State Archives; the Maryland State Archives; the Mississippi Department of Archives and History; the North Carolina State Archives; the Oklahoma State Archives; the Oklahoma Historical Society; the South Carolina Archives; the Tennessee State Library and Archives; the Texas State Archives; the Library of Virginia; and the Special Collections and Archives at Johnston Memorial Library of Virginia State University and its director, Lucious Edwards Jr.

My debts are even deeper to the staffs of two major collections of materials on the Rosenwald building program. Cynthia Wilson and Sandra Peck at the Tuskegee University Archives and Museums shepherded me through their collections during two long research visits. For many years now I have relied on the professionalism and kindness of Beth Madison Howse, director of Special Collections at Fisk University, and I cannot thank her enough for her assistance over the duration of this project.

My work has benefited greatly from the encouragement and challenges of other scholars, readers, and preservation activists. V. P. Franklin, Robert Lowe, Marta Gutman, Ning de Coninck-Smith, Linda Wynn, and participants at the 1995 Rosenwald School Conference and the 1995 History of Education Society meeting, as well as the National Trust's 2004 Rosenwald schools conference, offered valuable commentaries that have pushed me to think both more broadly and deeply about these school buildings. Angel David Nieves, Leslie M. Alexander, Marta Gutman, Ning de Coninck-Smith, and Peter M. Ascoli have been supportive critics for my writing about Rosenwald schools as well. Peter Ascoli has been very generous with his knowledge of Julius Rosenwald and the school-building program, for which I am most grateful. I owe particular thanks to the readers who reviewed this work for the University Press of Florida, and to Meredith Morris-Babb for her unflagging support throughout the entire process of creating this book.

Rosenwald schools have many advocates, and I thank all of the many people who have telephoned and written to me about their schools or stopped to talk with me on the grounds of the Rosenwald schools in their communities. They have taught me the meaning of a Rosenwald school. Others on the Rosenwald school trail have offered me directions and shared their discoveries, including Tom Hanchett of the Levine Museum of the New South, Jeanne Cyriaque of the Georgia Historic Preservation Division, Susan Pearl of the Maryland-National Capital Park and Planning Commission, Karen Riles of the Austin History Center, Alicestyne Turley-Adams of Georgetown College, and the late Diane Granat. Special thanks must go to education activist Phyllis McClure for her insights into Virginia's Rosenwald schools and her good cheer. I am grateful to Nyoni Collins of the Sankofa Center in Wake Forest, who has been an inspiration as well as a sounding board. Tracy Hayes and John Hildreth at the southern office of the National Trust for Historic Preservation and all of the members of the Rosenwald School Initiative task force have spurred me on and encouraged me to hope that my work can be of service to those who still labor for Rosenwald schools.

Family members have listened to this project for years and probably wondered when it would ever end. I thank them all for their encouragement—especially my parents, John and Sally Hoffschwelle; my sister, Ann Mullin, and her family; my brother, John Hoffschwelle, and his family; my godparents, Jerry and Johanna Kearns; and my extended family by marrige, the Van Hoosers and Wests—for sharing their time and homes with me during my research travels. Rosenwald schools have been a part of the background noise in the busy school lives of my children, Owen and Sara, and I thank them for every day they share with me.

This book is dedicated to my husband, Carroll Van West, often my partner on Rosenwald school adventures and always my partner in life.

Author's Note

To avoid confusion as much as possible, I have followed these conventions for the names of program and educational officials:

"Rosenwald school-building program," "Rosenwald building program," and "building program" refer to the overarching school-construction grant program funded by Julius Rosenwald from 1912 to 1932. Prior to 1930, this was also known as the "rural school-building program" or "rural school program," and after 1930 as the "southern school program," and I have used these terms as well in their appropriate contexts.

"Rosenwald Fund" and "the fund" refer to the Julius Rosenwald Fund, which Julius Rosenwald created in 1917 and to which he assigned the Rosenwald school-building program in 1920. Although records from the pre-1920 Tuskegee period of the Rosenwald building program often refer to a "Rosenwald Fund," those documents refer to the account in which Tuskegee officials kept Julius Rosenwald's monetary gifts for the Rosenwald building program.

"State agent for Negro schools," "state Negro school agent," and "Negro school agent" refer to the white men hired by southern state departments of education and funded by the General Education Board (GEB) who supervised all aspects of public education for African Americans. In the 1920s, the General Education Board also funded white men as assistants to Negro school agents; I refer to them as "assistant state agent for Negro schools" and "assistant Negro school agent." I use these rather cumbersome titles for the sake of consistency among the multiple job titles describing these men in early twentieth-century records: "agent for Negro rural schools," "supervisor," "inspector," and other variants. Furthermore, these selected job titles distinguish between the white state officials who handled black public school issues and the other General Education Board agents (for white secondary and elementary schools, and for schoolhouse planning, for example) who also worked for state departments of education.

"Rosenwald building agent" and "building agent" refer to the African American men hired with Rosenwald building-program support to conduct local campaigns and supervise building projects. These black men often held dual positions with a state's African American teachers' association, an African American college or university, or the state department of education, but this study covers only their activities on behalf of the Rosenwald building program.

"Agents" refers collectively to both white state agents for Negro schools and black Rosenwald building agents. For more information on the agents, see appendix 1.

"School patrons" refers to community members who supported schools through donations of time, labor, material goods, and cash, and who participated in school-sponsored events.

When transcribing quotations, I have followed the original texts, noting any changes for readability in brackets and using "[*sic*]" only to denote obvious typographical mistakes. Many of the rural black southerners who wrote about Rosenwald schools had limited educational opportunities, as reflected in their spelling and grammar. I have rendered their words exactly to capture their experiences and their aspirations. For similar reasons, I have quoted white people exactly to show the range of their social beliefs, for example, in their rendering of the term "Negro." Many white writers did not capitalize it, whereas virtually all African American writers did; capitalization of "Negro" by a white writer signaled a greater commitment to racial justice.

Introduction

Across the American landscape from Maryland to Missouri, and from Virginia to Texas, over five thousand Rosenwald school buildings once testified to the achievements of a remarkable coalition of activists. One of every five African American schools in the South was a Rosenwald school when the Rosenwald school-building program ended in 1932. By that time, Rosenwald schools alone outnumbered all the African American public school buildings that had stood in the South when the building program began twenty years earlier. Fittingly, Rosenwald schools are once again attracting public attention in the early twenty-first century, for many remain on the southern landscape where they still serve as essential community institutions.[1] This book aims to provide a backdrop against which both scholars and community activists can see the Rosenwald building program and its schools as an evolving, multilayered network of people and buildings that produced significant landscapes of identity and social change.

The Rosenwald school program followed a path blazed by African American southerners who for decades had been engaged in independent school-building campaigns. In the early 1900s, Tuskegee Institute staff began organizing school-construction projects as an integral element of community-based educational campaigns in the area around Tuskegee, for which Booker T. Washington solicited a combination of philanthropic donations and local contributions. Washington convinced Sears, Roebuck and Company president and Tuskegee trustee Julius Rosenwald to support the construction of six schools in 1912. These became pilot projects for a regional school-building initiative—funded by Rosenwald and administered by Clinton J. Calloway at the Tuskegee Institute department of extension—that offered matching grants for the construction of better public school buildings for African Americans. In 1920, Julius Rosenwald removed his building program from Tuskegee to Nashville, Tennessee, where Samuel L. Smith ran the southern office of his Chicago-based philanthropic foundation, the Julius Rosenwald Fund. After Julius Rosenwald reorganized his foundation in 1928 and brought Edwin R. Embree to Chicago as the fund's director, the Julius Rosenwald Fund broadened its philanthropic objectives beyond school construction. In the midst of an economic depression that constrained resources for school construction, and eager to move on to a new agenda for social change, Embree and fund officials terminated the building program in 1932.

By this time, Rosenwald schools had become an integral element of the institutional infrastructure in the African American communities they served and a focal point of community identity. The Rosenwald school-building program had not, however, offered a direct challenge to the discriminatory legal system of Jim Crow education that made such a program necessary. Rosenwald schools alone could not compensate for decades of inadequate funding or conquer the prevailing assertion of white supremacy that underpinned segregation and discrimination. That the people involved in building Rosenwald schools did not solve all of the problems of Jim Crow education is not a failure so much as an indictment of the forces of racism and indifference and the grim determination of black southerners to hammer away at those forces.

As a well-intentioned but limited effort to redress the South's neglect of its black children, the Rosenwald school-building program is a familiar element in historical studies of African American and southern education in the early twentieth century.[2] But the building program had other goals as well: to build new public institutions for African American community life and to remake African American schools into models for public school architecture. Furthermore, this program created a stage upon which many different people could act. For all the program's administrators' power to set policy and control the supply of money, their demands for state and local government involvement and African American self-help created opportunities for other activists to pursue their own goals. For some, the goal was to create model school designs that would promote modern educational standards for black and white children. Some wanted Rosenwald schools to help them make black education an integral part of the South's public school infrastructure, or to reinforce paternalistic white control over southern society. For others, the goal was to challenge the racist underpinnings of that society by creating alternative institutions and opportunities for black children. Looking closely at the Rosenwald school-building program from these multiple perspectives can help scholars better understand the significance of Progressive reforms in school design and their place in African American education and offers a historical framework within which today's Rosenwald school communities can assess their schools' meanings for the present and future.

This study examines the Rosenwald school-building program from the inside out, focused on the internal development of the building program and looking out from it to the broader arena of black education in the South, to understand its distinctive and enduring power as an agency for change. Two interrelated arguments demonstrate the enduring significance of the Rosenwald school-building program. First, the Rosenwald building program sheds light on the processes by which people create, use, and invest meaning in the material world, in this case the spaces and places, the sites and structures of schools. Julius Rosenwald and Booker T. Washington could have chosen to put all of Rosenwald's donations into teachers' salaries, training, or instructional materials for, as Edwin Embree realized when he transformed the Rosenwald Fund's educational program, a school's physical plant was but one part of its power to support change. The decision to invest in school facilities originated in Booker T. Washington's and Julius Rosenwald's desire to implement their vision of strong African American institutions in a successful multiracial society. It also defined a niche for Julius Rosenwald in the ranks of philanthropists concerned about education in the South. Their plan gained approval from reformers and educators who believed in the power of the material environment to shape individual experience and values, and in their own ability to engineer school buildings for social progress.

The thousands of African Americans across the South who labored to gain a Rosenwald school for their community believed in the power of the school environment as well. As black southerners marched into school superintendents' offices, appeared before school board meetings, enlisted state and philanthropic agency officials to endorse their campaigns and use their authority over local officials, and made contributions to their schools over and above their tax levies, they drew upon their "cultural capital," described by V. P. Franklin as "the sense of group consciousness and collective identity that serves as an economic resource for the financial and material support of . . . enterprises aimed at the advancement of an entire group."[3]

Rural black southerners, educators, and community leaders grasped the tool of the Rosenwald school-building program to force open public coffers and demand attention and resources from white public officials and educators. Although relatively powerless and often disadvantaged, African Americans claimed the power of citizens to secure the protections and benefits of the local and state governments that denied their civil and political rights and siphoned off the public revenues generated by black taxpayers to educate white children. Their cooperative efforts secured new spaces for a historic African American tradition and new places invested with their cultural capital that correlated education with community advancement. The Rosenwald building program gave black southerners another way to act on that tradition and thus shows us how people can forge alliances with outside agencies to change their worlds.

The second argument made here is embodied in the organization of the book itself, which replicates the operating structure of the Rosenwald school program to highlight the multiple meanings that people invested in Rosenwald buildings. The building program involved three broad groups of people: the program's benefactor and staff, who controlled its policies and designs; the state officials who coordinated grant applications and disbursements; and the local people who campaigned for and used the schools. This top-down hierarchy of region, race, gender, and financial power might have resulted in a building program that simply dropped modern school buildings onto the southern landscape. Yet the full success of the Rosenwald school-building program came from the interplay between these groups as they articulated their own visions of a Rosenwald school and used the building program for their own ends. The building program's policies and paperwork engaged all three groups, and their suggestions and complaints helped to shape the program over time. Administrators, state officials, and local people chose different strategies to pursue their aspirations for Rosenwald schools, and the rhythm of the school-building program varied accordingly. For example, the top officials of the building program frequently changed policies and building designs in response to personnel changes, administrative issues, and interactions with other philanthropies. At the local level, however, educators and school patrons incorporated the Rosenwald program into a continuous stream of activism dating back at least to the Civil War, updating some of the same self-help measures they had used for decades.

Consequently, the book consists of three parts that reflect these constituent groups and their distinctive understandings of Rosenwald school buildings as agents of change. This narrative explains how the Rosenwald building program developed as a philanthropic initiative over the course of two decades, how it operated through the state departments of education, and how African American southerners made the program work in their own communities. Part 1 traces what Samuel L. Smith called "The Evolution of the Schoolhouse construction Program" from its origins at Tuskegee Institute through its demise during the Great Depression. This administrative and architectural history of the Rosenwald school-building program emphasizes the intentions and actions of those who conceived and directed its operations: Booker T. Washington, Julius Rosenwald, Clinton J. Calloway, Samuel L. Smith, Francis W. Shepardson, Alfred K. Stern, and Edwin R. Embree. Local people and state-level educators appear in part 1 to indicate the times and ways that they too influenced the program's development; for example, in local and state pressure to widen the original program beyond Alabama, and in the ambivalent responses by local and state people to Rosenwald School Day.

Part 1 shows that, whether explicitly or implicitly, the administrators of the Rosenwald program continuously engaged in a discussion of race as they issued prescriptions for uplifting black southerners and made decisions about the relative power of whites and blacks to direct their initiatives. Their ideas and choices joined ongoing discussions among philanthropists and educators about the nature and purpose of education for African Americans and the South that have already received considerable scholarly attention. In this work, I argue that school architecture is an essential element for understanding the intersection of race, education, and philanthropy in the Progressive-era South. Booker T. Washington and Julius Rosenwald began the program with a conscious decision to promote buildings as a necessary condition for better instruction and learning. Rosenwald program officials studied and consulted with professional school architects, issued their own building plans, and tried to enforce ever-higher construction standards. Over the course of two decades, they redefined the building program from one that promoted better school facilities into one that claimed to create models for all schools, indirectly using Rosenwald buildings to subvert the material culture of Jim Crow.

Part 2 explains how the program operated at the state level. The white men who worked as state agents for Negro schools promoted the Rosenwald program and coordinated the paperwork and funds for the projects in their states. In nine states, African American Rosenwald building agents, partially subsidized by the Rosenwald building program, organized community building campaigns and supervised local fund-raising and construction. These white and black professional educators comprised the middle layer of the Rosenwald building campaign. They mediated between the program's administrators and local school officials and citizens. Moreover, in states that employed both state agents for Negro schools and Rosenwald building agents, these white and black men engaged in their own complex negotiations of professional status, expertise, and authority over other white and black southerners. Both white and black agents found the Rosenwald building program an effective tool for expanding black public education as an integral part of southern state school systems. They also used it to advance their own and their peers' interests as professional educators and in so doing built their own careers and pushed white teachers and school officials to consider black educational improvements as their professional responsibility.

No program administrator or state bureaucrat had the power to turn Washington and Rosenwald's idea into a blanket of over five thousand school facilities spread over fifteen states. That power came from the hundreds of local leaders and thousands of average people in the South's African American communities, which are explored in part 3. These black men, women, and children turned self-help prescriptions and idealized building plans into real places and invested them with meaning. They found themselves engaged in their own negotiations between state and Rosenwald program authorities and with local school officials. In addition, southern African Americans acted out their own debates over the sources of community identity and over the meanings of class and gender to a community's internal hierarchy and bumped up against obstacles of white opposition and economic hardship. Local people appear in the pages of parts 1 and 2 to make the case for outside help; they dominate the last pages of this book not only to replicate the building program's structure but also to ensure that they have the last word on its significance.

A Rosenwald school was a recognizable African American space of pride and achievement. Sometimes that school stood on a country lane surrounded by fields worked by the students and their families. Elsewhere in the rural landscape the Rosenwald school accompanied the church of a congregation that had spearheaded its building campaign. On the fringes of country towns, a Rosenwald school joined the churches, fraternal lodges, and funeral homes that marked African American residential and commercial enclaves. In cities, a Rosenwald school might look out over a bustling neighborhood. How and why those buildings came to mark the southern landscape is a story that begins in Macon County, Alabama, in the early years of the twentieth century.

PART I

The Rosenwald School-Building Program

1

The Rosenwald-Washington Partnership, 1912–15

Carpenters were busily working on a new school for the small rural community of Loachapoka, in Lee County, Alabama, when L. Pearl Rouseau published her report in the January 1913 issue of the *Messenger*. Notices of school-improvement and school-construction campaigns commonly appeared in this monthly publication from the extension department at nearby Tuskegee Institute. Rouseau's account, like others, mentioned a school rally and listed the names of all contributors and their donations, which ranged from five cents to over five dollars. But she could hint at a new source of hope for their project. "The ladies of Loachapoka are still striving to erect a new school building," Rouseau announced. "They are greatly encouraged because a friend has promised to assist them in this direction."[1]

This small notice was one of the first public references to an experiment in building schools for rural African Americans launched by Booker T. Washington and Julius Rosenwald. Significantly, Rouseau's account emphasized the community context in which the new school building was taking shape, a context of limited financial resources but firm resolve. Over the next twenty years, black southerners like Rouseau would join forces with Washington, Rosenwald, and fifteen state departments of education to address a glaring need in public education for black southerners.

The Rosenwald school-building program began with a shared conviction among all of its participants that school buildings embodied a community's commitment to the education of black children and a better future for all southerners. The administrators who led the Rosenwald building program expanded its operations and adapted its school designs to implement that belief. When the program's leaders lost faith in that strategy, they ended it—even though their own records showed that African American communities still labored for new school buildings as material expressions of their long-term quest for educational equity.

The origins of the Rosenwald school-building program lay in the paradoxical conditions of the post–Civil War South. In the late nineteenth- and early twentieth-century South, segregation, disfranchisement, and white supremacy starved rural black schools and stunted the learning of countless black children. At the same time, African Americans charted their own educational course, extending a social and cultural commitment to education forged by antebellum free and enslaved black southerners into the heady days of emancipation. Across the defeated Confederacy, African Americans flocked into the schools created by missionary societies, the Freedmen's Bureau, and their own efforts. As the Freedmen's Bureau and missionary societies left the South in the 1870s, white voters and politicians regained control of public education and circumscribed funding for black schools. White vigilantes attacked black schools and those who supported them, black and white, to suppress the drive toward equality. African American citizens protected the schools within their communities and valued the close connections between teachers, students, and school patrons. Their efforts transmitted the value of education to a new generation schooled in churches, fraternal lodges, and a host of ramshackle log buildings. Those conditions shaped the career of Booker T. Washington, founder and principal of Tuskegee Normal and Industrial Institute, and elicited the generosity of Julius Rosenwald, president of Sears, Roebuck and Company. When these men met in 1911, they would discover that they shared a commitment to "self-help" as well as a firm belief that education could improve the lives of black Americans in the rural South.

BOOKER T. WASHINGTON AND TUSKEGEE INSTITUTE

Booker T. Washington's own life history demonstrated the power of liberty and education.[2] Born a slave in Franklin County, Virginia, in 1856, Washington claimed to feel no antagonism against former slaveholders, despite the sexual exploitation of his enslaved mother by his white father, his family's miserable living conditions, and the joyful celebrations of emancipation described in his famous autobiography, *Up from Slavery*. Washington carefully crafted this account of his journey from slavery to the forefront of American public life, and it proved an effective tool for attracting support from sympathetic white readers as well as their donations to his beloved Tuskegee Institute. In its pages, Washington also recorded the determination of freedpeople to gain an education. Whether describing his altering the time clock where he worked at a West Virginia salt furnace so that he could attend evening school or his setting off for Hampton Institute with only a small bag of clothes and money from his brother and older black community members, Washington told of an individual's and a community's faith in education as their best chance to experience the benefits—and the rights—of citizenship.[3]

Once at Hampton Institute, Washington found a life mentor in its founder, General Samuel C. Armstrong.[4] Manual training, the development of physical skills that would benefit students as a complement to abstract thought and as a means to finance their educations, had had its advocates since the early nineteenth century. As Robert Francis Engs points out in his biography of Armstrong and Hampton, Armstrong drew upon this concept and a separate form of industrial education practiced in antebellum workhouses to train poor children for employment. But Armstrong envisioned industrial education as means of moral instruction in the value of work—"industry"—that Hampton-trained teachers would take out to the masses of African Americans in the rural South. Some African Americans had a different understanding of industrial education, seeing it as a supplement to the classical curriculum that provided a strategy for economic independence and the development of physical, mental, and moral skills for the advancement of their race. They too emphasized the training of black teachers as racial leaders for the rural masses, but for their own independent ends. Washington absorbed both Hampton Institute's moral vision, without Armstrong's racist assumptions about black inferiority, and its African American counterpart.[5] He would use industrial education to build independent African American institutions and communities, to make alliances with white northerners and southerners, and to propel himself into the role of race leader.

Washington graduated from Hampton in 1875, as Reconstruction drew to its close and most white northerners averted their gaze from the often brutal reassertion of white supremacy in southern states. He entered adult life at a time when ambitious African Americans like himself, eager for the advancement of black Americans, faced difficult choices about priorities and strategies. While he claimed to choose education over politics, in effect Washington used education to become a master politician. Supporters praised, opponents decried, and historians have dissected Washington's creation of his vast Tuskegee machine, with operatives across the country who promoted his leadership and his message, and his ruthless exercise of power behind the scenes to enforce loyalty. Yet as his biographer Louis R. Harlan has shown, Washington also used his carefully cultivated image to give him a platform for demanding that white Americans behave more justly toward black citizens. He outlined that platform in his famously problematic "Atlanta compromise" speech at the Atlanta Cotton State and International Exposition in 1895. Calling upon both white and black southerners to "cast down your bucket where you are," Washington told his white listeners that "there is no defence or security for any of us except in the highest intelligence and development of all." Thinking African Americans, he claimed, "understand that the agitation of questions of social equality is the extremest folly." Acceding to the segregation laws and disfranchisement campaigns sweeping through southern states, Washington asked instead for "education of head, hand, and heart" that would yield material progress for both races.[6]

This short speech detonated a storm of applause and criticism. Many whites, from South and North, would invoke Washington's compromise as evidence that African Americans would willingly renounce their quests for political and civil rights and accept second-class citizenship in return for schools and jobs. Some African Americans, such as W.E.B. Du Bois and Ida B. Wells-Barnett, were appalled by this message and the ensuing white lionization of Washington, as well as Washington's presumption to speak for all black Americans. Washington's public message itself, however, was quite complex, especially as he honed it over time. Louis R. Harlan has shown the "secret life" of Booker T. Washington as a lobbyist and financial contributor to many efforts at defending African Americans from injustice, as well as his continuing political activism, behind the "self-made" mask he showed to white Americans.[7] His apparent capitulation, thought Washington, would bind white southerners to their side of the compromise to respect the legitimate needs and aspirations of southern African Americans. African Americans could remain proud and retain their self-respect and positive racial identity under the withering onslaught of white violence and Jim Crow laws. Nonetheless, Washington could not admit that his own celebrity and political prowess in promoting racial accommodation allowed whites to maintain their domination over the very rural black southerners for whom he claimed to speak.[8]

Education, Washington believed, addressed the most serious needs of rural southern African Americans and promised immediate, tangible improvements in their life circumstances. After several years of teaching in Malden, West Virginia, and at Hampton Institute teaching night school and Native American students, Washington found himself in 1881 entrusted with the task of creating a normal school, partially funded by the state, at Tuskegee, Alabama. His students arrived expecting a traditional academic program, and that was where Washington began as well. Over the years, Washington would invest Tuskegee's curriculum with more of the industrial education he had experienced at Hampton, creating an educational program that emphasized what he called "dovetailing"—and what other educators of the time dubbed "correlating"—academic knowledge to practical skills in everyday life.[9] As Washington later described the process, he and teaching colleague Olivia A. Davidson, who would later become his second wife, strove to provide "an education as would fit a large proportion of [students] to be teachers, and at the same time cause them to return to the plantation districts and show the people there how to put new energy and new ideas into farming, as well as into the intellectual and moral and religious life of the people."[10] By the turn of the century, Washington had built the Tuskegee Normal and Industrial Institute into a striking campus of brick buildings, most paid for by wealthy white northern donors, designed by Tuskegee faculty, and built by Tuskegee students. Over 1,100 students were enrolled in Tuskegee's day and night schools, and Washington commanded a staff of eighty-six administrators and faculty whom he supervised closely and from whom he demanded constant work and complete loyalty.

At Tuskegee Institute, Washington put his educational philosophy into visible daily practice, having students construct the buildings in which they would learn and live. Tuskegee students studied a broad range of "industrial" and academic subjects, except foreign languages. Washington wanted them to see the connection between intellect and activity, but his educational philosophy was an integral part of his overall strategy for African American advancement. As he had told white educators gathered for the 1884 meeting of the National Education Association:

> Now in regard to what I have said about the relations of the two races, there should be no unmanly cowering or stooping to satisfy unreasonable whims of Southern white men; but it is charity and wisdom to keep in mind the two hundred years of schooling in prejudice against the Negro which the ex-slaveholders are called on to conquer. A certain class of whites object to the general education of the colored man on the ground that, when he is educated he ceased to do manual labor, and there is no avoiding the fact that much aid is withheld from Negro education in the South by the states on these grounds. Just here the great mission of Industrial Educa-

tion, coupled with the mental, comes in. It kills two birds with one stone, viz., it secures the co-operation of the whites and does the best possible thing for the black man.[11]

This strategy of accommodating education to white sentiment undermined Washington's intellectual argument for industrial education, yet it was the basis for his popularity.

Even when observers like Du Bois took him to task, he and Washington and all of their allies debated from the same premise: the transformative power of education. Tuskegee Institute by itself could not transform the South, however, and so Washington expected his students to take their learning and skills out into their own educational institutions and their communities. He wanted Tuskegee to do the same, for as he wrote in *My Larger Education*, "I have learned from later experience that it is just as important to carry education outside of the school building and take it into the fields, into the homes, and into the daily life of the people surrounding the school."[12] Many rural places had no school building, or only a rudimentary one, so Tuskegee Institute and its graduates would have to work with community members to build new schools.

PUBLIC NEED, COMMUNITY ACTION

As Washington explained in his 1884 NEA address, black schools suffered because white southerners opposed education as a threat to their established social and economic hierarchy. Before the Civil War, enslaved people like the young Washington had been excluded from the South's limited state public school systems. Although most states had laws that prohibited even private instruction, some slaves did acquire literacy and numeracy skills as part of their occupational training from more lenient whites or clandestinely from other African Americans, both individually and in secret schools. Free blacks also found their children banned from public schools and created their own institutions.[13] During the Civil War and Reconstruction, black southerners celebrated freedom by creating a multitude of their own schools and flooding into private academies run by missionary groups and religious denominations. As scholars James D. Anderson and David Freedman have argued, African Americans' antebellum school experiences fostered a deep commitment to education and prepared black southerners to lead the South's first movement for universal public education in the years immediately following the Civil War. Southern state constitutions and laws in the late 1860s and early 1870s did not always mandate racial segregation in public schools and often did provide equal funding for all schools. In practice and eventually by law, however, Reconstruction public school systems became segregated by race, which accorded with black goals for self-determination and aspirations for an educated professional class as well as white racism.[14]

Although not a direct political right like the franchise, black schools posed yet another threat to white supremacy in the wake of Confederate defeat and emancipation. Attacks on African American schools—and on the churches that often housed them—coupled with the violent intimidation of black and white educators who taught African American children, began in the 1860s and continued after Reconstruction. White violence circumscribed educational opportunities for many rural African Americans once again and provided yet more evidence that public education was a right of citizenship with far-reaching implications for social, economic, and political power structures. As a result, after Reconstruction ended, southern states and counties refused to appropriate any meaningful funds for black public education.[15]

Education returned to the forefront at the turn of the century, as the South felt the stirring of Progressive reform in the midst of widespread antiblack violence and white supremacist campaigns for expanding segregation and disfranchising black men. White southern Progressive reformers in fact supported segregation and disfranchisement, claiming that such measures would stem the tide of lynchings and restrain political corruption and demagoguery. As many scholars have demonstrated, white educational reformers refrained from pushing their agendas for African American education in the South until disfranchisement seemingly eliminated the political threat of an educated black citizenry. These developments overshadowed the positive record of black initiative in securing universal public education for southern children and control over their own public schools.[16]

Alabama schools, for example, followed a dual path of public need and community action repeated in other southern states. A new state constitution in 1875 imposed school segregation, which had not been a feature of the 1867 Reconstruction-era constitution. Subsequent legislation limited the allocation of poll taxes, and then all state school revenues, according to the race of taxpayers. A new state constitution in 1901 "thoroughly disfranchised" black Alabamians, in the words of scholar Horace Mann Bond, and allowed local school boards to distribute state school funds, who then diverted black schools' share to white schools. Thus Alabama's African American school patrons, who would build the first Rosenwald schools, entered the new century with decades of experience of running their public schools as "functionally private schools." As Robert G. Sherer writes, most black families had to make a significant sacrifice of their material and labor resources to send children to school: "For black families living at a subsistence level this sacrifice was comparable to that of middle-class whites who sent their children to more expensive private schools."[17]

Southern states buttressed segregation with discrimination by appropriating school funds on the basis of the scholastic population, a practice that encouraged county superintendents to count black children in the school census regardless of whether those children were enrolled in or attending school or if a school even existed for them to attend.[18] When state funds based on the school census arrived in the county, the superintendent and board had complete discretion over their allocation and used the money generated by the black scholastic population to pay for white schools.[19] States with relatively liberal provisions for African American schools emphasized the color-blind provisions in their school laws and passed the blame on to local whites. Kentucky, its state superintendent declared, "does not discriminate against one race or in favor of the other. The State school tax is levied on all alike; the State school fund is distributed for white and colored alike; the same salary schedule, the same course of study, and the same length of term, are provided for all alike." But he admitted that counties often "side-step[ped] their obligation to the colored" children by providing few schools and no high schools, and ignoring the legal requirements for the length of school terms. Whites in Kentucky towns used the mechanism of independent graded school districts to exclude black children—laws governing these schools allowed them to operate for whites only—and left black children to the mercy of the county even though they actually lived outside the county school system's boundaries.[20] Oklahoma had an unusual system of separate schools that ensured most black schools would receive no state funds, but in a few places African Americans could control public school resources. In each county, the regular public school system was that for children of the majority race—members of which ran the county school system. All state and local school funds went to schools for the majority race, whether black or white, and the county levied an additional property tax for "separate" schools serving the minority race.[21]

State legislators also wrote discrimination directly into school law. For example, in the decades after the Civil War, Maryland alternated between dividing state school revenues by race and devoting all public school revenues to white schools with a special appropriation for black schools. In the early twentieth century, the state enacted major school-reform laws that reorganized and expanded the state education department and mandated compulsory education. But the state also set different term lengths for white (nine months) and black (seven months) schools and allowed county boards of education to decide whether or not a school district's black population "warranted" a school.[22]

The persistent underfunding of universal public education, despite educational reformers' successes, allowed white school officials like Georgetown County, South Carolina's superintendent J. W. Doar to hide behind the claim that they could not afford to divide school funds according to scholastic population, for in his predominantly black county, "our white schools would run only about one-fourth the length of time they do now." Similarly, Arkansas state superintendent George B. Cook treated segregated schooling as a "necessity" and explained away the discriminatory nature of that segregation by claiming that "it is only now [1912] that the negroes are beginning by taxes to support their portion of the school expenditures to any appreciable degree." Alabama's state agent for Negro schools James L. Sibley believed that Progressive reformers' success in recruiting grassroots white support for public education had actually encouraged county school boards to raid black school funds. He explained that school boards needing more money for improving white schools simply appropriated $125 per black school to pay a teacher for five months, and then divided the remaining school funds among white schools.[23]

Disgruntled white taxpayers and politicians often called for allocation of tax revenues by the race of taxpayers, assuming that white schools would reap vast benefits and that black schools would be starved out of existence. Yet as Louisiana school officers pointed out, African American taxpayers paid in more than they received back in school funding. Alabama's state education officials provided detailed statistical evidence of the positive correlation between majority black populations and funding for white public schools. Even so, the potential threat to many impoverished black communities inspired African American activists and sympathetic whites to beat back attempts to divide tax revenues by race at the state level, but they argued unsuccessfully against similar practices at the local level.[24]

Under Jim Crow, the majority of African American schoolchildren and their teachers paid the price of Progressive reform in white public schools. Black southerners remained committed to education as a cultural value and a social right and kept up the sacrificial giving—the self-help—necessary to perpetuate their legacy of activism into a new century. The statewide campaigns for improved public schools mounted by white reformers obscured the African

American educational tradition from public view. As Horace Mann Bond observed for Alabama, "so far as educational campaigns were concerned, Negro children did not exist."[25] Discrimination and segregation meant that black schools remained housed in churches, fraternal lodges, stores, private homes, and farm buildings, while southern states began massive school-construction campaigns in the early years of the twentieth century. When available, public school buildings were often in poor shape. Publicly owned buildings often were former white school structures abandoned for a newer building, or decrepit postbellum schools like those in Franklin County, North Carolina: "absolutely worthless, and none of them . . . furnished with anything except a few old benches."[26] Without paint or maintenance funds to counteract the effects of human use and the elements, with a few unglazed narrow window openings and perhaps a bell tower, many rural black schools blended with the cottages and churches in their communities, their purpose and significance camouflaged to outsiders.

Consequently, when southern white reformers and northern philanthropic agencies turned their attention to African American public schools at the turn of the century, they assumed that they needed to remake black education from the ground up. They sought to remove black public schools from their roots in denominational and freedmen's schools and to abandon the classical education many African Americans had striven for since 1865. Instead, they contended, southern states should adopt true universal public schooling under state control and mandate industrial education for African Americans to secure long-term social and political order under a more enlightened Jim Crow hierarchy.[27] These reformers tapped into, yet generally did not acknowledge, black southerners' ongoing efforts for their own schools regardless of white support or opposition.

From Tuskegee Institute, Booker T. Washington counseled patience and self-help. Although Washington urged African Americans to seek their fair share of public-school dollars, he also pressed black southerners to address the appalling conditions in rural schools on their own rather than waiting for white officials to see the light. Washington declared that good school facilities were the place to start. "In many cases," he noted, "the schoolhouses in which children are taught are not fit for pigs to live in." A decent building, painted inside and out, its interior ceiled and plastered, and fitted with seats, blackboards, and a teacher's desk, was the sort that would attract better teachers and encourage longer school terms. Community members needed to get those good facilities however they could: by securing public funds, raising private funds, or donating labor and materials. He cautioned school patrons to use a formal architectural plan to ensure the quality of their new building, for "it is almost as cheap to build a good schoolhouse as it is to build a poor one."[28] Meanwhile, school patrons organized themselves to benefit their schools and watched for any sign of hope.

Philanthropic Agencies and Controversies

Even as southern African American men had their political rights wrested from them, and all black southerners faced new segregation laws and the constant threat of lynching, northern philanthropists began forging partnerships with moderate southern whites and blacks to counteract the South's destructive neglect of black education. This closely knit band of philanthropies and their administrators claimed to answer the needs of southern and African American education. Their efforts dated to the Reconstruction era, gained momentum as Jim Crow devastated black public schools in the late nineteenth century, and took off at the turn of the century when southern states simultaneously disfranchised black men and adopted Progressive reform initiatives. Booker T. Washington was a major African American figure in this burgeoning movement and guided Tuskegee Institute's own campaigns for black rural schools.

Consequently, by the time Julius Rosenwald turned his attention to African American education, many black and white activists and philanthropic agencies were already at work, and southern states had begun to address some needs in black public schools. Washington eventually helped Rosenwald carve out a niche for his own philanthropic endeavor among these interlocking reform programs, and by the mid-1910s they had crafted a rural school-building program that tackled the material conditions of school reform. Their strategy was to construct small, yet well-designed and better-equipped rural schools. These unadorned structures augmented the work already being done in southern black education by uniting the interests of educational reformers, sympathetic state and local school officials, and African American school patrons.

One of these northern-based philanthropic foundations was a survivor from the late Civil War and Reconstruction years, when many northern agencies like the American Missionary Association and the federal Freedmen's Bureau had sponsored black and white teachers in African American schools. The Peabody Education Fund was the creation of George Peabody, a Massachusetts native who had made a fortune in Baltimore and London as a merchant and banker. Peabody hoped that his foundation, created in 1867, would promote sectional reconciliation through public education for all southern children, which he saw as a critical first step toward the region's economic, social, and political reintegration into the national mainstream. Under the leadership of Barnas Sears, the former president of Brown University, then former Confederate officer Jabez Lamar Monroe Curry, and philosophy professor-turned-reformer Wickliffe Rose, the Peabody Education Fund helped southern state departments of education study their schools, expand public school systems, and train teachers to serve both white and black students. After decades of support for the Peabody Normal College in Nashville, Tennessee (where Rose was a faculty member), Peabody Fund trustees used most of the foundation's remaining assets to transform the school into the George Peabody College for Teachers, which began training white schoolteachers and administrators in 1914.[29]

Peabody Education Fund assets also went to the John F. Slater Fund, established by Connecticut textile manufacturer John Fox Slater in 1882. The Slater Fund focused specifically on the educational needs of African Americans in the post-Reconstruction South and, as shown by James D. Anderson, financed the rapid expansion of industrial education offerings in African American schools during the 1880s. Slater Fund aid went to private and public schools and colleges that taught both traditional academic and industrial subjects, for teacher training and salary support and for industrial equipment. J.L.M. Curry took over the administration of the John F. Slater Fund from Atticus G. Haygood in 1891 and merged its efforts with the Peabody Education Fund. Wallace Buttrick, a Southern Education Board member and secretary of the General Education Board, tied the Slater Fund to these two key agencies under his leadership of the Slater Fund from 1903 until 1910. His successor, James Hardy Dillard, also directed the Anna T. Jeanes Fund. As head of the Slater Fund, Dillard promoted county training schools for black southerners through grants for teachers' salaries and for vocational equipment and facilities. County training schools, often the only school in a county that offered any secondary grades to African American students, initially focused on providing teacher training as well as academic and industrial subjects. By the 1920s, many Slater Fund–supported county training schools had expanded their academic programs and were on their way to becoming four-year high schools.[30]

Whereas the Peabody and Slater Funds owed their origins to wealthy northerners, the Southern Education Board resulted from a series of meetings titled "Conferences on Education in the South" attended by both southerners and northerners. Philanthropic business leaders, ministers, and educators began meeting annually in 1898 to discuss the South's education needs, especially in African American schools. They concluded, however, that improvements in black education would be impossible unless white education received priority.[31] Led by New York merchant Robert Curtis Ogden, an executive committee formed the Southern Education Board in 1901 to implement the conferences' ideas, which named Booker T. Washington to a vague position as agent. The Southern Education Board and its Bureau of Information, established at the University of Tennessee in 1902, aided southern school authorities in building public support for the legislation and funding necessary to expand public school systems and sent school-improvement organizers into southern communities. Working with the Peabody Education Fund, the Southern Education Board also provided supervisors of rural schools to state departments of education.[32]

The Southern Education Board soon had a northern-based colleague, the General Education Board, created by John D. Rockefeller in 1902 and incorporated in 1903. John D. Rockefeller Jr.'s glowing report on the 1901 Conference for Education in the South, to which Ogden had transported him and other northern guests on a special railroad tour, led the senior Rockefeller to create a broad educational philanthropy. Baptist minister Wallace Buttrick administered the new foundation's programs, which initially included large contributions to the Southern Education Board as well as to teacher-training programs and vocational training. In 1905, the General Education Board began supporting secondary education professors at southern departments of education to promote and improve high schools. By 1914, the General Education Board had also undertaken initiatives in farm demonstration work and medical education and made grants to colleges and universities. After the dissolution of the Peabody Education Fund and the Southern Education Board in 1914, the General Education Board took over some of their work, including salary support for state rural school supervisors, and cooperated with both the Slater Fund and Jeanes Fund on initiatives in African American education.[33]

The Anna T. Jeanes Foundation had begun its work in 1907 and quickly became an integral part of this rapidly developing network of educational reform agencies. Anna Jeanes, a wealthy Philadelphia Quaker, was well aware of the work being done by those groups and their favored collegiate institutions, having already made donations to the General Education Board for Hampton Institute and Tuskegee, which Hollis B. Frissell and Booker T. Washington used for teacher-training projects, vocational teachers' salaries, and school buildings. She was especially interested in serving the needs of public schools for African Americans in small rural communities and shortly before her death gave a million dollars to this cause. Hers was the only major foundation of its sort that included African American leadership on its board of trustees. Its president, James Hardy Dillard, quickly focused its efforts on supporting county industrial supervising teachers, following the model created by Virginia Estelle Randolph of Henrico County, Virginia, near Richmond. Randolph emphasized industrial education, and she made school and community improvement major priorities as well as better instruction. By the early 1910s, southern counties could add supervising teachers like Randolph by matching a Jeanes Fund salary grant, and state departments of education could match salary grants for a state supervisor. Almost all Jeanes supervisors were female, and these women became powerful figures in local systems of black schools and the first black women to hold professional positions in southern state departments of education.[34]

The founders and members of these agencies comprised an interlocking directorate of southern education reform that, as scholars James D. Anderson and Louis R. Harlan have demonstrated, shared a common vision for African American education.[35] In addition to providing financial support for each other's programs and sharing common financial backers and trustees such as Robert Ogden, William H. Baldwin Jr., and George Foster Peabody, a small coterie of key figures dominated their administrative ranks. J.L.M. Curry, for example, was a founding participant in the Conferences on Education in the South and served on the Southern Education Board and the General Education Board in addition to his duties as administrator of the Peabody and Slater funds. His successor at the Slater Fund, Wallace Buttrick, was a member of the Southern Education Board and the secretary and later president of the General Education Board. Wickliffe Rose, who succeeded Curry at the Peabody Education Fund, served as executive secretary of the Southern Education Board and a trustee of the John F. Slater Fund; after joining the General Education Board in 1910, he succeeded Buttrick as its president in 1923. James Hardy Dillard administered the Jeanes and the Slater funds after 1910, and joined Buttrick and Rose as a trustee of the General Education Board in 1918. That pattern extended down through the ranks of these agencies and would continue through the 1930s. For example, William Taylor Burwell Williams of Tuskegee Institute was a field director for the Slater and Jeanes funds from the 1900s through the 1930s. State agents for rural black schools Jackson Davis of Virginia and Leo M. Favrot of Louisiana, first supported by the Peabody Education Fund and the Southern Education Board and then by the General Education Board in the 1910s, both became staff members of the General Education Board.

The common agenda that these philanthropic agencies set for southern Af-

rican American schools has generated controversy since the turn of the twentieth century. As the scholarship on southern education reform in this period has
demonstrated, these philanthropists and activists articulated a vision of African
American schooling as industrial education that was quite different from the
ideas of white and black educators in the late nineteenth century. Northern in-
dustrialists and their philanthropies joined forces with educational reformers in
the North and South to frame African American education exclusively as industrial education and used their financial leverage to enforce this limited agenda
on black schools. Trustees and staff of these philanthropies chose this route in
part out of a broader reevaluation of education by Progressive reformers and
in part out of their fear of southern white backlash, but they also shared the
assumption that black inferiority required white control. As many critics then
and since have charged, the philanthropists' agenda for industrial education cut
it loose from academic learning and instead emphasized vocational training to
keep black laborers on farms and in low-skill industrial jobs, where they would
undergird the region's economic development without challenging whites for
jobs or power. These reformers claimed that by accepting their version of the
educational models set at Hampton and Tuskegee, African American southerners could improve their economic well-being and develop a limited professional
class without precipitating continued racial violence. In their eyes, Booker T.
Washington's emphasis on educational and economic rights, and his message
of accommodation to white power, placed him at the forefront of black educational efforts.

The model for African American education espoused by the General Education Board and allied philanthropies placed them at the intersection of a multitude of contemporary class, race, and gender-based reform initiatives for education. They had many supporters, including African Americans, many of whom
upheld a different vision of industrial education that recognized the dignity of
manual labor and saw it as a potential springboard to social and political rights.
They also had many opponents, of whom white supremacist southerners were
the largest contingent, and who resisted any attempt to increase government
support for black education. Dissident African Americans from the South and
the North, and their more radical white (and northern) supporters, challenged
the philanthropies for coercing all black schools into industrial education,
and they challenged Booker T. Washington for trying to make his "Tuskegee
machine" the power broker for all African Americans. W.E.B. Du Bois made
himself the spokesperson of this group in *The Souls of Black Folk*, with its scathing critique of Washington, in 1903. By the 1910s, Du Bois and other African

American leaders had inaugurated the Niagara Movement, founded the National Association for the Advancement of Colored People with a small group of white allies, and created an alternative public forum for black Americans in the pages of the *Crisis*, which Du Bois edited.[36]

Historical and political debates still rage over the best strategies for using schools to achieve the promise of equality in American democracy. Most scholarly attention has been focused on issues of race, and many studies have exposed the racist assumptions of white philanthropists and their staffs and southern white educators and their political allies. Race cannot be separated from class, however, as the educational reformers also hoped it would produce a contented working class and farm population of native-born whites and immigrants as well as African Americans. Gender has provoked less controversy in studies of southern public education, although discussion of the gender roles embedded in, and challenged by, education reformers' leadership and programs has become an integral part of recent historical analyses.[37] Scholars and the original combatants in these controversies would likely agree, however, that southern African American public schools exemplified the glaring need for change in the early twentieth-century South. They also became problematic sites for all who sought to make that change happen, including participants in the Rosenwald school-building program.

TUSKEGEE'S MACON COUNTY PROJECT

As the major philanthropies in southern education marshaled their forces, Booker T. Washington pursued his own agenda for southern black education, using his favored status among white reformers and benefactors and staff resources at Tuskegee Institute.[38] Beginning in 1905, Washington and Tuskegee extension director Clinton J. Calloway used philanthropic funding to develop a public school program for Macon County, Alabama. What happened in Macon County gave Washington and Calloway important precedents for the early Rosenwald building program: securing the patronage of a single philanthropist, using matching grants and combining them with money from other agencies, cooperating with community activists, and linking instructional improvements to new school buildings.

In 1903, Washington became a favored recipient of Henry Huttleston Rogers's charitable giving. Rogers had amassed a fortune from Standard Oil, railroads, and other investments. As Louis R. Harlan explains, Rogers transformed himself from "a typically ruthless entrepreneur" into "a Santa Claus to those he liked and admired, and Washington was at the top of his list." In *My Larger Education* (1911), Washington recalled how he had interested Rogers in black schools by suggesting that southern whites would "not look upon the money spent for Negro education as a mere sop to the Negro race, or perhaps as money entirely thrown away," once they could see that better education produced better workers, better customers, and better citizens.[39]

Washington and Rogers demonstrated this proposition by focusing on Macon County, home to Tuskegee Institute. The county's first officially recorded black schools had opened in 1867 under the auspices of the Freedmen's Bureau. Soon afterwards, its white teachers had been thrown out of town by local whites, only to be replaced by the American Missionary Association's Cotton Valley School. Mount Olive, the first black public school, also opened in 1867. Since that time, Macon County's black schools had operated under siege from financial neglect and racial violence.[40] Beginning in 1905, resources from Rogers, Anna Jeanes, and Tuskegee Institute joined those from black residents flowing into Macon County schools.[41] Rogers's contributions helped to construct forty-six one-teacher schools, each costing about $700. Jeanes provided additional funds for school buildings and industrial supervising teachers. Local people contributed funding for teacher salary supplements in the expectation that a full year's school term and pay would improve the level of instruction. Altogether, Washington estimated, school patrons raised about $20,000 for better buildings and teacher salaries.[42]

Clinton J. Calloway "had charge of the experiment" as it spread across Macon County. Calloway, originally from Cleveland, Tennessee, joined the Tuskegee extension staff after his graduation from Fisk University in 1895 and became its director in 1901. He had already successfully organized the black residents of Kowaliga, Alabama, to replace a one-teacher school in "an old shanty" with a school campus of three new buildings staffed by eleven teachers.[43] In Macon County, Calloway expanded his school-building strategy into an ambitious plan for community uplift. He and extension colleague William M. Rakestraw campaigned for new school buildings among community members, patrons, and teachers, using Rogers and Jeanes funds to match local patrons' contributions. Calloway then publicized the school projects to attract African Americans from other parts of the state and region to a county where their children could enjoy a strong educational system. Washington claimed that Calloway had sold land to fifty families, and that others who could not afford their own farms had moved to Macon County as well, preferring to labor on farms near good schools.

After H. H. Rogers died in 1909, Washington attempted to transform his patron's personal giving into a family responsibility. The Rogers family agreed to support the Macon County project for the full period originally planned, which expired in the fall of 1910. Washington pushed Calloway to forge ahead, telling him at the beginning of 1910 to "place a good schoolhouse in each school district in the county."[44] In the meantime, Washington plied Henry Huttleston Rogers Jr. with letters of thanks for additional donations and appeals for continued aid. When the younger Rogers offered only that "at some future day, I hope to be able to render a certain amount of assistance along the same lines," Washington tugged at the son's filial heartstrings, writing that, "Your father sometime before he died, spoke of extending the work into other counties," but to no avail.[45] Washington still had access to Jeanes money, which the Tuskegee extension department continued to use intensively in Macon County. But in 1911, Washington was looking for a new patron who could grasp the possibilities in rural public school buildings.[46]

JULIUS ROSENWALD: A NEW PHILANTHROPIST FOR TUSKEGEE

That patron awaited him in Chicago, where Julius Rosenwald was just beginning to broaden his philanthropic concerns to include African American needs. Rosenwald was one of the most famous and influential business leaders of his time, a man who had risen to great wealth and believed strongly in personal initiative as well as social responsibility. Born in Springfield, Illinois, in 1862, the son of German immigrants to the United States, Julius Rosenwald had grown up working in his father's clothing store and other sales jobs. He attended high school for two years before going to New York in 1879 to learn the clothing business from his uncles, never resuming his formal education. With his younger brother Morris, Julius Rosenwald in 1884 set up his own store, J. Rosenwald & Bro., in New York. Hoping to profit by the region's growing demand for lightweight summer men's clothing, the brothers moved a year later to Chicago and established a new company, Rosenwald and Weil, with their cousin Julius Weil. Rosenwald married Augusta Nusbaum, the daughter of another clothing merchant, in 1890. To support their young family amid the uncertainties of the depression that began in 1893, he founded a separate company, Rosenwald and Co., in 1894, with financial backing from the New York clothing firm of Newborg, Rosenberg, and Co.[47]

In 1895, Rosenwald's brother-in-law, Aaron Nusbaum, approached him about an offer he had received from Richard W. Sears to buy the half-interest in Sears, Roebuck and Company being given up by Alvah C. Roebuck. Nusbaum wanted a partner to share in this new venture, and Rosenwald provided half of the needed investment. Rosenwald joined Sears, Roebuck as vice president and a year later was involved in the company's management full-time. Sears and Nusbaum could not work together, however. In 1901, Sears asked Rosenwald either to help him buy out Nusbaum or to help Nusbaum buy out Sears; Rosenwald chose Sears over his brother-in-law. After Richard Sears resigned in 1908, Julius Rosenwald became president of Sears, Roebuck and Company and began two decades of remarkable business success.[48]

Rosenwald famously attributed success to 95 percent luck and 5 percent ability, but no one else would have agreed in his case. According to biographer Morris R. Werner, those who knew J.R., as he preferred to be called, concurred that he exhibited "a quick business acumen, a shrewd judgement of the worth of other men and an acute appreciation of the value of their ideas and projects."[49] Rosenwald realized that Richard Sears's grandiose advertising claims and overextended staff could not fulfill the potential of a mail-order catalog business. He improved Sears, Roebuck's business operations dramatically, toning down the promotional rhetoric and replacing it with honest information and prompt, courteous service that he believed would attract and keep customer loyalty. Rosenwald also masterminded the creation of a new company plant on the West Side of Chicago, where operations manager O. C. Doering finally brought the company's mammoth mail-order operations under control.[50]

By 1910, Rosenwald had become one of the most successful business executives in the country and had embarked on a new career in philanthropy. His biographers attribute Rosenwald's emerging social conscience to the influence of his wife, Augusta, and his rabbi, Emil Hirsch. From Rabbi Hirsch, Rosenwald heard that Judaism could best serve modern society by serving its needy citizens. He learned of those citizens' needs from friend Julian W. Mack, who introduced him to Jane Addams and Addams's colleagues at Hull House. Rosenwald made donations to Hull House and served on its board. He also became a major supporter of Jewish charitable causes, especially the Associated Jewish Charities of Chicago, which he served as president and its major donor.[51]

Rosenwald made his first important contribution to African American causes in 1910, when he surprised the planners of a YMCA building for black men in Chicago by offering $25,000 for the construction of similar buildings in any American city that raised another $75,000. Eventually twenty-six African American YMCA and YWCA facilities qualified for these challenge grants. Rosenwald had only recently become interested in African American issues after his friend Paul J. Sachs sent him a biography of William H. Baldwin Jr., the Southern Railway executive and philanthropist who had chaired the board of trustees of the General Education Board and Tuskegee Institute. African Americans, Baldwin thought, needed "improvement of their country life" to keep them in the South's rural and small-town communities "where they had a chance to render better service than in large cities." That improvement, he argued, could come in part from new rural schools for whites and blacks in southern states that would offer vocational training and serve as social centers.[52] Rosenwald had already read and admired Booker T. Washington's *Up from Slavery*, but Baldwin's ideas opened up a new arena for Rosenwald's philanthropy. When Booker T. Washington visited Chicago in the spring of 1911, Rosenwald hosted a lunch for him. That fall, Rosenwald and a group of friends, including Rabbi Hirsch, visited Tuskegee Institute. Spurred on by Baldwin's example, and captivated by both Washington and his institution, Rosenwald began promoting Tuskegee to potential contributors and joined its board of trustees in 1912.[53]

Rosenwald found Washington and Tuskegee so compelling for some of the same reasons as other white philanthropists and reformers of that time. Washington's insistence that he wanted fair treatment and the opportunity for advancement, rather than rights, paralleled the strategy that Rosenwald preferred all disadvantaged groups to pursue. Like other Progressive activists, he urged private organizations to cooperate with government agencies on projects that would improve the conditions in which people lived and worked. Yet he disagreed when Progressives blamed corporate capitalism for those conditions. Thus he did not feel personally responsible for the sweated labor that produced much of the clothing he sold. Instead, he believed in creating programs that would offer all individuals the chance to earn a better place in society and reward them for their efforts on the job. In his own corporation, for example, Rosenwald encouraged and rewarded employee loyalty, most notably by creating one of the nation's first profit-sharing programs to underwrite pensions for company employees in 1916.[54]

Rosenwald mused publicly that as a Jew he could sympathize with others stung by the barbs of prejudice, although he did not believe that agitation of legal rights was the only or the best way to promote racial equality. Rosenwald made numerous contributions to the National Association for the Advancement of Colored People from its earliest years, yet as he told Oswald Garrison Villard in 1914, "other phases of service for individuals of that race are of greater personal interest to me." His interest in African American issues developed only in part from a desire to redress past wrongs suffered by a single group, and more broadly from his conception of citizenship. "The negro should command himself to the highest standard of living and efficiency," he told the audience gathered for the 1913 dedication of the Chicago YMCA for Colored Men. "This cannot be done by brooding over injustice, nor by declaiming about it, but by living up to the full standard of American citizenship."[55]

Racial equality did not frighten Julius Rosenwald, as it did many other Progressive whites, for his concept of American citizenship rested on equality of opportunity and an individual's willingness to seize upon that opportunity to become a productive member of the economy and society. During his first visit to Tuskegee Institute, he told the assembled students that their accomplishments could "prove to any doubter that colored men and colored women are just as capable of good citizenship, of learning, as any of the white people who have come into my experience." But like that of most Progressive whites, Rosenwald's concept of citizenship for black Americans was dependent on blacks' class and access to education, limiting its potential to help blacks achieve full equality. One Rosenwald Fund official later wrote that "it was plain to him that there would be either ten million [black] Americans, a large part of them illiterate, unprogressive and perhaps criminal because of the lack of educational opportunities, or else there would be ten million with some degree of training for the responsibilities and obligations of good citizenship." Rosenwald himself explained in a 1920 interview that "too much injustice has been practiced against the negro. He needs education and a chance to earn a good living." After making these classic Booker T. Washington–style statements, Rosenwald continued with what he sought to achieve: "I have a strong conviction that the negro will ultimately attain a high place in the scale of civilization. I believe he deserves a fair chance to get a better environment, and I am going to do all I can to see that he gets it."[56]

Rosenwald chose schools as his contribution to "a better environment" that would afford African Americans their "fair chance." While his choice placed him squarely in the mainstream of white philanthropy embodied in the Peabody, Slater, and Jeanes foundations, as well as the Southern Education Board and General Education Board, the preferred tool of better school buildings—rather than teachers, curriculum, or funding—separated his efforts from theirs. Rather than quietly joining the ranks of wealthy trustees and donors like his model, William H. Baldwin Jr., Rosenwald forged a partnership with Booker T. Washington to create an architectural ideal for black schools. Together with other southern reformers and African American school patrons, they made "Rosenwald" a household name in southern African American communities and an adjective that defined a modern school building.

WASHINGTON AND ROSENWALD FOCUS ON RURAL SCHOOLS

The field of southern black education was already crowded, but Washington and Rosenwald believed that schoolhouses, the physical facilities where learning took place, had been neglected. They borrowed from the experiences of other philanthropic initiatives as well as their own projects to move rapidly from ideas to a program of action. The efforts of the Peabody Education Fund, the Slater and Jeanes funds, the Southern Education Board, and the General Education Board led Washington and Rosenwald to assume that the South's state school systems were primed to take up matching grant programs and that these other agencies were handling instructional needs, especially in funding the industrial education curriculum. They also could reasonably expect that public school officers and philanthropic agencies would be willing to add a new partner to their existing alliance.

Previous experiences with their own projects and their shared faith in personal initiative and community responsibility also drove the Washington-Rosenwald partnership toward school construction. Louis R. Harlan has characterized Booker T. Washington as a "materialist" who "believed that strong black institutions would bring forth strong black men and women."[57] Not only Tuskegee Institute but the rural schools of Macon County had put that belief into practice. School buildings had united the county's African American citizens for community improvement. Moreover, Washington had learned that these projects appealed to white philanthropists by creating tangible and lasting structures for progress. Julius Rosenwald also believed in the importance of public spaces where self-help initiatives could flourish and serve as a demonstration to all that black and white Americans could prosper side by side. Rosenwald's fledgling YMCA project confirmed that a challenge grant could inspire local effort and reward all for their contributions. Both men believed that education was a public responsibility and thus expected public funding in addition to community and philanthropic contributions. Not surprisingly, then, the two men soon began exchanging ideas about a new rural school-construction program that would combine outside philanthropy with community self-help to leverage public investment in black education. In the short term, they posited, better school buildings would expand access to public education for African American children. By insisting that communities cooperate with public school authorities, they reasoned, in the long term they would ensure that local and state authorities distributed tax revenues more fairly among black and white schools.

Washington and Rosenwald actually started with hats and shoes. Early in 1912, during Rosenwald's stay at Tuskegee and another visit to Chicago by Washington, they discussed how to address the needs of black public schools and simultaneously foster the work of Tuskegee "offshoots" or "branches"— schools founded or largely staffed by Tuskegee graduates that trained young black men and women for service in black schools. Rosenwald had sent shipments of discarded Sears, Roebuck shoes and hats that Tuskegee sold for small sums to its students. "In the future we are going to consider more carefully the matter of not only using a portion of the shoes and hats to help the small country schools," Washington wrote, "but also to help the branch schools which have grown directly out of the Tuskegee Institute."[58]

Three months later, Washington laid out his ideas about helping those "small country schools" in a lengthy letter that demonstrates how he cultivated Rosenwald as a successor to the H. H. Rogers school project but allowed the idea to develop as Rosenwald's own plan rather than merely substituting one benefactor with another.[59] Obviously both Washington and Rosenwald had been thinking about how to proceed. "I have considered carefully the suggestion which you made regarding the method of helping the colored schools of the South," Washington wrote. "I am convinced, as I suggested to you, that it would hardly be possible to help through the medium of the state." After painting a broad picture of the discriminatory funding of southern public education to his patron, Washington moved on to more practical suggestions that may have come from C. J. Calloway. Calloway, like Washington, earnestly desired to revive the Macon County program to supplement his ongoing school-building projects and had suggested to Washington that the new trustee from Chicago might be interested.[60] Washington's proposal that "a good, strong man [should] be employed" to supervise the use of contributed funds certainly seems modeled on Calloway's role in the Macon County project.

One difference already envisioned between Tuskegee's earlier school-building projects and the new proposal for Rosenwald was that this "strong man" would enlist southern public school officials as partners along with philanthropists, Tuskegee, and black southerners. Washington had learned not to expect much from state authorities. The Alabama Department of Education had only just hired a state agent for Negro schools and had previously done little for black public education. Furthermore, as Washington well knew, local school officers were the ones who decided whether and how much to spend on individual black public schools. Thus Washington proposed concentrating on local officials, writing that "the wisest plan would be for the man in charge of the fund to get in thorough touch with, say, a half dozen county superintendents and county boards who are in thorough sympathy with the plan, get them to work in the county, and in this way it would soon attract the attention of other county officials, and they would make application to have the same thing done in their counties. Beginning in this way with a few counties at first, I believe the plan would attract attention and gradually spread throughout the South."

At this point in the early evolution of the Rosenwald school idea, white public school authorities were the targets of the proposed self-help incentives as well as rural blacks, and school buildings were part of a larger program of educational improvement. Matching grants with local contributions worked, Washington and Rosenwald both knew. But county school authorities needed to provide more equitable public funding, and Washington was concerned that they not use either outside philanthropy or local self-help efforts as cover for their negligence. "There are some dangers to be guarded against," Washington warned. "The temptation in some places would be for the counties to lean on you, and do even less than they are now doing instead of more." An invitation to engage in a joint effort, rather than simply criticizing or bypassing white officials would be preferable, for "the Southern white man likes to be talked to, but does not like to be talked about. Great care should be exercised to let the county officials feel as far as possible that they are doing the work—in a word, to place the responsibility upon them."

Washington also seems to have used the Macon County program as his model in the way he linked instructional improvements to building projects. Macon County communities had extended the school term to eight or nine months, which not only benefited students but attracted more qualified teachers by offering better salaries. Jeanes supervising teachers offered industrial training and community organizing skills as well. But ultimately the prospect of new school facilities had been the key to the community self-help efforts that made all these improvements possible. Thus Washington urged Rosenwald to focus on buildings: "I should hope that the scheme would carry with it a plan for building school-houses as well as extending the school terms. Many of the places in the South where the schools are now taught are as bad as stables, and it is impossible for the teacher to do efficient work in such places." He attached an outline titled "Scheme for Helping Colored Schools" to serve as a starting point for implementing their ideas, creating a draft plan ready for action when the occasion presented itself.

That opportunity came soon after Rosenwald celebrated his fiftieth birthday by contributing $687,500 to various worthy causes, including $25,000 to Tuskegee Institute. The birthday gift picked up on earlier discussions of ways "to help the branch schools which have grown directly out of the Tuskegee Institute." In July 1912, a month before his birthday, Rosenwald asked Washington to prepare a plan for distributing $25,000 to selected Tuskegee offshoots, an idea that Washington eagerly endorsed as "a Godsend to these institutions."[61] Early in August, Rosenwald sent a formal letter laying out his wishes, asking Washington to distribute $25,000 in matching grants to "institutions that have grown out of Tuskegee Institute, or where officered largely by Tuskegee men and women, and are doing the same kind of work as Tuskegee branch schools."[62] Rosenwald announced his birthday gifts on 12 August, which received immediate and widespread newspaper coverage and elicited many letters of thanks (and a few objections) from recipients and observers. Even the outspoken Ida B. Wells-Barnett, who had little sympathy for Booker T. Washington, wrote a letter of "heartiest congratulations" on behalf of the Chicago Negro Fellowship League and thanked Rosenwald "for the birthday gifts you have given the Negro, along with other beneficiaries. We rejoice that Providence has raised up a man who knows no color line in his benefactions."[63]

Booker T. Washington, Clinton J. Calloway, and other African American educators saw in Rosenwald's benefaction an opportunity to launch a much larger public school project. By the end of August, Washington informed Rosenwald that he was working up a school-building plan that he would "submit to you pretty soon." In mid-September, Washington submitted a proposal that reflected his earlier "scheme" and experience with the Macon County project:

> We are giving some careful, and I hope serious attention to the suggestion of making a plan for the helping of colored people in the direction of small country schools. In connection with this idea, I am wondering if you would permit us to make an experiment in the direction of building six school-houses at various points, preferably near here, so that we can watch the experiment closely, out of the special Fund which you have set aside for small schools.
>
> You will recall that in our report [on distribution of the birthday gift], we left unappropriated $2,800. If we could try the experiment on six schools at an average cost, with the idea that we would spend $350 on

each school building, provided the people in the community or the public school authority would raise an equal amount, we feel that we would
then be in a position to recommend something more definite after this
experiment has been made.

After working out the matter pretty carefully, we feel that the houses
themselves can be built for $600., but we would require in the way of trav-
elling expenses on the part of the people from here or somewhere, about
$50.00 in order to get people stirred up and to keep them stirred up until
the school-houses have been built. I really think the experiment is worth
trying. If you could agree to this, that would leave $700 still unappropri-
ated. We shall make recommendations regarding this balance within the
next few days.

One thing I am convinced of and that is that it is the best thing to
have the people themselves build houses in their own community. I have
found by investigation that many people who cannot give money, would
give a half day or a day's work and others would give material in the way
of nails, brick, lime, etc. I feel that there is nothing just now more needed
in the education of the colored people than the matter of small schoolhouses and I am very anxious that the matter be thoroughly planned for
and well worked out and no mistake be made.

Washington's proposal drew upon his earlier "Scheme for Helping Colored
Schools" to establish several key principles that would shape the early Rosenwald school program. First, physical structures—new school buildings—would
provide the catalyst for further educational improvements. Second, Rosenwald
aid would provide an incentive for local support, both private and public.
Third, local support, both by black community members and white school authorities, would renew and expand everyone's commitment to black children's
education. Consequently, community members could donate time, labor, and
material in lieu of or as supplements to cash contributions for the grant match,
not only to accommodate their meager cash resources but also to encourage
their physical participation in schoolhouse construction. White school officials, on the other hand, could add a valuable property to their public school
plant with only a small investment of public funds. And fourth, community involvement would require expert leadership, in this case a Tuskegee-appointed
organizer who would provide the needed supervision and coordination.[64]

This plan embodied several key assumptions as well, most obviously the belief that environment shaped the human experience, a belief shared by Progres-

sive educators with other reformers and, to some degree, the broader American culture. Another Progressive assumption was that education was a public responsibility, and access to public education an essential right of citizenship. The plan also assumed that local people had the capability for self-help but needed professional guidance to implement it successfully. These presumptions reflected African American traditions of educational activism and support for their own educated leaders, as well as newer Progressive concerns about the authority of professionals. Once Rosenwald found Washington's proposal "entirely satisfactory," the first, experimental stage of the building program was underway.

Another significant precedent for the later Rosenwald building program soon appeared as African American and white educators flooded Tuskegee Institute's mail with requests for help. Washington was not the only person trying to divert Rosenwald's birthday gift to another agenda. Other educators swiftly realized the potential for their communities and eagerly sought its benefits, foreshadowing the local initiative that would sustain the Rosenwald school program. Letters came from across the South: from Caret, Virginia; Eufala, Plateau, Hayneville, Livingston, and Sawyerville, Alabama; Lawrence, Mississippi; Macon, Georgia; Avinger, Texas; and Asheville and Bricks, North Carolina. Some correspondents wrote simply to find out if and how their institutions might be eligible for aid, but A. M. Addison from Port Gibson, Mississippi, wrote out of desperation. "I am writing to ask you, to please, assist our school," he pleaded. "The enrollment is nearly three hundred but the building is very poor. The children are packed like sardines in a box. The parents are poor and not able to build a school house. In the name of the children, please, allow me to again ask you to help us."[65] In 1912, Washington turned aside such requests and withheld news of the school-building experiment until he could claim success.

THE ROSENWALD RURAL SCHOOL EXPERIMENT, 1912–14

Booker T. Washington moved quietly on the first experimental schools and carefully monitored their progress to develop a template for a larger construction program. From the fall of 1912 until the summer of 1914, Tuskegee officials concentrated on six rural communities in three counties in the vicinity of Tuskegee Institute. Their experimental program began with a debate over standardized building plans and materials, which would keep expenses down for poverty-stricken rural communities and maximize the number of schools constructed with its aid. Rural school design for its own sake was, at this point, secondary to the sheer need for new and better buildings.

Rosenwald was as eager as Washington to test their plan for using better school buildings to improve education and community life. His first instinct, as the executive of a national mercantile firm, was to leverage the benefits of his donation through standardization and volume purchasing. He had immediately taken Washington's proposal to Sears management, as he explained in his letter approving the building experiment:

> We might save quite a little money on each one of these buildings through having Sears, Roebuck & Co. furnish the lumber and some of the other materials, instead of contracting for each school separately—let us have the plan and the lumber will all be cut to length and delivered. Then of course the little hardware that would be needed, the paint and the school desks could all be furnished from here. These are only suggestions, and if they meet with your approval can be carried out. What might be advisable would be for you to have a plan made of about such a school house as you think will be required and we could then figure out exactly what we could deliver the material on the ground for.

At Rosenwald's request, F. W. Kushel, who headed up Sears, Roebuck's famous "Modern Homes" department, had his staff draw plans for three sizes of schools to accommodate between twenty and fifty students but also suggested using one of the company's portable houses from its "Ready Made Building Catalog" to save expense.[66] After C. J. Calloway complained that these would be too small, Washington offered to have Tuskegee staff draw up alternate plans and specifications so that Rosenwald could "determine which will be best to have the house gotten up by your firm and shipped to us, or whether it will be best to have them wholly built here."[67]

Robert R. Taylor, director of industries and staff architect at Tuskegee, transmitted the first set of plans for what would become Rosenwald schools in November 1912. Taylor had earned his degree from the architecture program at the Massachusetts Institute of Technology in 1892, where he was MIT's first African American student, and joined the Tuskegee faculty later that year. Over the next two decades, he designed over twenty buildings on the Tuskegee campus.[68] Taylor sent Washington and Kushel three plans and his own cost estimates for schools housing thirty-four, fifty-four, and seventy-two students. Not wishing to antagonize Sears, Roebuck staff or his patron, and anxious to demonstrate that he shared their concern to minimize costs, Washington assured Kushel that Taylor's estimates were "our opinion," and that "we might be in a position to make a definite recommendation to Mr. Rosenwald" only after

Kushel could estimate what the materials would cost if purchased from Sears, Roebuck.[69]

While Taylor designed the schools, Clinton Calloway recruited communities for the six experimental schools. He was already busy on school-building projects funded with Jeanes money, however, and needed an assistant. Calloway got Washington's permission to assign William M. Rakestraw, organizer of the extension department's Farmers' Conference, to the school campaigns. Washington's insistence that communities qualify for Rosenwald money as soon as possible sped up the pace of their efforts. As Washington wrote to Calloway, he was "anxious to encourage Mr. Rosenwald to give more money" and hoped that Rosenwald would "give considerable money later on for schoolhouse building if we can show that the people are so interested that they will meet his conditions speedily, and therefore I want nothing to stand in the way of our getting hold of just as many communities as possible to meet these conditions."[70]

Calloway quickly discovered that local enthusiasm ran far ahead of the school planners. He reported in late November that residents of Loachapoka in Lee County had raised $100, and several other communities "are rallying and raising money as fast as it seems that it is possible for us to get them to carry out our suggestions." Under Washington's orders, Calloway focused on raising money and delayed construction until the issue of Sears, Roebuck materials had been decided, but he questioned the wisdom of such a procedure and chafed at the delay: "I wish that you would let me know as early as possible whether or not Mr. Rosenwald is to be expected to furnish the building material or cash money for these various points [communities]. I feel quite certain if it is decided that he will furnish the building material, we will experience many inconveniences in getting the people to put in their part of the money due in putting up the building. There seems to be a feeling in most cases that some local sawmill and local business house shall get some of the benefit of the money spent in putting up the building."[71]

After another flurry of memoranda from his staff, Washington carefully withdrew the project from complete dependence on Sears, Roebuck materials.[72] Anxious not to appear ungrateful, he proposed that "all of the rough and heavy lumber, bricks, etc. be gotten in the vicinity of the schoolhouses." But materials such as window sash, doors, nails and screws, paint, and blinds, he suggested, could still come from Sears, Roebuck & Company, as "we find that it will be an advantage to purchase these from your firm." Rosenwald issued a gallant response: "the only thing to do is to build these [schools] at the lowest possible cost without sacrificing quality. By this I do not mean a cheap build-

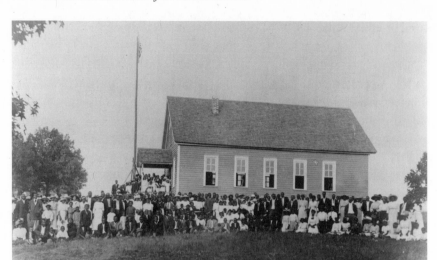

Figure 1. Dedication of the Loachapoka School, the first Rosenwald school, completed in March 1913. (Julius Rosenwald Fund Archives, Fisk University Franklin Library, Special Collections)

ing of course, but a good building at a low price. The cost of the building will of course be a great consideration as to the number we can erect, and I do not want Sears, Roebuck & Co., to be considered in the purchasing except as a factor toward reducing the cost."[73]

Thus Julius Rosenwald resolved an important early question about the relationship between his personal philanthropy and his corporate interests. In so doing, he allowed Calloway and Taylor to chart an independent course for the building program's designs and construction materials and to create more opportunities for African American self-help through donations of lumber and materials. Rosenwald had not agreed to the rural school experiment in order to benefit his business operations and certainly did not wish others to think that he had. His initial suggestion to involve Sears, Roebuck had been, as he said, just a suggestion. Rosenwald found the reward he sought from the communities that labored to build schools. In January 1913, Washington sent him a copy of the extension department's *Messenger*, in which Rosenwald could read about the fund-raising efforts in Loachapoka and Notasulga. Washington's steady stream of reports kept Rosenwald apprised of the progress of their experiment and "show[ed] that the people are so interested that they will meet his conditions speedily."[74]

And indeed they did: the schools at Loachapoka in Lee County (figure 1) and at Notasulga and Brownville in Macon County were finished by May 1913, and the Little Zion, Big Zion, and Madison Park schools (figure 2) in Montgomery County stood complete by the following spring.[75] Ever anxious to cultivate warm relations with their patron and project an image of interracial goodwill, Washington and Calloway sent Rosenwald letters of thanks from leading white citizens. Rosenwald particularly liked the photographs Washington sent of the first three schools, which he found "tremendously interesting," and which he thought could inspire more communities to build such schools and attract other donors. "There is no telling what the result might be if these photographs were given wide publicity with just the right kind of write-up," he enthused.[76]

The story of the Notasulga school did receive such a "write-up" in newspaper accounts of a mass meeting at Tuskegee in 1915. Its central character, Mary

Figure 2. *Clockwise from left:* Eli Madison, a Madison Park student, the Madison Park Farmers' Club, and the Madison Park School, 1915. One of the six experimental schools constructed in 1913–14, this school shows a plan for two classrooms with a dropped-gable entrance seen in later Rosenwald schools. (Julius Rosenwald Papers, Special Collections Research Center, University of Chicago Library)

Figure 3. The old Notasulga School, Lee County, Alabama. Mary Johnson led a nine-year campaign to replace this structure with one of the six experimental Rosenwald schools. Like many African American schools in southern states, this building had no visible identity as a school and blended into the rural landscape. (Julius Rosenwald Fund Archives, Fisk University Franklin Library, Special Collections)

Johnson, bore witness to rural African Americans' determination to educate their children and testified as to how that determination might be united with a philanthropic initiative and expressed in a modern schoolhouse. One cold day, Johnson had decided that she could no longer allow Notasulga's children to sit in a school building with wide cracks in its walls and floor, and without heat or windows (figure 3). She wrote to Booker T. Washington to ask how she could get a new building, and in return received instructions from the division of extension. "Amid the jeers of the men of her community and the disbelief of her own husband," a Boston newspaper recounted, Johnson organized the women of her community, who raised money by selling "pies and other dainties." After losing all their earnings to a dishonest treasurer, Johnson started over and raised enough money to buy the necessary lumber, "but not having enough to pay for the building of the structure, the men of the community let the lumber rot on the ground."[77]

Undaunted, Johnson began the project a third time. Clinton Calloway took a direct role in the project, probably thanks to Rosenwald's gift, and a new teacher, Fannie A. Wheelis, added her organizational skills. Wheelis reported that in less than six months she and "a few willing workers" held a Thanksgiving rally, an entertainment at a private home, a school concert, and a birthday party to which the invited guests brought bags of pennies. Patrons and "friends" made private donations, as did the Shiloh Baptist Church, Buleah Baptist Church, Macedonia Baptist Church, the Ebenezer Association, and the Mosaic Temple; patrons donated $100 in labor, and a church donated the building site. As the *Montgomery Times* reported, "they again bought lumber—not to rot this time. No outsider was employed. Each patron who could weild [*sic*] a tool, came and put in his day or days on the building." They did so under the watchful eye of Mary Johnson, who visited the building site daily "and passed planks and shingles to the carpenters."[78]

Mary Johnson's nine-year struggle culminated in the dedication of Notasulga's experimental Rosenwald school in May 1913. Johnson's and Notasulga's story would be repeated many times in the years to come, as African American women and men challenged each other and their communities to action on behalf of their children's future, and joined forces with teachers and outside organizers armed with Rosenwald money. One of "six acorns dropped into Alabama for a unique adventure in education," Notasulga's schoolhouse sprouted a plan for one hundred more schools in 1914.[79]

First Responses to the Rosenwald Rural School-Building Program

Booker T. Washington hoped stories like Mary Johnson's would convince Julius Rosenwald to support a larger rural school-building program. He hinted at this as early as October 1913, when he told William C. Graves, Rosenwald's personal secretary, that "it is likely from year to year the scope of the scheme will be broadened." Rosenwald had already signaled his own interest in June 1913, telling Washington, "When the . . . schools are erected I shall be glad to have your opinion as to the value of any further work along the same line." Once the last experimental schools had been completed, Washington scheduled a tour of the Madison Park, Big Zion, and Little Zion schools to generate quick publicity material. Clinton J. Calloway organized the day's events, distributed a poster announcing Washington's tour schedule, and urged Alabama Negro school agent James L. Sibley to attend as a show of official state support as well as a reporter from the *Montgomery Advertiser*. Afterwards, Washington sent Rosenwald a packet of photographs showing the construction of the schools and the resulting newspaper story.[80]

Booker T. Washington's careful preparations paved the way for a successful meeting with Julius Rosenwald in Chicago on 10 June 1914, where Rosenwald promised up to $30,000 toward the construction of as many as one hundred school buildings. Two weeks later, Tuskegee Institute secretary Emmett J. Scott circulated a press release to selected African American newspapers, including the *New York Age*. "Create Fund to Build Rural School Houses," announced the *Age*. "Rosenwald of Chicago Will Duplicate All Money Raised for Country Schools." Articles based on the press release identified Julius Rosenwald as the silent patron of a pilot project in schoolhouse construction, proclaiming that "the report made by Dr. Washington was so satisfactory that Mr. Rosenwald has decided to go ahead with the experiment on a large scale, and has agreed to duplicate dollar for dollar whatever sum is raised in any rural district in the South for schoolhouse buildings."[81]

This announcement unleashed another flood of requests for Rosenwald aid but also created a crisis because of its inaccurate characterization of Rosenwald's philanthropy. Educators and activists, most of them African American, started writing letters as soon as they read the published announcement of the rural school-building program. Booker T. Washington was gratified to find white officers at several state departments of education among the correspondents, for they offered just the sort of evidence that he needed to justify his strategy of accommodation and to elicit more white support. Certainly the white men whom the General Education Board had placed as state agents for Negro schools in southern education departments recognized the potential of this matching grant program for redressing the neglect of black school facilities. Arkansas state superintendent George B. Cook and state agent for Negro schools Leo M. Favrot suggested to Julius Rosenwald that he might want "some assurance from disinterested parties or state authorities" on the merits of building applicants. Favrot assured Booker T. Washington that they were "anxious to place this Department at your disposal, in the distribution of this money, in any way which you can use it."[82] Kentucky's state Negro school agent, Frank C. Button, and Tennessee's Samuel L. Smith also applied directly to Rosenwald and Washington, only to meet polite rejections.[83] A few white county school officials also wrote, generally to demonstrate support for requests being made from black schools under their supervision.[84]

Such letters indicated that Rosenwald's building program was attractive to a small number of sympathetic southern whites, but the majority of letters came from southern African Americans who wanted new schools. Their constant stream of letters would continue for almost two decades. Black correspondents included local leaders, the sorts of individuals who had already been at the fore-front of community school projects and now would prove central to grassroots Rosenwald building campaigns. Some had already tried for Rosenwald money from Tuskegee in 1912, such as J. M. Beverly of Caret, Virginia. Others had es-tablished careers and leadership roles to which the Rosenwald program seemed a natural addition, including Virginia E. Randolph of Henrico County, Vir-ginia, the model for the Jeanes industrial supervising teacher program. Many correspondents, like Georgian L. H. Brown, were teachers who faced dire cir-cumstances in rural schools. "The surrender of Gen. Lee has been 49 years ago last April 9th, and it is both a pity and a shame to know that we have Rural Dis-tricts in this County, thickly settled with Colored people, without any school houses whatever for the instruction of their children," Brown declared. "I beg to ad [*sic*] that this Haralson District has been under the Local supervision of white school officers for 20 years, and while they have received and handled all the Public school funds, all these years, they have comfortably provided for the whites good buildings, but not a *shingle* for the Negroes. . . . There are *Moun-tains* of *Race* Prejudice yet against the education of Negroes in many of these *back* corners."[85]

Like teachers, ministers held great respect and authority in rural African American communities. Their support and organizational skills were essential to community endeavors. Not surprisingly, announcement of Rosenwald's offer for schools caught their attention as well. Georgetown, South Carolina's Afri-can Methodist Episcopal minister, J. E. Beard, offered his assistance: "I shall be pleased to give some of my time in getting around advising my people as to how best to raise money for this particular purpose. . . . I shall be pleased to work where I can anywhere in the state."[86] Women also were already key figures in lo-cal school-improvement groups and community fund-raising and prepared to tackle Rosenwald projects. Louella M. Brown, president of the Mothers' Club and Parent-Teachers Association in Loudon, Tennessee, asked Rosenwald to match her group's efforts in having raised $962, which she hoped would amount to $1,200 after another rally.[87]

African American college presidents also seized on the program's possibili-ties for schools in their states and were eager to demonstrate that they already had white officials' support. E. L. Blackshear of the Prairie View Normal and In-dustrial College wanted Texas schools to benefit from Rosenwald's generosity, as did some superintendents who had heard his announcement of Rosenwald's matching grants at the white state teachers' association meeting.[88] From Louisiana, Southern University and A&M College president J. S. Clark wrote at the state superintendent's request to assure Washington that Louisiana's white leaders were sincerely interested in black schools and would see to it that Rosenwald's offer met a positive response.[89]

Even activists of the stature of W.E.B. Du Bois sent letters of inquiry. Du Bois asked Rosenwald for "an authoritative statement of this most important philanthropy" that he could run in the *Crisis*. His letter, like others Rosenwald received, was forwarded to Booker T. Washington for a formal response.[90] The August 1914 issue of the *Crisis* quoted an editorial from the *Nation* praising Rosenwald's largesse, and the following month's "Education" section quoted directly from "an authoritative statement sent out from Tuskegee."[91] In spite of Du Bois' long-standing public debate with Washington and his opposition to harnessing all black schools to industrial education, Du Bois continually publicized the Rosenwald building program in the *Crisis*.

Time and time again, these correspondents quoted and paraphrased the June press release statement describing Rosenwald's offer "to duplicate dollar for dollar whatever sum is raised in any rural district in the South for schoolhouse buildings." But an open-ended dollar-for-dollar gift to any community was not what Rosenwald had promised or what Washington wanted. With requests coming in from Virginia to Oklahoma, and from Kentucky to Louisiana, Rosenwald's and Washington's office staffs scrambled to contain the damage to their fledgling program. Washington used Tuskegee's own publications to issue modified announcements that restated Rosenwald's offer as duplicating "a stipulated amount."[92]

Despite this public relations glitch, Rosenwald, Washington, and their staffs were far more interested in articulating the procedures by which Tuskegee would administer Rosenwald's matching grants and communities could qualify for assistance. In mid-July, Washington sent out draft guidelines for review by Julius Rosenwald and other officials. One of them was James L. Sibley, who had been working closely with Calloway and Alabama Jeanes supervisors on community school-building projects. As one of Washington's guidelines called for approval from the Alabama department of education and local school officials before construction began, Washington asked Sibley for assurance of the state superintendent's support. Another copy went to James Hardy Dillard, who headed the Anna T. Jeanes Fund, to ensure his cooperation with Washington's plan for using Jeanes supervisors to help with local Rosenwald campaigns.[93]

Simultaneously, Washington hinted at the possibility of aid to other states by seeking advice on school buildings from state Negro school agents in Georgia and Arkansas. Their ready responses, including Leo Favrot's trip from Little Rock to Tuskegee to present his ideas in person, indicate that Washington's requests only increased expectations for Rosenwald aid across the region.[94]

THE PLAN FOR ERECTION OF RURAL SCHOOLHOUSES

Hammered out in the summer and fall of 1914, the "Plan for Erection of Rural Schoolhouses" spelled out the building program's initial guidelines to potential participants. It also served as the foundational document for program administrators Booker T. Washington, Clinton J. Calloway, and Tuskegee's executive council. As with the experimental schools, Rosenwald and Washington centered their plan on school buildings for rural communities and required the active involvement of local residents and school officials at both the local and state levels. First, as the "Plan for Erection" explained, its grants were to assist "public school officers and the people in the community in erecting schoolhouses in rural and village districts by supplementing what the public school officers or the people themselves may do." This language couched the new initiative in rural school construction within the same expectations of greater public support that outside philanthropies like the Peabody Education Fund had called for since the 1860s. In addition, community members had to secure approval from school authorities before starting on a project, as well as active participation by Jeanes supervisors and state Negro school agents. To address the inaccurate publicity about Rosenwald's own contributions, another proviso carefully spelled out that the grants were conditional on a community securing at least as much funding from public revenues or its own members but would not exceed $350 each, inclusive of expenses incurred in "working up interest" and supervising construction. At Rosenwald's request, Tuskegee officials added that Rosenwald had agreed to give up to $30,000 in grants of no more than $350 to "about 100 rural schoolhouses" over the next five years and warned that any notices about a dollar-for-dollar match "without limitation as to number and location [have] been made without Mr. Rosenwald's authority or knowledge."

The 1914 plan also mandated that the Tuskegee extension department approve all building plans and, if necessary for state aid, the state department of education would as well—a vague rule that would become much more important as communities began their construction projects. Where to construct the schools was more problematic. This initial plan of aid specifically identified

Lee, Lowndes, and Montgomery counties in Alabama, but Rosenwald program planners left several doors open to other areas of the state, suggesting that larger schools such as the Snow Hill Normal and Industrial Institute might serve as organizers for countywide schoolhouse construction programs, and that other Alabama counties could apply for aid.[95]

The scope of the initial plan changed almost immediately. Tuskegee officials broadened the number of eligible states under pressure from other educational activists and from rural correspondents. Booker T. Washington had originally envisioned a county-by-county campaign, but James Hardy Dillard advised a wider field of action.[96] Although Washington demurred, he invited Dillard to recommend deserving applicants from Florida, Georgia, and Mississippi, where Washington thought conditions were especially serious.[97] Yet Washington immediately offered Rosenwald aid for a model school in Georgia.[98] By the late summer, Washington informed Dillard that Louisiana, South Carolina, and possibly Arkansas would also be acceptable, although he still felt that North Carolina, Tennessee, and Virginia "have not such strong claims."[99] Washington had to justify this deviation from his own plan to Rosenwald and had Calloway produce letters from white officials to support his claim that white southerners had been inspired by the schoolhouse project. He also argued that poor economic conditions required Tuskegee to cast a broader net across the region. But the volume of correspondence in general, and the discussions with Dillard in particular, suggest that Washington was moving toward a regional program. Rosenwald sensed this too, and had Graves ask Washington to send a "suggested plan in detail for his consideration before taking any definite steps."[100]

The "Plan for Erection of Rural Schoolhouses" transformed the experimental building project into a limited statewide program with regional aspirations. Washington and Rosenwald had settled key issues raised by their six experimental schools. They had applied their personal interests in public buildings to a major area of need in a way that complemented the work of private and public agencies. Their philanthropic colleagues had welcomed the new initiative and the state and local officials responsible for black public schools had proved willing to add Rosenwald grants for buildings to their agendas. Thus the building grants would come from a central agency authorized by Julius Rosenwald and then flow from Tuskegee to state education departments and local school authorities. These officials would coordinate Rosenwald grants with moneys from other agencies and use them as incentives for greater public support.

The overwhelming response from black educators and school patrons, as well as the work of Calloway and Taylor, also shaped the early program's development. It would have a centralized administration in terms of design and approval of Rosenwald grants but a decentralized implementation coordinated by state agents for Negro schools and Tuskegee's community organizers. Its success would depend on local initiative through self-help and local effort in constructing the schools. Mary Johnson's story and Washington's correspondents demonstrated that rural African Americans were ready to put the Rosenwald plan into action.

New Schools

The Rosenwald Rural School-Building Program at Tuskegee,
1914–20

Between 1912 and 1914, Booker T. Washington and Julius Rosenwald had forged a partnership that would open a new chapter in African American education. The first of their new schoolhouses in rural Alabama communities had introduced the rural school-building program to black and white southerners and invited more participation. When Julius Rosenwald made his annual visit to Tuskegee in February 1915, he found proof that the fledgling building program could benefit the entire region (figure 4). Accompanied by a who's who of Chicago reformers, including Hull House luminaries Jane Addams, Edith and Grace Abbott, and Sophonisba Breckinridge; Jenkin Lloyd Jones of the Abraham Lincoln Center; and representatives from Jewish charities, Julius and Augusta Rosenwald enjoyed a series of entertainments and observed student life at the Tuskegee campus. Then they took a tour of rural schools recently built with Rosenwald grants, organized by Clinton J. Calloway, James L. Sibley, and Jeanes supervisor Lula Thomas. Jenkin Lloyd Jones described the scenes at Little Zion, Big Zion, Madison Park, and Davenport, where "not only the children but all the colored community in the vicinity and many whites were there to greet the party. They were lined along the road several tiers deep, waving evergreen branches and singing the old plantation refrains of their fore-elders" (figure 5).[1] These songs, the simple decorations that adorned the schools, and reports of community improvements appealed to the white northerners' stereotypical, yet sympathetic, images of what the South had been and might become.

The school tour suggested how Rosenwald schools might meet this future promise. At this time, only Tuskegee officials used the term "Rosenwald school," as Julius Rosenwald generally avoided publicizing his contributions with displays of his name. The earliest usages of "Rosenwald school" come in Tuskegee's internal correspondence. Clinton Calloway described three Montgomery County school buildings as "Rosenwald schools" in February and

Left: Figure 4. Julius Rosenwald and Booker T. Washington at Tuskegee Institute, 1915. (Julius Rosenwald Papers, Special Collections Research Center, University of Chicago Library)

Below: Figure 5. Davenport School patrons awaiting the Rosenwald party's visit, 1915. The shop building follows plan 14 in *The Negro Rural School and Its Relation to the Community* (1915). (Julius Rosenwald Papers, Special Collections Research Center, University of Chicago Library)

March 1914.[2] This terminology simply helped Tuskegee officials distinguish between their multiple school projects and patrons. A year later, however, Tuskegee staff had begun to use the term publicly in promotional efforts for the building program that targeted rural African Americans. The cover of the 19 June 1915, issue of the *Negro Farmer*, published by Tuskegee Institute, illustrated the new and old Madison Park schools, together with a picture of school patron Eli Madison. The caption announced that the new building was a "'Rosenwald' School" and identified Madison as "one type of colored citizen who has helped secure one for his community."[3] After Tuskegee Institute published a schoolhouse plan book later that summer, "Rosenwald school" very quickly came to mean a particular type of school building, a public school facility for African American children that met modern standards.

Within six years, more than six hundred of these schools stood across the South, many constructed according to the first official "Rosenwald school" designs. Their construction generated a complex debate over the goal of the Rosenwald building program, its methods of operation, and the effectiveness of African American leadership. Clinton J. Calloway came to the fore as the Rosenwald program's chief administrator, presiding over its expansion across thirteen states. Although Julius Rosenwald deepened his commitment to the building program, he and other white reformers began questioning whether its schools for black children were good enough. Despite the First World War and its economic aftermath, which slowed Rosenwald school construction, the building program expanded beyond Tuskegee's administrative resources. The resulting problems, as diagnosed by white professional reformers, provoked Julius Rosenwald into a complete reorganization of the building program and pushed Calloway and Tuskegee Institute to the sidelines.

The Rosenwald Rural School-Building Program in Alabama and the South, 1914–16

Julius Rosenwald's visit must have led to a private agreement with Booker T. Washington on a more expansive building program, for Washington soon reported that his staff had been working on the suggestions about "the extension of the schoolhouse building" made during Rosenwald's stay. In consultation with James L. Sibley, the Tuskegee executive council proposed extending the offer of Rosenwald aid to more Alabama counties "thoroughly ripe for such a movement." Two months later, Calloway, Sibley, and the executive council had approved at least fourteen Alabama counties for possible Rosenwald aid. They also agreed to accept small numbers of applications from Arkansas, Florida, Georgia, Mississippi, North Carolina, and Tennessee, setting a precedent for the annual allocations of specific numbers of buildings to individual states that would become a standard practice for the Rosenwald program.[4]

Washington and Clinton J. Calloway negotiated with Rosenwald for the staff needed for such an expansive program. Calloway and William Rakestraw could no longer meet the demand for their time and travel generated by Jeanes and Rosenwald school projects, as well as their other extension department responsibilities. Tuskegee's 1914–15 Jeanes Fund appropriation still included special building campaigns in Lee and Montgomery counties, and Calloway used both Jeanes and Rosenwald money to hire field agents to handle community organizing.[5] Subsequent Rosenwald building grants replaced the Jeanes funds used for construction projects, and Julius Rosenwald allowed Tuskegee to use his donation to hire a full-time assistant for Calloway. Booker T. Washington Jr. began work as the program's first Rosenwald building agent in the late spring of 1915, but the demand for community organizers still outpaced staff resources. By the end of the year, Calloway had asked for and received Rosenwald support for another field organizer.[6]

Meanwhile, the "Plan for Erection of Rural Schoolhouses" underwent repeated revisions to bring it in line with developments in the field and in Tuskegee's operational procedures. Updated guidelines issued in 1915 clarified that each one-teacher school would receive a construction grant of $300, with an additional $50 to cover administrative and promotional costs. Although Alabama would remain a major focus, applications from all eligible states would be accepted and reviewed in the order in which they were received. The most important new provision warned, "In no case will the Rosenwald aid be given until the amount raised by a community and that to be given by Mr. Rosenwald is sufficient to complete and furnish the schoolhouse to be built. In estimating the amount of money raised by a community, cash, land, labor and material shall be included."[7] Communities would not receive a grant from Rosenwald until they had raised their corresponding contribution, and they must outfit their new building as well. But their matching contribution could comprise any combination of resources that they had to offer, whether public or private money, in-kind contributions, or land.

What the buildings should look like was unclear. Tuskegee Institute agreed to distribute approved "pamphlets and plans," which would appear that summer as *The Negro Rural School and Its Relation to the Community*. Otherwise, the only hint about school design was that the one-teacher schools should cost on average $800, inclusive of the completed building, two sanitary toilets, and "sufficient desks, heater, etc." and possibly the site.[8] This short list set important precedents for later requirements that Rosenwald schools have proper sanitary facilities and be fully furnished. But the average cost also suggests how simple the structures were meant to be. Given that Alabama schools could expect a Rosenwald grant of $300 and another $200 in state aid plus patron contributions, this estimate also suggests that, despite the insistence that local authorities approve all Rosenwald projects, program planners initially expected little public funding at the local level.[9]

Booker T. Washington's own expectations were deliberately restrained, as his anxiety over the initial cost estimates for the six experimental schools showed. He believed that better school facilities would encourage teachers and students to perform to higher standards, foster community unity through self-help, and attract white support for black education. Just what those buildings could or should look like, for Washington, depended on how much the program's sponsor and local people were willing to give and what southern whites could tolerate. As he explained to J. L. Sibley, "The cheaper we can build these schoolhouses, the more Mr. Rosenwald is going to be encouraged to let us have additional money." The visual message his buildings might send to whites also concerned Washington. As Rosenwald himself had already noted, in some places even these humble new black schools would outshine white facilities. Washington suggested to Sibley that they all take care "not to put so much money into a building that it will bring about a feeling of jealousy on the part of the white people." "The more modest our school buildings are at present at least," Washington believed, "the more we are likely to avoid such a difficulty," doubtless referring to arson, a commonly used white tactic to destroy African American advancement through education.[10]

Designing Tuskegee Schools

Although the "Plan for Erection of Rural Schoolhouses" offered little guidance for building and equipping a school, it did require communities to use approved plans and thus promised to set new design standards for African American country schools.[11] The designs of Rosenwald schools, like the rural school program itself, developed from an unusual interracial partnership and created spaces for black schoolchildren that blurred the color line. Tuskegee architect Robert R. Taylor had already prepared the first plans for Rosenwald schools during the negotiations with Sears, Roebuck and Company in the fall of 1912. In May 1913, Calloway submitted Tuskegee's building plans to Negro school agent James L. Sibley to secure the state aid available under Alabama's school laws for the extension division's construction projects, including the experimental Rosenwald schools.[12] The Negro school agent's influence and the promise of both state and Rosenwald aid, Calloway hoped, might overcome the "considerable indifference" white school authorities often displayed toward black school facilities.[13]

Actually, most objections came at first from black school patrons. Some balked at the state requirement that their school property, which was usually privately owned, must be deeded to the state to qualify for state aid. African American Alabamians had subsidized schools when local and state governments would not, and they continued to suffer under the weight of state-imposed segregation and disfranchisement, hence their reluctance to place these community places under state control. As Calloway observed, "It is difficult to get the people to feel that they are not turning their birth right over into the hand of their enemies," even if he himself believed "it is the very best thing that we can do."[14]

Calloway also asked Booker T. Washington's approval for using some of the leftover Rosenwald money from the experimental schools to produce "a good leaflet on 'How to Build a Schoolhouse' with suggestive plans."[15] That suggestion escalated into a two-year project culminating in the 1915 publication of *The Negro Rural School and Its Relation to the Community*, a book of building plans with prescriptions for school and community improvement. Tuskegee's project became entangled with the Alabama State Department of Education's proposed plan book for white schools, for which J. L. Sibley wanted Calloway and Robert R. Taylor to collaborate with him on at least one design "suitable for both colored and white schools."[16] To Calloway's dismay, cooperating with the state department retarded Tuskegee's design work. Sibley wanted more than just one or two building plans. In the fall of 1914, he asked Tuskegee's famous agricultural scientist George Washington Carver to write on "about 15 topics" and had Taylor prepare plans for an industrial building and a teachers' home. William A. Hazel, head of Tuskegee's architectural and mechanical drawing division, was so overwhelmed by Sibley's repeated requests that at times he had to cancel his classes.[17] The finished bulletin finally appeared in print in August 1915.[18]

The Negro Rural School and Its Relation to the Community circulated widely, offering its readers new images of black education that paralleled contemporary developments in white public schools. Official reaction noted its contribution immediately. "That pamphlet . . . is one of the best things of its kind I have ever seen," Arkansas Negro school agent Leo M. Favrot congratulated Sibley. "I am going to fasten mine to my desk in some way so it will never get away from me."[19] North Carolina Negro school agent Nathan C. Newbold sent a copy to his new assistant agent to use as he inspected school buildings. Black community leaders seized upon its designs as well. In 1917, C. Dillard Jr., principal of the Columbus Literary, Normal and Industrial School in Whiteville, North Carolina, wrote Tuskegee officials that "we are anxious to follow diagram on pages 89–90 in your book on the Negro Rural School and its relation to the community."[20]

The Negro Rural School stressed what were already standard prescriptions for rural school planning by Progressive school architects and educators. Its authors—probably a combination of Sibley, Calloway, and Carver—echoed the advice pouring out of southern departments of education and from schoolhouse architects for white as well as black rural schools. State superintendents of education in southern states were reviving a campaign for new school construction standards that dated to the Reconstruction era. Florida state superintendent C. Thurston Chase had introduced hygienic and instructional factors to southern school architecture in an 1868 bulletin illustrating buildings designed or influenced by such architects as Andrew Jackson Downing and Calvert Vaux. Over subsequent decades, southern educators articulated their own rhetorical and aesthetic principles. Arkansas state superintendent James L. Denton in 1880 argued that "the school-house has a language of its own, that the superficial observer finds no difficulty in interpreting. It is the inarticulate speech of a people. It discriminates civilization from barbarism, breathes of culture and refinement, and is a silent yet powerful protest against ignorance and crime."[21]

Progressive educators and designers in the early twentieth century added the mandate of science and the aesthetics of efficiency to school design. These experts invoked a functionalist aesthetic that rendered modernity and progress in light, airy, and hygienic classrooms arranged within simple, symmetrical floor plans and facades. All agreed that the first step in building a new school should be the selection of a centrally located site of sufficient size to accommodate the school and necessary outbuildings, play spaces, and practice gardens. Then professional educators advised local school officials to seek out an architect or at least use plans prepared by a professional architect for their state department of education. Those expertly designed structures took the classroom as the basic unit of design. "When the room is bright and attractive and the air pure," advised the architects who prepared North Carolina school plans, "the scholars are always bright and attentive, and the teachers can do better work. With a poorly lighted room and bad air, the scholars are dull, inattentive and irritable." Thus the classroom had to provide adequate lighting, mostly if not exclusively falling from above and the left of students' desks. School architects recommended tall double-hung windows massed together into a single "battery" rather than strung at regular intervals along the walls, both to provide the needed light and for proper air circulation. Cloakrooms kept dirty or wet outer garments from the clean and dry classroom, and sanitary outhouses discreetly disposed of human waste.[22]

Educators described these modern designs in language that demonstrated their enduring belief that the school spoke in a "language of its own," arguing that the appearance of school buildings expressed their communities' values. As the authors of Kentucky's 1917 school design compendium contended: "The historian of the future will doubtless record it as a marvel of the age that intelligent, moral, patriotic citizens suffered their children to spend six hours a day in the antiquated, insanitary, weather-beaten shacks that are alleged to provide shelter for the 'deestrick' school. . . . It is dawning upon us . . . that the school property is an index to the enterprise and culture of any community—rural or urban."[23]

The authors of *The Negro Rural School and Its Relation to the Community* would have added "black or white." Thanks to the collaboration between Tuskegee staff and the Alabama Negro school agent, their publication used the same rhetoric and design elements that southern educational writers applied first and foremost to white schools. *The Negro Rural School* described schools as community centers where adults' and children's clubs could meet and children could play, supported by an active school-improvement league. Its plan for a two-acre school site showed areas for separate girls' and boys' playgrounds, a baseball diamond, and a garden—elements that promoted student health through organized physical activity, community use at the ball field, and vocational training for both genders in the school garden. The text of George Washington Carver's "topics" explained how schools should be landscaped to model the lawns and flower beds that rural African Americans could emulate at home, as well as to offer practical education in fruit and vegetable production.[24]

Large sections of the booklet's text and illustrations, as well as some industrial building plans, reappeared early the following year in the Alabama Department of Education's bulletin aimed at white schools, *Rural Schoolhouses and Grounds*.[25] Although their educational and design principles overlapped, *The*

Negro Rural School focused only on African American schools and presented an industrial curriculum as the best vehicle for student and community advancement. Thus *The Negro Rural School and Its Relation to the Community* and *Rural Schoolhouses and Grounds* replicated the separate yet related and unequal ideology that underlay Progressive attempts to uplift black schools. The two publications shared a Progressive faith in the uplifting power of an expertly planned environment as well as the power of practical manual training to correlate abstract learning with tangible experience. Yet when this shared ideology addressed black schools, its focus and application narrowed to a low-cost vocational program.

TUSKEGEE'S SCHOOL PLANS

The Negro Rural School's designs for schools, teachers' homes, and industrial buildings featured design elements that came to typify Rosenwald schools in the Tuskegee era: hipped and clipped-gable roof lines, and central entrances protected by projecting gable or shed porch roofs. The plans also exhibited many features that reflected contemporary design standards and would characterize Rosenwald school plans well into the 1920s. Sanitation, lighting, and ventilation—critical aspects of Progressive school design—received serious attention from the start. School planners, this text advised, should avoid poorly drained land and seek a clean water supply. Once they had settled on a state-approved plan, they must orient it on the building site to secure light from the east or west.[26] Tuskegee designs grouped windows into "batteries" of four to seven double-hung sash windows to maximize natural lighting and air circulation. Their buildings stood on short piers, which also allowed for ventilation and moisture control.

The arrangement of interior spaces set important precedents as well. Acting on advice from John R. E. Lee, head of Tuskegee's academic department, Calloway had proposed that the plans have a minimum of two rooms, even for the one-teacher school, to accommodate the industrial classes and exhibits required for the intended Tuskegee-style curriculum.[27] The completed designs most often provided a smaller classroom for girls' domestic science work as part of the school building and located boy's vocational work in a separate structure. All offered libraries to supplement classroom instruction, and cloakrooms to safeguard classroom hygiene. Tuskegee plans also incorporated features that made the building conducive to community events, such as folding doors between rooms, reflecting Progressive educators' belief that schools

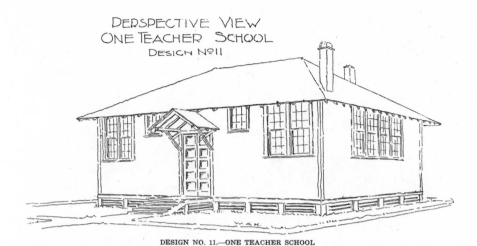

PERSPECTIVE VIEW
ONE TEACHER SCHOOL
DESIGN Nº 11

DESIGN NO. 11.—ONE TEACHER SCHOOL

Figure 6. Design 11 for a one-teacher school. (*The Negro Rural School and Its Relation to the Community* [1915])

should serve as social centers.[28] The same principles would guide the Rosenwald rural school-building program, which not only incorporated these ancillary spaces into its one-teacher schools but would always classify its buildings by the number of teachers, rather than the number of classrooms, to emphasize that its building designs met the curricular, health, and social needs of a community.

Three types of schoolhouses received the greatest attention in *The Negro Rural School*: a one-teacher school, a central school, and a county training school. The smallest design, numbered 11, would become the archetypal Rosenwald school of the Tuskegee years, when the rural school program concentrated on one-teacher schools (figures 6–8). It was a far cry from the one-room school typically in use for either white or black schoolchildren in the rural South. That kind of school, with its "one bare room," readers learned, "must go and in its place, must come the one-teacher school, housed in a building equipped with cloakrooms, library, and workroom in addition to the classroom proper." Design 11 included a classroom for academic instruction, a smaller industrial classroom, a kitchen, a library, and cloakrooms. Drawings of the building's exterior and its floor plan showed a rectangular block with the classroom located on its long axis next to the workroom on its short axis. The library, cloakrooms, and kitchen sat to either side of the central front entrance, which had a gable roof projecting over the steps leading up to the door. Folding doors between the

Figure 7. Welsh School, Jefferson Davis Parish, Louisiana, 1917. A typical early Rosenwald school following Tuskegee's design 11. (Jackson Davis Papers [#3072], Special Collections, University of Virginia Library)

Figure 8. Rally for the Rosenwald school at Welsh, Louisiana, 1917. Churches played an important part in the construction of Rosenwald schools across the South. The school patrons assembled here had already raised their $300 matching contribution, and state agent for Negro schools Leo M. Favrot then approved their application for Rosenwald aid. (Jackson Davis Papers [#3072], Special Collections, University of Virginia Library)

workroom and classroom could be opened to create a larger space for special events.[29]

Although the writers of *The Negro Rural School* believed that "for a long time to come, the majority of negro schools will be of the One-Teacher type," some communities needed larger buildings. At the time of *The Negro Rural School*'s publication, consolidation of small school districts into a larger, allegedly more efficient, and better-equipped school was a major tenet of the reforms proposed for rural schools by Progressive educators and state departments of education. Most consolidation programs in the South addressed white schools first or exclusively. Consequently, as *The Negro Rural School*'s text conceded, the cost of building and transportation combined with local school authorities' refusal to fund black schools adequately in the first place meant that "a consolidated school embracing all grades is practically out of the question for the majority of negro pupils." In its place, Tuskegee offered a plan for a "central" school that would offer four years of largely vocational instruction to "larger boys and girls" residing in a four to five-mile radius of the school.[30] The central school's planners probably envisioned the students as coming from the upper elementary grades; such a school would have alleviated some of the overcrowding at smaller elementary schools, where students typically were clustered at the lower grade levels, by siphoning off the older pupils.

The central school arranged a school building, a separate industrial building for blacksmithing and carpentry, and a teachers' home within a larger site that included practice farm plots. Tuskegee provided two alternative floor plans. The one-story plan in design 12 consisted of two classrooms separated by a large central hallway along the front and three rooms across the back (figure 9). While this rectangular one-story plan lit the classrooms along the front and back of the building, the two-story plan in design 13 had window batteries on the sides for the first-floor classrooms and across the front on the second story (figure 10). A long, narrow hall with a staircase ran between the two classrooms on both floors. The library, office, and additional cloakrooms ran across the back of the second story, while a single room for domestic science projected from the center rear on the first floor.

Two more Tuskegee school-building designs for county training schools, numbered 17 and 20, accommodated secondary instruction. Their inclusion hinted that communities could stack a Rosenwald building grant with aid from the John F. Slater Fund, and possibly the General Education Board, for teachers' salaries and vocational equipment. Tuskegee county training-school designs and their supplementary building plans clearly were intended to meet the Slater

Figure 9. One-story central school plan 12. (*The Negro Rural School and Its Relation to the Community* [1915])

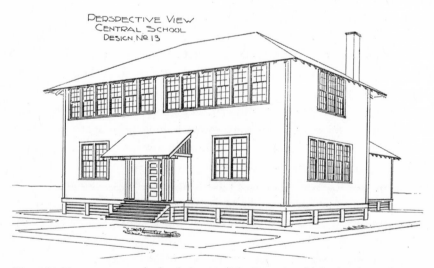

Figure 10. Two-story central school plan 13. (*The Negro Rural School and Its Relation to the Community* [1915])

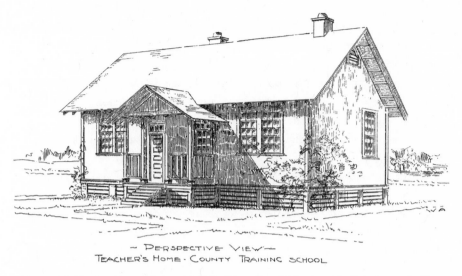

~ PERSPECTIVE VIEW ~
TEACHER'S HOME · COUNTY TRAINING SCHOOL

Figure 11. Teachers' home design 18. (*The Negro Rural School and Its Relation to the Community* [1915])

Fund's requirements with their ample spaces for "advanced training in home economics for girls, agriculture and trades for boys, and teacher-training courses for those who expect to become rural teachers."[31] Design 17 set a teachers' home and an industrial building, both one-story structures, at the sides of the two-story academic building, connected by open porches. The battery windows and clipped gable roof of the boy's industrial building echoed the windows and roof line of the classroom building. The central block of the school complex accommodated five classrooms, two large ones laid end to end across the front of the building, with a boy's cloakroom across the hall to the rear between the two sets of stairs. Upstairs, another large classroom was arranged on the left, perpendicular to the classroom below it, to allow two of the smaller classrooms across the central hallway to sit side by side over the right side of the building. In the distribution of window and floor space, the building's exterior appearance and interior layout in its central block resembled the Alabama education department's plan 5–B, designed by Montgomery architect Frank Lockwood.[32] Design 20 for a freestanding two-story academic building could be supplemented by design 19, a structure that housed both girls' industries and dormitory facilities, and a boys' trades building built to design 14.[33]

At this time, the Rosenwald building program was limited to one-teacher

rural schools and did not make grants specifically for central or county training schools, or for freestanding industrial buildings like design 14 or teachers' homes. The teachers' homes shown in designs 15, 16, and 18 (figure 11),
another item on Progressive educators' wish list for rural schools, provided a
housing incentive for a principal or teachers to stay in the community and a
model home for other families in the community to imitate. Some communities nevertheless did construct industrial buildings to supplement their smaller
Rosenwald-aided schools, like the Tuskegee plan 14 structure at the Davenport
School (figure 5).

Inside its school buildings, *The Negro Rural School* called for much more
than the Rosenwald "Plan for Erection of Schoolhouses" and gave concrete
form to the plan's vague references to furnishings and sanitary privies. Tuskegee's publication called for single desks in three different sizes to accommodate the range of student sizes and ages and promote discipline, along with
a teacher's desk and three recitation benches. Indirectly admitting that most
black schools could not afford commercially produced patent desks, the writers included a design for a homemade desk. Commercial blackboards were
recommended both for the classrooms and the workroom, however. Rather
optimistically, the booklet also described window shades, maps, charts, sand
tables, library books and magazines, and pictures for classroom use.[34] Turning
to health issues, Tuskegee's school planners explained the need for a protected
water supply, illustrating a well and well house, and for at least two sanitary toilets. Again their suggestions varied widely, with illustrations of internal plumbing for water fountains side by side with instructions for proper maintenance
of a well, and explanations of bucket and pit privies.[35]

The Negro Rural School's section on school furniture reflected a renewed
debate at Tuskegee about commercial patronage, especially of Sears, Roebuck
and Company. Julius Rosenwald had asked that no one consider using Sears,
Roebuck goods to build a school to which he contributed except as a cost-sav-
ing measure, yet Washington continued to push such purchases himself and
to use them as evidence of his loyalty to his patron. Clinton Calloway had encouraged school patrons at the first experimental schools to buy the necessary
hardware from Sears, Roebuck; at his suggestion, G. P. Madison had placed
an order for the Madison Park School through Tuskegee Institute's business
agent.[36] Apparently Washington found this insufficient, reminding Calloway
six months later, "I hope you keep in mind the suggestion about buying schoolhouse furnishings just as far as possible from Mr. Rosenwald's firm." Calloway
got in touch with James L. Sibley, who conveniently provided a letter claim-

ing that both black and white teachers were buying Sears, Roebuck desks for their schools and that "I believe in the erection of these new schools [under the new Rosenwald building program], it would show our appreciation as well as save the people money, by purchasing patent desks from the above firm." Washington forwarded Sibley's letter to Julius Rosenwald, and, after hearing that Rosenwald had been pleased, he ordered copies of the Sears, Roebuck and Company school furniture catalog sent to all county and state officials handling Rosenwald school construction. In a form letter accompanying the catalog, Washington carefully noted that "Mr. Rosenwald has given no intimation in this matter . . . but nevertheless I think it would very much encourage him if you will act upon the suggestion" of furnishing Rosenwald schoolhouses with Sears, Roebuck products whenever possible.[37]

R. T. Clayton of the Educational Exchange, a school supply house in Birmingham, Alabama, begged to differ. Clayton inquired about the desks Sibley would be purchasing for black schools, which he had heard would all come from Sears, Roebuck because of "the attitude of one Rosenbush, head of that concern, towards Negro schools of the South." Sibley reminded Clayton that one Rosenwald-aided school had already purchased desks from the Educational Exchange, and local school committees decided where to buy materials.[38] Calloway also equivocated with black school patrons, suggesting to one correspondent that he write for a Sears catalog and "mention to them that your school is being aided by Mr. Julius Rosenwald," but that he also consult the Educational Exchange in Birmingham.[39] Thus Calloway was understandably frustrated when Booker T. Washington then reversed course and asked him about using homemade desks rather than Sears, Roebuck patent desks to save money in Rosenwald schools. As Calloway pointed out, "we have led Mr. Rosenwald to believe that we would order that much of the schoolhouse furnishing, as far as possible, from the Sears Roe Buck [*sic*] Co."[40]

The real significance of school furniture was not where it came from but rather was implicit in the choice between commercially manufactured patent desks and locally produced low-cost versions. On the one hand, the Tuskegee Rosenwald program promoted new rural black schools that met the standards accepted for white schools inside and out. On the other hand, program administrators cautiously sought to minimize costs and keep appearances so modest as to avoid controversy. Early Rosenwald schools exhibited the same tension. In addition to schoolhouses erected on the plans illustrated in *The Negro Rural School*, the official "Plan for Erection of Rural Schoolhouses" allowed Clinton Calloway to approve other designs from state departments of education.[41] The

Tuskegee Rosenwald program also awarded Rosenwald grants to buildings already under construction and for remodeling of existing schools.[42] Consequently the early Rosenwald schools differed widely in appearance and quality.

Almost in spite of their planners and builders, these structures created the first public visual images of a Rosenwald school. One-teacher design 11 first embodied that image: a rectangular structure standing on short piers, often covered with a hipped roof, and pierced by massed windows whose white frames contrasted strongly against a darker facade. In the next few years, the Rosenwald rural school-building program would aid larger schools, some of which would follow the plans in *The Negro Rural School*. Uniting these disparate buildings and transcending their irregular quality was a common goal of bringing African American public school facilities up to contemporary standards. Those modern standards began to shift the building program's goal from the modest new schools Washington had envisioned to schools that suggested a more ambitious goal of modernization. Negotiating that transition would pose the next challenge for those who funded and operated the building program.

EXPANDING THE ROSENWALD BUILDING PROGRAM AT TUSKEGEE, 1916–19

Booker T. Washington's unexpected death in November 1915 and uncertainty about his successor troubled but did not immediately undo the Rosenwald building program. While Washington struggled with his final illness during a trip in the North, Rosenwald made a quick visit to Tuskegee after attending the inauguration of Fayette Avery McKenzie as president of Fisk University. Washington sent instructions to ensure that Rosenwald saw the new Chehaw school, about which Rosenwald sent a positive report back to his sick friend. That long-distance exchange proved to be Washington and Rosenwald's last shared effort for the schoolhouse project, for Washington's condition deteriorated rapidly, and he died on his return to Tuskegee.[43]

Deeply saddened, Julius Rosenwald hoped that Tuskegee's board of trustees would appoint the institute's secretary and Washington's close associate Emmett J. Scott as principal. Other influential trustees, however, believed Tuskegee needed new leadership, and the board selected Robert Russa Moton of Hampton Institute to the post.[44] Julius Rosenwald did not approve of Moton, but with the experienced Clinton J. Calloway and the trusted Emmett

J. Scott to provide continuity, Rosenwald saw no reason to question Tuskegee's operation of his rural school-building program. Instead he made even greater commitments, offering another $30,000 in matching grants and administrative support for a second set of one hundred schoolhouses in February 1916. Nine months later, when over 180 schools had been approved for assistance and Calloway estimated that another hundred communities were organizing to apply for aid, Rosenwald agreed to make grants for a total of three hundred schools.[45]

As the Rosenwald school-building program expanded, Robert Russa Moton and a Rosenwald committee of key Tuskegee administrators handled the correspondence with Julius Rosenwald and his secretary, William C. Graves, in Chicago. They also worked closely with James L. Sibley and, when approving aid for schools in other states, handled their applications through the Negro school agents there as well.[46] Thus, despite Washington's earlier dismissal of state authorities, in practice the regional Rosenwald building program depended on state agents for Negro schools as much as its own field organizers. Nevertheless, the real burden of coordinating the program—reviewing applications, collecting information from the state agents for Negro schools and Rosenwald building agents, corresponding with educational officials and community activists, and conducting field surveys of completed schools—remained on Clinton Calloway's shoulders.

Calloway had been overshadowed by Booker T. Washington's powerful personality and close relationship with Julius Rosenwald. Now he offered much-needed continuity for the building program and played a key role for African American leadership in southern school reform. Calloway's authority as the chief administrator of the early Rosenwald program required him to monitor the efforts not only of Rosenwald building agents but also the white men who served as Negro school agents—and their compliance with his authority. Calloway also saw himself as a gatekeeper for industrial education in Rosenwald schools, which would replicate the Tuskegee curriculum for fostering the work ethic and skills for economic independence. For example, when reviewing a Clemson University plan modified by Negro school agent J. Herbert Brannon, Calloway asked for folding doors between the classroom and workroom to open up the interior space for "demonstrations," more windows, and a dedicated space for industrial classes.[47]

His position also accorded him great influence over the reshaping of African American community landscapes. Calloway asserted this authority and influence through his oversight of the building plans and specifications used for Rosenwald schools. The requirements he imposed on non-Tuskegee plans ensured that Rosenwald schools met the same standards and produced similarities among their designs. Calloway's instructions to North Carolina county superintendent Charles L. Coon indicate how he enforced Tuskegee's design standards by tracing his authority back to Julius Rosenwald: "It is one of Mr. Rosenwald's requests that those who are in charge of the building of the schools which he aids, shall guarantee to him or those administering his aid, that the school building be painted inside and out, furnished with plenty of blackboard space and fairly well furnished with desks, heater, maps, charts, etc., and that this be done at the time or before the receipt of his aid."[48]

Periodically, Calloway conducted field inspection tours to follow up on grant projects and critique design and construction standards. Tours like his summer 1917 visits to Alabama, Louisiana, and Mississippi schools allowed Calloway to meet with local school patrons and become personally acquainted with community leaders, state agents for Negro rural schools, and Rosenwald building agents.[49] After a tour of Tennessee schools in which he found only one of the five schools reported as finished to have actually been completed, Calloway offered state Negro school agent Samuel L. Smith a candid assessment of each structure's shortcomings.[50] Calloway's correspondence with Smith also illustrated the leverage that Rosenwald aid gave him over white state and local school officials. The following summer Calloway "beg[ged] to advise . . . that the type of building of the Rutherford County Rural Schools, as a one-teacher school does not come up in outside appearance to the standard which we are trying to set for the Rosenwald schools" and concluded with an implied threat: "We are required to send a photograph of these schools to Mr. Rosenwald, and the type of schools being put up in Tenn., as far as I have seen, is behind other States."[51]

Some issues did require a ruling from a higher authority. School leaders and state officials plied Calloway with requests for exceptions to the guidelines and new ideas for the program. Leo M. Favrot, now Louisiana's state agent for Negro schools, wanted to see the Rosenwald program add incentives for school consolidation with grants for larger buildings, for example. Periodically Calloway received requests for aid to demonstration schools for teacher-training programs at African American colleges, such as Southern University and A&M College outside Baton Rouge and the Tennessee Agricultural and Industrial Normal School in Nashville. Generally Calloway received such requests politely and took them up with the Tuskegee Rosenwald committee, which in problematic cases sought a final ruling from Julius Rosenwald. In return, when applicants tried to bypass the Tuskegee committee and contacted Julius Rosenwald directly, Rosenwald went back to the Tuskegee committee for its advice.[52] Although Calloway, the Tuskegee Rosenwald committee, and Rosenwald himself were reluctant to approve exceptions to current guidelines, such exchanges would eventually bring new ideas into the Rosenwald program.

By the fall of 1917, the program's success inspired more revisions to the "Plan for Erection of Rural Schoolhouses." Almost three hundred schools had been constructed or approved for aid, without any sign that the demand for Rosenwald schools had abated. Julius Rosenwald decided to reorganize the building program and, rather than starting with the Tuskegee Rosenwald committee, initiated the process by convening a meeting with the state agents for Negro schools. They appointed a committee to make additional recommendations, an all-white committee composed of Jackson Davis of the General Education Board, Alabama's James L. Sibley, and Tennessee's Samuel L. Smith. Sibley drew up the committee's formal report, which recommended that Tuskegee form a "special Department of Rural School House Extension" headed by "a man . . . who is in a position to co-operate with the various school officials in the southern states" and could offer larger grants of $400 for one-teacher schools and $500 for two-teacher schools to offset the increasing cost of building materials. Smith sent his own informal version of the committee's deliberations, which included an additional recommendation that Rosenwald add support for extension of school terms and introduced his own idea of matching grants for school libraries.[53] Both state Negro school agents advocated that Tuskegee Institute continue to manage the building program, a very important recommendation as Rosenwald's secretary, William C. Graves, had recently asked Moton for detailed explanations of Tuskegee's expense claims and procedures for approving projects and inspecting construction.

Sibley's committee concluded its report with the suggestion that another committee, this time an interracial one composed of Tuskegee's Robert Russa Moton and Emmett J. Scott, along with Sibley himself, develop a new plan for future Rosenwald school construction. The trio had already begun work, for Sibley sent his report from the state agents' committee with a letter notifying Rosenwald that he'd already met several times with Moton and Scott. Interestingly, given that Graves had recently been interrogating Moton about Tuskegee's handling of the school program, Sibley noted that "our committee"—referring to Davis, Smith, and himself—had also decided that Tuskegee should operate the program "until further conditions developed," and furthermore that "I found, after a conference with the other Rural School Agents, that there had been very little trouble in working directly through Tuskegee." His comments suggest that Rosenwald was seriously considering aid to a dedicated department of rural schoolhouse extension at Tuskegee, but that perhaps others had questioned Tuskegee's management.[54]

Clinton Calloway's own recommendations to Emmett Scott indicate how much stress the building program placed on the extension department. Impatient with hearing from various state Negro school agents about what Rosenwald had said at the August meeting, he wanted either Moton, Scott, or himself to meet directly with Rosenwald every three months, as well as a small advisory committee that could handle matters quickly. Calloway also wanted Moton to work with the General Education Board to clarify how Tuskegee and the state Negro school agents should work together. "A wide awake Negro agent in each state," more clerical assistance, and better salaries for all involved with the program would speed up the work, he believed. Perhaps feeling that Rosenwald schools were not as important to Moton's agenda as they had been for Booker T. Washington, Calloway urged that Tuskegee "should, perhaps, now look upon the importance of the rural schoolhouse building in the south with as much importance as the General Education Board looks upon similar work."[55]

Moton, Scott, and Sibley drafted an ambitious new version of the "Plan for the Erection of Rural School Houses" that offered aid to two-teacher schools as well as one-teacher buildings and expanded the program's reach across the region from Maryland to Arkansas.[56] The 1917 plan offered what by now was a familiar description of the Rosenwald program:

> The money given by Mr. Rosenwald is to be used in providing school houses in rural districts, preferably for one and two teacher schools, on condition that the people shall secure from public school funds, or raise among themselves, an amount equivalent to, or larger than, that given by Mr. Rosenwald. It is understood that in no case will the sum exceed $400 for a one teacher school, and $500 for a two teacher school. By the term "one teacher school" is meant not necessarily a one room school building, as these school buildings in every instance should be provided with rooms for industrial work; which means kitchen, library, manual training work, etc. By furnishing is meant providing the school with two sanitary toilets and equipping the building with desks, blackboards, heaters, etc.

Procedural changes likewise reflected the expansion of the program. Now Calloway and the Rosenwald committee would review applications in the order in which they arrived at Tuskegee and work with the state departments of education in deciding on the annual quotas for the number of schools to be funded. A last and significant new feature of the 1917 plan offered a matching grant of at least $30 a year to extend the school terms to six or seven months in communities that had built Rosenwald schools or to supplement the teacher's salary at schools with a seven-month term. Term-extension grants would be available for a three-year period, with a possibility of renewal, both to attract better teachers and to encourage school authorities to provide a full scholastic term for black students. In practice, the term-extension offer had a very important side effect of requiring Rosenwald schools to have at least a five-month school term.[57]

After Rosenwald approved the revised plan, the Tuskegee executive council sent him a proposed budget for another three hundred schools intended to entrench the rural school-building program at the institute. They proposed to reinforce the existing vertical hierarchy that connected Julius Rosenwald to Tuskegee to rural communities with a horizontal central layer linking Tuskegee and its African American building agents to white educators across the region. Calloway and the extension department would report to a Rosenwald committee, whose policy recommendations would go to the institute's executive council and then to Julius Rosenwald for final approval. In addition, as Calloway had suggested, the director of extension would work closely with the agents for Negro schools in participating state education departments. Though the council withdrew the earlier proposal for a rural school extension department, its members still wanted Rosenwald to fund the additional staff needed for a regional program. As the building program spread across the region, Tuskegee officials realized, so would its administrative burden, so they asked for a new assistant director, a combined secretary and bookkeeper's position, half of the salaries of building agents to work in nine states, and the costs of office expenses, conferences, and building plans and specifications for a total $144,030.[58]

Julius Rosenwald had instigated this reorganization process at the same time that he restructured his personal giving into a charitable foundation. The Julius Rosenwald Fund, incorporated for "the well-being of mankind" on 30 October 1917, began its work with an endowment of twenty thousand shares of stock in Sears, Roebuck and Company. Although the Rosenwald Fund provided him with a separate institutional structure through which to manage his gifts, Julius Rosenwald at first used it as a clearinghouse for his donations to social service agencies other than black public schools.[59] He remained deeply involved in the school-building program, still working through the indispensable William C. Graves, still committed to building rural schools for black children, and yet starting to question its operations.

In November 1917, Rosenwald approved three hundred additional school grants, $14,030 for Tuskegee extension division salaries, and $6,000 for the extension of school terms, as Tuskegee officials had proposed. But he also asked Abraham Flexner, secretary of the General Education Board, to review the new plan. Rosenwald's request reflects his growing familiarity with the broad network of philanthropies focused on southern education, led by the General Education Board, and his new position on the board of the Rockefeller Foundation. Flexner suggested that Rosenwald put more force behind the program's requirement of public support and build a more valuable facility requiring a 1:3 match to both community contributions and public school funds rather than matching his grants to local contributions. Flexner added a postscript to his letter noting that "there appeared to be a general agreement [at the General Education Board] to the effect that, as its educational work is now organized, Tuskegee is not a sufficiently important factor in the training of teachers."[60]

Flexner's proposal met a cold reception at Tuskegee Institute. R. R. Moton and his staff disagreed with Flexner's formula, pointing out that "there are a few communities in some states where they have no funds for the building of schools. This gives us a chance, if it seems best, to put schools into communities where the colored people would not otherwise have one. The end is served when the school authorities take over the property and guarantee to forever maintain a school for colored people." Tuskegee staff knew that the original formula had the benefit of flexibility, allowing projects to proceed with little public funding in communities hamstrung by the local conditions Moton described. On the other hand, a required 1:3 match might elsewhere encourage local authorities to depend on black contributions and outside aid instead of treating the Rosenwald grant as an incentive for investing tax revenues into black schools. Appealing to Rosenwald's fond memories of earlier days, Moton suggested "that for the good of the movement we had better stick to the original plan as worked out by Dr. Washington and his associates here; that has seemed to be so successful."[61] Moton prevailed, but this exchange, together with Sibley's comments a few months previously, suggests that Rosenwald was beginning to hear criticism of Tuskegee's operations and was taking it to heart.

Rosenwald's expanded southern program received a more positive response from its potential new members. John C. Wright, academic dean of Florida A&M College, asked Clinton Calloway on behalf of the black state teachers' association "what Florida must do in order to get in line for the Rosenwald aid."[62] Wright had also heard about the salary grants being offered for state Rosenwald building agents, and asked Calloway to consider him for such a position.[63] Arthur D. Wright, the state agent for Negro schools in Virginia, told Calloway that "this appropriation is the best news I have had for a long long time" and wrote Julius Rosenwald that "this is, I can safely say, the finest gift that has ever been made to the cause of better Negro schools in Virginia." Virginia had already been the recipient of eight Rosenwald grants, but prior to the fall of 1917, Tuskegee's unofficial stance had been "that Hampton [Institute] can take care of Virginia easily," while other states had greater needs. Now the state had an appropriation of $11,100 for Rosenwald schools.[64]

Clinton Calloway distributed this new largesse on behalf of Julius Rosenwald and Tuskegee Institute. He also controlled the funding for up to nine Rosenwald building agents, who would mediate between the state agents for Negro schools and rural communities, disseminate information about the building program, organize fund-raising events and committees, and oversee construction. Three were already in the field: Booker T. Washington Jr. continued as Alabama's building agent, North Carolina's Charles H. Moore now added Rosenwald agent duties to his work as field agent of the North Carolina Teachers Association, and O. W. Gray had just started work in Louisiana. In letter after letter for the next two years, Calloway strongly encouraged other state Negro school agents to hire Rosenwald building agents, an important step that created new professional positions in state governments for African American men. By 1920, Calloway finally had his nine building agents in place in Alabama, Arkansas, Georgia, Kentucky, Louisiana, Mississippi, North Carolina, Tennessee, and Virginia.[65]

QUESTIONS AND PROBLEMS, 1917–19

The successful expansion of the Rosenwald school-building program into ever more southern communities strained rather than strengthened Julius Rosenwald's relationship with Tuskegee Institute. Although his support for the institution remained strong, Rosenwald's enduring dislike of principal Robert R. Moton probably contributed to the developing tension. He also became increasingly upset by complaints from white officials about the building program and its black administrators. Certainly the swift expansion of the project across the region put tremendous pressure on Calloway and other Tuskegee staff and almost inevitably resulted in administrative errors. At the same time, some of the problems were beyond anyone's control. Local observers testified to worsening agricultural conditions as the boll weevil cut into southern farmers' limited incomes and made it harder for rural African Americans to raise cash or make in-kind resources available as contributions. Inflation, triggered by the war in Europe and demand for American products, boosted prices for building materials so that the overall cost of school construction rose dramatically, adding to the difficulty of matching local contributions. Many African Americans responded to these general conditions by moving out of the South altogether, creating the "Great Migration" and reducing the ranks of school patrons available for self-help.[66]

The war posed yet another challenge to Rosenwald school campaigns when the federal government curtailed domestic construction to redirect all labor and materials to the war effort. Moton sought relief from U.S. commissioner of education Philander P. Claxton, who advised the Tuskegee principal to "exercise great care" and build schools only if laborers "could not possibly go elsewhere." He suggested that state agents for Negro schools review projects first, then get a ruling from the state superintendent and the state council of defense.[67] Wartime Rosenwald construction programs varied accordingly. Tennessee authorities, for example, rejected only one project, for a school at Goodlettsville in Davidson County that would have competed for laborers with the nearby DuPont powder plant and area farmers. But in Alabama, the state superintendent approved work only on existing buildings.[68]

Consequently, Moton reported, only 249 of the 300 schools planned for 1918 had been completed. The armistice brought little relief, as prices remained high and the influenza pandemic infiltrated the rural South, keeping Rosenwald building agents from their community campaigns.[69] Monthly reports from the building agents demonstrated that, despite the best efforts of Tuskegee extension staff and Rosenwald building agents, the pace of schoolhouse construction slowed dramatically through 1918 and did not improve in 1919. Although some building-program officials, including Clinton Calloway, tried to pin the schoolhouse program's poor showing on rural black "slackers" who allegedly would not give as freely to school campaigns as they did to Liberty bond drives, more followed Moton's lead in blaming wartime government policies or the boll weevil.[70]

Rosenwald surely understood the war-related conditions facing his school-building program. He had turned over management of Sears, Roebuck to vice president Albert Loeb to devote himself to the war effort. Rosenwald served on the advisory commission to the Council for National Defense in 1916–18 and chaired its committee on supplies. He also represented the council on the War Industries Board, created in 1917, and in 1918 undertook an official tour of YMCA service centers in France for white and black soldiers.[71] Yet the program's difficulties and criticisms from observers disturbed and disappointed him.

Some of Rosenwald's concerns came from his own dealings with Tuskegee. The school-building program had always had its fair share of problems, such as the erroneous announcement of an open-ended dollar-for-dollar match in 1914, and Rosenwald reviewed its every step with the same watchful eye for inefficiency and wasteful expenditures that he cast over all his activities. But starting in 1917, Rosenwald's secretary, W. C. Graves, questioned Moton repeatedly over his handling of the program. How could Booker T. Washington Jr.'s salary and expenses always total exactly $125 each month regardless of variations in his travels as Rosenwald building agent for Alabama? If Rosenwald approved an additional gift to the five-teacher Frissell School in Evergreen, Alabama, would that not set a dangerous precedent for larger buildings? What had happened to the Rosenwald committee recently appointed to assist Calloway? Why did Tuskegee waste postage responding to each letter it received about a project rather than gathering together correspondence of a day or more on the subject before answering? Was Tuskegee sending Rosenwald money out before schools were completed? And how did they know a building was finished? "Will you kindly ask the proper official to go into details in answering so that we may thoroughly understand the policy at Tuskegee, regarding the status of building operations, when requisitions are made on us and when payments are made by you?"[72]

Such concerns would have resonated with several of the state agents of Negro schools with whom the Tuskegee staff cooperated in administering building grants across the South. From their office in Montgomery, Alabama, James L. Sibley and his successor, James S. Lambert, who had the closest ties to the Rosenwald program at Tuskegee, complained about redundant paperwork and increasing delays in processing applications and grant checks. They made their criticisms known to their superiors at the General Education Board, whose officials took them to Rosenwald. Warnings from the influential Abraham Flexner, the man who could claim to have reformed American medical education, carried great weight at a time when Rosenwald was serving on the board of another Rockefeller philanthropy, the Rockefeller Foundation.[73] And their timing was propitious for their own interests during a period of postwar instability. By 1919, the Great Migration of African Americans from the rural South to northern urban centers was underway, adding urgency to any measures like school construction that promised to produce content black southerners happy to stay in their small towns. Furthermore, as racial violence surged again at the war's end, white northern and southern Progressives looked to schools as positive models for orderly change.[74]

Early in March 1919, James Hardy Dillard penned a confidential letter to Robert Russa Moton to inform him of a recent meeting Julius Rosenwald had called with Wallace Buttrick, Abraham Flexner, Jackson Davis of the General Education Board, and Tuskegee trustee William G. Willcox. He reported that Rosenwald "seemed to desire a little more organization for his work." One suggestion was that the executive committee of the Anna T. Jeanes Fund act as the board for the Rosenwald Fund, and then hire James L. Sibley, Nathan C. Newbold, or Clinton J. Calloway as field agents. Dillard, who headed both the Jeanes Fund and the John F. Slater Fund and had recently become a trustee of the General Education Board, reported that he preferred Newbold, with Calloway to continue "if possible as at present" in a revamped program that would tighten construction standards and require more public tax funds. An official warning came on 13 March 1919, when William C. Graves sent Robert Russa Moton a telegram ordering him to stop all new Rosenwald school projects.[75]

Although Rosenwald soon lifted the ban on new construction, he did embark on a two-pronged review of Tuskegee's handling of the rural school-building program's finances and construction projects. Accountants from Arthur Young & Co. pored over the financial records from 1913, when the last audit of the building program had been conducted, through the summer of 1919. After receiving their report, William Graves summarized it for Principal Moton: "Kindly state to the Committee that the auditors seriously criticize the failure to keep books of account, the confusion in the files, the loss of valuable data, including checks, check stubs and expense accounts, the failure to reconcile bank balances, the temporary use of Rosenwald money for Jeanes fund disbursements and vice versa, and the payment of money to schools that had not made requisitions. An unexplained Rosenwald surplus of nearly $1,000 was found. The auditors believe the Fund was administered honestly, the conditions criticized being due to lack of knowledge of bookkeeping." The auditors also blamed the mess on the "originators of the rural school work" who had failed to set up a proper governing body with a board of directors or establish clear lines of responsibility for staff. Basic accounting procedures and the assignment of an accountant to the building program could solve its financial reporting problems, they concluded.[76]

Rosenwald was just as concerned about how efficiently and effectively his money was transformed into properly constructed school buildings. He complimented state Negro school agents and Rosenwald building agents on the resolutions urging proper building standards adopted at their annual meeting in July 1919: "This is of the *greatest importance* and I would suggest that it be insisted upon so that no slip-shod buildings be undertaken or accepted." The agents had called upon the Tuskegee Rosenwald committee to maintain its standards for lighting, ventilating, heating, and painting school buildings and to enforce the requirement for a fully equipped industrial room, and recommended that Tuskegee publish a new bulletin of floor plans and specifications for schools that would be "recognized Rosenwald types."[77]

Rosenwald had reason to suspect that the existing "Rosenwald types" did not meet his or the agents' standards. He had hired Fletcher B. Dresslar, professor of school hygiene and architecture at Nashville's George Peabody College for Teachers, to assess the Rosenwald schools completed under Tuskegee and state supervision. Dresslar was one of the few educational professionals who specialized in rural school design and was the author of two bulletins for the U.S. Bureau of Education: *American Schoolhouses* (1910) and *Rural Schoolhouses and Grounds* (1914).[78] After an early career in public school teaching and administration in his native Indiana, Dresslar had earned a doctorate at Clark University, studied in Munich and Berlin, and embarked on a new career in schoolhouse planning. He taught at the University of California and the University of Alabama, where he was dean of education, before becoming a founding faculty member at George Peabody College for Teachers. By this time, Dresslar had established a national reputation as an expert on school hygiene and building design who insisted on functional school designs for simple, unadorned, one-story buildings.

Dresslar was well known to the General Education Board, which contributed to George Peabody College and paid the salaries of some of its students who now worked in state departments of education. Not surprisingly, the General Education Board's secretary, Abraham Flexner, recommended Dresslar to Rosenwald for an evaluation of school-building design and construction.[79] Flexner, who had begun raising questions about Tuskegee with Rosenwald two years earlier, had collected a number of complaints about improperly constructed Rosenwald schools from North Carolina Negro school agent Nathan C. Newbold.[80] Flexner also relayed criticism about North Carolina Rosenwald schools from Frank P. Bachman, another General Education Board staff member, asking Rosenwald "whether the planning of these buildings should not be in more experienced hands. I doubt if Major Moton quite takes in the situation. . . . . Undoubtedly Mr. Dresslar's report will decide the issues involved."[81]

Flexner was correct, for Dresslar's report launched a fundamental reordering of the Rosenwald building program that wrested it from its birthplace at Tuskegee. Dresslar approached his Rosenwald school assignment with different expectations and goals than the "Plan for Erection of Rural Schoolhouses." Booker T. Washington's small, inexpensive experimental schools had represented a major improvement over most black public schools in the rural South, and Tuskegee staff like Clinton J. Calloway and Robert R. Taylor had introduced modern school-design standards into the regional building program. Their goal was to use these improved schools as vehicles for community self-help and public commitment to black public education. Fletcher Dresslar, however, was one of the national experts who instituted and then increased modern standards, a professional who judged buildings by their adherence to strict architectural and hygienic rules and not by the social value of the process that produced them.

Dresslar inspected forty-seven schools constructed under the Rosenwald program at Tuskegee during August and September 1919. He visited schools in all stages of construction in six of the ten states where the program operated: Alabama, Georgia, Kentucky, Louisiana, North Carolina, and Tennessee, accompanied by the state agents of Negro schools rather than Calloway. In his published *Report on the Rosenwald School Buildings*, Dresslar prefaced his comments with an admission that "the types of buildings, now being erected with Rosenwald aid, are so much better than those which preceded, that one is loath to criticise or in any way to point out faults. Nevertheless in the interest of progress and economy, both in planning and construction, there is still room for much improvement." He proceeded to lambaste the Rosenwald buildings that he had seen. The Tuskegee plans, although decent, did not meet his standards for lighting, ventilation, and sanitation. For example, while Tuskegee design 11 for a one-teacher school properly used batteries of tall windows to light its classroom and industrial room, the plan did not specify the building's orientation on its site and, like the other Tuskegee plans, placed windows on two sides of a classroom so that either the teacher or the students would have to ruin their eyesight by looking into the light.[82]

Worse yet, in Dresslar's judgment, county school officials and contractors altered the plans at will and bought cheap materials to stretch construction dollars further. When local citizens did the work, he claimed, they often were not skilled carpenters and had little or no supervision, so that they frequently made mistakes in interpreting the plans. Consequently, the windows might be grouped together as shown in the Tuskegee plan or spaced out across the facade, and they were not always set high enough in the walls to provide proper

CANADAVILLE SCHOOL, FAYETTE CO., TENN.
1. This is a two-teacher building with two industrial rooms, two cloak rooms and a teacher's room with library.
2. In the center of a prosperous Negro settlement, where the land is owned by the colored people, and all are deeply interested in the education of their children.
3. It will be difficult to make suitable additions to this building and this is a growing community.
4. Workmanship on this building above the average, but the fenestration is faulty and the sash too light.

Figure 12. Laborers at Canadaville School, Fayette County, Tennessee, 1919. Although patrons could donate labor to match a Rosenwald grant, Fletcher B. Dresslar mistrusted local labor and blamed construction problems on lack of supervision. (Dresslar, *Report on the Rosenwald School Buildings* [1920])

light for students' work (figure 12). Dresslar had little regard for county superintendents and school boards to begin with, and he blamed ignorant, if well-meaning, superintendents for most of the construction mistakes he observed in Rosenwald schools. Without proper supervision by either superintendents or other officials, workmen used whatever lumber came to hand, and their handiwork was slipshod. The building materials, especially the window sash and hardware, were substandard because Rosenwald school builders chose the least expensive items to save expense or to get a larger building for their money.[83]

Sometimes builders introduced their own ideas about what a schoolhouse should look like, a practice that Dresslar abhorred. He believed that the purpose of school-building design was to support instruction and promote health; everything else was irrelevant and undesirable. His ideas visualized Progres-

PROSPERITY SCHOOL, MOORE CO., NORTH CAROLINA

1. This is one of two buildings found not fronting on the road and properly so. But the L to the left faces the wrong direction. This method of making an addition always introduces this if the original structure was correctly placed.
2. But what of the cupola? Think it away and you will feel how much better the building would be without it. These are remnants of church architecture, and have no reason for continuance.

Figure 13. Prosperity School, Moore County, North Carolina, 1919. Fletcher B. Dresslar objected to cupolas as "remnants of church architecture." (Dresslar, *Report on the Rosenwald School Buildings* [1920])

sive educators' concept of the public school as a civic institution that unified a community rather than dividing it as private and church-affiliated schools did. Dresslar thought that America's school designers, including many of his own peers, had incorrectly drawn their imagery from church architecture, and wanted to strip away any visual references to church design. About the Prosperity School in North Carolina, Dresslar asked: "But what of the cupola? Think it away and you will feel how much better the building would be without it. These are remnants of church architecture, and have no reason for continuance" (figure 13).[84]

The use of Rosenwald facilities also concerned Dresslar, for he found many one-teacher buildings functioning as two-teacher facilities, which meant that the industrial room was serving as a regular classroom. As Dresslar himself pointed out, this problem resulted from the very success of Rosenwald schools and rural African Americans' commitment to the education of their children, who flocked to the new facility. He prescribed typical solutions offered by many Progressive educators for rural and black schools, beginning with school consolidation so that larger buildings in central locations would replace scattered one-teacher schoolhouses. Such schools might become the county training schools for African Americans being promoted by the John F. Slater Fund, with an industrial curriculum he thought "more nearly in line with their needs and social demands than any other." For any facility to be used properly, its interior spaces had to be properly prepared and equipped. Dresslar disliked the Tuskegee homemade desks and benches because they were, he felt, uncomfortable and could not be adjusted to students' height, unlike most patent desks. He also criticized the use of painted walls as blackboards, as well as the low-cost commercial blackboards he saw in most schools.[85]

Dresslar recommended that the Rosenwald program officials require more on-site supervision, multiple inspection reports, and complete adherence to its approved designs as conditions of financial assistance. He also suggested new plans that would allow school authorities a wider choice of designs and permit future expansions such as an auditorium and classroom additions, as well as offering full basements for heating systems and septic tank systems for toilets.[86] Both his criticisms and his proposals showed how the context of the Rosenwald building program had changed since 1912. Rosenwald school designs and buildings had already raised the bar for black country schools, but professional standards by 1919 had moved even higher. The building program had outstripped Tuskegee's administrative capacity, and its benefactor had moved beyond the terms of his original partnership with Booker T. Washington. Rosenwald and Tuskegee officials had worked with hundreds of rural black communities to redress one of their most pressing needs with better school buildings. Now Rosenwald was moving toward a new vision of his school-building program as the leading force in the modernization of black education in the South through model school architecture.

REJECTION AND REMOVAL

Most of the officials involved in building Rosenwald schools knew that Dresslar's evaluation would be a harsh one well before its publication and expected it would rebound on Tuskegee more than the state or local participants whom

Dresslar had also indicted. Both the auditors and Dresslar had spread the blame widely, but Rosenwald and many other white educators focused on Tuskegee's inconsistent supervision and the need for higher building standards. Some believed that Rosenwald would turn over the building program to the Anna T. Jeanes Fund, as James Hardy Dillard had told Robert Russa Moton that March. Initially Moton and even Calloway acquiesced to this proposal, and in June 1919 Moton asked Dillard to call a meeting of the Jeanes trustees' executive committee to discuss the transition: "We are of the opinion here that inasmuch as it is going to be done, the sooner the better, everything else being equal."[87]

Then Moton reversed course and began a last-ditch effort to hold on to the Rosenwald program as an important tool of African American—and Tuskegee's—leadership for southern black schools. Previously he had not been "very strong either one way or the other but rather simply wanted to do what you thought best," he wrote Julius Rosenwald in July. But now he claimed to have realized the broader implications of such a change: "The effect on Tuskegee in the minds of a great many colored people and white people would be that things were going to pieces, and that your interest in the School was not as strong as hitherto." He told Rosenwald and Flexner that his change of heart came after meeting Rosenwald school teachers and the state Negro school agents and Rosenwald building agents at their annual summer conferences. "I have been surprised," he admitted, ". . . how strong the feeling is among that group of people that Tuskegee owes it to itself and to the colored people to continue to administer the Fund, and there is a feeling also that I would be derelict in my duty if it were taken away, especially now." Alerted to the threatened loss of African American influence over the building program, Moton now believed that "the moral effect on the whole Southern situation of having this Fund administered through a Negro school is very great in bringing about better race relations."[88]

Others tried to dissuade Rosenwald from this drastic step. After hearing more from Rosenwald about his plan to move the rural school-building program, fellow Tuskegee trustee William G. Willcox questioned the implications of such a move. Rosenwald had explained his thinking to Willcox in business terms, writing that "there is, I believe, a great lesson to be taught, especially to the Southern people, as to thoroughness. The South is inclined to slipshod methods and I believe there is a chance to demonstrate the value of good workmanship, which would be beneficial to the entire community, White as well as Black." Willcox agreed, but he realized that not every observer would interpret the change in that light: "I think the value of such a demonstration will be increased if it emanates from Tuskegee. I know you will consider this point of view and I have entire confidence that it will be recognized in your ultimate decision."[89]

Moton succeeded in convincing Rosenwald to put his plans for a new administration on hold, but he still had to overcome the audit and Dresslar's report. He openly embraced both to limit their damage. "I wish frankly to admit that our records have been faulty and we should have had a competent accountant in Mr. Calloway's office," he confessed to W. C. Graves, "but the work began small and has grown more rapidly than has our machinery." Furthermore, he and his staff had compounded the problem by skimping on administrative costs to put more money into school buildings. Tuskegee's accountant, W. H. Carter, would henceforth handle Rosenwald building-program funds at Tuskegee to keep matters in order. To demonstrate his newfound zeal for school buildings, Moton himself wrote the introduction to Fletcher B. Dresslar's report, which was printed at Tuskegee Institute, and expressed a desire to hire a new staff member who would ensure that buildings followed approved plans.[90]

Behind the scenes, Clinton Calloway also tried to buttress Tuskegee's commitment to strict standards of school construction. Calloway was more familiar with the shortcomings of individual building projects than anyone, having critiqued school construction across the region since the program's inception. He had already tried unsuccessfully to interest Moton in a new plan book to supplement *The Negro Rural School and Its Relation to the Community*.[91] Following discussions with Julius Rosenwald and Abraham Flexner at the Tuskegee summer school in early July 1919, and anticipating Dresslar's survey, Calloway had asked Alabama Negro school agent James S. Lambert to bring some school-building plans to Tuskegee for the upcoming agents' conference. "Both Mr. Rosenwald and Dr. Flexner seemed anxious about the type of school building being erected," he reported. "They expressed themselves as anxious that every building being erected should have the industrial feature and should be perfectly built; that is, the workmanship and material of the building and furniture should be as nearly perfect as possible."[92] The result had been the set of resolutions on building standards adopted by state Negro school agents and Rosenwald building agents that so pleased Julius Rosenwald.

Calloway now strove to improve Tuskegee's administrative practices and reputation. In the fall of 1919, he followed in Dresslar's wake in his own travels with state agents for Negro schools and the Rosenwald building agents. The following spring he drafted new forms for county superintendents and state Negro school agents to certify that school buildings met all Rosenwald building-program requirements. In the meantime, he was left in limbo about ongoing and new construction projects and became the target of many complaints from the state agents for Negro schools, county superintendents, and school patrons anxious for Rosenwald grants that had been approved but for which there was no appropriation.[93]

Julius Rosenwald could or would not see a deeper racial message in a possible split from Tuskegee, only a business decision to improve the quality of his philanthropy's products by replacing a sloppy, inefficient management team.[94] Although Moton and his staff promised changes, their financial and statistical reports did not improve quickly enough for Rosenwald and William C. Graves, who continued to complain about the organization and accuracy of Tuskegee's reports, and especially about new applications for schools being accepted on the basis of Tuskegee's proposed 1919 budget for another three hundred schools, which had not been formally approved.[95] When he sent in Tuskegee's proposed construction budget for 1919–20, Moton probably erred in congratulating Rosenwald as the inspiration for Pierre S. du Pont's $2.5 million donation for school construction in Delaware. Moton did not need to tell Rosenwald that du Pont's gift paid all construction costs and exceeded the total of his own grants, but more important, Rosenwald heartily disapproved of this sort of philanthropy that relieved local people and governments of their own responsibilities. Rosenwald ignored the budget request, and as the program limped into 1920, its future at Tuskegee was in grave doubt.[96]

Julius Rosenwald met with Moton and Flexner in Washington, D.C., early in 1920 to review Fletcher Dresslar's report and plan for a conference of all state Negro school agents and General Education Board officials at Tuskegee that summer.[97] After their meeting, Moton expressed his hope that "the arrangements for keeping the machinery intact here at the Institute . . . may have your approval." Moton also reported to the state agents for Negro schools on the new goals set for Rosenwald schools, whereupon the controversy over Tuskegee's management erupted once again. He reported that no new grants would be forthcoming until Julius Rosenwald decided on the details and budget for a revised program. States that employed Rosenwald building agents would continue to receive salary support for their positions, and all Negro school agents were informed of the number of schools already approved that must be completed before the new budget went into effect. Dresslar's report would guide the formulation of a new program to produce "as nearly as possible *model* school buildings," Moton reported, his choice of words suggesting the new direction anticipated for the Rosenwald program. "While we may not, with the new program, build as many schools to begin with as we have been building heretofore," he continued, "it is our earnest desire that hereafter each new school building will be a model from every point of view of what a good country school should be."[98]

Most state agents for Negro schools took a wait-and-see approach to Moton's news.[99] But Louisiana's Leo M. Favrot challenged both Moton's and Rosenwald's new emphasis on "model" school buildings, charging that the building program's "lack of flexibility" was a more pressing problem than the problems Dresslar had observed, and that professional school designs might exclude the neediest rural southerners. "These folks have to crawl before they can be expected to walk," Favrot contended. "They have had nothing in the past; they cannot be expected to go from this condition to full perfection at one bound."[100] Favrot was one of the few white men who considered the effect of the proposed change not only on Tuskegee but on rural African American communities. His own state superintendent was complaining to the General Education Board about Julius Rosenwald's "unwise" decision to operate his building program through Tuskegee and predicting that southern school authorities would withdraw from the program because of "the petty and unwise annoyances resulting from the action of the negro committee." Favrot had his own reactionary opinions about African Americans, evidenced in his description of rural blacks crawling before they walked, but he had seen rural black poverty and white indifference first-hand. "I am solicitous lest this vastly improved Rosenwald school be placed out of the reach of the people who can derive the greatest benefit from it," he wrote to Rosenwald. Favrot apparently was the only state agent for Negro schools who argued on behalf of the poor rural communities that would be left behind when the Rosenwald program demanded larger local contributions to match grants for more expensive model buildings, and who openly supported Clinton Calloway's continued leadership of the program.[101]

For his trouble, Favrot was appointed to a committee charged with planning the program's removal from Tuskegee, together with Wallace Buttrick and Abraham Flexner of the General Education Board, R. R. Moton and C. J. Calloway of Tuskegee, Fletcher B. Dresslar, and the state agents for Negro schools in Alabama and Tennessee, J. S. Lambert and S. L. Smith. Julius Rosenwald prepared for a May meeting in New York with Moton, Margaret Murray Washington, Buttrick, Flexner, and the Jeanes Fund's James Hardy Dillard. Flexner realized the delicacy of the situation he had helped to create and entreated Rosenwald, who had been ill, to attend that meeting to reassure Moton and Margaret Murray Washington: "A word and a look from you will convince them of the absolute sincerity with which the entire matter is being considered."[102] Two weeks later, sitting in Flexner's New York office, Tuskegee representatives heard from Julius Rosenwald that he would be removing the building program from the institute and operating it independently as a program of the Julius Rosenwald Fund.

The planning committee delivered its report at Tuskegee early the next month, although Rosenwald stayed away because of ill health. He did send his "Thoughts about Rural School Building" that show he had carefully read letters from state Negro school agents, for he suggested having state education departments "handle the details of the local work," as Favrot had requested, and added the grants for teachers' cottages that S. L. Smith had been advocating for some time. He also made some proposals for handling the program's money, including making deposits with state officials against which they could draw grant funds as needed after each school passed inspection.[103]

Committee members took turns making their own statements. Wallace Buttrick noted that Rosenwald had spoken to him several times in recent years about creating "a corporation of his own" that would "develop this work into a greater work." Favrot issued a last call for maintaining the program's connection with Tuskegee "because it seems to me that the very spirit of the Rosenwald Fund school idea is after all the idea brought to fruition by Booker T. Washington, and that belongs particularly to Tuskegee, and although it may be expedient now, in the interest of the larger work . . . to have this as a separate and distinct fund, I do not think it ever should be separate from Tuskegee." Moton restated many of the points he had been making to Rosenwald and Graves for a year or more: he attributed Tuskegee's administrative problems to excessive economizing and expressed concern that "nothing be done to shake the confidence of the colored people in this movement" and compared the building program to a daughter about to leave her mother's home to wed: "We wonder if it would not be better for her stay in her mother's home. . . . We are sure she is safe if she stays at home, but the probabilities are that it is better for her to go into other hands."[104]

If Margaret Murray Washington had been that mother, she would not have let go so easily. She had already penned a bitter letter to Wallace Buttrick after their May meeting with Rosenwald, blaming the situation on white officials who could not bear having to take instructions from black men at Tuskegee. Although she did sign off on the new arrangement, she clearly felt that Tuskegee's and her husband's contributions were being shortchanged. Julius

Rosenwald, who considered himself a friend as well as one of Tuskegee's most loyal white supporters, tried to smooth matters over. He sent a personal letter to assure Margaret Murray Washington that "in looking over the plan for distributing aid to rural schools . . . I am happy to see among the list of those signing the document the name of one woman. It is, in fact, the name of the one woman whose advice on that subject would be most convincing to me. That name is yours."[105]

Rosenwald referred to the first of a new series of guidelines for the building program, the "Plan for the Distribution of Aid from the Julius Rosenwald Fund for Building Rural School Houses in the South." The plan that emerged in the summer of 1920 marked a fundamental shift in the Rosenwald building program. To be sure, some aspects would not change, such as the key roles played by the state agents for Negro schools and Rosenwald building agents who implemented the program at the state level, and the outpouring of local African American support for Rosenwald schools. But after its relocation from Tuskegee to the Julius Rosenwald Fund's offices in Chicago and Nashville, the building program became increasingly distant from the communities it served and its staff increasingly white. Those changes would, ironically, allow the Julius Rosenwald Fund to develop into an aggressive philanthropy that would overshadow the school-building program and eventually return to its biracial roots. What had begun in 1912 as an effort to produce better school buildings for African American communities became in 1920 an intensive campaign for model schools that could lead the South's drive for modern public education.

Ideal Schools

The Julius Rosenwald Fund Rural School-Building Program
at Nashville, 1920–27

In the summer of 1920, southern state superintendents of education received a "Plan for Distribution of Aid from the Julius Rosenwald Fund for Building Rural School Houses in the South." Like the "Plan for Erection of Rural Schoolhouses" that it replaced, this document became a touchstone for all involved in the school-building program. Widely circulated to public school authorities and reprinted by state education departments, educational journals, and the black press, the "Plan for Distribution of Aid" told readers exactly what to expect and do, beginning with the program's fundamental objective: "The Julius Rosenwald Fund co-operate[s] with public school authorities and other agencies and persons in the effort to provide and equip better rural school houses for the Negroes of the Southern states."[1]

In 1920, the words "better rural school houses" had a new meaning for the Rosenwald school-building program. Better now meant ideal, or model, schools designed by professionals, informed by modern architectural standards, and constructed under close supervision by agents of state departments of education. The 1920 plan of aid inaugurated this new ideal, championed by a new leadership for the program dominated by white men, and implemented through a broader repertoire of incentives for new public schools for southern African Americans.[2]

THE 1920 "PLAN FOR DISTRIBUTION OF AID"

The plan of aid necessarily addressed the program's new administrative procedures, as well as its new emphasis on school architecture. As Leo M. Favrot had suggested, the Julius Rosenwald Fund's officers in Chicago and Nashville would administer the program through state departments of education and their agents for Negro schools. Florida, Oklahoma, and Texas joined the list of southern states eligible for aid. Rosenwald Fund trustees and state education officials now determined how many schools to build each year, for which the fund provided each state with $5,000 in working capital—Rosenwald's own idea—replenished as needed to fulfill the year's construction allotment. Plan guidelines reiterated that communities had to raise an amount "equal or greater" than the Rosenwald grant from any combination of public and private sources and clarified that "labor, land and material may be counted as cash at current market values."

Thus the building program still did not specifically require state or local government funding, although the increasing size and cost of its model schools would make public support above and beyond local contributions almost essential, boosting the percentage of Rosenwald school costs paid out of public coffers. The Rosenwald building program's catch-all definition of local contributions seemingly undercut its objective of a more equitable distribution of public funding, yet for the time being it kept the program accessible to communities where state school laws constricted funding for building projects or white opposition made tax support impossible. The 1920 plan of aid did specifically require a minimum term of "at least five consecutive months," which indirectly mandated improved public funding for instruction. And schools that ran a minimum eight-month term were eligible for grants for the construction of teachers' homes, as Samuel L. Smith had suggested. The plan also warned that the Rosenwald program was not an endless fountain of money, as the Julius Rosenwald Fund "reserve[d] the right to discontinue its operations in behalf of rural schools after reasonable notice to the Departments of Education of the several co-operating states."

The 1920 plan of aid was much more specific and demanding about what would constitute a "better rural school house." Its provisions for sites and building plans addressed complaints about the design problems and inconsistent quality of the Tuskegee-era Rosenwald schools. They also reflected the fund's new resolve to support only new construction and not the remodeling projects that Tuskegee had allowed. Rosenwald had listened to state agents who called for larger grants and schools, and thus the 1920 "Plan for Distribution of Aid" offered not only $500 for one-teacher schools and $800 for two-teacher schools but also up to $1,000 for three-teacher school buildings and the possibility of even larger amounts for consolidated schools or county training schools.

Furthermore, in addition to the usual requirement of public ownership of both the sites and the buildings, the plan stipulated that both "the Agent of the Fund" and the state department of education must approve building sites. Sites were supposed to provide room for playgrounds and "such agricultural work as is necessary for the best service of the community"—a vague prescription for vocational education that could be implemented or sidestepped. As for the buildings, communities were reminded that "plans and specifications . . . shall be approved by an authorized representative of The Fund before construction is begun," for which "The Fund will consider it a privilege to furnish general suggestions, plans and specifications." And schools must be fully furnished, because the fund considered "such equipment as desks, blackboards, heating apparatus, libraries and toilets . . . of equal importance with the schoolhouses themselves."

THE JULIUS ROSENWALD FUND TAKES CHARGE

As the 1920 plan of aid made clear, the Julius Rosenwald Fund had assumed oversight of the rural school-building program. For its first three years, Julius Rosenwald had used his foundation to coordinate his philanthropic gifts, primarily to support Jewish and social service organizations. In 1920, he began reorienting his foundation to focus on the restructured building program, initially under his personal supervision and then with a small staff.[3] He still supported other projects from his private purse, including Jewish causes and the Museum of Science and Industry he envisioned for Chicago.[4] Although he and his assistants tried to direct all requests from African American schools to the Rosenwald Fund, Rosenwald also made personal gifts to favored educators and African American schools. For example, Rosenwald added his own contribution to the fund's 1927 grant to the Coffin Point school on St. Helena's Island, South Carolina, because of his admiration for its major sponsor, Rossa Cooley of the famous Penn School.[5]

Rosenwald and his personal secretary, William C. Graves, soon needed help with the building program. As secretary and acting director of the fund, Rosenwald hired Francis W. Shepardson, a former professor of history at the University of Chicago and the first head of the Illinois Department of Professional Regulation. Rosenwald and Shepardson had been involved with the Chicago Commission on Race Relations that investigated the city's 1919 race riot, on which Shepardson had served as vice-chair.[6] Shepardson served in his Rosenwald Fund post until 1926, when he was succeeded by Alfred K. Stern, Rosenwald's son-in-law.[7] Rosenwald remained in constant communication with Shepardson and Stern about operational and policy matters, although he placed day-to-day activities in their hands.

These administrative changes in Chicago followed in the wake of Rosenwald's relocation of the building program's leadership from Tuskegee Institute to a new headquarters in Nashville headed by a southern white man. Tennessean Samuel L. Smith was, perhaps, a dark horse candidate for the fund's new position of general field agent, for which Rosenwald had also considered the more outspoken Leo M. Favrot of Louisiana, Nathan C. Newbold of North Carolina, and Alabama's James L. Sibley. Smith had been an active supporter of African American and industrial education in his early career as Montgomery County school superintendent. As the Tennessee agent for Negro schools, Smith had a strong record of building Rosenwald schools and had hired a Rosenwald building agent to promote construction projects. General Education Board officers also vouched for Smith, who had impressed president Wallace Buttrick at their first meeting. So could his mentor at George Peabody College for Teachers, Fletcher B. Dresslar, with whom he had designed school plans for the Tennessee Department of Education.[8] The prospect of a southern office located in Nashville, with Dresslar on hand to assist with school-building design, must have been appealing to Rosenwald.

Smith's own persona, later described by Edwin R. Embree and Julia Waxman as "disarming, sincerely friendly, instinctively tactful," also surely appealed to Julius Rosenwald, who knew Smith's style and substance from the planning committees that had advised him on the building program in 1917 and again in 1920. Smith was an eternal optimist who wholeheartedly believed in the essential goodness of his cause and those who supported it. He reaffirmed his enthusiasm in letters to Julius Rosenwald on each anniversary of his hiring. In June 1930, he exclaimed: "He who builds a school closes a prison! You have closed 5000, and, in doing this, have inspired new faith and hope in the lives of 600,000 rural Negro boys and girls."[9] Smith's effusions sometimes bemused more worldly Rosenwald officials. Edwin Embree, who became president of the fund in 1928, wrote on one of Smith's letters: "statements must be discounted somewhat, for to Smith *all* our work is good. He has much the attitude of Jehovah toward his creation of the world, reported in Genesis."[10] Smith would need optimism and faith in the fund's good works as he began the difficult process of transferring the building program from Tuskegee to his own office and establishing his leadership of the building program.

These tasks required a new working relationship with Clinton J. Calloway, who endured several months of uncertainty before he could announce in September that "my new position is Field Agent for the Rosenwald Schools and Director of the Extension Department at Tuskegee Institute."[11] The removal of the Rosenwald program was a blow to Tuskegee Institute's prestige that directly hit at Calloway's stature as a key figure in the program's formative years. Now it was Calloway's turn to prepare and file a monthly report of activities and expenses like those he had previously reviewed and approved from the Rosenwald building agents. Accompanied by the state Negro school agent or Rosenwald building agent, he visited communities for rallies and construction inspections, met with county superintendents, and tracked the progress of applications and construction projects.[12] As S. L. Smith spent most of his time at the Nashville headquarters, Calloway's visits reassured communities of the Rosenwald Fund's commitment to African American advancement through the building program, even as they demonstrated his reduced status in a new hierarchy headed by a white man in a distant office.

Smith's and Calloway's first tasks were to close out the Tuskegee building program and implement the new plan of aid.[13] Julius Rosenwald had not formally consented to Tuskegee's proposed building program budget for 1919–20, but the extension department and state Negro school agents had nonetheless approved a number of projects. Rosenwald authorized a "cleanup" budget for 1920–21 for these Tuskegee building projects, as well as a separate 1920–21 budget for new Rosenwald Fund projects.[14] Continuing difficulties caused by the boll weevil and an economic recession that limited African Americans' access to credit cost seventy-five schools their Rosenwald grants under the regular 1920–21 budget. Yet by the end of June 1921, Rosenwald aid had supported a total of 1,069 school buildings—640 under the Tuskegee regime, 84 from the cleanup budget, and 345 under the fund's first regular budget year—the largest number of Rosenwald schools built in a single year up to that time. The Rosenwald Fund's total contributions to the cleanup budget and 1920–21 budget schools alone exceeded the total amount Julius Rosenwald had contributed to the Tuskegee schools, $356,335 compared to $263,515, but it had been a very difficult year.[15]

School officials and patrons struggled to keep building projects from foundering during this long transition. From Alabama, Autauga County superintendent Mrs. R. L. Faucett wrote in January 1920 that she was already "distressed beyond measure at the delay" in getting the Rosenwald grant for Hunter Hill School. Nineteen months later, Escambia County superintendent L. K. Benson had lost patience with the new Rosenwald regime, expostulating, "I am almost prepared to say with regard to Rosenwald aid, 'NEVER AGAIN.'" He claimed not to have known that the new Mason School had to have patent desks for eighty students and protested: "Those colored people ought not to be forced to raise more money now. They simply are not able to do it at present."[16]

Benson may have been rationalizing his own mistake, but he was also frustrated at being crossed up by the program's new lines of authority and blindness to local conditions. Alabama Negro school agent James S. Lambert had tried to help out by transferring a grant appropriated for another Escambia County project to the Mason School, which then got him and Clinton Calloway in hot water with S. L. Smith and with each other. Lambert warned Calloway, "Our county superintendents, as well as the colored people, are becoming very much discouraged over the situation and technicalities are only adding to the confusion."[17]

This small dispute hinted at a larger contest over reordering the building program's racial hierarchy. Smith planned to administer the program with a common racial strategy employed by white reformers and philanthropic programs, a strategy that gave first priority to white expectations and adjusted plans for black education accordingly. Tennessee Rosenwald building agent Robert E. Clay aptly described Smith's working technique: "being a Southern white man, [Smith] knew that before he could make any progress he would have to change the attitude of the white people in the communities, counties, and in the State toward Negro education; so he mapped out a definite, practical, workable program for contact, confidence and cooperation between the white and colored people in the communities, counties and State."[18] Smith shared his reluctance to challenge white supremacy and demand racial justice with most of his white colleagues and some African American activists like Clay. They believed, not without reason, that they stood on racial minefields where one false step would obliterate all hope of change. Lynchings and other forms of mob violence against African American southerners continued, gaining national attention with the postwar wave of antiblack riots, including Chicago's in 1919. The Ku Klux Klan had reemerged as a national and very public organization with a broad array of social and moral, as well as political, targets for its own forms of intimidation. Threatened by unceasing violence and intimidation and encouraged by the promise of a better life outside the South that they had glimpsed during the First World War, African Americans continued their great migration to the cities of the Northeast and Midwest. One response came from the Commission on Interracial Cooperation, a biracial coalition of southern Progressive activists founded in 1920 that attempted to halt the violence and establish positive relationships between blacks and whites within a more safely segregated South.[19]

The Rosenwald Fund faced an early test on these issues soon after Smith established the Nashville office when the Tennessee Interracial Committee, the state branch of the Commission on Interracial Cooperation, asked Smith to serve as its chair. The building program was already associated with the Interracial Committee through Clay, who was one of its African American officers. Smith himself later served on its executive committee, and the Rosenwald Fund would later support the national Commission on Interracial Cooperation. But in 1921, leading the Tennessee Interracial Committee would require a public activism that Rosenwald Fund officials feared would rebound negatively on their program. William C. Graves and Francis W. Shepardson warned that Smith might embarrass Julius Rosenwald and become distracted from his real duties. Smith acquiesced, expressing his own concern about an issue usually left unspoken among Rosenwald program staff. As chair of the Interracial League, Smith would have had to challenge the Ku Klux Klan and address lynching openly, topics that he had avoided discussing in public for fear of attracting Klan attention to the building program and its Jewish benefactor.[20]

Moreover, Rosenwald Fund officials, including Julius Rosenwald, had made an important shift in their approach to interracial cooperation. African American deference and accommodation had been integral to the early years of the rural school-building program. But Booker T. Washington and Clinton Calloway had understood that public displays of deference could shield African Americans when they asserted themselves with white southerners, such as when Calloway drew authority from Julius Rosenwald to enforce the program's dictates on the state agents for Negro schools, or as black school patrons used self-help contributions to leverage resources out of white public school boards. The Rosenwald Fund's new plan put a greater emphasis on white paternalism and white leadership on behalf of African Americans.[21] For Smith, asserting his leadership of the Rosenwald building program meant claiming authority by virtue of race as well as professional expertise. Consequently, as Rosenwald Fund officers heightened their emphasis on professional expertise for model schools, they simultaneously concentrated authority within their own white leadership, marginalizing Clinton Calloway in the program he had constructed.

Adjusting to his new position was not easy for Calloway, as no one seemed clear about the precise nature of his responsibilities or the extent of his authority. He described the situation to Tuskegee principal Robert Russa Moton at the end of 1920 as "pleasant but not yet what I hope it will be. I am asking Mr. Smith to outline some specific work for me to do rather than have me up in the air as to what I am expected to do." Calloway was sympathetic to Smith, who was "getting his hands on the work as fast as possible so that he can help me to find my bearing," but the transfer of leadership must have been difficult.[22] Not too long before, Calloway had been doling out Rosenwald grants to Smith and chiding him about the lackluster quality of Tennessee's Rosenwald schools. Now Smith controlled the money and expected Calloway to report to him. Although he was restless and dissatisfied, Calloway was reluctant to leave the building program. In 1921, he told a correspondent that he had not resigned as field agent "because I have had no definite information of any source which affords as large a[n] opportunity of service."[23]

Within two years, Calloway's job with the Rosenwald Fund was on the line, and with it the place of black professional leadership in the rural school-building program. In the late spring of 1923, he warned his brother Thomas Junius Calloway that "Tuskegee Institute and the Negro generally, I am of the impression, will have less and less to do[,] so far as the officials of The Julius Rosenwald Fund are concerned[,] in the general administration of The Fund." At almost the same time as he penned this letter, the state agents for Negro schools were holding their annual meeting with representatives of the General Education Board and the Julius Rosenwald Fund. Although Calloway's fate was not an official item of business, the only African American present at the meeting, W.T.B. Williams of the Jeanes and Slater funds, made a pointed comment. "Mr. Williams (Negro) thought it would be a great mistake to eliminate Negro workers from the Rosenwald movement," noted Francis Shepardson. "While he did not mention Calloway, I thought he had him in mind as Mr. Williams has his headquarters at Tuskegee." Calloway also could have counted on Leo Favrot's continued support. Favrot had written S. L. Smith in late 1922 that Calloway offered a "decidedly worthwhile" service and an important "psychological effect" for the Julius Rosenwald Fund among their African American constituents.[24]

Julius Rosenwald took a different view. In July 1923, Rosenwald "decided definitely that one man can serve as General Field Agent . . . and that a colored man is not needed," Clinton Calloway reported to his brother Thomas. "I am [not?] sure that it has been left to him to originate the idea, but he has at least acted in the matter. I have written some letters which are in shape of a protest, but I am pretty sure that they will do very little good except to let the people know what I think of the action." Indeed, when North Carolina's Rosenwald building agent received one of these letters, he showed it in confidence to his white superiors and declared no interest in taking up Calloway's cause. While Calloway realized that his attempts to keep the field agent's position were self-serving, he also was disappointed and disillusioned. "My contention is not for the job for myself," he claimed, "but that promises made at the reorganization of The Rosenwald work have been either forgotten or disregarded."[25]

Calloway's services as field agent may well have been redundant now that state agents for Negro schools and Rosenwald building agents processed applications and inspected the completed schools, yet his complaint addressed another key point. By cutting the building program's last official ties with Tuskegee, Julius Rosenwald and the Rosenwald Fund had removed the program's African American leadership. Furthermore, the African American Rosenwald building agents lost their direct connection to both Tuskegee and Julius Rosenwald. Whereas Julius Rosenwald or his representative had routinely attended meetings of Rosenwald building agents during Tuskegee's annual Farmers' Conference in the late 1910s and early 1920s, by 1928 Rosenwald Fund director Alfred K. Stern could propose a building agents' conference as a new idea. Samuel L. Smith corrected him but admitted that he himself had not attended the Farmers' Conference for the past three years and did not think that the building agents had been attending the meeting as much as they had "when Mr. C. J. Calloway was assisting in the work of the Fund."[26] As had happened in 1920, an administrative decision, made most likely in the name of efficiency, took on a racial dimension when applied in the context of southern states and communities.

COMMUNITY SCHOOL PLANS

As he negotiated leadership roles, Samuel L. Smith also prepared a fresh set of plans for what would become the archetypal Rosenwald schools of the 1920s, the Julius Rosenwald Fund's *Community School Plans*. These building plans physically expressed the program's shift from promoting better schools to creating model schools, and the related emphasis on professional expertise in rural school architecture that had begun when Julius Rosenwald hired Fletcher B. Dresslar to assess Rosenwald-aided school buildings. Some of the *Community School Plans* incorporated and updated Tuskegee designs. Most came from earlier "Community School Plans" that S. L. Smith had developed for Tennessee public schools with Dresslar's assistance. Smith had already used some of those plans for Rosenwald-aided buildings, such as an H-plan used for the 1916 Fayette County Training School at Somerville.[27] The first Tennessee school built under the Rosenwald Fund's 1920 plan of aid, the one-teacher Krisle School in Robertson County, utilized another design Smith had prepared after his course work with Dresslar, featuring a "modern well-lighted classroom . . . excellent industrial room, and fuel room, and two cloakrooms." Tennessee's department of education would publish Smith and Dresslar's designs in an official *Community School Plans* bulletin in 1921.[28] Meanwhile, Smith took the designs with

Figure 14. Building a Rosenwald school, Gregg, Texas, 1921. *Community School Plans* and other approved designs for Rosenwald schools featured batteries of windows. These tall, narrow windows with minimal framing maximized natural lighting; consequently all designs for Rosenwald schools positioned the classrooms to face east or west. (Jackson Davis Papers [#3072], Special Collections, University of Virginia Library)

him to the Rosenwald Fund, had Dresslar and state Negro school agents review them again, and hired J. E. Crain and E. M. Tisdale to redraw them.

The Julius Rosenwald Fund published its own *Community School Plans* in the fall of 1921.[29] Although the fund published several revised and expanded editions of *Community School Plans*, the 1921 series of plans remained at the core of this influential architectural pattern book.[30] The fund's *Community School Plans* reflected contemporary discussions of school architecture and Smith's specialized training in rural school design under Fletcher Dresslar. Dresslar was especially concerned about lighting, an essential aspect of school hygiene for the conservation of children's eyesight and general sanitation. In *Community School Plans*, Smith eliminated the cross-lighting Dresslar had criticized in the Tuskegee plans by limiting windows to one side of a classroom. In addition, *Community School Plans* maximized natural light by using batteries of much taller windows that stretched from the interior wainscot cap to the eaves, and with narrower framing than seen in Tuskegee designs.[31] Thus, a single stream of light falling from left to right would illuminate the blackboard and desks, preventing eyestrain caused by inadequate and inconsistent light levels (figures 14, 15).

Figure 15. Class in the Florida Agricultural & Mechanical College practice school, Tallahassee, 1923. The glare at the top left corner of the photograph shows how the battery windows, oriented to east and west, brought in light over the students' left shoulders. Florida A&M received one the first grants for practice schools at teacher-training programs in the 1920s. This building, which no longer stands, became a teachers' cottage after construction of the Lucy Moten Practice School, another Rosenwald grant structure, in 1931–32. (Jackson Davis Papers [#3072], Special Collections, University of Virginia Library)

Because the building had to be laid out to maximize the natural lighting provided by each classroom's battery windows, the orientation of the building on its site would ensure that windows faced either east or west.[32] Dresslar had faulted Tuskegee plans for not addressing building orientation. *Community School Plans* corrected this omission by devising alternative plans for each size category according to the school's orientation. A building with an entrance that faced east or west had its classrooms arranged along the front or the back wall. In a building with an entrance facing north or south, the classrooms filled the east and west sides. For example, the one-teacher Community School Plan 1 faced east or west only so that its windows would illuminate the industrial and cloakrooms at the front, and the classroom at the back (figure 16). Community School Plan 1–A, designed for a one-teacher school oriented north-south, placed the entrance in one gable end and the classroom and industrial room along one side of the building (figures 17, 18).

Proper windows, according to Progressive school designers like Smith and Dresslar, provided much-needed ventilation as well as light. Double-hung sash windows could be raised at the bottom and lowered at the top to ensure that

COMMUNITY · SCHOOL ·
· ONE TEACHER PLAN · NO · 1 ·

· TISDALE ·

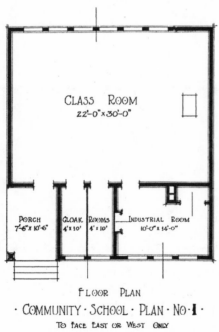

CLASS ROOM
22'-0" X 30'-0"

PORCH
7'-6" X 10'-6"

CLOAK ROOMS
4' X 10'   4' X 10'

INDUSTRIAL ROOM
10'-0" X 14'-0"

FLOOR PLAN
· COMMUNITY · SCHOOL · PLAN · NO · 1 ·
TO FACE EAST OR WEST ONLY
Blue prints for wood only.

Figure 16. Community School Plan 1, to face east or west. (*Community School Plans*, rev. ed., 1928)

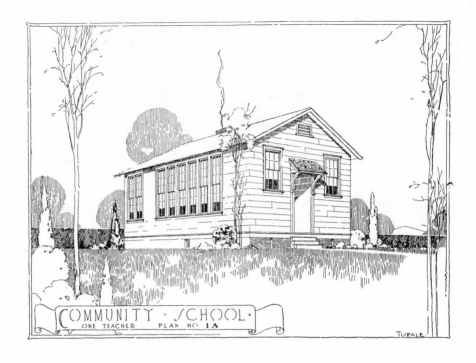

COMMUNITY · SCHOOL ·
ONE TEACHER   PLAN NO 1-A

TISDALE

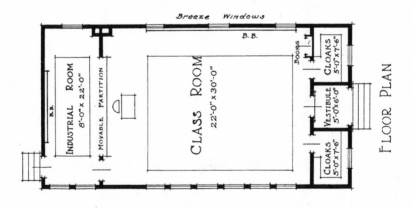

ONE-TEACHER

COMMUNITY SCHOOL PLAN No 1-A

TO FACE NORTH OR SOUTH ONLY

Figure 17. Community School Plan 1–A, to face north or south. (*Community School Plans*, rev. ed., 1928)

Figure 18. Cedar Creek School, Bastrop County, Texas, 1923. Like many Rosenwald schools, this Community School Plan 1–A structure stands next to a church, the Hopewell Primitive Baptist Church. (Photograph by author)

students and teachers would have plenty of fresh air. The Tuskegee plans had featured such windows, but Dresslar did not think they afforded enough circulation. Following his mentor's advice, Smith added "breeze windows" high under the eaves on exterior walls (to avoid cross-lighting) or above the blackboard on interior walls. Breeze windows pulled air across the room and into a hallway or adjacent classroom. The buildings still sat above the ground on short piers to limit moisture from creeping up into the building from the ground. Now they were to be enclosed, which Dresslar taught was essential for student and teacher health as well as building sanitation and longevity. To ensure this combination of ventilation, health, and construction benefits, the instructions accompanying *Community School Plans* ordered builders to pay careful attention to window framing, double flooring, and the building's underpinning.[33]

Community School Plan facades generally were unadorned, limiting decorative details to a bare minimum that might suggest the Mission or Colonial Revival styles familiar from early twentieth-century residential neighborhoods. Simplicity was a key Progressive design principle signifying order and rationality. School architects like Dresslar and Smith also incorporated simplicity into a functionalist aesthetic that made Rosenwald buildings more affordable, modern in appearance when compared to the vernacular buildings they replaced, and modest in comparison with most white schools. Their floor plans take the classroom rectangle as a basic organizational unit. Each floor plan assembles

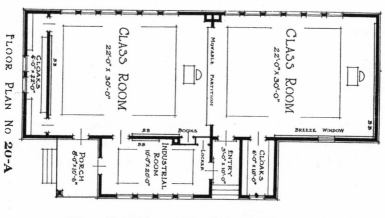

Figure 19. Community School Plan 20–A, to face north or south. (*Community School Plans*, rev. ed., 1928)

one or more classrooms with an industrial classroom and cloakrooms in such a way that they can obtain the essential unilateral lighting.

Floor plans tended to have one of two basic schemes, rectangular or H-shaped, although larger rectangular structures evolved into T-plans. Smaller structures typically were variations on the rectangle. One-teacher plan 1 adapted an earlier Tuskegee building plan that had a similar distinctive incised corner porch. Plan 1 grouped the cloakrooms and industrial room in a series of small interior rectangles in front of the classroom, creating an almost square exterior block (figure 16). Its alternative, plan 1–A, lined up the classroom and industrial room behind the two cloakrooms and recessed entranceway to create a more elongated rectangular outline (figures 17, 18). The 1–A plan also served as the basis for the two-teacher plan 20–A, which extended the rectangle with another classroom (figure 19). Perhaps the most popular two-teacher school was plan 20, identifiable by the projecting industrial room in the center of the front facade that gives the building the appearance of a squat triangle (figures 20–22). Its core sits behind the industrial room in another elongated rectangle of two classrooms arranged end to end. Unilateral lighting usually necessitated that this building face east or west, with one set of windows in the front projection and two battery windows along the rear wall. A north-south version of this plan, 2–C, located the classroom windows on the sides of the building and had less satisfactory north or south lighting for the industrial room in the center.

Most plans could be expanded easily by adding a room or rooms to the rear or side, as Dresslar had recommended.[34] Three- and four-teacher buildings expanded on the rectangular classroom block, and some larger designs joined several blocks together. Plan 3 showed another simple rectangular building, two classrooms wide and two deep, with battery windows stretching across the front and back. Plan 30 was very similar, with a steeper gable over a narrower front door, and entrances in the gable ends (figures 23, 24). An alternative three-teacher plan, 3–A, turned the rectangle on its end in a long, narrow building with a dropped-gable porch entrance that faced north or south. Four-teacher plan 400 turned the rectangle back on its long axis in a bilateral floor plan of four classrooms with industrial rooms and side entrances set within the dropped-gable ends. This version of the four-teacher plan echoed a Tuskegee-era plan that placed a central gable over the classroom windows, and variations on it continued to be built through the 1920s (figures 2, 25–29). A rectangular block of classrooms dominated the front of plan 4 also, but an auditorium projecting at right angles from the back of the building created a T-plan. These designs allowed for expansion simply by lining up more classrooms at the ends,

COMMUNITY SCHOOL
TWO TEACHER PLAN Nº 20

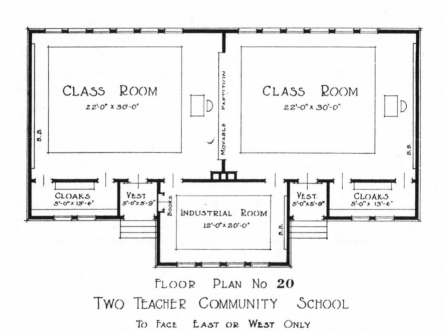

CLASS ROOM
22'-0" X 30'-0"

CLASS ROOM
22'-0" X 30'-0"

B.B.

MOVABLE PARTITION

B.B.

CLOAKS
5'-0" x 13'-6"

VEST.
5'-0"x5'-9"

BOOKS

INDUSTRIAL ROOM
12'-0" X 20'-0"

B.B.

VEST.
5'-0"x5'-9"

CLOAKS
5'-0" x 13'-6"

FLOOR PLAN No 20
TWO TEACHER COMMUNITY SCHOOL
TO FACE EAST OR WEST ONLY

Figure 20. Community School Plan 20, to face east or west. One of the most popular designs for a small Rosenwald-aided school, this arrangement of classrooms became a standard floor plan for two- and three-teacher schools in many southern states. (*Community School Plans*, rev. ed., 1928)

Figure 21. Julius Rosenwald School, Okfuskee County, Oklahoma, 1924–25. This school follows Community School Plan 20. The blank end wall prevented cross-lighting in the classrooms, which had window batteries in the rear facade. The small windows in the front left of the building provided lighting in one of the cloakrooms, and the front center window battery lit the industrial room. (Julius Rosenwald Fund Archives, Fisk University Franklin Library, Special Collections)

and indeed later editions of *Community School Plans* included T-plan structures accommodating four to twelve classrooms, some with wider front entrances to allow for a projecting auditorium at the rear. All of these larger plans, organized around a rectangular block of classrooms lined up to either side of the entrance, had to face east or west.

The *Community School Plans* also suggested the H-plan for bigger schools, such as plans 4–A, 5–A, 5–B, and 6–A. Smith borrowed the H-shaped floor plan from turn-of-the-century urban schools, whose architects had to fit large numbers of rooms on relatively small sites and yet provide windows for each classroom (figure 30).[35] Community School H-plans ranged from four to twelve classrooms plus vocational rooms. Classrooms occupied the "arms" of the *H*, which could be expanded by additions to the front or back. The "bar" of the *H* featured an auditorium and, in larger schools, office and library spaces. This was the floor plan of choice for larger buildings that had to face north or south.

Community School Plans also had their own color schemes and specific requirements for interior appointments. The building program's continued in-

Figure 22. Old school replaced by the Julius Rosenwald School, Okfuskee County, Oklahoma. (Julius Rosenwald Fund Archives, Fisk University Franklin Library, Special Collections)

sistence on exterior and interior paint represented a huge improvement in appearance for many rural black schools, and the furnishings it mandated created spaces much more conducive to teaching and learning. Especially in the early years of the building program at Tuskegee and Nashville, school facades were often painted with a nut brown, or "bungalow," stain with white trim; white with gray trim and light gray with white trim were also recommended. By 1922, the fund had begun sending paint chips to illustrate its recommended color schemes, and its plan books gave specific instructions on paint application. Interior paint schemes employed bands of color to accentuate the effect of the battery windows on light levels and students' vision. Walnut-stained wainscoting ran along the lower section of classroom walls, surmounted by gray or buff painted walls and light cream or ivory ceilings.[36] The resulting horizontal bands of color reflected and intensified natural light entering from the windows set above the wainscot, while the darker wainscot minimized

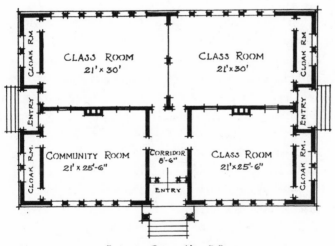

FLOOR PLAN No. 30
THREE TEACHER COMMUNITY SCHOOL
TO FACE EAST OR WEST ONLY

Figure 23. Community School Plan 30, to face east or west. Simple rectangular structures like these easily accommodated classroom additions, for which matching grants were also available. (*Community School Plans*, rev. ed., 1928)

Figure 24. Community School Plan 30 structure at Voorhees College, Denmark, Bamberg County, South Carolina. The Rosenwald Fund contributed $700 to a school in Denmark in 1930–31. (Photograph by author)

glare at desk level for seated pupils. Light tan and translucent window shades also aided in controlling light levels.

School equipment made one of the program's most direct connections between the building and instruction. Blackboards along three walls served the teacher and students. Modern patent desks were supposed to replace the rough wooden slabs, pews, and benches typical of many other black schools. White county school officials often wanted to bypass this requirement as well so that they could transfer used furnishings from white schools over to black ones, a practice that African American school patrons and Rosenwald Fund officials despised. But when school authorities would not allocate public funds for new furniture, black community members often had difficulty paying for patent desks in addition to their contribution to the building. S. L. Smith, the fund's plan of aid, and state agents for Negro schools simply called for modern desks so that public school authorities would not ignore the requirement but quietly allowed Tuskegee-style homemade desks when necessary to complete a building.[37]

Two other essential pieces of equipment were the sanitary privies required for all Rosenwald schools, for which the fund continuously published the same plan and instructions for a four-seat pit privy with a latticework grill under the

COMMUNITY · SCHOOL ·
FOUR TEACHER   PLAN NO 45

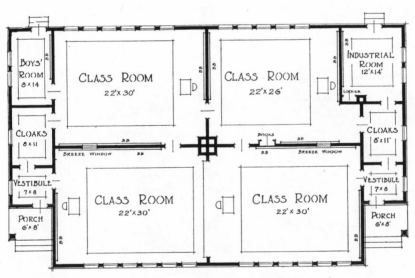

BOYS' ROOM 8'×14'	CLASS ROOM 22'×30'		CLASS ROOM 22'×26'	INDUSTRIAL ROOM 12'×14'
CLOAKS 8'×11'		BREEZE WINDOW	BOOKS BREEZE WINDOW	LOCKER CLOAKS 8'×11'
VESTIBULE 7×8	CLASS ROOM 22'×30'		CLASS ROOM 22'×30'	VESTIBULE 7×8
PORCH 6'×8'				PORCH 6'×8'

FLOOR PLAN No 45
FOUR TEACHER COMMUNITY SCHOOL
TO FACE EAST OR WEST ONLY

Figure 25. Community School Plan 45, originally numbered 400. (*Community School Plans*, rev. ed., 1928)

Figure 26. Prosperity School, Newberry County, South Carolina, 1923–24. Known in its community as the Shiloh School because of its historic ties to the Shiloh AME Church that stands beside it, this school follows Community School Plan 400. The building still stands, although it is no longer in use. (Julius Rosenwald Fund Archives, Fisk University Franklin Library, Special Collections)

Figure 27. Old school at Prosperity, Newberry County, South Carolina. Two-story structures such as this often accommodated fraternal lodges as well as schools in African American communities. (Julius Rosenwald Fund Archives, Fisk University Franklin Library, Special Collections)

Figure 28. Lincoln Park (Addor) School, Moore County, North Carolina. Constructed in 1922–23, this Community School Plan 400 building now serves as the Addor Community Center. (Photograph by author)

Figure 29. Center Star School, Dinwiddie County, Virginia, 1927–28. The dropped-gable design in Community School Plans 3, 45, and 400 resembled an earlier Tuskegee plan seen at Madison Park, Alabama, in fig. 2, and here in Virginia. (Photograph by author)

Figure 30. Camilla School, Mitchell County, Georgia, 1930–31, known in its community as the Rockdale School. An excellent example of the 1928 Community School Plan 6–B, this brick school was eligible for a permanent construction bonus. Community School Plan 6–B was identical to the earlier 6–A but was updated to show a brick exterior. Today the Brown Chapel CME Church congregation owns and worships in Camilla's building, and the Kiddie Kollege day care center operates in one wing. (Julius Rosenwald Fund Archives, Fisk University Franklin Library, Special Collections)

Figure 31. Sanitary privy at the Camilla School, Mitchell County, Georgia, 1930–31. (Julius Rosenwald Fund Archives, Fisk University Franklin Library, Special Collections)

Figure 32. Community School Plan sanitary privy. All Rosenwald-aided schools had to have two sanitary privies, for which the Julius Rosenwald Fund provided this plan or referred school builders to their state board of health. (*Community School Plans*, rev. ed., 1928)

eaves for ventilation and a high fence along two sides for privacy (figures 31–32). At a time when most rural African American schools had no toilets at all, and many white rural schools had only squalid facilities, two properly constructed and painted privies advertised a Rosenwald school as a model school.[38]

ROSENWALD SCHOOLS AND STANDARDIZED SCHOOL DESIGN

Tuskegee's Rosenwald schools had first suggested that African American school facilities might become models of school construction for white public schools, if only because improved black schools would inspire local whites to demand that their schools look even better. Fletcher Dresslar agreed, noting in his report on the Tuskegee buildings that "the best rural school buildings for Negroes are now serving as both incentives and models for those in authority who build for white children."[39] By the middle 1920s, many state agents for Negro schools claimed that the Rosenwald Fund's *Community School Plans* had not only raised the bar for African American schools but had prompted better school plans and construction standards for white schools as well. Observers used a consistent vocabulary to describe Community School Plan buildings: "modern, well-lighted, sanitary"; "modern, model schoolhouses for negroes"; "modern buildings following the Rosenwald plans"; "modern and correct negro rural school buildings"; "the very best that is known in school house lighting and ventilation."[40] The Rosenwald schools of the 1920s embodied the efforts of professional school designers to standardize what they meant by "modern, model schoolhouses." Their ambivalent messages about racial standards—did or should the standards of professional school architecture differ across racial categories?—meant that observers saw Rosenwald schools variously as neutral learning environments, "safe" Jim Crow facilities, and spaces of African American achievement.

State departments of education used Rosenwald grants and *Community School Plans* to make public investment in black schools more palatable and to argue that black schools should meet the same standards expected for white schools. Georgia Negro school agent Walter B. Hill Jr. stressed the cost-effectiveness of model black schools: "The buildings are not expensive, and have no features not essential to a properly built school house. It has been found that the money given by Mr. Rosenwald more than pays for the good features embodied in the plans. In other words, the Rosenwald money pays for the difference in cost between a modern school building and the kind that is usually built without Rosenwald aid." Texas state officials emphasized the quality of Rosenwald schools, which "when erected according to plans and specifications agreed upon by the Fund and the State Department [compare] favorably with the best, most lasting, and most attractive type of rural school building to be seen in Texas." Florida's Dewitt E. Williams trumpeted the buildings' professional credentials: "The plans for the Rosenwald Schools are drawn by Mr. S. L. Smith, who was trained for this work by Dr. F. B. Dresslar, possibly the Nation's greatest and most reliable building expert."[41]

Community School Plans, by establishing professional standards for model school buildings serving African American students, questioned the racial boundaries that Jim Crow had inscribed on the southern landscape. If, as scholar Grace Elizabeth Hale has suggested, "segregation materially and metaphorically grounded the South's new racial order," then the construction of schools specifically designed for African Americans certainly reinforced the region's racial hierarchy. Similarly, Michael McGerr has pointed out that white Americans used segregation to confine African Americans in separate and unequal spaces and to exclude them from many "white" spaces in a calculated effort "to put African-Americans in their 'place' once again."[42] Yet the Rosenwald Fund's *Community School Plans* became an integral part of white school construction. Rosenwald schools created a visual vocabulary for southern rural schools that crossed the color line and suggested that all students could and should learn in professionally designed instructional environments.

Several factors account for the resemblance between Rosenwald plans and designs for white schools and the increasing use of Rosenwald plans for white school facilities. Fletcher B. Dresslar's role in training Samuel L. Smith and reviewing Rosenwald school plans lent his professional stature to the *Community School Plans*. The 1924 publication of Dresslar's new bulletin for the U.S. Bureau of Education, *American School Buildings*, further enhanced the reputation of his designs.[43] Smith took his mentor's training into his career in black public education, thereby bringing Rosenwald schools into the mainstream of 1920s professional design. Furthermore, Dresslar and Smith saw themselves as leaders in a growing movement to set modern standards for school architecture. Progressive educators in general and school planners in particular had been calling for greater state control over public school architecture and the hiring of professional schoolhouse planners to implement it.[44] Simultaneously, educators and designers began to develop specific, measurable standards by which to assess current facilities and plan future ones. Their efforts typify the efforts of Progressive reformers in the 1920s to apply to society the methods of scientific management used in the factory.[45] The school planners' concept of "standards" was consequently broad, ranging from standard sizes of lumber and nails, to standards determining the size and arrangement of classrooms, to general standards that assessed a building's efficient use of space, all of which was intended to create cost-effective and highly "productive" school environments.

The National Education Association's Committee on Standardization of Schoolhouse Planning and Construction, led by Boston architect Frank Irving Cooper and funded by the General Education Board, attempted to set those standards. Samuel L. Smith represented the Julius Rosenwald Fund on Cooper's committee, which included other leaders in the field, such as George D. Strayer and Nickolaus L. Engelhardt of Teachers College, Columbia University, who used standardized scorecards to rate school buildings in their surveys and plans for school-construction programs across the nation.[46] The Committee on Standardization of Schoolhouse Planning studied state school-building laws and reviewed research studies on proper classroom illumination, heating and ventilation, toilets, and clothing storage. The committee's 1925 report included guidelines for every aspect of planning and constructing a school building, replete with checklists and flow charts.[47]

Standardization, as professionals like Smith understood it, did not mean uniform buildings but rather a consistent, predictable combination of design elements that reinforced their shared educational purpose and demonstrated school builders' up-to-date knowledge of professional practice. The *Community School Plans'* repetition and recombinations of rectangular spaces and consistently restrained decorative styling clearly exhibit this understanding. Smith drew attention to his plans' adherence to professional school-design standards, assuring viewers of the 1924 and 1927 editions of *Community School Plans*, "Much time has been spent in planning these buildings with a view to furnishing modern schoolhouses meeting all the requirements for lighting, sanitation, classroom conveniences, etc." He used the Committee on Standardization's guidelines to prove the efficiency of Rosenwald Fund designs, even borrowing Frank Cooper's "Candle of Efficiency," a chart that rated the efficiency of a school plan by the ratio of its "production area" to its total floor area. The "Candle of Efficiency" called for a minimum 50 percent ratio between instructional floor space and total floor space, but, Smith emphasized, the *Community School Plans* all offered at least a 65 percent ratio and often more than 75 percent.[48]

As Smith's reassurances suggest, cost-efficiency also promoted the use of Rosenwald school designs as models. Southern public school authorities usually were not lavish in their spending on any facilities, white or black, in rural districts. The Rosenwald Fund chose not to exercise copyright privileges and made *Community School Plans* available free of charge, both in small pamphlets of plans and specifications and in blueprints.[49] Free distribution of plans and blueprints was essential to appeal to state and local school officials and to secure the desired standards for black school construction. The ready availability of Rosenwald school plans also encouraged their use for white school buildings and handed the Rosenwald Fund a major public relations tool for asserting both the quality of its designs and their effect in producing interracial goodwill.

Plans developed and circulated by state departments of education in the late 1910s and throughout the 1920s certainly show an affinity with the *Commu-*

nity School Plans. Some have more elaborate ornamentation, but the provisions for fenestration, ventilation, and community space follow Dresslar's precepts. In 1921, Memphis architect Raymond B. Spencer and his associate Henry J. Kramer designed a clipped-gable roof variant on plan 20 for the Mississippi Department of Education. Architect H. F. Kuehne of Austin, Texas, devised a hipped-roof version, "from designs suggested by" the state agent for white schools, published in 1922 and already constructed in Circlesville, Williamson County. Schools designed by Dresslar's students, like Oklahoma's Haskell Pruett, predictably imitated the *Community School Plans* and demonstrated their continuing utility and appeal in the later 1920s. Pruett's "Mildred" offered a Colonial Revival version of Community School Plan 20 with rearranged cloakrooms and a stage at one end; his "Keyes" three-teacher plan was a modified version of *Community School Plan* 30, in which he converted a classroom into an auditorium.[50]

"Standardized" schoolhouse design allowed cost-conscious southern school boards to pick and choose among a variety of plans without having to hire a professional architect or pay for architectural drawings. Some state and county school authorities simply translated Rosenwald designs wholesale into their regular building programs for white students. State agents for Negro schools and Rosenwald building agents in Arkansas, Florida, Georgia, Kentucky, Louisiana, North Carolina, Oklahoma, South Carolina, and Texas reported that county superintendents had built white schools using *Community School Plans* on their own initiative as well as at the agents' urging, sometimes because they were the only plans available in the state education department's office.[51]

S. L. Smith also believed that the continued practice of approving state plans and architect-designed buildings that met Rosenwald Fund standards, instead of restricting grants to *Community School Plans* only, acted as a further impetus to the crossover between black and white school buildings. This practice, which began under Tuskegee's administration, created a diverse set of images for Rosenwald schools that only deepened the architectural parallels between black and white southern schools. For example, early in 1921, Alabama Negro school agent James S. Lambert sent Smith copies of the Alabama state plans that originally had been designated as white versions of the Tuskegee plans for Rosenwald schools. Smith critiqued the plans, mostly on the issues of orientation and lighting, but approved them for continued use.[52] Even though originally designed and printed as Jim Crow "white" plans, these designs were now officially "black" Rosenwald schools as well.

THE ROSENWALD PROGRAM MATURES

Between 1920 and 1927, the Julius Rosenwald Fund's officers extended the school-building program across the rural South, administratively and financially through modifications of the plan of aid, and architecturally through revisions and additions to *Community School Plans*. The building program matured over the course of the 1920s as its leaders gained experience in using model buildings to address a broader range of educational needs. The resulting proliferation of school-building types, as well as new initiatives for supplementary buildings and instructional resources, brought Rosenwald schools into the mainstream of educational reform and reaffirmed the rural school-building program's leadership in setting design standards for southern public education.

Grants for large consolidated school facilities sent the clearest signal of the conceptual shift away from the modest goals of the program's early years, when Rosenwald and Tuskegee officials concentrated on improving schools in small rural black communities. Between 1920 and 1927, the types and number of grants fluctuated as fund officers encouraged consolidated rural schools and provided new *Community School Plans* for them. The 1920 plan of aid specified $500 for a one-teacher school, $800 for a two-teacher building, $1,000 for a three-teacher structure, and $1,500 for anything larger, plus $1,000 for a teachers' home. Specific grants for four-, five-, and six-teacher schools came in 1921–22.[53] In 1927, the fund amended its grant categories again to encourage larger buildings and, even more significantly, began designating aid to secondary schools. Grants for small, rural elementary schools now ranged from a mere $200 for a one-teacher school to $1,400 for a six-teacher one. County training schools and high schools housing seven to ten teachers were eligible for grants between $1,500 and $2,100.[54]

The restructured grants paralleled the expansion of *Community School Plans* options, which elaborated on the precedents set by earlier and smaller designs in several new plans for seven-teacher schools. Plan 7 for schools facing east and west followed the T-plan, featuring a rectangular classroom block with classrooms arranged along the east and west walls and divided by a corridor, and an auditorium that extended from the back. Plan 7–A followed the 6–A plan very closely, both being H-plans for north-south schools. The seven-teacher plan simply subdivided one classroom into two smaller recitation rooms and pushed the industrial room to the rear of the building.[55] Any

Figure 33. Teachers' home at Collierville School, Shelby County, Tennessee, 1921–22. In addition to providing comfortable living spaces that would attract good teachers to a community's school, teachers' homes often functioned as home economics classrooms and meeting places for community groups. This early rendition of Community School Plan teachers' home 301 displays the dark exterior stain favored by some communities. The Collierville School had been built with Rosenwald aid the previous year, and its teachers' home was one of the first built under the new aid plan. (Julius Rosenwald Fund Archives, Fisk University Franklin Library, Special Collections)

of these designs, like many preceding *Community School Plans*, could have additional classrooms put on to secure the largest Rosenwald grants.

The Rosenwald Fund also instituted new grant categories for structures other than classroom buildings, thus putting into practice its long-standing assertion that new school buildings should stand at the center of improved educational programs and exert a broader influence over community life. A good example is the teachers' home. Tuskegee's *The Negro Rural School and Its Relation to the Community* included plans for the teachers' homes endorsed by Progressive educators across the nation to attract and retain better-qualified and effective teachers. Nevertheless, experience proved that southern school boards resisted spending additional funds for such facilities at African American schools. James L. Sibley had asked Clinton Calloway in 1916 to interest Julius Rosenwald in giving $100 grants for teachers' homes, and Samuel L. Smith made another proposal for teachers' homes directly to Rosenwald in 1919. Rosenwald was more interested this time and had even suggested to Robert R. Moton that Tuskegee staff design a teachers' home plan for consideration.[56] The idea resurfaced as part of the 1920 plan of aid and remained a consistent feature of the grant program (figure 33).

Initially the Rosenwald Fund staff "left the plan of Teachers' Homes, largely in the hands of the local people," according to Clinton Calloway, "only insisting, as far as possible, on such homes being built so as to include modern conveniences now or later; that is, sanitary toilets and bath."[57] After first offering as much as $1,000 in 1922, the fund scaled its maximum award back to $900. The 1923 plan of aid clarified that the grants were for one-half of construction costs up to $900, and that only Rosenwald schools could qualify for teachers' homes, which also had to be public school property. Over the following years, fund officials repeatedly adjusted teachers' home grants to match the designs offered in *Community School Plans*, which by 1927 included plans for homes of four, five, and six rooms.[58] Community School Plan teachers' homes looked like, and were, comfortable middle-class homes. Their facades blended with the adjacent school plant with hints of cottage, bungalow, and Colonial Revival styling (figure 34). Domestic amenities included welcoming porches on the exterior and modern bathrooms indoors, but designers had not forgotten that teachers' homes were instructional as well as visual models. Separate entrances into their kitchens made them accessible for possible home economics class use.[59]

Vocational buildings followed a similar path as the Rosenwald Fund developed its model school program. Industrial education—part and parcel of the building program's dual origins in the white-dominated southern educational reform movement and the racial uplift agenda promoted by Tuskegee Institute—was supposed to be an integral part of the Rosenwald school curriculum. The subject gained additional currency with the federal Smith-Hughes Act of 1917, which provided matching federal aid for secondary school vocational programs, and the shift from manual or industrial training to vocationalism by 1920s educators, who promoted a full curriculum of job training.[60] Consequently, Rosenwald school plans continued to include industrial rooms, most often used for girls' domestic education. But the program offered no specific grants for vocational buildings until 1927, even though its administrators realized that many schools turned their industrial rooms into regular classrooms because of overcrowding, local preference for academic training, or the lack of resources for vocational equipment.

When Alfred K. Stern joined the Rosenwald Fund in 1926, he toured

Figure 34. Wilson School and teachers' home, Mississippi County, Arkansas, [1925?]. The school building to the right is the second school, constructed 1923–24; the first Wilson School burned the night before its dedication. The bungalow styling of this teachers' home, a slightly modified Rosenwald Fund plan 302, modeled middle-class domestic architecture for its residents and the community. (Julius Rosenwald Fund Archives, Fisk University Franklin Library, Special Collections)

southern schools with Samuel Smith and became convinced that vocational facilities for girls outstripped those for boys. Stern made vocational training his personal cause within the building program. By this time, Smith-Hughes vocational education programs had become entrenched in public schools. Although most Smith-Hughes money paid vocational teachers in white schools, African American county training schools in particular had been able to win inclusion in this program. Stern proposed that the Rosenwald Fund join this movement by supporting an updated program of vocational training with new financial incentives for boys' agricultural and trades facilities. Fund officials sanctioned grants of between $200 and $400 for freestanding vocational shops of one or two rooms, but only if built according to Rosenwald plans, fully equipped, and properly staffed.[61] The resemblance between shops and schools in the *Community School Plans* was, naturally, more pronounced than for teachers' homes. Rectangular structures with gabled entrances and battery windows, shop plans A and B might have be mistaken for school plans 30, 4, or 5 but for the garage door (figure 35).[62]

The new shop plans pointed to the Rosenwald Fund's renewed interest in industrial education, which did not go unnoticed by African American critics. Early in 1927, Stern's advocacy for vocational education at a meeting of state education agents had angered North Carolina's African American high school supervisor, W. A. Robinson, who also served as president of the National As-

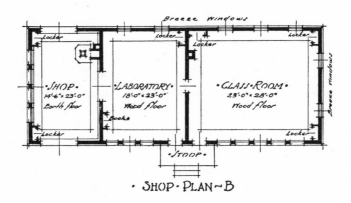

Figure 35. Shop plan B. Beginning in 1927, the Julius Rosenwald Fund offered matching grants for vocational buildings like this. (*Community School Plans*, rev. ed., 1928)

sociation of Teachers in Colored Schools. Robinson contended that "in view of the present social situation of the Negro people . . . we would hardly be justified in the South in an effort to perpetuate the present industrial, economic and social status of any group in wholesale way by establishing a system of education definitely looking toward an industrial caste system for any group of people."[63] Stern responded that his own experiences as "a member of a Race" subjected to persecution allowed him to "appreciate" African Americans' problems, and that he had no intention of creating "an industrial caste group." Yet his comparison of the manual training program in the school system of Ravinia, an affluent suburb of Chicago, to the black schools of North Carolina indicates the inherent blinders of class, region, and race that shaped Stern's and other Rosenwald administrators' vocationalist agenda.[64]

Another building category added to the revamped Rosenwald program was the practice, or demonstration, school. These were model schools not only in architectural design and appointments, but teacher-training institutions that modeled the newest and best instructional and administrative methods (figure 15). Several African American colleges and universities had petitioned Julius Rosenwald and Clinton Calloway for grants to fund practice schools during the Tuskegee era of the building program, to no avail. After the Rosenwald Fund staff enlarged the scope of the building program to include consolidated schools and teachers' homes, they were more open to include demonstration schools— as long as they followed the fund's standard plan of aid. Thus, when Robert R. Moton asked for special appropriations to fund demonstration schools at Tuskegee and Hampton, fund officers refused to consider anything other than their standard incentive grants.[65]

Rosenwald and the fund's staff in Chicago and Nashville took additional steps to ensure the longevity of Rosenwald schools both in physical and instructional terms. Starting in 1922, communities could apply for aid for classroom additions to existing Rosenwald schools, a very helpful opportunity given the endemic overcrowding in African American public schools and Rosenwald schools' tendency to encourage higher levels of attendance. What to do when a Rosenwald school was destroyed by fire (whether an accident or arson) or natural disaster had become an issue by 1922, when the fund agreed to support a replacement building under the same terms as the original, minus a portion of any insurance payment. In 1927, fund officers applied the same terms to replacements of deteriorated Rosenwald school buildings, minus a portion of the value of salvaged materials from the original structure.[66] That same year, flooding along the Mississippi River destroyed and damaged numerous African American schools in Arkansas, Mississippi, and Louisiana, and ruined furniture and equipment. As teacher Henry H. Weathers wrote to Julius Rosenwald from Rolling Ford, Mississippi, the flood was "such a set-back." The Rosenwald Fund made special appropriations for replacing buildings and furnishings in these states, which could even be applied to non-Rosenwald black public schools.[67]

By this time, the Rosenwald Fund had begun to sponsor instructional initiatives independent of its school buildings. The school library program began in 1927 under a new fund staff member, Clark Foreman. Its primary goal was to increase the number of books available to African American children and secondarily to provide books selected by professional librarians for their quality and positive portrayals of African Americans and peoples of other cultures. Any elementary school for black children with two or more teachers could purchase a set of 155 volumes and then a supplemental set. The Rosenwald Fund paid $40 and the shipping expenses of the $120 cost of the first set and $30 plus shipping for the $90 second set; later, white schools could purchase these libraries as well but at full cost. Another $120 set of books selected for high school libraries came under the same plan. Elementary school books included Arna Bontemps' *Sad-Faced Boy* along with *Boy of Old Virginia—Robert E. Lee*; high school sets featured titles celebrating the cultural diversity of the United States and documenting the countries of Latin America and the world. To help teachers and principals care for and manage their book collections, the fund hired librarians to offer on-site instruction.[68]

The Rosenwald Fund also offered substantial grants of up to $2,500 for book purchases to qualifying colleges with teacher-training programs. Conditions of aid insisted that at least two-thirds of the titles came from a list of books selected by Hampton Institute librarian Florence Curtis and contain children's literature for the benefit of future teachers, and that they would be housed in a proper facility and managed by a professional staff. South Carolina's Colored Normal, Industrial, Agricultural and Mechanical College (now South Carolina State University) was one of the institutions that garnered a Rosenwald library grant after agreeing to match the fund's $1,000 with another $2,000 for books "selected under the Rosenwald plan." As with the public school program, the fund offered training, in this case fellowships for training library staff at participating institutions.[69]

Rosenwald Fund staff in Nashville and Chicago celebrated the building program's continuing growth with celebrations at a selected school each time that another thousand Rosenwald schools reached completion. Dubbed the "Thousandths Rosenwald Schools," these sites included the three-teacher Dora School in Walker County, Alabama, at one thousand in 1921–22; the five-teacher Brunswick School in Shelby County, Tennessee, for two thousand in 1923–24; the two-teacher Riverside School in Walker County, Texas, for three thousand in 1925–26; an eleven-teacher structure at the Berry O'Kelly Training School in Wake County, North Carolina, at four thousand in 1927–28; and the six-teacher Greenbrier School in Elizabeth City County, Virginia, at five thousand in 1929–30.[70] Each "thousandth" celebration included a special dedication event attended by Julius Rosenwald or a member of the Chicago staff, S. L. Smith, representatives from the state department of education, local educators, and county school authorities, as well as schoolchildren and the general public, and generated a flurry of special publicity.

Which school earned this honor was something of a judgment call, which Smith and Chicago fund staff used to encourage and reward particular states. Thus, in 1927, Smith remarked to William F. Credle, who supervised North Carolina's Rosenwald building program, that the fund expected to reach the four thousand mark soon, adding, "It would be interesting if it could be in N.C. this time." So it was, and the celebration rewarded not only the state with the largest Rosenwald building program but also African American business leader Berry O'Kelly, who had first helped state education officers petition for Rosenwald grants in 1914. In 1930, S. L. Smith asked Alfred K. Stern to decide between two candidates for the fifth "thousandth," the Carroll School in York County, South Carolina, or Virginia's Greenbrier School; the latter's proximity to Hampton Institute favored its candidacy.[71]

As the tenth anniversary of the creation of the Julius Rosenwald Fund and fifteenth anniversary of the first experimental Rosenwald schools approached, fund officers believed it was time to take stock of their achievements. Noted African American historian Carter G. Woodson accepted a commission in 1926 to write a history of the Rosenwald Fund, with particular attention to its rural school-building program. Woodson was the nation's second African American scholar to hold a Ph.D. in history and had published his first monograph, *The Education of the Negro Prior to 1861*, in 1915. Shortly thereafter he founded the Association for the Study of Negro Life and History, on whose advisory council Julius Rosenwald served, and the *Journal of Negro History*, to which Rosenwald contributed. Woodson punctuated his historical narrative of the fund's operations with long quotations from official files and commentaries by participants and observers of the building program. His analysis and selected quotations emphasized both self-help and interracial cooperation, an interpretive strategy that Woodson hoped would elicit greater Rosenwald Fund support.[72] Consequently, his manuscript, "The Story of the Fund," provides a rich compendium of firsthand accounts of building campaigns and insider perspectives on the building program's development and achievements.

Despite the manuscript's generally laudatory tone, and perhaps because of its measured assessments of the building program's success, Woodson failed to convince Julius Rosenwald and fund staff to publish his work. Alfred Stern sent a copy to Tuskegee principal Robert R. Moton, who appreciated its detailed stories. Yet Moton felt that Woodson's text came across as a "colorless philosophical analysis" rather than "the living record of noble generosity, farsighted statesmanship, of passionate longing and sometime pitiful sacrifice which are the heart and core of the movement inaugurated by the Rosenwald Fund," and that its negative portrayal of the shortcomings in black public education in the early 1910s would antagonize some white southern readers. Ultimately, the Rosenwald Fund paid Woodson $500 for the manuscript and put it away.[73]

Woodson's typescript remains a fascinating albeit obscure text in which Rosenwald schools and their supporters struggle heroically against the long-term deprivation of southern black education. As Woodson began work on his project, W.E.B. Du Bois was publishing the results of a study of black public education in Georgia, Mississippi, and North Carolina in the *Crisis*. These essays also stressed the debilitating effects of white supremacy on black public schools, especially in funding and school facilities. While Rosenwald schools represented "the best colored schools in the state" and "the one encouraging sign" amidst otherwise deplorable conditions—and other pages in the *Crisis* reprinted the Rosenwald Fund's plan of aid—Du Bois concluded that only full state funding could guarantee "equal opportunity for advancement."[74] Ironically, perhaps, after spending the next half-dozen years fighting more battles over industrial education and model school architecture, a new set of Rosenwald Fund administrators would come to the same conclusion. While local school patrons would continue to wage their long-term battle for schools, the leadership of the Rosenwald Fund would broaden its agenda beyond the rural school-building program and the material conditions of southern black life.

Southern Schools and Race

New Leadership and the Demise of the Building Program, 1927–32

In 1927, Julius Rosenwald began transforming his philanthropic foundation, opening a new and final era for the school-building program. Up to this point, the rural school-building program had dominated the Julius Rosenwald Fund's expenditures, consuming all but $620,496 of the fund's $4,049,974 spending. Julius Rosenwald, the fund's president, participated actively in the administration of the fund with Francis W. Shepardson, Alfred K. Stern, and Samuel L. Smith. Rosenwald, who was familiar with other philanthropies, such as the Rockefeller Foundation, that operated more as charitable corporations than as personal benefactions, concluded that the time had come for a professional staff to chart new directions for his foundation.[1]

Once again, as he had done with the rural school-building program's reorganization in 1919–20 and throughout his business career, Rosenwald decided that a new system was needed, moved quickly to order dramatic changes, and trusted his staff to implement them. No extraordinary complaints about his foundation or its building program moved Rosenwald to action in 1927 and 1928, however. Rather, he had refined his personal philosophy of philanthropy to require a more vigorous application of aid on a wider scale and had identified Edwin R. Embree as the right person to lead that effort. This new course would transform the Rosenwald Fund and the place of the building program on its agenda. Within four years, the building program would expand its reach to and beyond all southern black schools and then give way to Embree's more aggressive campaign for social change.

NEW LEADERSHIP FOR THE JULIUS ROSENWALD FUND

Rosenwald had more time and opportunity to focus on philanthropic issues in the later 1920s because he had wound down his business career. The death of Sears, Roebuck vice president Albert Loeb in the fall of 1924 had suggested to Rosenwald that the time had come to plan for his own succession. He eventually settled on Robert E. Wood, former vice president of merchandising at Montgomery Ward and Company, whom he had hired for Loeb's job. Although he remained as chair of the corporation's board, Rosenwald curtailed his direct involvement in the company's operations.[2]

Julius Rosenwald followed these corporate changes with a reorganization of the Rosenwald Fund to update its administrative structure in a similar fashion and make it conform to his philosophy of self-extinguishing philanthropy. Rosenwald admired the corporate organizational model employed by other philanthropic foundations but did not endorse the concept of a perpetual endowment. As the Rosenwald Fund's official history explained, Julius Rosenwald "had a firm belief that the generation which contributed to the making of wealth should be the one to profit by it. . . . He wanted dollars to be spent for clear needs today rather than left to accumulate until they had multiplied even a hundredfold for possible uses in the remote future." He became more emphatic in his belief that philanthropy could best serve the needs of the present and determined to make his foundation a model philanthropic agency.[3]

Late in 1927, Rosenwald selected Rockefeller Foundation vice president Edwin R. Embree to become president of the fund, and early in 1928 the two men began overhauling the fund's policies and programs. Rosenwald expanded the board of trustees beyond family members to include business leaders and civic officials. Continuing members consisted of Julius Rosenwald and his wife, Augusta Nusbaum Rosenwald, son and Sears vice president Lessing Rosenwald, and fund director and son-in-law Alfred K. Stern. New trustees included Adele Rosenwald (Mrs. David M.) Levy, son-in-law and New Orleans Cotton Exchange president Edgar B. Stern, University of North Carolina president Harry W. Chase, University of Chicago Medical Clinics chief Franklin C. McLean, Enterprise Paint Manufacturing Company vice president Frank L. Sulzberger, Swift and Company vice president Harold H. Swift, and Rosenwald Fund president Edwin Embree. The Rockefeller Foundation's Beardsley Ruml joined the board later in 1928.[4]

Now chair of the board of trustees, Julius Rosenwald gave his foundation another twenty thousand shares of Sears, Roebuck and Company stock, as he had when he created the fund in 1917, to stimulate its broader platform of African American and race-relations issues. By late 1928, the Julius Rosenwald Fund held more than 227,000 shares of Sears, Roebuck stock with an estimated value of about $40 million. Rosenwald also instructed his foundation's administrators and trustees to expend all of the fund's resources within twenty-five years of his death. "By adopting a policy of using the Fund within this generation," Rosenwald advised the trustees, "we may avoid those tendencies toward bureaucracy and a formal or perfunctory attitude toward the work which almost inevitably develop in organizations which prolong their existence indefinitely. Coming generations can be relied upon to provide for their own needs as they arise."[5] Of course, that did not mean that he, the staff, or trustees would allow external events, most notably the stock market crash of 1929 and the ensuing Great Depression, to wipe out the fund's financial resources. Rather, they would carefully husband those resources to ensure their dispersal as productive social investments.

Social change became the ultimate goal of the Julius Rosenwald Fund under Edwin Embree. As scholar John H. Stanfield has observed, "the career of Edwin R. Embree as President and a trustee of the Julius Rosenwald Fund can be explained only within the context of the characteristics, contradictions, and limitations of the southern white liberal worldview."[6] Indeed, although he was born in Nebraska and spent some of his childhood in Colorado and Wyoming, Embree identified himself as a Kentuckian and modeled himself after the examples set by his paternal ancestor, Tennessee antislavery newspaper publisher Elihu Embree, and his maternal grandfather, John G. Fee, an abolitionist minister and founder of Berea College in Kentucky. Berea College admitted African American and white students until the passage of the state's Day Act in 1904, which required even private educational institutions to adopt a single racial identity. Embree attended Berea's preparatory school and undertook some collegiate courses there during its early interracial period, then earned his undergraduate degree from Yale University. After a brief stint as a reporter, Embree spent a decade working for Yale's alumni association, pursuing graduate studies in philosophy and education as well, before joining the staff of the Rockefeller Foundation in 1917. Within ten years, Embree had risen from secretary to vice president of the Rockefeller Foundation and linked the foundation's existing health and medical programs to the social sciences. He also had established a relationship with Julius Rosenwald, who joined the foundation's board of trustees in 1917.[7]

When Embree accepted the presidency of the Julius Rosenwald Fund, he brought with him a strong belief in interracial cooperation between liberal southern whites and moderate African American southerners. He also brought the influence of Charles S. Johnson, a pioneering African American sociologist with his own philosophy of interracial cooperation and racial pride. Johnson's mentor, University of Chicago sociologist Robert E. Park, had worked with Booker T. Washington and Julius Rosenwald in the early 1910s. Johnson studied with Park before and after the First World War and worked with Julius Rosenwald and Francis Shepardson on the Chicago Commission on Race Relations. As the commission's associate executive director, Johnson had formulated the group's research plan and was the principal author of its report, *The Negro in Chicago: A Study of Race Relations and a Race Riot.*[8] Johnson moved to New York to work for the National Urban League and edit its publication *Opportunity*, where he became an influential promoter of Harlem Renaissance artists and writers. In 1927, he organized a two-week conference on race relations that brought together philanthropic foundation officials, including Embree, with such African American leaders as A. Philip Randolph, W.E.B. Du Bois, Robert Russa Moton, and James Weldon Johnson. The conference inspired Embree to envision a holistic program for achieving full equality of opportunity by improving social, economic, educational, and medical programs for African American southerners.[9]

Embree brought that vision to the Rosenwald Fund, and not the assumptions about school buildings as environmental agents of change that had inspired the Rosenwald rural school-building program. After touring Rosenwald schools, Embree wrote Julius Rosenwald in February 1928 that the building program had wrought an "unbelievable" change in black schools and had had a positive influence on white schools as well, but "we are in the embarrassing position of having good school buildings for mediocre work."[10] Embree outlined a wide range of projects in African American education for the Rosenwald Fund, as well as programs that reflected his experience with the Rockefeller Foundation's public health work and his own scholarly interest in Latin America. At Julius Rosenwald's home in April 1928, the trustees agreed to embrace "the whole field of Negro education, including industrial high schools and institutions of higher learning," as well as initiatives in medicine, school counseling, and public education in Mexico.[11] New ventures in African American education and medicine would quickly outpace the school-building program, which Embree and the Rosenwald Fund trustees terminated in 1932—but not before they had erected a new set of model schools on the southern landscape.[12]

EXPANDING PROGRAMS, 1928–30

During the first years of Edwin Embree's leadership, Rosenwald Fund staff supplemented the initiatives already launched in the 1920s with another flurry of proposals intended to solidify the rural school-building program and its connections to instruction as well as professional architecture. Fund officials tightened their control over building-program money by ending the distribution of working capital to the states, which intensified the Nashville office's control over financial operations.[13] They also added incentives that would enhance the South's financial investment in Rosenwald buildings and ensure their lasting influence. "Permanent construction" grants for brick or concrete buildings, offered for the first time in the 1928–29 plan of aid, allowed an additional $50 per room over the regular grant allotment for a two-teacher or larger school, vocational building, or addition to an existing structure, and $25 per room for a teachers' home. These building materials would extend the life and reduce the maintenance of a school building and make the building more fireproof. After 1 July 1929, the fund also required public school authorities to carry insurance on all new Rosenwald-aided schools; earlier structures were still covered by the previous policy allowing a small rebuilding grant.[14] While certainly these new guidelines indirectly addressed the destruction of Rosenwald schools by racist vigilantes, they were also meant to ratchet up the buildings' construction standards and bring Rosenwald schools in line with standard practices for white public school facilities.

A parallel initiative sought to ensure that the Rosenwald building program reached as many southern communities as possible. By the summer of 1928, 193 counties in fourteen southern states still had no Rosenwald schools, although African Americans accounted for more than 5 percent of their populations. Noted the trustees, "These counties represent the most backward ones in the South as far as Negro education is concerned," and the remedy they approved in the fall of 1928 became known as aid to "backward counties." The Rosenwald Fund offered backward counties a bonus of 50 percent over the standard grant for their first two-teacher or larger Rosenwald school.[15]

One of the major obstacles to Rosenwald schools in areas with small numbers of African Americans, and to larger consolidated Rosenwald schools everywhere, was the lack of transportation. School wagons, trucks, and buses had become an integral component of white public education in the 1910s and 1920s. Few school systems offered any public funding for transportation of black students, however, and parents either had to hire a driver and vehicle themselves or let their children walk. Beginning with the 1929–30 school year, the Julius Rosenwald Fund offered grants to support bus service for black pupils at two-teacher or larger schools with terms of at least eight months that paid teachers a minimum monthly salary of $60. Qualifying counties received half of the cost of the bus and a portion of its operation expenses for a trial three-year period, after which the local school board had to assume the full cost. Kentucky "start[ed] out on high" with applications from twelve counties for twenty-three buses that totaled almost $16,000, with just under $7,000 coming from the Rosenwald Fund.[16] Although Alabama Negro school agent James S. Lambert eagerly sought transportation grants as well, he advised that the fund not push too hard. The superintendents he dealt with preferred to contract with drivers who owned their own buses rather than use county school funds to purchase buses for black students; they might be wrong, but "human nature does not change over night." For black schoolchildren, the change could not occur quickly enough. Whereas Ruth Johnson had to live with her grandmother to avoid a daily six-mile walk to and from the Rosenwald school in Murfreesboro, North Carolina, Ada Mae Stewart rode a Rosenwald bus to the Preston School in Georgia.[17]

Some of the new initiatives of the late 1920s recognized improved instruction as an independent goal within black schools rather than the logical outcome of new facilities. Instructional issues had never been absent from a program that sought to embed a vocational curriculum into its buildings and sites and mandated modern desks and blackboards. Effective teachers were essential to the Rosenwald building program, which depended on Jeanes industrial supervising teachers, principals, and classroom teachers to organize community school campaigns and had paid Rosenwald school teachers to attend summer classes at Tuskegee or Hampton. Throughout the 1920s, grants to African American colleges and universities had supported construction of model schools for teacher-training programs, and school library programs. Now instructional time and materials became the subjects of renewed attention. School term-extension grants, which had been part of the Tuskegee program, came back into the building program. Once again, the fund helped schools reach an eight- or nine-month term with a series of matching grants over three years that would grow smaller as the county picked up its contribution. The fund's library programs added an ambitious county demonstration project, in which eleven communities used Rosenwald grants to establish central libraries for blacks and for whites and countywide systems of branch libraries and bookmobiles.[18]

Radio grants, added in 1929, were probably the smallest new instructional initiative. Schools with four or more teachers could receive a $25 grant if they paid the remainder of the $75 purchase price of a seven-tube battery radio, or $30 toward a nine-tube electric radio.[19] Radios exposed students to a wider world of news and popular culture and served community gatherings as well. As D. Lillian Poignard rhapsodized:

The sun shines bright on our Rosenwald school,
The pupils are happy and gay,
The time has come when education is in bloom,
And the radio makes music all the day.[20]

Two more instructional initiatives addressed Alfred K. Stern's interest in vocational education. Stern had instigated the Rosenwald Fund's grants for vocational buildings in 1927. Beginning in 1928, the fund offered matching grants of one-third, or as much as $100, of the cost to equip each vocational room of a school or shop as long as a trained vocational agriculture or home economics teacher was on the teaching staff. The fund also offered salary support for itinerant vocational education teachers, who toured schools in specially equipped trucks. Known as vocational supervisors or shop supervisors, these men focused on trades instruction for boys, in pointed contrast to the agricultural instruction already offered by vocational agriculture teachers and extension agents, as well as vocational home economics training for girls under the 1917 federal Smith-Hughes Act.[21] The Rosenwald initiative overlapped with federal and state-funded Smith-Hughes vocational programs, however, provoking a small controversy in Oklahoma when the fund tried to place the vocational supervisor in the state extension service rather than the state education department.[22] State conditions also shaped Mississippi's response to this initiative. State Negro school agent Perry Easom sought funding for a vocational supervisor but not the truck because he wanted agricultural rather than trades instruction, for example.[23]

URBAN INDUSTRIAL HIGH SCHOOLS

Edwin Embree's expansive agenda gave Alfred Stern a chance to amplify his own vision of vocational education for African American schools. In a short-lived experiment with urban industrial high schools, Stern and the Rosenwald Fund attempted to weld their updated model of vocational education to the increasing number of black public high schools in southern states. As white philanthropists and reformers had done in the early years of the school-building program, Stern and Embree drew upon a contemporary educational movement and interpreted it within their own vision of a modern racial and economic order. However, African American southerners would prove even less receptive to this particular incarnation of industrial education, which offered little promise for advancing their economic status and community institutions.

Historian James D. Anderson has explained how the expansion of public secondary education for southern blacks in the middle 1920s, especially in cities, surprised the officials of philanthropic agencies that had been engrossed in elementary and county training schools. While the success of the black high school movement might seem to have made Rosenwald aid superfluous, fund officers saw it as an opportunity. In 1925, Francis W. Shepardson had floated a trial balloon with Jeanes Fund director James Hardy Dillard. If the Rosenwald Fund was to offer matching grants to urban high schools, he asked Dillard, would they be welcomed by state agents for Negro schools and southern cities?[24] Three years later, Alfred K. Stern and George R. Arthur, a former YMCA official who now headed the Rosenwald Fund's "Negro Welfare" programs, revived the urban high school idea and added a vocational plan. Urban industrial high schools, Stern and Arthur suggested, would update the Rosenwald building program to the economic needs of the 1920s. The goal was to increase black southerners' skill levels and incomes, but without changing their occupational status in relation to white workers or employers.[25]

Critics of industrial education had long charged that vocational training was demeaning in its presumption that all African Americans faced an inevitable future as laborers, and that it did not provide the skills needed by the modern worker of any race.[26] Stern and the Rosenwald Fund denied the first charge and focused on redressing the second. "With the gradual industrialization of the South and a consequent influx of skilled mechanics from the North, Negroes may expect to advance in industry only as they are prepared to compete both mentally and manually in a highly industrialized system," Rosenwald Fund trustees reasoned.[27] Thus "the erection of adequate school buildings combining both literary and trade features would be further evidence of the South's present tendency toward bettering the general surroundings of its colored people." Young black men could advance in the "carpentry, brick masonry, plumbing, plastering, and auto mechanic work," and young black women in the "housework, needlework, millinery, and cooking" trades that their elders already dominated.[28] At their fall 1928 meeting, the fund's trustees authorized an urban industrial high school initiative that offered grants of 25 percent of the total cost for city high schools that incorporated a full trades program. Ultimately only five schools would be constructed under this initiative, at Little Rock, Arkansas; Winston-Salem, North Carolina; Maysville, Kentucky;

Figure 36. Dunbar High School, Little Rock, Arkansas. One of the handful of urban industrial high schools constructed with special appropriations from the Julius Rosenwald Fund between 1928 and 1931. (Photograph by author)

Greenville, South Carolina; and Columbus, Georgia, at a cost of slightly over $200,000 to the Julius Rosenwald Fund.

Urban industrial high schools failed, as James Anderson has shown, largely because Rosenwald Fund trustees and staff, with Stern leading the way, rekindled and lost the debate over industrial education that had raged at the turn of the century. That debate erupted again in Little Rock, Arkansas, site of one of the first urban industrial high school projects, where the school superintendent warned that "you will find our School Board more willing to do than you will find the negro people willing to accept the thing we would offer them. . . . You will find the negroes here wanting only the literary courses."[29] W. A. Booker broached the topic from an African American perspective, asking, "Just why now should we have to hide behind the scheme of 'industrial' training to get for the Negro youths of Little Rock what justice urges and what we as the tax payers and the fathers ahead of us have long since earned?" He and other black citizens wondered why their new high school had to drop the name of M. W. Gibbs, an African American man who had served as a city judge, for "Negro Industrial High School" after years of waiting "for a real high school, one that would not be a subterfuge; one that would give a thorough educational train-ing and literary back ground, and a curriculum upon which a college education could be well predicated." As Booker also noted, the term "Industrial" bore a distasteful resemblance to "certain Negro penal institutions in the State." After considering a suggestion to name the school after Julius Rosenwald, the school board settled on a new name, the Paul Lawrence Dunbar High School (figure 36).[30]

The Rosenwald Fund's experience in Little Rock included two other signifi-cant features for the urban industrial high school initiative and for the overall Rosenwald school-building program. As part of their complex negotiations with Little Rock residents, Rosenwald officials activated a network of local Jewish businessmen to use their influence on the school board. Harry B. Salm-son organized a luncheon with "leading Jewish members" of the Little Rock white community to boost the prospects of the vocational program at the new school. This event brought onboard M. L. Altheimer, president of North Little Rock's Twin City Bank, who offered to help find opportunities for trained black workers at North Little Rock's railroad yards.[31] Similarly, in New Or-leans, Alfred Stern would work through his brother-in-law Edgar B. Stern and sister-in-law Edith Rosenwald Stern to reach school board member Isaac S. Heller.[32]

In both of these cases, Stern was able to use personal contacts with the Jewish business communities, but the significance is not only the religious connection but the class-based practice of cultivating allies among influential whites. As Embree observed in a penciled note in the margin of a letter from Altheimer, "Its [*sic*] fine to get these important people interested in such a project. We do a great deal more on this personal side than the General Education Board care to. I believe we are right and that this kind of help often counts for more than our contribution in money." Embree knew that "the personal side" could also work in the opposite direction and across the color line, with high-status locals using personal contacts at the Rosenwald Fund to advance their cause. The catalyst for the urban industrial high school at Maysville, Kentucky, was a letter from principal N. H. Humphrey reminding Embree that they had attended Berea College together during its interracial period, and that the new school would bear the name of Embree's grandfather and Berea founder John G. Fee.[33]

Another influential practice from the Dunbar High School project was the use of outside experts. Rather surprisingly, the first set of building plans for the Little Rock school had no vocational facilities for the senior high school unit other than home economics. Stern and Arthur brought in Frederick E. Clerk of the New Trier High School in Winnetka, Illinois, and Franklin J. Keller of the East Side Continuation School in New York City as consultants for the vocational program and hired architect Walter R. McCornack of Warner-McCornack & Mitchell in Cleveland to revise the design. The Rosenwald Fund also commissioned a report on industrial employment for African Americans and the attitudes of black and white citizens in the city.[34] Thereafter the fund dispatched teams of outside experts to cities seeking aid for urban industrial high schools, and McCornack would so impress the Chicago staff that they later commissioned him to review the *Community School Plans*.

The building program's need for expert advice on industrial employment also gave Edwin Embree an opportunity to bring Charles S. Johnson into the Rosenwald Fund, reestablishing a black presence at the upper levels of the fund. The two men began to weave a web of interracial personal and professional relationships for the Rosenwald Fund, anchored at Johnson's academic base at Fisk University in Nashville, where Johnson had just joined the faculty in 1928. Most of the sociological studies of cities applying for urban industrial school grants would come from Charles S. Johnson and the Department of Social Sciences at Fisk, especially economist Mabel Byrd. These paved the way for many sociological studies that Johnson and his staff at Fisk would conduct for the Rosenwald Fund in the 1930s and 1940s.[35] The industrial employment studies thus brought African Americans back into the upper levels of the building program, initially as outside experts, and tied the building program into the Rosenwald Fund's expanding array of social initiatives.

Ultimately, Dunbar High School would serve as Little Rock's premier secondary school and junior college for African Americans until 1955.[36] While a vocational program remained in place, Dunbar continued to offer Little Rock's black youth the strong academic preparation insisted on by citizens like W. A. Booker. Thus its success demonstrated that the urban industrial high school program could succeed only when it supplemented a strong traditional curriculum, and not as a fully integrated vocational curriculum. Nonetheless, the urban industrial high school project was doomed to failure. Rather than serving as a model demonstrating how vocational and academic programs could be conjoined in a single high school setting, the schools created problematic debates over their purpose and expense. Most of the cities that applied could not afford—or would not afford, for a black high school—the costly buildings and vocational equipment that McCornack, Clerk, and Keller advised. Once the Great Depression began, neither white educators nor favorably disposed African Americans would support trades schools that did not expand their students' job opportunities. White workers became increasingly hostile to black vocational training as well. The fund stopped accepting applications in 1930 and terminated the project the following year.[37] Most of the cities involved and their black citizens eventually opted for a smaller grant toward an industrial department within a regular high school setting under the new guidelines of Rosenwald Fund's new "southern school program."

THE SOUTHERN SCHOOL PROGRAM AND ROSENWALD SCHOOL DAY

In the late 1920s, new initiatives like the urban industrial high school revealed the Rosenwald Fund's movement away from an exclusive focus on school buildings, especially rural school buildings, and broadening concern for instructional programming and economic issues. Rosenwald Fund officials began to express ambivalence about the building program even as they authorized new initiatives for it. When Alfred Stern announced the urban high school concept at the 1928 meeting of the state agents for Negro schools, he "stated that the Rosenwald Fund was seeking a way to begin to draw out of rural school construction, and that The Fund was becoming interested in better construction."[38] Fund officers had already started that process by reducing the amount of Rosenwald aid for one-teacher schools to $200 in 1927, and early in 1928 S. L. Smith announced he would no longer allow states to transfer unused Rosenwald grant money allocated for other building types to one-teacher projects.

The overt purpose of these actions was to promote larger consolidated schools, but the state agents for Negro schools saw it as a cutback. "Poor negroes! How they have 'bled' to raise their part of the money for this little building. Must they now be disappointed? God forbid—and the Rosenwald Fund, too!—if it can," Negro school agent James S. Lambert implored Smith about a rejected one-teacher school in Alabama. Behind Smith's back, Lambert and Walter B. Hill Jr. of Georgia discussed how to cope with the changes. "Isn't it awful—the way the little one-teacher schools are begging for help," Lambert wrote, and he advised Hill to "slip in one or two 1–teacher buildings on your budget whether you need them or not."[39] But small schools were on their way out. Aid for one-teacher buildings ended completely in 1930; aid to two-teacher schools was reduced by $100 that year and discontinued in 1931. State Negro school agents protested again, in vain. From Maryland, state Negro school agent J. Walter Huffington pleaded, "May I urgently request that you [S. L. Smith] intercede for us with the Fund *not* to cut us down ... on the small schools just now, it simply means that in all probability we will have a number of negro schools constructed which are not suitable for the instruction of children."[40]

After 1928, small rural African American schools did not qualify as model schools for the Rosenwald program. Large schools, often in urban settings, would play that role instead. In the middle 1920s, applications for Rosenwald schools located in large towns or small cities raised eyebrows in the Chicago office, even if the project represented a consolidation of smaller schools or a county training school serving mostly rural students. State Negro school agents and building program director S. L. Smith in Nashville had used their own discretion in deciding whether such schools were rural enough to qualify for Rosenwald aid, and by 1927 they had explicitly separated the rural elementary school allotments from those for county training and high schools in the plan of aid.[41] The 1927 Dunbar High School in Fort Myers, Florida, illustrated "the kind of schoolhouse now emphasized by the Rosenwald Fund" in the state's 1930 Rosenwald School Day Program. Designed by L. N. Iredell, this two-story structure for eighteen teachers offered elementary and secondary grades and was the only high school available to African American youth in Lee County (figure 37). Its Spanish Mission styling and gleaming white stucco, with contrasting dark window frames and detailing, bore little resemblance to Robert R. Taylor's Tuskegee designs or Smith's *Community School Plans*.[42]

The demonstration schools on the Florida Agricultural and Mechanical College (FAMC) campus in Tallahassee offered direct testimony of changes in the material definition of model schools (figure 15). The first one, built in 1921–22, was a rectangular frame structure with four classrooms known as the Junior High School. After the construction of a handsome new facility in 1931–32, the former school appropriately became a teachers' cottage. The second building, named the Lucy Moten School after the prominent Washington, D.C., African American educator, was designed by a white architect, Rudolf Weaver, the head of the University of Florida's architecture department and staff architect of the state's Board of Control. Weaver used Colonial and Georgian Revival styles to provide stylistic unity for the buildings he designed at the FAMC campus.[43]

Figure 37. Dunbar High School, Fort Myers, Florida, designed by L. N. Iredell, 1927. This building is one of the larger schools in urban locations that received Rosenwald aid because it offered the only secondary education for African American youth in Lee County. It also exemplifies the Julius Rosenwald Fund's policy to approve designs other than its own *Community School Plans* and the trend toward aiding larger buildings in the late 1920s. (Photograph by author)

Faculty, teachers-in-training, and students only had to look from the older building to the new one to measure the Rosenwald Fund's higher standards for model African American schools and their supporters at the state and local levels.

At the end of the decade, the Rosenwald Fund officially recognized the building program's expanded scope by renaming it the "southern school program." Fund trustees voted to support school buildings in large towns and cities that offered at least two secondary grades and vocational training to all students, as well as to rural and small-town schools. Still clinging to Stern's vocational concept, all applications for seven-teacher and larger schools had to undergo mandatory reviews for vocational training and consolidation opportunities.[44] Town and city African American schools had long been more complex and expensive buildings than their rural counterparts, and so for the southern school program to succeed, the Rosenwald Fund had to provide larger grants to at-

Figure 38. Lincoln School, Springfield, Greene County, Missouri, 1931. Large schools such as this became the preferred type in the last years of the Rosenwald building program. Lincoln was the first Rosenwald school constructed in Missouri after its admission into the Rosenwald program in 1929. (Julius Rosenwald Fund Archives, Fisk University Franklin Library, Special Collections)

tract the significant investment of public school funds required. The early 1930s plans of aid offered matching grants from $700 for a three-teacher school up to $4,200 for a twelve-teacher school. Grants for teachers' homes began at $400 for a five-room house and went up to $800 for nine-room dwellings; vocational building aid ranged from $300 for a one-room shop to $900 for a four-room vocational building. All were eligible for permanent construction bonuses, but school buildings larger than the six-teacher type, like the Lucy Moten School, had to be of permanent construction.[45] The results could be seen most clearly in Missouri, which Rosenwald Fund trustees approved for building aid beginning in 1929. Missouri built only three Rosenwald schools and one shop, but they served twenty- eight teachers and 1,260 pupils and had a combined value of $257,959 (figure 38).[46]

The southern school program also required more staff in Nashville. In 1930, former Arkansas agent for Negro schools Fred McCuistion became associate director of the fund's Southern Office, joining Samuel Smith and veteran secretary Bessie Carney as a permanent, full-time staff member. McCuistion spent as much effort on research as school construction, analyzing the discriminatory distribution of public education funds in southern states and the teaching staffs at African American schools and publishing his findings in *Financing Schools in the South* (1930) and *The South's Negro Teaching Force* (1931).[47]

The southern school program signaled that Rosenwald Fund officers had re-defined a Rosenwald school to mean potentially any African American public school in any southern community. Simultaneously, Rosenwald Fund staff and state departments of education broadened their annual Rosenwald School Day celebrations, which began as commemorative events for Rosenwald schools and almost immediately expanded to include all African American public schools and even a few white ones. Several states had begun to hold annual events hon-oring Julius Rosenwald and the building program at community Rosenwald schools.[48] The state agents of Negro schools seem to have intended that these events would subsume the annual rally days, patrons' days, or field days that African American communities and their teachers had long celebrated to sup-port their local schools. They also may have drawn upon the work of Jeanes teachers, who had become expert school fund-raisers, and the proliferation of competitive projects for rural and domestic reform undertaken by federal and state extension service agents in the 1920s.[49]

Rosenwald School Day refocused these events from the community and its school to the Rosenwald building program and its place in the philanthropic pantheon for southern black education. Louisiana's 1927 Rosenwald Day pro-gram included printed speeches such as "Educational Progress in the Negro School during the Last Ten Years" (by a teacher) and "What the Rosenwald School Building Movement Has Meant to the Negroes of Louisiana" (by an "advanced" pupil), extemporaneous speeches by "a prominent colored citizen" and the white school superintendent or another white citizen, as well as a read-ing of Ephrim D. Tyler's poem "A Tribute to Honorable Julius Rosenwald," and the singing of the national anthem, the Negro National Anthem, and spiritu-als.[50] S. L. Smith tried to encourage other states to follow suit, and a commit-tee of Negro school agents from Texas, Louisiana, and Arkansas developed a Rosenwald Day template for all states aided by the fund. Annual grants of $100 to pay for printing programs and for prizes became available to state educa-tion departments in 1929.[51] Boilerplate copy sent out from Nashville contin-ued Louisiana's precedent with prepared addresses for speakers, such as "Some Ways in Which Mr. Rosenwald Has Helped and Is Helping to Provide Better Educational Facilities" for the principal or a teacher. Sample speeches also in-cluded explanations of the other philanthropic agencies aiding black public education: the John F. Slater Fund, the Anna T. Jeanes Fund, and the General Education Board. Pictures provided included a portrait of Rosenwald; a mon-tage of portraits of Rosenwald, Wallace Buttrick, and James Hardy Dillard; and a photograph of Rosenwald posed with Dillard. The Nashville office also supplied a scorecard that awarded up to 700 points for various features such as whether the school had a protected drinking supply, properly hung window shades, or a Parent-Teacher Association. The school scoring the highest points in a county won a prize, often a portrait of Julius Rosenwald.[52]

As with the building program in general, the Rosenwald School Day initiative seemingly was a centralized and standardized project administered by the fund's Nashville office, but in practice it was completely dependent on the interest of state agents and especially local school patrons. The event's planners at the state and local levels chose how much of the fund's program material they wanted to use, and tailored at least some of the copy to their own conditions, especially in the facts about black education. Florida, Georgia, and North Carolina state agents for Negro schools preferred to draw attention to their own black education initiatives.[53] Louisiana offered one of the more creative alternative programs, a dramatized boat ride up the Mississippi to visit Julius Rosenwald in Chicago. Participants dressed to represent their schools, for example, wearing a hat full of holes to suggest a leaking roof.[54] In Kentucky, state agent for Negro schools L. N. Taylor used his $100 for a "Rosenwald issue" of the African American teachers' association's *KNEA Journal*.[55] All seized upon the opportunity to publicize recent construction projects and to show off their Rosenwald-funded school buses, with photographs such as that of Conway County Training School students gathered in front of their bus in Menifee, Arkansas.[56] Florida's 1929 program cover featured the Boynton School, a simple frame Community School Plan 3–B. But as the precariously leaning trees around it indicate, the school had been one of the few frame buildings to survive a recent hurricane and was credited with saving the lives of those who had taken refuge inside.[57]

Rosenwald School Day offered the fund and the state agents for Negro schools and Rosenwald building agents who orchestrated the events an opportunity to promote their work in public ceremonies and newspaper coverage.[58] Obviously the printed programs were intended to reach a broader audience than just the children, teachers, and patrons in Rosenwald schools. By the early 1930s, the Rosenwald Fund and state agents for Negro schools had opened Rosenwald School Day programs to all African American public schools, and Oklahoma had become the first state to open the program to white schools. State Negro school agent E. A. Duke announced that the 1931 Rosenwald School Day bulletin contained information that "should be familiar to every person in the state, especially to Negroes," and his 1932 report to the Nashville office listed Rosenwald School Day events in twelve counties with no black residents.[59]

The Fund's Rosenwald School Day programs created rituals in which African American communities would simultaneously act out their dependence on white philanthropy and build pride in their own schools. Yet even as they included and acknowledged African American community members for their contributions to the schools, Rosenwald School Day planners glossed over the reality of a much older tradition of community self-help and local response. The fund's limited success with Rosenwald School Days suggests that local people may not have wanted to turn their familiar self-help projects into highly structured exercises in deference. Florida Negro school agent D. E. Williams acknowledged this from his own paternalistic viewpoint when he suspected that many schools "went through the whole affair in a very perfunctory manner missing the object entirely," although he did admit to getting the printed program out only one week before the event. How local people responded is difficult to say, but statistics reported by the state agents for Negro schools show that although several thousand patrons attended each year's celebrations, the number of participating schools was usually rather small—between one and two hundred in most states—except for the events held in 1932, the year of Julius Rosenwald's death.[60] Those figures were below the total number of Rosenwald schools in a given state, suggesting that some of the event's core audience—the same people who had been willing to accept the fund's dictates on school architecture—saw less value in its standardized programming. Whether it was local people or Rosenwald School Day planners who were "missing the object entirely" remains unclear.

Designs and Standards for Southern Schools

The southern school program and Rosenwald School Day events welcomed urban African American communities and all black public schools in the South into the Rosenwald program. By the later 1920s, model schools for southern African Americans had become identified with a standardized school architecture that could be applied to country, town, and city—and potentially to white as well as black schools, to northern and western as well as southern schools. Rosenwald Fund staff members began to rethink their designs accordingly.

One of the more intriguing new projects of the late 1920s was a commission awarded to Frank Lloyd Wright, the nation's leading modernist architect, for a Rosenwald school to be constructed at Hampton Institute. Wright listed this among a number of new commissions that he had undertaken in 1928: "a school-house for the Rosenwald Foundation,—you know,—the negroes in the

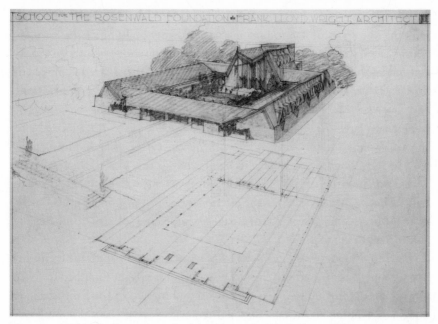

Figure 39. Frank Lloyd Wright, *School for the Rosenwald Fund*, 1928. (Reproduced from the Donald D. Walker Collection, Prints and Photographs Division, Library of Congress, with permission of the Frank Lloyd Wright Foundation. Drawings of Frank Lloyd Wright are copyright © 1957, 2005, Frank Lloyd Wright Foundation, Taliesin West, Scottsdale, Arizona)

South." He explained to architectural critic Lewis Mumford: "I have tried to make this one theirs. The Yankee things they have been getting seem to me rather hard on them: this is another modest excursion into the nature and feeling of an alien race such as was the Tokio [*sic*] hotel on a grand scale."[61] The association of Chicago's most famous architect with one of the city's most prominent philanthropies must have seemed natural. Although Wright dismissed the existing Rosenwald school plans as "Yankee things," his own work and the *Community School Plans* shared a commitment to function and simplicity that would come to fruition in Wright's later Usonian house plans.

Wright's proposal for Hampton was a complete departure from the current aesthetic of the *Community School Plans* (figure 39). He offered no explanation of how this sketch represented "another modest excursion into the nature and feeling of an alien race," but the comparison to the Tokyo hotel aptly describes his approach to interpreting another culture. Wright grafted his version of African design elements—angles and planes organized into triangles and diamonds—onto his standard interpretation of an "organic" American building as a series of flat and open spaces. For the building's basic form, he appropriated the quadrangle from the vocabulary of school architecture to accommodate banks of classrooms along its long sides. On the exterior, instead of neat clapboard, brick, or concrete, Wright called for a sheathing of "fieldstone and rough boards." He marked off sets of four classrooms along the facades by joining two larger triangles, one the window hood and the other incised into the wall beneath it, into a diamond and then using the diamond to punctuate a series of smaller and narrow triangular hoods that shaded the rest of the windows. The front offered a low flat canopy over a wide entrance, through which one would gain access to the interior corridors or the inner plaza. Rising from the back of the quadrangle was a tall asymmetrical structure, probably the auditorium or gymnasium.

Much to Wright's disgust, his proposal remained on paper. When he later gave one of his pencil sketches to Albert Kahn, Wright inscribed it "N.B. (Never built Not 'Colonial')," indicating his failure to transform the aesthetic imagination of the Rosenwald school program.[62] Nevertheless, new initiatives in school construction and vocational training did trigger a major architectural reassessment of the Rosenwald building program in the late 1920s and early 1930s. The fund culminated its efforts at standardized school design by sponsoring the Interstate School Building Service (ISBS), a school-design service that circulated building plans for general use. Simultaneously, fund officers engaged in an internal debate over architectural styling that also turned on aesthetic opinions about the "Colonial" styles Wright abhorred and their applicability to modern school design.

The Rosenwald school-building program had fostered the development and application of Progressive school architecture since Robert R. Taylor designed the first Rosenwald schools in 1912. Samuel L. Smith, who had made the Rosenwald Fund's *Community School Plans* an integral part of the developing professional standards for model school buildings, now allied the Rosenwald Fund with the state schoolhouse planning agents funded by the General Education Board at southern departments of education. Schoolhouse planning agents brought professional expertise in school-building design to the states, and many had studied with Fletcher B. Dresslar. They spent as much time on black schools as their state superintendent and their own interests allowed, creating new state building plans that communities could use as alternatives to *Community School Plans*.[63] These men, and a few women, helped to embed school architecture in the nation's educational bureaucracies. Their professional organization was the National Council on Schoolhouse Construction, founded in 1921, of which S. L. Smith was a life member and later president. The council's leadership overlapped with the membership of the Committee on Standardization of Schoolhouse Planning and Construction of the National Education Association, further allying the architects with educators.[64]

During the 1928 conference of the National Council on Schoolhouse Construction, Dresslar protégé and Oklahoma schoolhouse planning agent Haskell Pruett proposed the formation of a multistate organization, the Interstate School Building Service.[65] The other schoolhouse-planning agents took up Pruett's suggestion and selected an executive committee composed of Fletcher B. Dresslar, Samuel L. Smith, and Pruett to find sponsors. Smith and Pruett secured an agreement for the new organization to have its headquarters at their alma mater and Dresslar's home base, the George Peabody College for Teachers in Nashville. Smith unsuccessfully petitioned the General Education Board for funding but had better luck with his own employer, the Julius Rosenwald Fund. Smith's request for the Interstate School Building Service was timely, coming soon after the reorganization of the Rosenwald Fund and just as Edwin Embree began implementation of his broader agenda. It dovetailed the schoolhouse-planning profession's increasing emphasis on standardization with the Rosenwald Fund's growing interest in better school-construction standards. Thus in his solicitation letter, Smith argued that "as I see it, we [the Rosenwald Fund] would simpl[y] be assisting in greatly enlarging the service which we have been doing for almost 9 years, reaching a much larger group and tying up with the building program for Negro schools, this new group, which might otherwise feel it their principal duty to look after building white schools."[66]

The Interstate School Building Service, established with a $5,000 appropriation from the Rosenwald Fund, served as a clearinghouse for school-building plans from and to state departments of education and hosted annual conferences on building plans and construction standards. An ISBS fellowship supported a Peabody graduate student in his studies who also handled the agency's office work and served as an "associate" temporary staff member in the fund's Nashville office. The holders of these fellowships included men with positions at state departments of education, either in Negro education or schoolhouse construction, who were already familiar with the Rosenwald building program, including not only Haskell Pruett but William F. Credle of North Carolina.[67] The tie that bound together the early ISBS was Fletcher B. Dresslar, mentor to ISBS fellowship holders and schoolhouse planning agents; the Rosenwald Fund's S. L. Smith; and a new generation of Peabody education faculty supported by the Rosenwald Fund.[68]

In 1929, Fletcher Dresslar and Haskell Pruett compiled the Interstate School Building Service's first major publication, *For Better Schoolhouses*. This compendium featured the Rosenwald Fund's *Community School Plans* together with plans from state departments of education across the nation, as well as the U.S. Bureau of Education and private sources.[69] The purpose was to offer models of public school designs from which school officials could choose the one best suited to their site, building size, curriculum, and finances without either having to resort to inadequate traditional school styles or incurring expensive architectural fees. Its pages made clear that the Rosenwald Fund's *Community School Plans* and the principles that guided their design remained well entrenched in the mainstream of American school architecture. In each category where they appeared, Rosenwald plans were among the least elaborate in their styling, yet the layout of their facades and floor plans reverberated throughout the collected designs.

While the Interstate School Building Service placed the Rosenwald *Community School Plans* in a wider context of national standards for school design, the Rosenwald Fund's Southern Office also took steps to update its architectural plans. S. L. Smith brought back J. E. Crain and E. M. Tisdale to prepare a revised edition of *Community School Plans*, published in the fall of 1928.[70] The reorganization of the bulletin alone sent a message, for now *Community School Plans* began not with the smallest schools but with two ten-teacher plans and then worked its way down to one-teacher buildings. Moreover, all three-teacher and larger buildings now appeared with brick facades as a visual hint meant to encourage permanent construction.

Larger school designs maintained the basic organizational patterns of the earlier *Community School Plans* but in more solid and varied exterior appearances. Plan 10 combined the massing of space from both the rectangular and H-plans. Its long central rectangular block repeated that of plan 8, then added two-room rectangles set perpendicular to the central block, each with entrances recessed into the end walls. The building gave the visual effect of an H-plan even though the window batteries faced east and west rather than the north-south orientation associated with that floor plan. Shop plan D, a four-room dropped-gable design resembling what was now designated as school plan 45, and an L-plan three-room shop, labeled plan C, joined the 1928 collection,

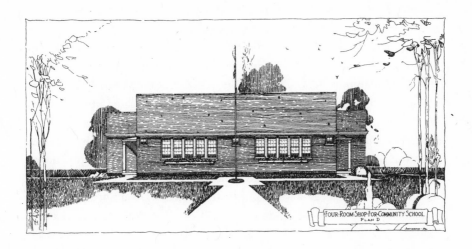

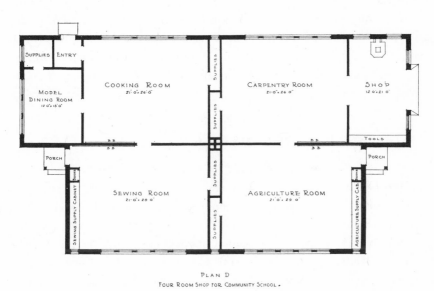

PLAN D
FOUR ROOM SHOP FOR COMMUNITY SCHOOL .

Figure 40. Shop plan D housed classrooms for girls' vocational home economics and boys' vocational trades and agriculture courses. In 1928, the Julius Rosenwald Fund began offering grants for supervisors and equipment to support the classes in facilities like this one. (*Community School Plans*, rev. ed., 1928)

along with more extensive specifications reflecting Smith and his profession's growing preoccupation with standardization (figure 40).

Crossover designs from the revised *Community School Plans* and state education departments continued to blur the distinction between segregated schools. Community School Plan 5–A now boasted arched entrances into the wings of its H-plan. Another version of this design appeared in the Tennessee Department of Education's new *Building Plans for Rural School Houses* by Memphis architects George Mahan and Everett Woods. Similarly, Arkansas plan 5–E in many respects followed Community School Plan 5–B while rearranging the central interior space to provide a fifth classroom. Both plans oriented the building east-west, and their outlines were almost identical T-plans, with the classrooms arranged in parallel rows in the main rectangular block for proper lighting and a projecting auditorium with stage at the back. The facades and interior spaces differed, however, as the Community School Plan still sought to identify vocational instruction with Rosenwald school construction. The Arkansas plan had three classrooms across the front separated by doorways, which created a tripartite front wall accentuated with dormers; the Rosenwald plan used a central gabled entrance adjoined by an office and an industrial room.[71]

Aesthetics and Instruction in Community School Plans

Yet another design review followed hard on the heels of Smith's 1928 update and provoked a rare internal battle over building standards among the program's staff. Fund officers' experiences with the urban industrial high school initiative suggested that the *Community School Plans* also required an outsider's professional opinion to keep them at the forefront of public school design. The fund turned to Walter J. McCornack for this task. Pleased with McCornack's work on urban industrial high school designs, Rosenwald Fund officials began insisting that he evaluate other special projects as well. When asked to support new buildings at the Arkansas Agricultural, Mechanical and Normal College at Pine Bluff, Embree advised: "In connection with our cooperation with certain industrial high schools for Negroes, we have found that a good deal of benefit came from having building plans gone over by a consulting architect. . . . In so important an undertaking as the new buildings at Pine Bluff I should think it might be very well worth while for an outside consultant to be brought in." In other words, do it and hire McCornack for the job.[72]

Walter McCornack reviewed the *Community School Plans* late in 1930 and became embroiled in the ensuing debate over the aesthetics of Rosenwald schools. Alfred Stern sent Julius Rosenwald a summary of McCornack's critique, mostly on functional issues, to which Rosenwald responded: "This sounds great.... Pity Mr. McC did not come along several years ago." At Stern's request, Smith organized meetings with McCornack, Nashville fund staff, and several state schoolhouse-planning directors; Stern himself joined the Rosenwald Nashville staff for a follow-up meeting early in 1931. The participants reached general consensus on several of McCornack's key points, such as the need to reduce the number of plans, to reduce the size of cloakrooms and provide several sizes of classrooms, to revise the specifications to include modern materials such as wall board instead of plaster, and to standardize elements such as blackboards and hardware. Toilet facilities occupied much of their time, as they debated whether to require indoor flush toilets and ultimately specified them for larger buildings only. Discussants agreed on two of McCornack's more interesting suggestions, given the Rosenwald program's tradition of emphasizing industrial education and community use in its buildings: to move all vocational rooms back into school buildings and to include an auditorium in all schools for six or more teachers.[73]

Rather than have McCornack himself redo the existing plans or design new ones, the fund again hired J. E. Crain for the design and drafting, and E. M. Tisdale for perspective drawings. Based on McCornack's suggestions, and "after consultation with and agreement of the staff of the Southern Office" and the Interstate School Building Service's executive committee, Crain amended the plans for eight-, ten-, and twelve-teacher schools.[74] Not surprisingly, his designs maintained the pattern of massing classroom rectangles, with schools facing north or south organized into an H-plan, while east-west schools kept their essential rectangular block exteriors, but with significant modifications based on McCornack's recommendations.

Changes included the location of a small library area behind French doors at the back of one classroom and the designation of a community room "which may be used for group meetings, improvised health clinics, home economics, etc." All designs could be expanded by the addition of more classroom rectangles at any end of the building. Furthermore, the text informed readers that they could call upon the schoolhouse construction agents at their state departments of education for help with supervising construction, at least on large buildings.

The proposed plans embodied McCornack's vision for reincorporating vocational classrooms into the main school building. Plans for eight-, ten-, and

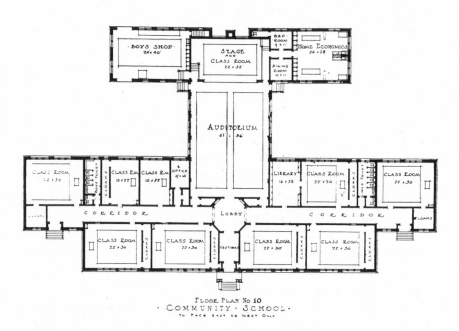

Figure 41. Community School Plan 10, to face east or west. The final revision of the *Community School Plans* in 1931 reattached the vocational classrooms to the main school building and retitled the former "industrial" rooms as "community" rooms. When originally designed, these large-scale plans included cupolas. Chicago Rosenwald Fund staff insisted that the "belfries" come off, resulting in the emphatically horizontal appearance of these schools. (*Community School Plans*, rev. ed., 1931)

twelve-teacher schools maintained the 1928 *Community School Plans* T-plan layout but added another bar to the end of the *T*'s stem, suggesting a modified I-plan. The auditorium, as usual, projected from the center of the back of the building, with vocational rooms for trades and home economics extending to the left and right of a combination stage and classroom at the rear of the stem. Plan 10 gained rooms for additional teachers by extending the stem of the *T* at the rear, and abutting single rooms to each end of the *T*'s forward bar (figure 41). Tisdale's perspective and the floor plan show these single rooms as small, one-room appendages, looking like cottages and set back along the rear half of the classroom block.

Plans 8–A and 10–A offered alternatives for schools facing north or south that turned the typical Community School H-plan into a pavilion school (figure 42). The main classroom structure was the standard H-plan with three window batteries along each side. Small dormers marked the roof of the central bar, which included an office, library, and small classroom at its front and the auditorium in its usual position across the rear of the bar. But instead of a central entrance at the front, students entered through recessed doorways set into the front facade of each wing and could proceed down corridors past the classrooms and then outside along a "cloister," or covered walkway, on either side of an open courtyard that attached a vocational building to the main structure.

Crain also amplified the hints of Colonial Revival styling in those earlier designs, triggering the internal debate about architectural styles. A description of the revised plans, drafted by S. L. Smith or W. F. Credle, explained their decorative schemes: "Realizing the importance to the community in having architectural character in these buildings, the Georgian-Colonial style prevails throughout, which is well-defined in the east west plans, but blends into the classical in the north south plans, but this has been done without much ornamentation."[75] These designs achieved the "Georgian-Colonial" style with a projecting pediment supported by columns that marked the entrance, accentuated by a centrally placed cupola rising above the roofline. Small dormers set above each battery of windows allowed ventilation of the attic space. Thus the front facade created a visual effect of three horizontal bands. First, the regular spacing of the four window batteries dominated the lower classroom wall. Second, the four dormers punctuated the angled plane of the roof and led the eye upward to the central and only feature of the third level, the cupola.

Chicago fund officers recognized the improvements but wondered about the stylistic details. "I am not so sure about the belfry," mused Alfred Stern about the cupola. "It looks sort of stuck on as an afterthought. Otherwise these sketches

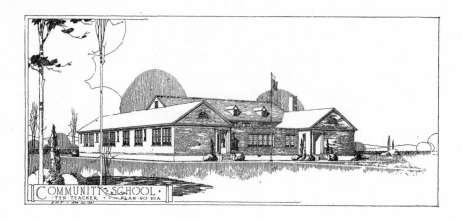

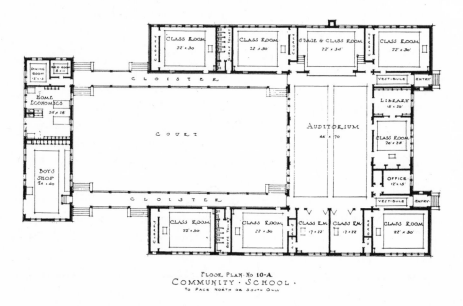

Figure 42. Community School Plan 10–A, to face north or south. Covered walkways that connected the vocational building to the main school building created a pavilion school plan. (*Community School Plans*, rev. ed., 1931)

strike me as very attractive." George Arthur tried to explain that cupolas, or lanterns, were commonplace "on a great many of the (white) school buildings in the South—Southern atmosphere, one might say." Embree offered a functionalist critique. "The simpler the more beautiful is the fundamental rule of architecture," he wrote. "The belfry looks pretentious and silly."[76] When Smith defended the cupolas as necessary for ventilating large buildings in the southern climate, and as an expression of the South's "rich architectural heritage," Embree scoffed. "'Rich architectural heritage my eye. Pretentious architectural excrescence [*sic*] is a better description." A battle of the experts ensued: Smith called in Walter McCornack and Nashville's leading architects, and Stern got a second opinion from George Carr of Nimmons, Carr, and Wright, an architectural firm that handled many Sears, Roebuck buildings. Embree and Stern held firm against the "belfries" and all such "frills," and the cupolas disappeared from the new building plans.[77]

Heavier ornamentation that conveyed specific historical styles was, despite Embree's and Stern's modernist preference for functional design, endemic in contemporary school-building design. Not everyone wanted a school like the new Webster County Training and Rosenwald City High School, featured in the journal of the Kentucky Negro Educational Association and reprinted on the reverse of Kentucky's 1931 Rosenwald Day report form. Described as "one of the typical Rosenwald Schools," the building was an exceedingly plain two-story rectangle, its facades broken only by windows and doors. The windows were neither grouped into batteries nor restricted to one side of a classroom, violating the Rosenwald building program's own standards. Alfred Stern saw the publication and complained to S. L. Smith: "If this is the picture of a typical Rosenwald School in Kentucky, I think we had better stop doing business there. I cannot see any application of architectural standards other than those applied to a box."[78]

Smith may well have sighed at the irony of Stern's comments so soon after their "belfry" debate, yet he and Chicago Rosenwald staff did agree that their larger buildings required at least some ornamentation to make them aesthetically pleasing. The 1931 *Community School Plans* might not sport cupolas, but they counteracted the monotonous effect of repeated window batteries along the facades of larger school buildings with more detail at the windows and entrances, an approach often seen in plans for large rural schools published in contemporary professional journals or by state schoolhouse-planning divisions.[79] The 1931 edition of *Community School Plans* offered the new designs for larger schools as well as the latest renditions of smaller schools, teachers' homes, and shops. A few early designs disappeared or underwent a make over: plans 2–C, 3, and 400 vanished, along with the seven-teacher plans, although the simple Colonial Revival pediment from plan 3 now appeared over the entrance to plan 30. A new teachers' home design for a nine-room home incorporated more Colonial Revival features, such as a columned front porch and gable dormers, accompanied by the more restrained Colonial Revival seven-room home and the bungalow-style five-room home from earlier collections.

More important, the "industrial room" designation shifted to "community room," reflecting another McCornack suggestion. The debate over industrial or vocational education was over. Vocational training had not disappeared from the fund's curriculum plans, as designated areas for trades and home economics education appeared in larger designs and the shop plans remained. In smaller schools, fund officers now saw the auditorium and community room as multipurpose areas that could serve vocational or social purposes. But the old-fashioned "industrial room" designation that had distinguished Rosenwald schools from their white counterparts had given way to the vocational education routinely found in American public education, while the "community room" label encouraged school administrators to see Rosenwald Fund designs as racially neutral and thus suitable for white or black students.

BEGINNINGS AND ENDINGS, 1930–32

The Rosenwald southern school program soon came up against the gathering storm of the Great Depression.[80] First the stock market crash sliced into the Rosenwald Fund's assets. Then, as the banking system collapsed and the economic crisis widened, state and local governments abandoned school-construction projects. Perennially underemployed and underpaid, many rural African American southerners did not have much more to lose, but their middle-class and professional peers, including teachers and principals, soon lost pay and then jobs. Even though African American interest in the building program never waned, resources for self-help and public funding dwindled and often disappeared.

The economic depression accelerated the developments that destroyed the Rosenwald building program. In the summer of 1930, Edwin R. Embree, Julius Rosenwald, and the fund's trustees engaged in yet another reassessment of the Rosenwald Fund's overall philanthropic purpose. In a "Special Confidential Memorandum on the Kinds of Things That Should Be Supported by Foundations," Edwin Embree called on the trustees to move beyond the safe familiarity of the school-building program: "Our own rural school program has been well conceived and effectively carried out, but we can easily drift into the position of simply helping Southern communities do what from now on they should be ready to do for themselves." Instead of becoming "a crutch rather than a stimulus," Embree suggested that the fund engage in social experimentation.[81]

Social experimentation in African American education, Embree had told the state agents for Negro schools a month earlier, "calls for leadership which is not complacent but which is dissatisfied, since all progress arises from dissatisfaction." Embree thought that leadership should also be white: "Mr. Embree said that in his opinion white leadership was more necessary at this time than Negro leadership." Embree was not opposed to black leadership. Indeed, under his administration African Americans returned to the upper levels of the Rosenwald Fund. Already the fund had commissioned studies by Horace Mann Bond as well as Charles S. Johnson and the Fisk University Department of Social Sciences; Johnson would join its board of trustees in 1934. Embree had also inaugurated what would become a far-ranging fellowship program to support emerging black professionals, scholars, writers, and artists and would lead the fund to embrace full social, economic, and political equality among peoples. However, Embree believed that, in the United States of 1930, white people bore responsibility for solving the problems created by racist white domination. Thus the "Conspectus of Present and Future Activities of the Julius Rosenwald Fund" argued that "Negro welfare . . . may be regarded as the classic program of the Fund," and that to succeed, the foundation had to contribute to the "general social situation and to the development of white leadership."[82]

Could the southern school program meet that test? Embree thought not, and that, furthermore, the Rosenwald Fund could not fulfill its potential as long as the building program consumed the bulk of its assets. The time had come, he suggested, for gradually eliminating it. In the fall of 1929, some trustees had asked when the school-building program would end, given that they had already voted to discontinue grants to one-teacher schools in 1930 and were now reducing the amount awarded to two-teacher schools. Eight months later, Embree raised that possibility again. As "it has been understood that the Fund proposed to retire gradually from its extensive program of aid to Negro schools," he suggested the foundation should also limit the moneys allocated to the building program so that it could "stimulate further developments such as consolidated schools, better teachers, sound industrial education."[83]

In May 1931, Clark Foreman and Horace Mann Bond submitted a preliminary report on their study of children's learning commissioned by the Rosenwald Fund that further spurred the staff in Chicago and trustees to change tactics. Although titled *Environmental Factors in Negro Elementary Education* when published in 1932, the study would only briefly discuss school buildings. The researchers dismissed professional school planners' complicated building standards in favor of six basic requirements: adequate upkeep, heating and ventilation, window lighting, sanitary water supply and toilets, seats and desks, and a blackboard. They focused more on teaching methods and student intelligence as the key "environmental" ingredients for learning. While Foreman and Bond's statistical analysis showed a significant correlation between poor facilities and substandard student performance, they contended that "better education would probably result from a good teacher in a bad building than from a bad teacher in a good building." Foreman and Bond claimed that, because good teachers gravitated to good facilities, the relationship between environment and teaching effectiveness was hard to measure, turning one of the Rosenwald building program's claims for the instructional value of new facilities on its head.[84]

Having heard what they could expect from Foreman and Bond, Rosenwald Fund trustees appointed a committee of W. W. Alexander, Edgar Stern, and Beardsley Ruml to make recommendations for the building program's future. Edwin Embree, meanwhile, kept offering justifications for ending the building program. In a memo to Julius Rosenwald, Embree repeated the same arguments he had been making for three years: "I think it may be that in the reasonably near future we may wish to discontinue further general building of school houses. The housing of schools is now in a good deal better position than the teaching and the learning that goes on inside them." Noting that the building program had now exceeded Rosenwald's original goal of five thousand schools, and still holding out the possibility of extending aid until every county had one Rosenwald school, Embree carefully suggested that the time had come to move on. "Of course we shall make no hasty changes in our long established programs, but I am sure you will be as eager as any of us to make sure that the Fund is doing the most it can do to promote sound elementary education for Negroes. School houses are only a means toward the general end of good schooling." Julius Rosenwald penciled his response directly on Embree's memo: "I am greatly pleased with the idea of the plan [outlined?] for the Negro schools."[85]

Rosenwald and Embree's exchange marked a devastating change in the thinking behind the Rosenwald school-building program. The fund's termination of aid for one-teacher schools as of July 1930, and then for two-teacher schools as of July 1931, eliminated 60 percent of the building program. Grants for building additions ended in 1931 as well, and the "backward county" bonus fell to 25 percent of the regular grant amount, with the qualification raised to counties with at least a 10 percent African American population.[86] The fund also cut its allotments for individual building types, even though its new designs would entail greater cost. Embree and the Rosenwald Fund staff recommended further cuts to the fund's overall program for black education, which had already been reduced in the 1931–32 budget from a proposed $350,000 to $208,000 for the first six months of the new budget year. Of that total, $142,000 had been earmarked for school-building construction. The committee charged with reorganizing the building program recommended a new construction budget of a mere $25,000 for the rest of the year and greater emphasis on "the work inside the schools."[87]

Embree had already dispatched Nathan W. Levin, the Rosenwald Fund's comptroller and assistant treasurer, to Nashville to double-check that all schools receiving grants for the past year had been completed according to the fund's requirements. In part, Embree was responding to controversies about misuse of Rosenwald grants in Mississippi and Louisiana, and to guard Smith's well-known soft heart, upon which Walter Hill and James Lambert had already been playing to get more small schools. But he also acted on his own belief that the time had come to force state governments to shoulder their financial responsibility instead of counting on outside aid, and to stop the proliferation of small schools.[88]

Economic circumstances reinforced those policy changes as the principal and interest from the fund's stock holdings withered away.[89] Officially the Rosenwald Fund glossed over the Depression's effect on its programs and used the falling costs of materials and labor as justifications for reducing its annual allotments of building projects.[90] Others could read between the lines and were dismayed. North Carolina's Nathan C. Newbold, the region's heaviest user of Rosenwald school grants, voiced the concern of many. Having received a vague account of what would happen after the fund's six-month construction appropriation for 1931–32, Newbold remonstrated with Edwin Embree: "This statement does not inform us if the Rosenwald program will be continued, or is to be discontinued at some early date. Even the mention of the latter possibility is discouraging and disheartening, extremely so when we consider the distressing period through which we are now passing." Newbold documented that black North Carolinians in nineteen counties had more than $6,000 in bank deposits earmarked for fifty-one Rosenwald schools, representing in some cases three years of community effort. He also pointed to the inevitable negative impact on white public school officials, but Embree was unmoved. While promising to distribute copies of Newbold's letter to the reorganization committee, Embree repeated his concern that the building program had become "a crutch rather than a stimulus," and restated his desire to shift the focus away from buildings and on to "what goes on inside of them."[91]

The reorganization committee offered no reassurance to advocates of the building program. Alexander, Stern, and Ruml proposed new programs in teacher education, a curriculum for "Negro life," and countywide demonstration projects correlating all social institutions for both races. As for the southern school program, the three trustees took cutbacks for granted and left the details to the fund's officers, "who would be expected to give due consideration to maintaining the momentum of the progress which the Fund has so greatly stimulated, and to maintaining the morale of southern officials engaged in this work."[92]

While fund officials debated the building program's future, Julius Rosenwald was seriously ill. Rosenwald's death on 6 January 1932 ended a great American philanthropist's personal involvement in reshaping the South. Tuskegee University's newspaper clippings files document how the black and white press memorialized Rosenwald in articles celebrating his business success and his many philanthropic causes.[93] The 1932 Rosenwald School Day celebrations became memorials to Julius Rosenwald at which the biographical sketches typically included in community programs gained special poignancy. The Arkansas printed program cover featured Commissioner of Education C. M. Hirst quoting Jesus Christ, "I am come that they might have life, and they might have it more abundantly," and proclaiming, "It was another Jew, Julius Rosenwald, who showed that this abundant life may be attained through cooperation." Alabama Rosenwald Day planners suggested that school patrons gather for "appropriate memorial exercises" at the end of the day. North Carolina issued a special memorial program featuring tributes to Julius Rosenwald from leading black and white citizens of the state. Rosenwald building agent George E. Davis's testimonial asked school day participants to "rededicate ourselves to high public service, good citizenship, true living, and unswerving loyalty to his ideals."[94]

Rosenwald had given more than 200,000 shares of Sears, Roebuck and Company stock to his foundation to achieve those ideals, but the value of the foundation's assets was small and its obligations many. As Rosenwald had specified when he reorganized the fund in 1928, the officers had a mandate to expend the Rosenwald Fund's assets within the next twenty-five years. With the fund's Sears, Roebuck shares worth only $30 each by December 1931, they were already expending the fund's principal as well as its interest income, but, as S. L. Smith reported, "the trustees of the Fund are convinced that to sell capital stock at the present ridiculously low market prices is simply to dissipate resources which otherwise will continue to serve 'the well-being of mankind.'" Embree and the rest of the Rosenwald Fund staff worked with the trustees' approval to stop the drain on their liquid assets. Loans from the General Education Board and a grant from the Carnegie Corporation, as well as bank loans backed by the fund's holdings in Sears, Roebuck stock, allowed the fund officers to meet basic obligations and to rededicate what they hoped would soon be increasing amounts of interest income and principal to their wider platform of educational improvement, field studies, and health projects.[95]

Julius Rosenwald had approved Embree's new directions for his foundation's activities, and his death so soon after reaching the 5,000–school mark made it even easier for fund officers to declare victory and move on to other fields of action. Soon after Rosenwald's death, Edwin Embree was reported to have announced that the building program was "nearing an end." By April 1932, the Julius Rosenwald Fund was giving notice that the school-building program would stop with that year's appropriation. Fund officials always portrayed this as the logical result of the school-building program's success: "With this achievement together with the momentum created in building the 5000 and more schools, the Fund's purpose in schoolhouse construction may be considered accomplished, making it unnecessary to continue a scheduled program of aid except possibly in a few backward counties and selected centers." The Depression was referred to as a state and local problem—"Because of greatly reduced school revenues but few buildings could be erected next year even with the Fund's aid"—that mooted any matching Rosenwald grants.[96]

At the end of the 1931–32 fiscal year, S. L. Smith notified state superintendents of education that no further aid for school buildings would be forthcoming from the Julius Rosenwald Fund and advised them to seek assistance from the General Education Board for the few remaining projects that had been approved but were still under construction. State agents for Negro schools like Georgia's J. Curtis Dixon negotiated with S. L. Smith and the General Education Board's Jackson Davis about these grants, which Smith described as taking care of a "moral hang-over" for the Rosenwald Fund.[97] The Slater Fund's Arthur D. Wright still felt it proper to assure Edwin Embree that he did not intend its new county training-school projects to encroach on the Rosenwald Fund's building program, but Embree simply replied, "We shall probably never reenter that field [school building]."[98]

For Embree, these dark times held the promise of a better future. Embree was focused on his fledgling initiatives for African American higher education, which included grants for selected university centers and medical training hospitals; for studies in public health, medical economics, and rural education; and for race-relations projects. The school-building program simply did not fit into the Rosenwald Fund's emerging identity as a participant in social progress—what Embree called "direct effort" by the foundation that would "promote fresh attacks on social complexes." His text for the fund's annual report in 1933 was full of hope and new ideas, featured in an essay entitled "A World of Interesting Peoples: Education as an Instrument of Racial Growth and Cultural Adjustment."[99]

For others, it was a cruel blow, a "serious" and "grievous loss."[100] Rosenwald Fund officials believed that they had taken the school-building program to its proper conclusion, and that their five thousand school buildings had created a more conducive setting for more wide-scale efforts to achieve equal opportunity for southern African Americans. Their partners at the state and local levels were not yet ready to abandon school-building campaigns, however, and would find new allies in the federal government in the 1930s.

PART II

Rosenwald Schools and Public Education in Southern States

5

Rosenwald Schools and the Professional Infrastructure for Black Public Education

The Rosenwald school-building program forged a coalition of people that stretched from one of the nation's wealthiest men to some of its humblest citizens. Julius Rosenwald and a small circle of regional administrators shaped the building program into a centralized agency that moved standardized designs for southern black schools into the mainstream of professional school architecture. Part 2 takes a closer look at the next layer of the Rosenwald school coalition, the white men who served as state agents for Negro schools and the African American men who served as Rosenwald building agents.

Rosenwald schools were only one of the responsibilities of the white state agents for Negro schools, who also coordinated aid from philanthropies like the Slater Fund, General Education Board, and Jeanes Fund and supervised instruction. The African American Rosenwald building agents also had multiple responsibilities, usually holding joint appointments at African American colleges and universities or with state teachers' associations. Both groups acted as agents of the state, and their interaction in the Rosenwald school program illuminates how these projects created opportunities for professional and social activism across the color line.[1] Standing at the center of the Rosenwald school coalition, these officials mediated between the agencies that financed and controlled African American public education on one side, and the communities that wanted new school buildings for a better future on the other. Agents also used the Rosenwald building program to further their own professional goals, shedding light on the ways that white and black educators worked to incorporate African American education into the developing southern public school bureaucracy.[2]

State agents for Negro schools and Rosenwald building agents used their professional and bureaucratic power to forge a model of interracial cooperation. These men viewed their work through their own lenses of racial, class, and regional identity, which complicated their working relationships with their superiors at state departments of education and philanthropic foundations, as well as with each other. Neither group of agents wanted to attack legal segregation directly, preferring to use their professional expertise and access to philanthropic largesse to call for equity within Jim Crow school systems. Rosenwald schools offered them the most tangible expression of the beneficent power of education for gradual social change and the opportunity to demonstrate their favored strategy of interracial cooperation.

THE STATE AGENTS FOR NEGRO SCHOOLS

Some account of the roles of white agents for Negro schools is essential to understand how the Rosenwald school-building program operated at the state level, and how state action for Rosenwald schools proved significant for African American public education in the South. As Edwin R. Embree explained, the Negro school agent was "the one upon whom the Fund relies for information and advice."[3] Rosenwald program administrators depended on the staffs of southern state departments of education, which in turn depended on financial support from the powerful General Education Board. All fifteen departments of education that participated in the Rosenwald building program employed state agents for Negro schools to oversee public educational institutions for African Americans. The Peabody Education Fund and Southern Education Board had funded the first Negro school agent, Jackson Davis of Virginia, in 1910. By 1914, the General Education Board had taken over support for such positions across the South, adding them to board-supported agents for white secondary schools and white rural elementary schools. In the 1920s, additional white state officials supported by the General Education Board, especially the assistant agents for Negro schools and state schoolhouse planning agents, co-operated on Rosenwald projects as well.[4]

White philanthropists, educational reformers, and school officials never questioned that state agents for Negro schools should be white men. Some African American educators challenged that presumption, such as William J. Edwards, founder of Alabama's Snow Hill Normal and Industrial Institute. He argued that the state superintendents of education should appoint "the most competent Negro educator" as state agent "because in order to really help the people one must go amongst them and know of their hardships, struggles, desires, sorrows, and their joys, must talk with them, eat and sleep with them and know their hearts. It would be asking too much of the Southern white man to do this." Most African American educational reformers and officials accepted white leadership as the price of philanthropic largesse, or as a ploy to reach otherwise unsympathetic whites—or at least told white officials that they did. According to Samuel L. Smith, former Tuskegee academic director John R. E. Lee had observed that African Americans' opposition to white state agents for Negro schools diminished with the realization that "a white man could do much more for them than a negro could do in securing the cooperation of the county superintendents and boards of education." Alabama black educators later took a more pragmatic view, explaining that the white state agent for Negro schools had served "as a spokesman for Negroes in meetings where Negroes were not permitted attendance."[5]

The General Education Board stressed that state superintendents of education had full authority to hire and supervise state agents for Negro schools. Nevertheless, the board actively participated in the hiring process and continuously monitored the agents. Officers of the General Education Board guided the selection process to ensure that Negro school agents would support the board's approach to black education and have the confidence of the state superintendent. For example, the board approved Texas state superintendent Annie Webb Blanton's choice of L. W. Rogers as state Negro school agent only after a series of interviews determined that the former newspaper editor, high school teacher, and county superintendent "isn't especially keen on negro education, but believes it is the next great step to be taken in Texas, and does his part of it in the day's work."[6] The General Education Board also intervened when state politics threatened its agents. Thus when a new governor tried to replace Leo M. Favrot as Louisiana's secondary school agent, the General Education Board simply terminated its support for the position and reassigned Favrot as state agent for Negro schools in Arkansas. Favrot later returned to his home state as its first Negro school agent in 1916.[7]

African American southerners tried to influence the selection of a state agent for Negro schools as well. When Alabama's white Negro school agent, James L. Sibley, left his position in 1918, a committee from Tuskegee Institute, headed by Clinton J. Calloway, offered its own slate of candidates to the state superintendent. Calloway had a major stake in the selection of a new Negro school agent, as he had worked closely with Sibley to develop the early Rosenwald building program and to coordinate Alabama's Jeanes teacher program with the Tuskegee Extension Department's projects. Tuskegee Institute also had a major stake in placing its students in the teaching profession and using the state department to advance the cause of black education. After hearing that state superintendent Spright Dowell had already chosen James S. Lambert, Calloway voiced his institution's desire to protect black women professionals. Fearing that Lambert "would be brusque or blunt in dealing with the ladies of our race," Calloway secured Dowell's assurance that he would discuss this issue with his new state agent.[8]

The first group of white men who, like Alabama's James L. Sibley, became state agents for Negro schools usually were well-educated former teachers, principals, and county superintendents with strong track records in African American education. As a recent graduate of the University of Georgia, J. L. Sibley's participation in the 1902 Conference for Education in the South gave him the contacts and the inspiration for black educational reform.[9] Tennessee's Samuel L. Smith held a bachelor's degree from Southwestern Presbyterian University and later earned a master's degree from George Peabody College for Teachers. He met Wallace Buttrick, then executive secretary of the Southern Education Board and the General Education Board, at a National Education Association meeting. At Smith's invitation, Buttrick toured Montgomery County's white and black schools, which led to Smith's selection as Tennessee's Negro school agent.[10]

Later state agents for Negro schools had similar educational and professional backgrounds, as well as prior experience with Rosenwald school construction. Ollie H. Bernard, who succeeded S. L. Smith as Tennessee's state agent for Negro schools, had four years experience in building Rosenwald schools as Robertson County superintendent. Oklahoma's E. A. Duke followed the typical route from teacher to principal to county superintendent to the position of state agent for white rural schools in 1916. The hiring of an assistant agent for white schools in 1919 allowed Duke to add black schools to his agenda. He oversaw Oklahoma's Rosenwald school program from 1920 to 1932, and held the Negro school agent position from 1927 to 1947.[11]

As the Rosenwald building program expanded across the region, state Negro school agents combined Rosenwald school-construction efforts with their Jeanes Fund and Slater Fund work. But the Rosenwald program required so much travel, correspondence, and financial oversight that it occupied much of a state Negro school agent's time. As early as 1915, J. L. Sibley reported that he spent most of his time out of the office organizing Alabama's Rosenwald projects and inspecting completed schools. As a result, one General Education Board official noted "with a smile," "The G.E.B. pays the State Agents for certain work and they don't do it because of their interest in building Rosenwald schools."[12]

Several education departments lightened the burden by hiring another white man as assistant state Negro school agent, also with support from the

General Education Board, who took over the extensive correspondence and inspection tours required by the Rosenwald program.[13] Coming from similar backgrounds and with direct experience in Rosenwald school projects, these men resembled the second generation of Negro school agents. W. A. Schiffley became South Carolina's assistant supervisor of black schools in 1925 as a graduate of the University of South Carolina and a former teacher, principal, and county superintendent who had expanded secondary education for whites and built black schools in Orangeburg.[14] In Texas, the General Education Board authorized the temporary appointment of George T. Bludworth as assistant Negro school agent to handle Rosenwald school work when state Negro school agent Rogers became assistant state superintendent in 1923. The temporary appointment became permanent in 1925 with the hiring of Douglas B. Taylor, who had studied black education in Texas for his master's thesis, as assistant Negro school agent for black secondary schools.[15]

With the tacit support of their General Education Board sponsors, state agents for Negro schools took on the administrative burden of coordinating statewide Rosenwald school-building campaigns. Especially after the 1920 reorganization, most of the building program's operational tasks fell to the state agents of Negro schools, which reinforced the Rosenwald Fund's concentration of administrative power in white hands in the 1920s. Even though building-program officials at Tuskegee and Nashville addressed the plan of aid and construction budget appropriations to state superintendents of education, Negro school agents were the ones who actually distributed the plan of aid, drafted annual construction budgets, reviewed individual applications, and prepared the necessary reports.[16] From 1920 until 1928, the state agents for Negro schools handled the "working capital" deposited with each participating state government as well. State Negro school agents also could shift money between building types and projects within their Rosenwald allotments, as long as they remained within their overall budget for the year.

State agents for Negro schools shouldered the additional burden of enforcing Rosenwald building standards. Agents for Negro schools had always contacted Rosenwald staff asking for building plans and seeking advice and rulings on specific projects. J. L. Sibley had consulted with C. J. Calloway on everything from building plans to Booker T. Washington and Julius Rosenwald's tours of rural schools. His successor, J. S. Lambert, continued the incessant letter writing with Calloway and then S. L. Smith. Like most state agents for Negro schools, Sibley and Lambert interpreted Rosenwald policies more broadly than the program's officials liked; for example, both Calloway and Smith had to press them to ensure that Rosenwald schools met the program's requirements for furnishings and sanitary toilets before receiving grant payments.[17] Surviving collections of Negro school agents' correspondence in other states include similar exchanges about building plans and construction standards as well as furnishings and financial matters.[18]

The attitudes and talents of the state agents for Negro schools varied widely, with direct consequences for the Rosenwald building program's implementation by state departments of education and for southern African American communities. In 1929, Rosenwald Fund secretary William B. Harrell described the Negro school agents as not "especially reactionary concerning race matters," although they differed in their personal attitudes. Overall, he thought, "The point of view of the group as a whole is remarkably sane. The idealogy [sic] of the missionary is almost entirely lacking."[19] But initially, some of the state agents for Negro schools had been more of the "missionary" sort. The first white men who accepted these positions recognized that they risked their social status and future job opportunities by aligning themselves with African American interests. Both S. L. Smith and N. C. Newbold hesitated before accepting their positions, weighing the prestige of association with the leading philanthropy in southern education against alternative job offers and the threat of ostracism by other whites.[20] They took up their new jobs with the same strong sense of white southern paternalism expressed by the Southern Education Board, emphasizing that they were white men of the South who understood and could mollify other white southerners and could convince southern African Americans to accept their dependence on white goodwill.[21] Once they made a commitment, many Negro school agents remained in these positions for decades, such as Maryland's J. Walter Huffington (1917–45), J. S. Lambert of Alabama (1918–42), South Carolina's Joseph B. Felton (1919–47), Virginia's W. D. Gresham (1920–36), Louisiana's A. C. Lewis (1923–40), and L. N. Taylor of Kentucky (1924–43).

Agents like these invested time and effort in building Rosenwald schools both to exercise their authority as white professionals and to entrench black education in southern public school bureaucracies. The Rosenwald building program and the General Education Board shared the common goal of building a white consensus for black education as an integral feature of southern state education departments. Over time their achievement of this goal could turn state agents for Negro schools from evangelists into bureaucrats and reveal their lingering racist presumptions. Thus African American teachers acerbically recalled the longtime Maryland Negro school agent as "the pleasant

Mr. Huffington," a "small very abrupt, very rude" man who offered them little encouragement.[22]

Other Negro school agents' success as Rosenwald campaign administrators helped to launch them on remarkable individual careers. Leo M. Favrot in 1923 left his Louisiana Negro school agent position to become a field agent of the General Education Board. S. L. Smith, of course, became director of the Rosenwald Fund's Nashville office thanks to his experience as Tennessee's Negro school agent and his training in school architecture. Arkansas Negro school agent Fred McCuistion also joined the staff of the Rosenwald Fund before moving to the Southern Association of Colleges and Schools. Arthur D. Wright, Virginia's Negro school agent from 1915 to 1920, went on to become president of the Jeanes Fund and Slater Fund in 1931, and then president of the board of the Southern Education Foundation.[23] John Curtis Dixon of Georgia attracted the General Education Board's attention while a county superintendent with his campaign for a new Rosenwald school, shop, and dormitory. After a board fellowship took him to Teachers College, Columbia University, he returned to Georgia public schools and became state Negro school agent in 1930, director of rural education for the Rosenwald Fund in 1937, and executive director of the Southern Education Foundation in 1947.[24]

THE ROSENWALD BUILDING AGENTS

Nine states—Alabama, Arkansas, Georgia, Kentucky, Louisiana, Mississippi, North Carolina, Tennessee, and Virginia—also hired African American men as Rosenwald building agents.[25] Rosenwald building agents were some of the first African American men to hold professional positions in post-Reconstruction southern state departments of education, just as state Jeanes supervisors were for black women. Like the state agents for Negro schools, the African American Rosenwald building agents drew upon the public power of the state and the financial influence of the Rosenwald program to bolster their professional authority and embed black education in state public school systems. As they campaigned for Rosenwald schools, they established new leadership roles for African American men as educational agents of the state and tied their individual labors to the advancement of black higher education as well. Within the Rosenwald building-program coalition, these men provided an important continuity of African American leadership linking the local and state levels that counterbalanced the loss of black leadership at the program's top levels in Nashville and Chicago.

Rosenwald agents initially worked for Tuskegee Institute as community organizers who coordinated local fund-raising and construction activities. They took Tuskegee's message of uplift through self-help into rural communities, where they expected that school patrons would defer to their cultural authority as educators. From the start, Booker T. Washington told Julius Rosenwald that he wanted travel expenses for "people from here [Tuskegee Institute] or somewhere" who would "get people stirred up and . . . keep them stirred up until the school-houses have been built."[26] Beyond a flair for inspiring people to action, these community organizers had the educational and professional backgrounds that rural African American southerners already valued and a paternalistic sense of their own mission.

Calloway himself initiated the building agent role in 1913, orchestrating local campaigns for Jeanes- and Rosenwald-aided schools along with Tuskegee colleague Rev. William M. Rakestraw.[27] Rakestraw worked for the Tuskegee extension department as organizer of the institution's annual Farmers' Conference and local farmers' conferences. His experience in community organization prepared him well for school-construction campaigns. Rakestraw's status and oratorical skills as a minister proved especially helpful; local reports described his speeches as sermons that inspired community action on churches, schools, and homes. At the end of the decade, Rakestraw was campaigning for Rosenwald schools in Tennessee and Mississippi as well as Alabama.[28]

The intense interest generated by the 1914 press release about Julius Rosenwald's purported dollar-for-dollar grant offer gave Calloway more ammunition for his repeated requests that Booker T. Washington hire "lecturers in the field." He envisioned the lecturer as a professional educator skilled in the strategies of interracial cooperation and grassroots organizing, a combination already familiar to Jeanes industrial supervising teachers. "In order to make the schoolhouse building which Mr. Rosenwald is encouraging a success," Calloway told Washington, "it will be necessary to have . . . the kind of help which understands how to interest the colored people and the white people in each county and each community in the building of schoolhouses" and "who will understand how to get the people in each community to raise money for schoolhouse building."[29] Calloway experimented with his "lecturer" concept after Julius Rosenwald agreed to provide salary support in the fall of 1914. Cornelius B. Hosmer, one of Tuskegee's fund-raising agents, joined the extension department as a field agent. Within a year, Calloway had also put Tuskegee graduate Vernon W. Barnett into the field and then dropped Hosmer. These first field agents assisted both Calloway and Rakestraw in their office work and coordinated school-improvement and school-construction campaigns with local communities, the Tuskegee extension department, and J. L. Sibley at the Alabama education department.[30]

Calloway also experimented with another kind of agent, an individual who would work in a specific community selected for Rosenwald schools. These community-based agents fanned local enthusiasm, contracted for materials and labor, and supervised the building process, for which Calloway paid them $25 of the $50 promotional fee charged to Julius Rosenwald for each school. Calloway employed local agents in consultation with Alabama Negro school agent James L. Sibley, who provided references for them and directed their activities.[31] Most were men, like N. E. Henry, who built schools in Conecuh County, and R. H. Lee in Perry County. Some of the men were Jeanes teachers, and at least one female Jeanes teacher, Russell County's Mrs. J. I. Doggett, spent a summer building Rosenwald schools.[32]

Promotional expenses soon became a subject of debate and threatened the building agent concept when Rosenwald's secretary, William C. Graves, questioned the justification for the $50 dollars appropriated for each school. Washington tried to placate Graves with promises to reduce promotional expenses. But Tuskegee administrators remained convinced that a black professional had to take the initiative for rural African Americans, organize and supervise their building project for them, and serve as mediator between them and local white officials.[33] Washington and Calloway pressed Rosenwald to support a new type of staff position devoted to school construction, buttressing their request with support from Alabama Negro school agent James L. Sibley. As they described it, "the duties of the additional man would be confined, very largely, to keeping in touch with the County Superintendents, County [Jeanes] Supervisors, and local teachers, as far as practicable; in seeing that everything is done properly and economically," a combination of interracial cooperation and cost-efficiency they hoped Julius Rosenwald would find appealing.[34]

This proposal became the template for the Rosenwald building agent. Even before Rosenwald approved funding for the new position, Booker T. Washington had awarded it to his son and namesake. Calloway received a detailed set of instructions for training Booker T. Washington Jr. for the job the day before he sent his salary request to Julius Rosenwald. Vernon Barnett and the community building agents continued their work in Alabama for the next two years, and one of Booker T. Washington Jr.'s responsibilities was to inspect their completed school buildings and report back to Calloway and Sibley.[35]

During the 1917 revision of the Rosenwald building program, officials reorganized Tuskegee's multiple building agent positions into a regional system. Julius Rosenwald's increased financial support allowed Clinton Calloway to distribute matching grants for the salaries of Rosenwald building agents in up to nine southern state departments of education. Not all the white state agents for Negro schools were interested: South Carolina Negro school agent J. Herbert Brannon asserted that the money would be better spent on more buildings, while Maryland's J. Walter Huffington came up with a list of candidates but never hired anyone for the position.[36] State officials who did hire building agents quickly came to rely on them for local Rosenwald school campaigns. After Booker T. Washington Jr. left Tuskegee Institute in 1918, leaving only William Rakestraw to help sporadically with Rosenwald projects, Alabama Negro school agent J. S. Lambert lamented, "WE MUST have a man." At a time when the entire Tuskegee Rosenwald building program was suffering from the postwar economy and complaints about shoddy construction, Lambert saw the implications for his own work. "I realize now that the work is suffering for lack of a good Rosenwald agent to follow up on the work subject to my direction," he told Calloway. In 1919, former field agent Vernon W. Barnett became Tuskegee's assistant director of extension and took over responsibility for Alabama's Rosenwald school campaigns.[37]

State agents for Negro schools like Lambert and state school superintendents selected the Rosenwald building agent, but Tuskegee and Rosenwald officials, as well as leading African Americans, sought to influence the hiring process. Calloway recruited and recommended candidates himself. For Mississippi, Calloway suggested Reuben Scott on the basis of a recommendation from Jackson attorney Perry W. Howard. Howard's warning to Calloway that he suspected that white authorities would overlook Scott and instead "pick up some worthless 'good nigger'" is revealing. The two men realized that cooperation with philanthropic funds and white authorities gave them cover for African American advancement, but it also could mean submission to white patronage. Indeed, Negro school agent Bura Hilbun did hire someone else, and despite its later problems with Hilbun, the Mississippi Department of Education maintained a Rosenwald building agent on staff until 1932.[38]

Early Rosenwald building agents included highly educated and experienced educators who had been teachers and principals of prominent black schools. Some held offices in black state teachers' associations, such as Alcorn University alumnus Richard S. Grossley, who held the presidency of the Mississippi Teachers Association simultaneously with his appointment as Rosenwald building agent from 1918 to 1922, and Vincent H. Harris, executive director of the Georgia Teachers and Educators Association and Rosenwald building agent from 1930 to 1932.[39] During the building program's years at Tuskegee, African American teachers' associations and colleges often shared the cost of the agent's salary and expenses with Julius Rosenwald. Thus many Rosenwald agents held faculty positions at black colleges and worked from those campuses, such as Arkansas' Percy L. Dorman, whose office was at the Pine Bluff Agricultural, Mechanical, and Normal School. Louisiana's O. W. Gray was a faculty member at Coleman College in Gibsland, paid in part by Southern University and A&M College, whose president was a Coleman alumnus.[40] Kentucky's Francis M. Wood took the position with him as he moved up the professional ladder. Wood had been principal of elementary and secondary schools and had briefly served as president of his alma mater, the Kentucky Normal and Industrial Institute, from 1923 to 1925, simultaneously working as a Rosenwald agent from 1918 to 1924.[41]

In the 1920s, most states employing Rosenwald building agents assumed the salary match, and some hired a second round of building agents, who took up their positions in the midst of the building program's reorganization and the reassignment of its top leadership to white men. With Clinton J. Calloway sidelined in 1920 and out of the Rosenwald school program in 1923, Rosenwald building agents became the ranking African Americans in the construction program. They labored under a double layer of white supervision, one by state education department officials and the other by Rosenwald Fund administrators in Nashville. Like their predecessors, these men held college degrees and positions in state teachers' associations and had professional experience in teaching and administration at the secondary and collegiate levels. John S. Jones, Louisiana's second Rosenwald building agent, had excelled in the classics at Leland College in New Orleans and also had studied at Selma University, Knoxville College, Hampton Institute, and Tuskegee. He was principal of the Boston High School in Lake Charles before joining Southern University and A&M College in 1914, where he served as director of teacher training and dean. Jones also was editing-secretary of the Louisiana Colored Teachers Association.[42] In Arkansas, Rufus C. Childress, who had been in the first graduating class of Philander Smith College in 1888 and taught there for a dozen years, became Rosenwald building agent in 1921. He was a founder of the Arkansas Teachers Association and its president from 1920 to 1923. Marquis H. Griffin succeeded V. W. Barnett as Alabama's Rosenwald building agent in 1921; the Alabama State Teachers Association elected Griffin president for the 1925–27 term and later noted that "his gospel was the establishing of the Rosenwald schools and long school terms."

Mississippi's W. W. Blackburn followed R. S. Grossley's precedent, serving as the state teachers' association president from 1926 to 1928 and as building agent from 1926 to 1932.[43]

Rosenwald building agents, like the Negro school agents, used their affiliation with the building program for individual professional advancement, but they also found it a helpful tool for African American higher education. Building agents based at African American colleges provided their institutions with immediate access to the state department of education and Rosenwald's philanthropy, as M. H. Griffin did for Alabama State Teachers College, F. M. Wood did for Kentucky Normal and Industrial Institute, Robert E. Clay for Tennessee Agricultural and Industrial College, and J. S. Jones for Southern University. Mississippi's R. S. Grossley later became president of Delaware State College; the tenure of his successor, B. Baldwin Dansby, as building agent from 1923 to 1926 garnered him a General Education Board fellowship to the University of Chicago, after which he became president of Jackson State College in 1927.[44] Dansby later recalled that "there was a close connection between his duties [as a Rosenwald building agent] and the later development" of Jackson State College during his presidency:

> In the first place, it afforded him first hand information as to the needs and deficiencies of the various regions of Mississippi. This became the means of helping him and his associates to formulate the kinds of program best suited for the teachers who would finally graduate from the College and serve those same communities. It allowed the Administration to construct a curriculum that was deductive in nature and drawn from the experiences developed in three vigorous years of field work. Not only did this connection give him vital information, but it also allied the Institution to the Rosenwald Fund.[45]

SUPERVISING THE AGENTS

With so much at stake—the financial commitment and prestige of philanthropic agencies and state departments of education, public and private support for African American institutions of higher education, and public perceptions of Progressive educational reforms—both General Education Board and Rosenwald building-program officials policed the ranks of their agents to ensure that they all followed the same agenda. The agents' monthly reports and annual conferences allowed their supervisors at state education departments and philanthropic agencies to judge agents' effectiveness. Typical personnel problems arose when agents failed to meet their superiors' expectations, raising questions about the chain of command among state and philanthropic agencies, and becoming especially difficult when the problems crossed racial lines.

Those states that employed Rosenwald building agents created a novel set of experiences as white and black education professionals figured out how to work as a team. They engaged in rituals of respect and deference grounded in their own understandings of their respective professional, class, and race positions. Overall, Rosenwald building agents enjoyed the support of the state agents for Negro schools, but white state agents clearly perceived themselves as supervisors of black building agents who, as J. S. Lambert had put it, would "follow up on the work subject to my direction." Their working relationships hinged on the Rosenwald building agent's ability to meet white expectations of both professional competence and black deference. African Americans sometimes described Rosenwald building agents as having jurisdiction over the Rosenwald building program in their state. But only one white official seems to have done so, Kentucky's Frank C. Button, who referred to Rosenwald building agent F. M. Wood as "State director of this fund."[46] In all-white professional settings, state Negro school agents gave short shrift to their black colleagues. Notes of the Negro school agents' annual meetings in 1920 and 1923 indicate that they spent but minutes considering their black counterparts, although it was to offer their "unanimous consent" to the value of supporting building agents' salaries.[47] Rosenwald building agents also gathered periodically, but, with the Negro school agents and some state superintendents in attendance as well, the building agents left no recorded commentaries on the contributions made by the white state agents for Negro schools.[48]

A successful Rosenwald building agent possessed consummate skill in balancing personal and professional pride against the demands of interracial cooperation, as those who lacked that ability quickly learned. In Louisiana and Alabama, the first African American Rosenwald building agents had to negotiate new working relationships with the white Negro school agents and adapt to the Rosenwald building program's changing demands. Clinton Calloway had paved the way for Louisiana's building agent during a 1917 tour with state Negro school agent Leo M. Favrot, who "was surprised at the value of having a colored agent or representative to go among the colored people and arouse interest in this particular line of work." When Favrot asked for another Tuskegee representative to help him, Calloway put him in touch with Southern University president J. S. Clark and suggested that they cooperate on hiring a building agent.

O. W. Gray began work in November and quickly developed a problematic relationship with Favrot.[49]

Gray's monthly reports detailed the routine of any Rosenwald building agent: convening meetings to kick off local building campaigns; recording donations and pledges of money, lumber, and labor; and checking back on construction progress and workmanship.[50] When not on the road, Gray conducted his office work in Gibsland, where he also preached and led religious programs at the Palestine Baptist Church.[51] Nevertheless, after his first month on the job, Gray met infrequently with Leo Favrot and rarely spent time at Southern University, whose administrators may have felt that their sponsorship of the position offered little in return. Gray and Favrot clashed on their interpretations of Rosenwald aid to consolidated schools and on state support for Gray's work. Gray repeatedly called on C. J. Calloway to pressure Favrot into securing state payment for a camera to document building projects, and for travel expenses to the Tuskegee agents' meeting, and to match Rosenwald's support for Gray's salary. As a black southerner, Gray believed he knew the reason for Favrot's reluctance all too well: "I live in La. so this will explain its self," he confided to Calloway. Certainly Favrot's racial paternalism was the major factor, but Gray also did not meet the professional expectations either of Favrot or the black leadership at Southern University.[52]

Indeed, when Favrot pushed Gray out early in 1919, Southern University president J. S. Clark had his own replacement candidate in mind, A. E. Perkins from McDonogh School No. 6 in New Orleans. Behind the scenes, Perkins contacted Clinton Calloway, and his comments suggest that Favrot was willing to allow Clark the final say on the hire, perhaps to make up for Southern's failed investment in Gray and perhaps to ensure the selection of a man whom both Clark and Favrot could respect as a professional. "When I last saw Mr. Clarke [*sic*] he was pressing upon me for my acceptance of the Rosenwald place here which is now vacant it seems. Mr. Favrot also seemed to desire me to take the place," Perkins related. "Though I think he will finally let it go under the auspices of Southern if he fails to get such a man as he wants and perhaps or very probably will let it run thus even if he should be able to find such a man."[53]

Although Perkins declined the offer, Southern University's president did make the appointment. John S. Jones, Southern's teacher-training director, added Rosenwald building agent work in March 1919. Gray still had his supporters: B. W. Gray of Gibsland, perhaps a relative, complained to Tuskegee principal Robert Russa Moton that, "We were indeed sarry when Mr. Gray gave up the work and most especially as he thought that he was not treated just right in the matter." But Tuskegee officials hesitated to object, especially at a time when Calloway needed supporters like Favrot, one of his few white allies, for the institute's management of the building program. Calloway advised Tuskegee Institute secretary Albion Holsey to avoid the issue, observing that "getting along with colored people and getting along with white people are two essential requisites for a Rosenwald Schoolhouse Agent. Not getting along with white people, as I understand it, was one of Mr. Gray's weaknesses." As for Favrot, he was "such a fine man that we do not question his sincerity."[54]

Alabama's Vernon W. Barnett followed Gray out of the Rosenwald building program a year later, a victim of the revamped Rosenwald program's new construction standards. Barnett wrote his white supervisor, Negro school agent J. S. Lambert, a frank letter asking if Lambert was, as Barnett had been told, looking to replace him. He defended his record and "boosting ability," offering to study "if you feel that I do not know enough about building plans." Lambert claimed that Barnett had "been misinformed to a certain extent," although he acknowledged that "the policy regarding your work has been changed." Barnett remained on the job through the summer but left Alabama altogether that fall.[55]

In both states, the African American men who next became Rosenwald building agents proved far more successful in meeting the expectations of both whites and blacks and remained in their positions for the rest of the Rosenwald building program. John S. Jones and Marquis Griffin were models of the successful black Rosenwald building agent who adeptly balanced acquiescence to the racial hierarchy in their dealings with white officials and their own assertions of leadership in African American education. They met their white and black supervisors on a common ground of professionalism that bridged the worlds of black and white educators. John S. Jones's monthly reports document how a Rosenwald building agent gained and maintained support from his black and white superiors. Jones's position at Southern University guaranteed his close ties to the programs at its Scotlandville campus. Jones also met several days each month with Leo M. Favrot, and together they developed a clear understanding of their goals for Rosenwald schools. His careful reporting of each building and its grounds, equipment, and sanitary measures more closely matched the rising expectations of Rosenwald program officials.[56] In Alabama, Marquis H. Griffin, a former coal miner, schoolteacher, and principal of the Corona Training School in Walker County, began a similarly successful career as Alabama's new Rosenwald building agent in 1921. Like Jones, he excelled at enforcing the higher construction standards of the revamped building program.[57] Both of the new Rosenwald building agents also succeeded by highlighting interracial co-operation by whites. Their reports emphasized the roles played by supportive white county superintendents, planters, and businessmen in Rosenwald school campaigns and won the admiration of white officials at state departments of education and the Julius Rosenwald Fund for eliciting white sympathy to black needs.

As long as the white state agents for Negro schools kept Rosenwald construction projects running smoothly, Rosenwald building-program officials had no need to challenge their handling of personnel issues or financial management or to criticize them to the General Education Board. If a state agent for Negro schools went astray in his handling of Rosenwald projects, however, all parties concerned trod carefully across the blurred lines of authority between state and philanthropic foundation officials. State Negro school agents continued to run afoul of state politics and politicians, such as when Georgia's state agent for Negro schools, Walter B. Hill Jr., lost his job in 1924. State superintendent Nathaniel H. Ballard alleged that Hill was unqualified for his position and had failed to improve the state's black schools, pointing to the reversion of federal Morrill Act and Rosenwald funds appropriated for Georgia but not spent. Hill and his supporters alleged that his dismissal was in retaliation for his whistle-blowing on state misuse of federal funds at the Georgia State Industrial College. As Hill was the son of two well-known educational reformers—former University of Georgia chancellor Walter Barnard Hill and state school-improvement organizer Sallie Barker Hill—his case drew immediate media attention that both he and Ballard sought to control. Hill defended his record of Rosenwald school construction and argued that the governor could not dismiss him as his salary came entirely from the General Education Board and he had been hired by the state board of education. The state attorney general agreed, and the state board of education voted to keep Hill in his position. But Hill did not return until a new state superintendent took office at the start of the next scholastic year.[58]

The Rosenwald building program was not so fortunate in Mississippi. John R. Ellis, the state's first Negro school agent, resigned after he was unexpectedly sentenced to a four-year prison term for technical violations of state law in building schools while a county superintendent.[59] His replacement, Bura Hilbun, was nothing but trouble for the Rosenwald building program. After his late 1919 inspection tour of Mississippi Rosenwald schools, Clinton J. Calloway complained to R. R. Moton about both Hilbun and Rosenwald building agent R. S. Grossley. At a time when both he and Moton knew that Julius Rosenwald was dissatisfied with their efforts, Calloway must have been chagrined when "every house which I had the pleasure of seeing that had been reported to me by Mr. Hilbun as being completed and furnished, failed to come up to the requirements." In several cases, Hilbun had already transferred Rosenwald grants to schools where insufficient local funds had been raised, and the buildings were neither furnished nor painted.[60] Calloway may have been attempting to create a paper record of his own attention to the building program's standards, but in retrospect his criticism would seem prescient.

The "ghost school" debacle began almost a decade later, soon after Hilbun resigned his position. As a personal friend of demagogic governor Theodore Bilbo, Hilbun won a new position as agricultural service commissioner.[61] Soon after his successor, Perry H. Easom, took office, anti-Bilbo politicians launched investigations of several Bilbo cronies that included Hilbun's alleged embezzlement of $1,600 of $3,200 sent by the Nashville Rosenwald office for a school in Tunica County. Ultimately investigators uncovered seven "ghost schools," nonexistent buildings for which the Rosenwald Fund had sent grants, as well as the embezzlement of larger sums of General Education Board funds. Forwarding a clipping titled "Bura Hilbun Now Faces Charge of Diverting Funds" to the Chicago Rosenwald Fund office, S. L. Smith confided that Hilbun had caused "much inconvenience and concern" with his financial carelessness while Negro school agent.[62] Moreover, Smith repeated rumors that Bilbo planned to run for state superintendent and Hilbun for governor and asked if he should issue a statement of support for the incumbent superintendent, which drew an immediate command from Chicago that Smith stay clear of Mississippi politics.[63]

Hilbun was acquitted of grand larceny in his first trial late in 1930, despite testimony from Samuel Smith and Yazoo County school officials showing that Hilbun had received a $700 Rosenwald grant for a two-teacher school that had never been constructed. Hilbun faced eight other indictments and survived them as well. A year later, Hilbun's trial for embezzlement of $50,000, most of it from the General Education Board and Slater Fund, ended in a mistrial. A third trial became problematic when a new audit of state funds revealed that Hilbun had deposited some of the disputed money into state accounts from which county superintendents could withdraw funds. As one reporter dryly commented, "Mississippi politics have been effective in the case." However, Hilbun was finally convicted on one count of embezzlement and sentenced to a five-year prison term.[64]

Although Hilbun allegedly embezzled much more money from the General Education Board than from the Julius Rosenwald Fund, newspaper stories emphasized the Rosenwald school allegations. The undesirable publicity irked building-program administrators, especially at the fund's Chicago headquarters, because of their dependence on state agents for Negro schools. Consequently, Rosenwald Fund officials bristled at the revelation of another set of problematic schools authorized by Louisiana Negro school agent Arthur C. Lewis.[65] Lewis had taken over as state agent for Negro schools from Leo Favrot in 1923 after several years as assistant Negro school agent. In 1931, Lewis admitted approving a Rosenwald grant to refurbish a six-room white school in Armant into an African American school. After a number of white families moved into the school's vicinity and petitioned for its retention as a white school, Lewis feared it would fall prey to arsonists if turned into a Rosenwald school. He now wanted to build an entirely new facility instead and asked Samuel L. Smith if he should return the original appropriation.[66]

Lewis's request came as a shock because the Rosenwald Fund had forbidden grants to remodeled schools since 1920. As Edwin Embree observed of this case, renovating former white school buildings in effect allowed local officials to sell their old facilities to the Rosenwald Fund to raise money for new white schools. A review of all Louisiana applications identified several other irregular projects, including two others that had been funded as new construction when they were renovations of school buildings previously used for white children. Smith was furious, not only because of Lewis's ineptitude but because the Rosenwald Fund still smarted from Hilbun's trials in Mississippi. He called in Leo Favrot to handle the matter, both as the former Louisiana Negro school agent who had supervised Lewis's early career and in his new capacity as an official of the General Education Board that paid Lewis's salary.[67] Favrot reassured Smith that "it has been understood from the beginning that the state agents financed by the General Education Board should direct the program of the Julius Rosenwald Fund. . . . I am sure you can depend upon us [at the General Education Board] to cooperate with you in every respect to correct any defect in the work in Louisiana or in any other state in which difficulties of this kind may arise." Favrot also brought in Louisiana state superintendent Thomas H. Harris, who ordered Lewis to return all Rosenwald money in question.[68] Rosenwald Fund officers in Chicago were angry too. Embree admitted, "Our faith in the state agents has been shaken," a particularly chilling comment at a time when fund officials were scaling back the school-building program and testing alternative strategies for the fund's social agenda.[69]

Furthermore, as Texan George T. Bludworth discovered, the major philanthropies in black education would close ranks against state agents who questioned their policies. Bludworth certainly was blunt, as evidenced by his descriptions of Texas counties eligible for the Rosenwald Fund's "backward county" construction bonus: "almost hopeless," "scarcely any chance at all," "very backward," "those Germans and people of another Faith than of Protestantism will not cooperate." He voiced unspecified grievances with Edwin Embree and the Rosenwald Fund at the 1931 meeting of Negro school agents, perhaps about the fund's reduced allocations for all types of building projects and the elimination of grants for small schools, or Embree's plans for a broader social agenda. Afterwards Leo Favrot hastened to assure Embree that the General Education Board barely tolerated Bludworth and that "the Julius Rosenwald Fund has been too much of a benefactor to the cause of the Negro education for its officers to be subjected, at an open meeting, to such expressions of dissatisfaction as came from the representative from Texas." A gracious reply from Embree ensured that a single agent's tactlessness would not threaten the relationship between two powerful philanthropic allies.[70]

CONSTRUCTING A STATE ROSENWALD PROGRAM

Embree could be magnanimous because the state agents for Negro schools, the assistant Negro school agents, and Rosenwald building agents had built a generally positive record of cooperation that boosted professional and educational opportunities across the South. North Carolina offers perhaps the best example of how white and black state officials used General Education Board and Rosenwald programs to create a professional infrastructure for black public education. In the process, however, the state officials responsible for North Carolina's black public schools struggled to resolve the racial questions raised any time that white and African Americans came together in a common effort in the Jim Crow South. They used the Rosenwald building program to develop strategies for working across the color line—strategies that set limits on African American independence yet set new precedents for cooperative activism.[71]

North Carolina agents created the region's most dynamic state program of Rosenwald school construction. Nathan C. Newbold assembled the strongest staff devoted to black education in the region. A graduate of Trinity College, Newbold left the superintendency of Washington County schools to become state Negro school agent in 1913 after being recruited by both Wallace Buttrick and Jackson Davis.[72] He skillfully used the Jeanes and Slater funds and the General Education Board's resources to enlarge his staff, which in time included two white assistant Negro school agents and four African Americans as a state Jeanes agent, a supervisor of Negro secondary schools, a Rosenwald building agent, and a public health nurse. In 1919, he had hired one of the first assistant Negro school agents, former Pamlico County superintendent T. B. Attmore, to handle the fieldwork for Rosenwald projects. Two years later, when Newbold reorganized his staff into a Division of Negro Education, William F. Credle replaced Attmore as assistant state agent for Negro schools and took over responsibility for the Rosenwald construction program in addition to duties as assistant director for schoolhouse planning. A graduate of the University of North Carolina, former Hyde County superintendent, and World War I veteran, Credle took a leave of absence from 1930 to 1932 to complete a master's degree at George Peabody College for Teachers and worked in the Rosenwald Fund's Nashville office, then returned to North Carolina as director of schoolhouse planning.[73]

North Carolina's Rosenwald building agents likewise boasted impressive backgrounds and experience in education. Charles H. Moore, who had been born into slavery, was educated at Howard University's preparatory department and at Amherst College, from which he graduated in 1878. Moore left his position as vice president and head of the academic department at North Carolina Agricultural and Mechanical College in 1907 to become an organizer for the National Negro Business League. In 1915, the North Carolina Teachers Association, the state organization for African American teachers, appointed Moore as director of its rural school extension department, to which Moore added Rosenwald building agent duties in the spring of 1918. His successor, Dr. George E. Davis, earned his undergraduate degree at Biddle Institute in Charlotte, pursued graduate studies at Howard University, then returned to Biddle University for his doctorate and became its first African American faculty member. While at Biddle, Davis also served as dean of faculty and as an officer of the state teachers' association. He retired in 1920 and that fall began his new job as Rosenwald agent, remaining in that position until 1932.[74]

Newbold, Credle, Moore, and Davis were affluent, highly educated, and well-connected in their separate worlds. Their common experience of social and economic privilege, combined with their Progressive commitment to educational reform, made them all paternalists—men who believed that they could and should lead others to a better future. They were also paternalistic in their dealings with each other, operating with authority in parallel white and black settings but positioning themselves as benevolent white supervisors and deferential black employees in interracial contexts. Typical of other state education departments, North Carolina's Rosenwald program administrators operated at some physical distance from each other. The white agents worked out of the department's Raleigh office, and the African American agents were located separately, Moore in Greensboro and Davis at Biddle University in Charlotte. They all traveled a great deal across a large state; hence they corresponded with each other extensively as well as making out their required monthly reports, creating a rich record of the ways in which the Rosenwald program allowed black and white educators to negotiate the boundaries of paternalism, professionalism, and social activism.

The white state agent for Negro schools N. C. Newbold and African American Rosenwald building agent C. H. Moore initially seemed to have an affable working relationship. Yet their interactions became more openly hierarchical and critical in contexts where Newbold's role as Moore's supervisor intersected with an underlying conflict between Newbold's increasing professionalism as a white educator and Moore's persistent activism on racial issues. Other white southerners' expectations about the agents' authority and black deference further complicated the situation, exacerbating the deterioration of their relationship.

Moore, like other early Rosenwald building agents, worked for two agencies simultaneously: the state department of education and the black teachers' state association. Thus he reported both to Newbold and to Dr. Aaron M. Moore, the secretary-treasurer of the North Carolina Teachers Association. Aaron Moore and his business colleague John Merrick were legendary figures in Durham's and North Carolina's African American business community, the founders of one of the nation's most successful black-owned businesses, the North Carolina Mutual and Provident Association. They hired schoolteachers to sell insurance policies for this business, but Dr. Moore took a direct interest in public education for African Americans. Charles Moore would have known Aaron Moore and John Merrick from his previous work with the National Negro Business League, and through the league both he and Aaron Moore knew Booker T. Washington as well.[75]

Charles Moore divided his educational work between interracial and all-black activities. He met regularly—and separately—with his white and black sponsors, N. C. Newbold and A. M. Moore. His efforts among whites included meetings with county superintendents and addresses to county boards of education, with whom he discussed black school buildings and opportunities for Rosenwald aid. His community campaigns among African Americans revolved around community meetings to organize school-improvement and fund-raising efforts, and speeches at denominational associations and fraternal lodge meetings to raise additional funds. Moore seems to have felt little compunction about expressing his views to Newbold. When he encountered problems, he reported them matter-of-factly, whether a division among school patrons over the location of a proposed consolidated school, or the apathy of county officials.[76] Surviving letters between the two men show that their styles differed: Moore wrote in a more conversational tone than the businesslike Newbold and couched his suggestions as requests to which Newbold responded with instructions. Newbold in return encouraged Moore to maintain pressure on seemingly hopeless county officials, noting that superintendents needed "cultivation, encouragement and sometimes a little criticism."[77]

When dealing with those superintendents, Newbold and Moore discovered how easily they could run afoul of white North Carolinians' expectations of proper black behavior, especially if it involved politics. Newbold prepared county superintendents for visits from Moore by sending a letter of introduction that carefully spelled out Moore's official position and why he would want to meet with the superintendent, and then asked for an account of the results of Moore's visit. Moore submitted his own reports, of course, but Newbold used his correspondence with superintendents to check on his black employee's dealings with whites. Thus Newbold asked Halifax County Superintendent A. E. Akers to "write ... frankly" after reading headlines about an article Moore had published in a Halifax newspaper that suggested that Moore had been "misunderstood or was a little critical in his statements."[78]

Although other superintendents wrote favorably about the Rosenwald building agent, Franklin County's E. L. Best expressed chagrin that Moore had "called attention to the fact that some of the colored schools did not receive justice in regard to the apportionment of the school fund" at a school gathering. Best claimed that he had cut short his own meeting with Moore because "many other reports were circulated this morning about his attempting to arouse a bad feeling and sentiment among the negroes." Newbold's reply defending Moore from allegations that he had made pro-German comments indicated that Best's confrontation with Moore had included an attack on Moore's patriotism. The United States was about to enter the First World War, and Moore, like other activists, would later contrast African American support for making the world safe for democracy with their treatment at home. Best retreated with a plaintive assertion that he had always been a good friend to Halifax African Americans and their schools, suggesting how white officials became defensive when black and white outsiders challenged their self-image as racial paternalists.[79]

Apparently news of this flap and other complaints from black North Carolinians reached Tuskegee, prompting Clinton Calloway to issue a private warning to Moore. The beleaguered Rosenwald agent attributed his problems to those white superintendents, like Best, who could not stand to hear the truth: "The reason for their feeling and desire is due to the fact that I reported them in my monthly reports to the State Superintendent of Public Instruction . . . for allowing their respective district school committeemen to use the colored peoples' money on white schools. . . . I am proud of such enemies . . . and I intend to make more of them mad, if uncovering their rascality, hypocrisy and thievery will do it." But Moore also had African American critics, whom he was equally loathe to please: "Now, as to my own people: While I would like to please them all, I am not anxious to do it and I am not going to try to do it, if in doing so will be to the disadvantage of the majority of our people to be served in the premises," he declared. "I care nothing about the criticism of irresponsible characters."[80]

His adversaries could not silence Moore, who published letters in the *Greensboro Daily News* calling on white North Carolinians to reward black veterans with "fair treatment" and to give up their limited notions of a "special and different education" for black children. Perhaps to forestall similar situations, Newbold petitioned Julius Rosenwald for a white building agent who could "reach county superintendents, and boards of education who might not be impressed by Professor Moore. The latter can appeal to the Negroes better." Moore recognized the implicit affront and let Tuskegee officials know his side of the story: "By the way, I've been thinking more or less about N[ewbold]'s wishing to put a *white man* in this part of the work to handle the school officials, while *I* handle *only the Negroes* just as if I cannot handle *both races*." Rosenwald rejected Newbold's request, and instead the General Education Board funded an assistant Negro school agent, T. B. Attmore, to handle Rosenwald building supervision. Meanwhile, in an April 1919 circular letter in which he offered superintendents the services of both Attmore and Moore, Newbold was careful to describe Moore as a graduate of Amherst and "a man of good judgment and . . . leader among his people."[81]

Trouble erupted yet again in the fall of 1919 during Clinton Calloway's inspection tour of North Carolina Rosenwald schools. When Newbold, Moore, and Calloway arrived for their scheduled meeting with Wilson County superintendent Charles L. Coon, Coon insulted Moore, reportedly saying that "he did not want to see him, and not to come to his office." Once again the root cause was Moore's outspokenness. Moore and Coon had previously met about Wilson County's plan to construct four Rosenwald schools in the next year. According to Coon, Moore "had much to say and caused much to be published detrimental to me" and "wanted notoriety which he shouldn't get through the public press." Newbold tried to smooth the situation over, but Moore refused to return to Coon's office.[82]

Charles Moore submitted his last report for May 1920. Probably Newbold forced him out, but Moore also had reasons of his own for resigning. In addition to antagonistic superintendents and Newbold's segregation of the state's Rosenwald work into black and white categories, the Rosenwald building program's increasing emphasis on modern school construction practices and its removal from Tuskegee may well have rankled the former National Negro Business League official. Certainly Moore's political activism—at the time of his departure, he was challenging the lily-white policy of North Carolina Republicans at the party's national convention—made him controversial to those who believed African Americans should privilege the right to public education over the right to vote.[83] In his school campaigns, Moore had exposed racists and demanded more of paternalist whites, refused to stop talking about politics and all the rights of citizenship, and welcomed the backlash against him as proof of the justice of his claims.

At the same time, a rift had developed between the state teachers' association and N. C. Newbold involving the Rosenwald agent position, a rift fraught with the ambiguities faced by activists like Charles Moore, Dr. Aaron Moore, and black teachers seeking educational equity. A. M. Moore informed Newbold of the association's decision not to appoint Charles Moore's successor but rather to send a delegation to lobby for matching state and Rosenwald funds for a Rosenwald agent. Assuring Newbold that he had their support for "tearing away the rubbish of inefficiency" and their understanding of his "embarrassment that you find in putting over this work," A. M. Moore intimated that black teachers would support the new Rosenwald regime and expressed hope that "God will give you strength to live and see the superstructure for our educational buildings erected on the ruins thereof." Moore's confusing statement that "we are only anxious to help you to work out our own destiny as any other group of citizens" resonates with the conflicts that white and black activists felt when working with each other. African American professionals realized that if they wanted to assert their right "to work out our own destiny as any other group of citizens" without losing their place at the funding table, they might have to distance themselves—at least in white eyes—from other blacks who had fallen from white favor. But they did not let white allies off the hook, however much they "appreciated the embarrassment" that white state agents for Negro schools experienced when confronted by other whites who suspected their racial loyalties. Black professionals framed their deferential protestations to shield their demand for a just share of financial support and their right as citizens to "work out our own destiny."[84]

Dr. George E. Davis took over as Rosenwald building agent and established an extraordinary professional relationship with his white superiors that illuminates how a skillful operator could use the Rosenwald program to extract concessions from a Jim Crow public school system. Historian Thomas W. Hanchett has described Davis as "a fascinating study in contrasts" of class, religious convictions, and racial loyalties.[85] Davis's sometimes paradoxical beliefs reflected his class, his membership in the black intellectual elite, his deep religious convictions, and his faith in racial uplift. North Carolina's African Americans, Davis assumed, needed and wanted his leadership and guidance and expected him to act on their behalf. Davis also was keenly attuned to his white audiences and calibrated his words to what he sensed they would or would not hear. Accordingly, his monthly reports to the Division of Negro Education and the Rosenwald Fund took the most accommodating tone, emphasizing black patience and faith in white friends. For example, Davis interrupted his report on the Negro Education conference at Winston-Salem in January 1927 to sermonize, "Thus all great movements are forward, though in any limited epoch we may not see the gain, yet the movement is forward though unseen for the moment, like the shadow on the dial or the heavenly body by which it is marked."[86]

In his communications with division director N. C. Newbold, Davis was more pointed, yet just as discreet, indicating that he was well aware both of Newbold's insistence on white leadership and his support for black professionals as well as black public schools. He praised Newbold's "wise and cautious direction" in building white support for black education and promotion of the Rosenwald building program and added his own claims that the school-building campaign benefited whites as well, for all would prosper when black citizens no longer had to "worry over legal disabilities and lack of educational advantages." Davis's language communicated a double-edged argument—whites could remain in control, he implied, but they had to recognize that African Americans deserved much better from them. Thus Davis invoked the benefits of self-help before he reminded Newbold of the true context for the black self-sacrifice that whites expected: "When we remember that the per capita wealth of the Southern whites is $885, while that of the Negro is, per capita, only $34; when he comes up with about $3.85 to the collection table he has made a sacrifice equal to the white man's contribution of about $100 toward the education of his child."[87]

Davis found his most receptive white audience in his immediate supervisor, W. F. Credle. The two men conducted a voluminous correspondence in which the older, more experienced Davis tugged at the younger, up-and-coming administrator's professional and personal sentiments. Both men spent a great deal of time in the field on the day-to-day process of building new schools, and consequently their letters contained detailed assessments of their meetings with school officials and community members, and especially of building-construction methods. Davis described the buildings carefully in accordance with the specific requirements of the Rosenwald plan of aid and the specifications given in *Community School Plans* so that Credle could determine whether and when to release Rosenwald grants. For example, the Parkton School initially did not deserve its Rosenwald money because it was "a bum job": "There is need of a middle girder under the shaky floor. There are not enough pillars and some of those put under are mere bricks piled up and wedged up with wooden blocks. There is an acute deficiency of black boards. The building is not painted inside. There are just about half the number of desks required.... The toilets(?) are a disgrace, just extemporized."[88]

Davis intermixed these factual reports with extensive commentaries, to which Credle replied in more formal and measured terms, always respectfully addressing Davis as "Dr."[89] Yet clearly Credle was the supervisor, and his own superiors expected him to monitor Davis's work closely, especially his building inspections. From the Rosenwald Fund office in Nashville, S. L. Smith asked that Credle chide Davis for submitting projects that simply remodeled older buildings in violation of Rosenwald Fund policy.[90] Credle also asked Smith to help him prevail over Davis, whom he described as "the best building agent in the South," when they disagreed on the necessity for single-story buildings.[91]

Like other Rosenwald building agents, Davis freely voiced criticism of local conditions, including white southerners. He could describe one county superintendent as "*absolutely* doing his duty by us," another as sympathetic but hamstrung by local prejudice (the black school had burned not once, but twice), but a third as "everything but sympathetic and just in dealing with his Negro schools."[92] Such reports helped Credle mete out the praise and criticism that Negro school agents used in their dealings with the county superintendents, such as when Davis suggested that Credle have "our folks in Chicago or Mr. Smith . . . write. . . a nice letter" to the Union County superintendent, whom Davis believed was leaving his office because of white criticism of "his liberal and absolutely fair treatment of the Negroes."[93]

While always careful to recognize white supporters, Davis's particular skill lay in knowing how to obligate Credle to use his power over white county officials on behalf of Davis's rural black constituents. For example, Davis wrote

Credle in April 1922 about the Woodrow School's imperfections, which included a thin coat "of *cheap* white something" on its exterior walls, and "some pine desks . . . strong, to be sure—but not 'modern'" as required by the Rosenwald Fund. Davis did not stop with his criticism of the building:

> Now I think these people are not getting a square deal. I think our Fund is not getting a square deal. These people gave of their poverty $350 in cash, 3000 feet of good framing, did all the hauling and much other work on building. They are allowed [their donations were valued at] $500 for money and work and material—very little I think. The county has put in 550. Now if Rosenwald Fund is giving nearly twice as much as the County it looks as if we might *at least* get two good coats of *real* paint inside and out for that building.

Davis had managed to critique not only the paint but also the county's education officials for their minimal effort and the state office for its own failure to acknowledge the significance as well as the cash value of local contributions. And he got the desired result, a promise from Credle to prod the county superintendent once again.[94]

Davis occasionally vented his frustration in more forceful terms, as in his response to a botched building and uncooperative superintendent in western North Carolina. He wanted one last chance to use his powers of persuasion on the man, but whether Davis could have used the arguments he posed for Credle is doubtful: "I want a little thing before you make final payment . . . to see if I can't induce Mr. Steppe to give the handful of Negroes who have sweat blood for that which every consideration of equity and justice should have given them as law-abiding useful citizens of the town, county & state; without the expenditure of a single dollar aside from their taxes." Forty African American families had contributed almost $2,500 toward the county's two black schools, Davis explained, while their children went to school only for six months compared to the white children's nine. "God looks with disfavor on such injustice," he preached. "His face will not always shine on those who take advantage of the poor and dependent people who seeing their wrongs have not murmured or sulked." He then explained how "white men 'shoe-stringed'" the Marion city limits to leave its black school outside the city boundaries and thus ineligible for the city's nine-month school term. "That's cowardly," Davis fumed. "That's contrary to Anglo-Saxon claims to *fair play*! I am wondering if the people of Marion are not mainly of German extraction. They act as if they were."[95] Such expostulations were not typical, but they suggest that Davis believed he and

Credle shared a vision of justice as well as professional expertise, and that their relationship could tolerate an honest appraisal of white intentions.

Davis also let his white superior know that he kept his distance both from Tuskegee Institute and the National Association for the Advancement of Colored People, probably out of a mixture of his own convictions, his awareness of Newbold's distaste for Tuskegee's management of the Rosenwald program, and his sense of the white agents' opinions of less discreet black activists. He had no sympathy for Clinton J. Calloway's ambiguous position as the new field agent of the Rosenwald Fund's building program. When Calloway asked for Davis's assistance with an inspection tour of North Carolina schools, Davis grudgingly accepted, telling Credle that he didn't "quite know his relation to North Carolina." A year later he forwarded another letter in which Calloway had apparently asked Davis to write on his behalf to Julius Rosenwald about keeping the field agent position. Davis refused to buck his North Carolina chain of command and instead informed his white superiors about Calloway's request. Later in the decade, when the *Crisis* published critical articles about North Carolina black schools that used material obtained from Davis, he told Credle: "personally I do *not* admire its editor—nor do I regard him as fair to the South in all respects. I gave him . . . only printed statistical information as I know his disposition to see things from his own perspective."[96]

The experiences of North Carolina's agents reveal the delicate nature of their work with each other and their constituencies, which played out with varying results in other state education departments aligned with the Rosenwald school-building program. From their state offices, the white agents for Negro schools and the black Rosenwald building agents transposed the school-building program into the standard operations of a southern state department of education. These agents shared an interlocking set of supervisors—state superintendents, the General Education Board, and the Rosenwald Fund—but operated within their own professional and racial hierarchy of Negro school agent over Rosenwald building agent. Their work, however problematic, illuminated the potential and the perils of interracial cooperation in a Jim Crow context.

Their central role as the conduits for Rosenwald school applications and grants certainly afforded both groups of agents some influence over the building program's policies and practices and magnified the significance of their mistakes. Both the white state agents for Negro schools and the African American Rosenwald building agents wielded their greatest influence at the state level. All of these agents used the Rosenwald school-building program to expand the range of state services to black education, whether by connecting it and state public school systems to African American higher education institutions or by enforcing the program's rules on unwilling local white authorities. State agents for Negro schools and Rosenwald building agents also sought to recruit a broader range of southerners to the cause of black education, and the Rosenwald building program served them well in that task as well.

Spreading the Rosenwald Message
in Southern Education

Across southern states, the construction of Rosenwald schools proceeded parallel with the construction of a professional bureaucracy dedicated to improving black public education. State agents for Negro schools and Rosenwald building agents also used Rosenwald schools as magnets to draw broader white and black audiences to the cause of African American advancement. They championed Rosenwald schools as models of proper African American education in the pages of bureaucratic reports, promotional pamphlets, and educational journals; at professional meetings; and in personal contacts. Agents most often labored to reach others like themselves: professional educators and sympathetic white and black southerners who were well-educated, civic-minded, mostly middle-class, and desirous of change without conflict. As a result, the Rosenwald Fund claimed, its schools fostered "a more general recognition of the Negro as a factor in the community, and a larger interest in Negro education."[1]

In the early years of the twentieth century, state school leaders and their allies in outside philanthropies, especially the Southern Education Board, had campaigned across southern states to win voter support for better white public schools and the increased taxation and state regulation necessary to support them. Having acquiesced in black disfranchisement and the misappropriation of public funds from black to white schools, southern educational reformers now waged a second, and quieter, crusade on behalf of African American schools. The Rosenwald school-building program was part of these state school reformers' campaign, for they needed local school authorities to approve the construction of Rosenwald schools and accept them into their public school systems. The Rosenwald program's insistence that local school authorities approve its school-building projects was indeed, as historians Eric Anderson and Alfred A. Moss Jr. have argued, a "defensive" strategy meant to deflect white opposition to an outside agency supportive of African Americans that gave local whites a "veto power."[2] Yet Booker T. Washington, Julius Rosenwald, and building-program participants also believed this requirement would build genuine systems of universal public education in the region. Consequently, the efforts of state agents for Negro schools and Rosenwald building agents to recruit other southern educators form a significant component of the Rosenwald building program and the history of public education in the South.

State Negro school agents and Rosenwald building agents strove to bring African American education into the mainstream of southern school reform by incorporating it into the professional agenda of both white and black school administrators and teachers. Rosenwald schools simultaneously served the agents' purpose as tools for building a professional consensus for African American education and benefited from their success with local school authorities. Rosenwald schools, the agents declared, offered tangible examples of the progress southerners could expect to see in public education. Agents exhorted their white and black colleagues to advance their careers and their communities by embracing the Rosenwald building program.

Recruiting Professional Support for Black Schools

State agents for Negro schools and Rosenwald building agents worked across the color line to publicize advances in black education through Rosenwald schools. The white men who served as agents for Negro schools, like other state bureaucrats, felt compelled to justify their work to state government and to taxpayers even though the General Education Board paid their salaries, and they potentially saved thousands of taxpayers' dollars by collecting grants from outside philanthropies like the Rosenwald school-building program. State agents for Negro schools viewed themselves as representatives of the advancing power of southern state governments and public school systems engineered by Progressive reformers.[3] They also realized that they symbolized a grudging acknowledgment of state responsibility for black citizens, made palatable by segregation and disfranchisement, and rendered practicable by white dependence on black labor and the use of outside aid to mask the transfer of state resources from black to white schools.

All agents for Negro schools wrote summaries of their work for the state superintendents' annual and biennial reports, which documented the department's activities for the governor and state legislature and interested educators across the state and nation. These narratives offered a venue for Negro school agents to explain their overall contribution to the state educational system, and the Rosenwald school-building program generated effective written and photographic evidence for that purpose. A typical annual report by a state Negro school agent included an overview of the Rosenwald building program and a table detailing recent Rosenwald school construction, sometimes accompanied by excerpts from the current plan of aid, located amid discussions of other philanthropic projects such as the Slater Fund's county training schools. For example, J. H. Brinson's "Report of State Agent for Negro Education" in Florida's 1922–24 biennial report explained: "The work of the Rosenwald Building Fund in aiding in the securing of modern and correct negro rural school buildings has been one of the outstanding features of American school work for the past few years." He described the building program's designs as having been "recognized as representing the very best that is known in school house lighting and ventilation," noting that "it is from this source that we have our only supply of stock blue prints and specifications for either white or colored school buildings." He continued with a list of Rosenwald schools built over the biennium and noted which of Florida's county training schools had been constructed with Rosenwald grants.[4]

This sort of text served the purposes of both a state Negro school agent and Rosenwald building-program administrators. Brinson's report detailed not only the initiatives sponsored by each outside agency in African American education but how their programs intersected, noting which county training schools had received assistance from the Rosenwald and Slater funds to demonstrate how his readers might combine Rosenwald grants with other philanthropic monies. Here Brinson identified school architecture as the Rosenwald program's unique contribution and a major achievement. And by describing Rosenwald blueprints and specifications as "the very best that is known in school house lighting and ventilation"—before he explained that they were the only ones available from the state department for either white or black schools—Brinson articulated one of the Rosenwald program's most important arguments for using its schools as models of standardized school design.

Negro school agents, and in some cases Rosenwald building agents as well, routinely submitted this sort of material for their state superintendents' annual reports. In Louisiana, agents excelled at recasting their standard reports into pamphlets and articles that reached wider circles of white educators. Leo M. Favrot led this effort from his first months as Negro school agent, working in tandem with assistant agent Arthur C. Lewis and Rosenwald building agents O. W. Gray and John S. Jones. In their publications, Louisiana agents used Rosenwald schools to offer reassurance, praise, and blame as positive and negative stratagems for recruiting support for African American education. Their writings exemplify not only the techniques agents used to spread the Rosenwald message but also how the Rosenwald message shaped their understanding of black education in the South.[5]

Like all state agents supported by the General Education Board, Leo Favrot submitted monthly reports to his state superintendent and to the board in New York that assessed individual schools and their prospects for improvement. In the 1910s, Louisiana's education department took the unusual step of publishing reports by all of its General Education Board agents in a monthly bulletin, *Field Force Reports*. This publication addressed a small audience of state administrators and educators with an interest in Progressive reforms and who were already knowledgeable about the General Education Board's agents and their work. Anxious superintendents and teachers may have scanned its pages for agents' reviews of their schools.

Leo Favrot's contributions to *Field Force Reports* used the Rosenwald program as one standard for judging individual schools and teachers. Favrot clearly expected that parish superintendents and Jeanes supervisors would respond appropriately to criticism or compliments. Thus his report on the rally for a Rosenwald school at Wildsville mentioned that the teacher had not attended, and "I could not refrain from suggesting to the superintendent that her absence from this meeting gives sufficient ground for cancelling her contract." A rally at Welsh earned Favrot's favor, as "the mayor of the town, the parish superintendent, and a large delegation consisting of the negro principal and pupils" met his train. School patrons had $300 ready, and the parish board had already purchased land and committed funding for a new school (figures 7–8).[6] *Field Force Reports* also allowed Favrot to introduce Rosenwald building agent O. W. Gray and explain his duties so that white parish authorities would understand his promotional work in African American communities.[7]

Seeking a wider audience of white educators across the state and region, Favrot and assistant agent A. C. Lewis issued their own pamphlets and bulletins, which the state superintendent distributed to parish superintendents and school board members.[8] Favrot began the series in 1918 with *Aims and Needs in Negro Public Education in Louisiana*. He used its text to promote an educational paternalism that acknowledged African Americans' right to public education within a safety net of white control—arguments made all the more urgent at the end of the First World War by African American migration out of the South. Favrot shared other white reformers' desire to recognize African American demands for justice and better opportunities and yet hold them under white leadership and keep them in the segregated South. In his pamphlet, he argued that black

Louisianans "are entitled to share in her public education" because education would only improve the labor force and universal education was necessary for democracy. A paternalist himself, he cast his discussion of African Americans in racial terms familiar to other moderate and Progressive whites: "he [the Negro] is a human being, with the desires and hopes of other human beings; ... he is among us, working with us and for us, dependent upon us for guidance and care, for protection and development." Then he introduced the element of fair play, explaining a statistical chart that showed not only that African Americans did not get their share of tax revenues, "which amounts to confiscation," but that school expenditures for whites increased and blacks decreased as the size of a parish's black population grew.[9]

Rosenwald Negro Rural Schools in Louisiana 1917 and 1918, Favrot's next independent publication, put Rosenwald schools at the forefront of his agenda for African American education. The pamphlet celebrated Louisiana's "achievement of the past two years" with numerous photographs illustrating the transformation of black public school buildings. Favrot correlated Rosenwald facilities with instructional improvements. The Rosenwald building program, according to Favrot, made it "possible to formulate with greater clearness and definiteness the ideals and standards towards which we are striving. . . . The aim of the Rosenwald school goes beyond the construction of modern schoolhouses and the establishment of school plants; it extends to the course of instruction, the work of the teacher and the life of the school."[10]

In addition to providing detailed instructions explaining how to apply for Rosenwald aid, Favrot offered his own commentary on the "Plan for Erection of Rural Schoolhouses" that linked its specific provisions to familiar issues in Progressive rural school reform. He outlined the bleak condition of southern African American schools, which he claimed Julius Rosenwald "must have been impressed with," as justifications for the Rosenwald plan's conditions of aid. "That a community should provide for its children a modern schoolhouse, on a suitable site, furnished and equipped for work" as the 1917 plan required, Favrot declared, would redress "the total lack of school plants for Negroes in many parts of the rural South" and in others "the unfinished, unequipped, unattractive, and improperly planned and constructed school plants that housed the Negro schools." After this description of black school facilities in the standard language that Progressive school designers applied to older buildings, Favrot went on to instruction. "The lack of relationship between the usual rural school plant and the purpose it was designed to serve"—another typical critique by Progressive educators concerned about country schools—would disappear in a Rosenwald school, thanks to the required "industrial room in which at least the home-making arts for girls should be taught, and in which agricultural home projects for boys and girls should be directed." Further emphasizing the building program's affinity with current discussions of improved rural schooling, Favrot claimed that Rosenwald schools would employ teachers "who know how to bring the school into close relationship with rural life."[11]

Favrot, and later A. C. Lewis, issued such pamphlets annually through 1924. The Negro school agents argued that modern school facilities were one of the "paramount needs of Negro rural schools" and repeatedly described how the Rosenwald building program operated, reprinted Rosenwald school plans, and listed recent Rosenwald school construction. Superintendents of the parishes where these schools were located could pat themselves on the back and others might be reassured about taking on Rosenwald projects, as the agents promised "no dictatorial type of supervision of the funds calculated to estrange good will." But those in parishes described in print as doing "little or nothing" had—perhaps for the first time—earned public criticism by other whites for their neglect of black schools.[12]

Not all Louisiana educators would have read these bulletins, so Favrot, Lewis, and Rosenwald building agent John S. Jones took their message to the state's white teachers and school administrators in the journal of the white state teachers' association.[13] Again Favrot and Lewis published the names of parishes that supported Jeanes teachers, county training schools, and Rosenwald schools and offered official recognition and praise for the parish superintendents and school boards that had joined their cause. They assured white readers that they would not lose power by supporting black educational reform programs, such as when Favrot introduced the Rosenwald program by claiming that African American citizens were "ready to put money into the building of schoolhouses for their children," although they would "need the guidance and direction of the trained white superintendent."[14]

As his own thinking evolved, Favrot supplemented his increasing demands for black schools, always couched in terms of white self-interest, with sporadic calls for justice. Galvanized by the First World War, Favrot began capitalizing the word "Negro" in his writings and called on white educators to reward black patriotism. Not that he had changed his paternalistic attitudes, for he could still write that "he [the Negro] has a knowledge of his own limitations and of his utter incapacity to perform unassisted this task [better education] that he has set his mind to" even as he demanded that whites do more. "As the dominant race we are anxious to do the thing that is best for the Negro. Let us show him that we are honestly striving to treat him justly, and to help him to climb," Favrot urged. "Such an obvious desire on our part will serve to knit him firmly into our civilization and our industrial life."[15]

When *Southern School Work*, the journal of Louisiana's white teachers' state association, instituted a "Department of Negro Education" early in 1919, Rosenwald building agent John S. Jones added his voice to Favrot's calls for better black education. While another Southern University colleague took the editorial position for this column, president J. S. Clark and Jones authored most of the copy, cementing their institution's reputation among whites as a state college that offered the appropriate "practical" education for blacks. In return, these black educators gained a forum in which they could influence white opinion about the necessity of improving all aspects of black education.[16]

Jones used this opportunity to elicit the sympathy of white educators, patiently explaining the Rosenwald program in articles that emphasized rural blacks' commitment to education and the opportunity for "an encouraging spirit of co-operation" between the races as well as the buildings' instructional and aesthetic merits.[17] He told white educators, "I find the people to be so deeply concerned in the matter of better school equipment that it is almost impossible to get Rosenwald Schools fast enough to meet the demands of the communities making application." To portray black educational aspirations as a noble cause worthy of white support, Jones also hit on the themes of black self-sacrifice and acceptance of the "proper type" of education. He found it "encouraging to note this tendency on the part of our people, not to waste or dissipate what they have but to invest it in the training of our boys and girls who will be the men and women of tomorrow."[18] In a 1920 article for *Southern School Work*, Jones correlated aesthetic appearance with pedagogical and health standards. Landscaped grounds outdoors and "pictures having educational value" indoors—primarily images of Booker T. Washington and Julius Rosenwald—were as integral as the structure's design and industrial instruction to what Jones called the "Rosenwald vision."[19]

Articles in their own professional journals certified the "Rosenwald vision" as a legitimate part of the Progressive agenda of southern educators and administrators. Few readers of these journals might ever set foot in a Rosenwald school, let alone become activists for black educational reform, but their reading suggested that white educators were supposed to know something about a philanthropist like Julius Rosenwald and how his program fit into the Progressive education agenda. Effective superintendents were supposed to be building Rosenwald schools. And white educators were supposed to show some level of respectful interest when addressed by their peers across the color line. The few who resisted in print suggest that white educators indeed did feel this pressure. A disgruntled DeSoto parish superintendent bluntly informed a *Southern School Work* reporter that he "holds that no outside funds, like the Rosenwald, will be acceptable to this parish . . . that the education of the Negro should be taken care of by the State, and rather resents than invites outside provision."[20]

African American teachers' organizations also offered professional audiences for the Rosenwald program's administrators. In many states, a portion of their members' dues went to pay part of the building agents' salary and expenses, and members often elected Rosenwald building agents as officers of their state organizations. Not surprisingly, members of black teachers' organizations were not merely the passive readers of articles about the Rosenwald program but took an active role in defining its place in their professional agenda. For example, the Kentucky Negro Educational Association (KNEA) embraced the Rosenwald building program and used news of its activities to advance black school interests, just as the Negro school agent used the KNEA's meetings and journal to advance the Rosenwald program.[21]

Rosenwald building agent and Kentucky Normal and Industrial Institute president Francis M. Wood had a long history with the KNEA, which he led from 1909 to 1916. One of his actions as president was to align the KNEA's meetings with the white Kentucky Education Association so that the organizations could share speakers and exchange delegates. Published proceedings of the KNEA's meetings in the 1920s listed speakers such as Negro school agents F. C. Button and L. N. Taylor; state Jeanes supervisor Florence G. (Mrs. T. L.) Anderson; Jeanes Fund president James Hardy Dillard; General Education Board officials E. C. Sage, Jackson Davis, and W.T.B. Williams; as well as E. Franklin Frazier, Charlotte Hawkins Brown, Alice Dunbar-Nelson, and Horace Mann Bond.[22] Wood himself served on the KNEA board of directors and spoke to KNEA members as "State Director of Rosenwald Fund." In 1923, simultaneously with his appointment as president of the Kentucky Normal and Industrial Institute, the state department of education took over Wood's building agent position and retitled it "Supervisor of Colored Schools," inspiring the KNEA to issue a resolution approving "a plan advocated for many years by this association." Another resolution instructed black teachers to "inform themselves as to the various outside funds available for supplementing the state and county funds," such as the Rosenwald and Jeanes funds, by contacting Button and Wood.[23]

For the KNEA, Wood's joint appointments created an essential bridge between the white-controlled state education department and African American professional leaders. When Wood's college presidency almost immediately ran afoul of state politics, the KNEA published resolutions of support. After both Wood and his replacement as Rosenwald agent, J. W. Bell, were dismissed, the KNEA protested with a set of published resolutions calling upon state education officials to hire another African American staff member, "since it is impossible for any man who has not lived with our race nor even been a part of them, to know our real condition, it would be impossible for him to sympathize with our conditions or needs." Five years later, the KNEA had not given up, including in its "Declaration of Principles" a call for the appointment of a "Negro supervisor" and "a workable relationship" between white and black school leaders "for the good of the state." Then, after calling for teacher salary equity, the KNEA concluded, "The magnanimous contribution to the cause of Negro education by Julius Rosenwald should be honored by our people in a celebration with special exercises."[24]

Kentucky's state department of education did not hire another black man as supervisor or Rosenwald building agent, but by the time the KNEA had expanded its published proceedings into a regular periodical in 1931, the better working relationship it sought was in place. L. N. Taylor, who had been state Negro school agent since 1924, saw the new *KNEA Journal* as a promotional organ for the Rosenwald building program, and the journal's editor in return featured newly built Rosenwald schools. Taylor used the periodical to remind African American educators of the "Funds Aiding Our Colored Schools," emphasizing "Our Rosenwald Buildings." He continued with a lengthy discussion of "How to Get Aid from the J.R.F." that instructed educators to "write to L. N. Taylor . . . and get information on how to proceed." Proceed they did: the *KNEA Journal* featured the Rosenwald school at Providence, Maysville's John G. Fee Industrial High School, Frankfort's May-Underwood School, Jefferson County's Newburg School, Harrodsburg's West Side School, and the Lebanon Colored School. The journal's article on the Harrodsburg school noted that "it stands as another fitting testimonial to the faithful service and persistent efforts of Mr. L. N. Taylor, representative of the Julius Rosenwald Fund in Kentucky, supplementing the faithful service and splendid cooperation of a community's educational sponsors," suggesting that the KNEA and the state department had overcome some of their past tensions.[25]

Thus Kentucky's black educators, like their white peers across the color line, heard the message from their professional organization that they should not only be knowledgeable about, but take action to use the philanthropic programs available through the department of education. But for these teachers and administrators, Rosenwald schools represented a new form of a familiar practice of educational and community service rather than a novel professional interest.[26] State agents for Negro schools and Rosenwald building agents who strove to bring "the Rosenwald vision" to black educators focused on guiding the independent efforts of these professionals into a newly opened channel, unlike their efforts to make white professionals simply acknowledge black education.

African American teachers, Jeanes supervisors, and principals certainly understood that such programs required a public display of industrial education and deference to white authority. Some members would have approved of those strategies, while others paid only lip service. In the case of the KNEA, members simultaneously endorsed the Maysville Industrial High School, constructed with aid from the Rosenwald Fund's controversial urban industrial high school initiative, and collected money for the NAACP's legal cases. In other states, those conditions led African American educational associations to keep the Rosenwald program at arm's length. In Virginia, Rosenwald schools moved on and off of educators' professional agenda as defined by the Negro Organization Society and the State Teachers Association. The Negro Organization Society, founded at Hampton Institute in 1912 as a coalition of voluntary groups, merged with the School Improvement League in 1917, creating a powerful state association supported by school patrons and many teachers. For the next five years, the Negro Organization Society cooperated on school-improvement issues with the Virginia State Teachers Association (VSTA), which had previously focused on professional development. The two groups separated again in 1921 to pursue their individual agendas. School improvement crept back into the VSTA in the mid-1920s, as its *Virginia Teachers' Bulletin* recorded two presentations by state Negro school agent W. D. Gresham at the organization's annual meetings, and a 1925 resolution calling on communities to make applications for Rosenwald aid.[27]

However, African American educators advocating educational equality, led by John M. Gandy, split with those who supported industrial education and school-building improvement, led by Thomas C. Walker. Walker was a long-

time African American Republican Party activist and attorney from Glouces-
ter, a Hampton Institute alumnus who served as the field agent for the Negro
Organization Society and Virginia's Rosenwald building agent. The tension
between the two associations erupted during a 1926 meeting of the State
Teachers Association Executive Committee, which suspended its agenda "in
order to hear from Lawyer T. C. Walker, who was charged with attempting to
inject the work of the NOS" into the teachers' association. Committee members William F. Grasty, John M. Gandy, and Luttrelle F. Palmer called for the
two groups to maintain their independence from each other, and Gandy suggested they "not even attend each others' meetings." On behalf of the committee, Palmer "complimented Negro state supervisor Gresham, saying that he is
taking the steps he knows best" and, snubbing Walker, "further explained that
Mr. Gresham should be given a colored assistant." The *Virginia Teachers' Bulletin* refocused its contents back to instructional issues until late in 1928, when
principals and teachers began regularly sending in news of their Rosenwald
school projects.[28]

Acting on their own convictions and paternalistic presumption of authority, the white state agents for Negro schools and their assistants easily crossed
over from their white professional organizations into the workings of African
American educators' associations, enjoying the hospitality of black educators in
search of white allies. African American Rosenwald building agents made the
reverse journey across the color line infrequently, constrained by the organizational and social barriers between the two sets of professional organizations
and their subordinate position to the Negro school agent. These interactions
were unequal, yet they served a purpose. White educators who read their association journals learned that black education had become a legitimate part of
the professional landscape, replete with not only new school buildings but also
new kinds of white and black state officials to support them. The white state
agents for Negro schools themselves gained experience in working with African American professionals, who then helped them to prepare other whites for
similar tasks in their communities, as did the black Rosenwald building agents
and educators who learned about working with white state and local officials.

Taking the Message to County Superintendents

Writing articles and attending professional meetings connected the state
agents for Negro schools and Rosenwald building agents with other groups
of educators. Communicating directly and effectively with individual county

superintendents proved to be a far greater challenge. First, all agents had to be persistent. As the Texas Negro school agent remarked: "sometimes several visits were required to interest one county superintendent. Where the office of the superintendent is political and changes occur frequently, the idea has to be sold anew several times."[29] Negro school agents kept close tabs on county superintendents. W. F. Credle's reports as North Carolina assistant Negro school agent repeatedly commented on individual superintendents like the "very hospitable man" in Robeson County, noting that "it is pleasant to be with him unless one is thinking of the thousands of colored children in his county who could, with a little effort, be provided with better schoolhouses."[30]

Rosenwald building agents recognized the narrower limits of their power over white school superintendents, as Charles H. Moore's unhappy experiences in North Carolina revealed. Rosenwald building agents from Booker T. Washington Jr. to Dr. George E. Davis used compliments and forbearance to keep themselves and African American locals in a favorable position. Davis himself rarely characterized his conferences with county superintendents or other local officials, although his comments in letters to Credle certainly conveyed which went smoothly and which did not. After a conference with a recalcitrant Lincoln County superintendent, Davis wrote, "I am well aware that he has the 'whip hand' there and that nothing can be forced—so I received his indifference blandly and begged that he help the people at Mt Vernon and Tuckers Grove to get their brick and rafting timbers up in shape for use."[31] With such blandishments, agents like Davis could press the needs of black schools without jeopardizing individual projects, even as they cannily maneuvered the Negro school agent into exercising state, professional, and race authority over local whites.

For their part, the state agents for Negro schools barraged county superintendents with letters, circulars, and forms that reiterated the Rosenwald building program's purpose and procedures and prodded them to take action. Letters constantly went out from every Negro school agent's office offering advice and monetary assistance. In Alabama, James L. Sibley dangled the prospect of state and Rosenwald aid before Superintendent W. P. Archibald: "I was wondering if we could not start a little campaign in your county this summer and encourage the negroes to erect at least ten industrial schools. . . . If your county board would grant $200 State aid for every $200 they [African Americans] raised, I think I could get you $300 additional [from the Rosenwald program]." In Florida, J. H. Brinson wrote superintendent W. M. Scruggs to ask, "I wonder how the building programme [*sic*] is coming on in old Jefferson?"[32]

Virginian William G. Rennolds left a cache of incoming correspondence that illustrates how the Negro school agents carefully solicited county superintendents' support. Circular letters from the state superintendent and board of education arrived with suggestions for "Negro School Activities," such as applying for Rosenwald grants, and copies of the Rosenwald program's annual plan of aid. State agent for Negro schools Arthur D. Wright wrote Rennolds frequently about the Jeanes supervisors under his employ, and the Jeanes supervisors themselves wrote Rennolds about their school-improvement work and the Rosenwald money Wright had promised for their new buildings. When Wright left the state department of education in 1920, he sent Rennolds a circular letter thanking the superintendents for their efforts "for a work which has not always been popular," as well as a personal note that he counted Rennolds "among the inner circle of my friends." After W. D. Gresham took over as Negro school agent, he too exchanged letters with Rennolds about the proper sort of desks and toilets for Rosenwald schools and the status of Rosenwald school applications and construction, as well as the distribution of Slater and Jeanes aid.[33] Streams of bureaucratic paperwork helped the state agents for Negro schools use Rosenwald schools to identify a network of sympathetic local school authorities to whom they also pitched their professional appeals.

PATERNALISM AND EQUALITY

Organizing statewide campaigns for Rosenwald schools prompted some state agents for Negro schools to redirect their vision of African American education from an emphasis on its subordination to white paternalists to modest calls for equality. Certainly the Rosenwald school program was not their sole inspiration, any more than it was their exclusive job responsibility. Rather, the agents continued to invoke Rosenwald schools as material evidence that validated their arguments about African American education. Rosenwald building agents still found it difficult to agitate the question of equality openly, but they shared their white colleagues' belief that Rosenwald schools could build truly equal, if separate, schools. By the time that the Julius Rosenwald Fund dropped the school-building program in favor of a broader campaign for African Americans, all of the agents had reached the limits of paternalism.

At the time that the Rosenwald building program began at Tuskegee Institute, some of the first state agents for Negro schools had taken a "missionary" approach, to use William B. Harrell's term, primarily to attract white support. Negro school agents like those in Georgia presented themselves as evangelists to both races, and ultimately the Rosenwald school-building program inspired some of them to question commonplace white assumptions about race and schooling. George D. Godard, the state's first Negro school agent, presumed that he could speak with paternalistic authority on behalf of other enlightened whites and claimed that "the negroes of Georgia are well grounded upon the fact that their best friends are their own neighbors, and that the white people, among whom they live, do now, and will for a long time, exercise that guidance over them." He could provide that guidance by reaching out to "the best and most influential members of the negro race," presumably the most receptive to white ideas and able to marshal local school patrons into their proper ranks under white and black authority. Rosenwald schools fit nicely into Godard's agenda, for he described the Rosenwald grants as "perhaps the best way of awakening interest in suitable school buildings among the negroes." With each year, more news of the Rosenwald building program appeared in Godard's annual reports, where he illustrated the "model school houses" that were "doing more to elevate the ideas of the colored people and to develop civic, county, and community pride in them than anything that has been done for them."[34] Clinton Calloway passed along some of Godard's reports to Tuskegee Institute principal R. R. Moton, dryly noting that Godard's comments had to be understood in relative terms: "I think Mr. Godard has a pretty up-hill business in Georgia, and he seems to be congratulating himself on the progress he is making. I presume that as far as Georgia is concerned, he is doing well."[35]

Godard's successor, Walter B. Hill Jr., took a more aggressive tack in promoting African American education, including the Rosenwald building program. In the 1920s, Hill's annual reports listed specific recommendations for state and local governments together with the Rosenwald Fund's current plan of aid. Whereas Godard had discussed Georgia's Rosenwald program as a two-step effort in which modern school plans galvanized black communities to accept white authority, Hill added a third step for his white readers to take—to increase their financial support for black schools. He stressed that the Rosenwald plans were "not fancy" and that they had "no features not essential to a properly built school house." Having assured white readers that they would not waste precious tax revenues in building Rosenwald schools, he argued that they had to spend more on black schools anyway. He called on county governments to build at least one Rosenwald school each year and to include black schools in bond issues. To whites who argued that African Americans did not pay enough local taxes to justify more county spending on their schools, he asked if county governments would wish the state to take that attitude toward them as well.[36]

When J. Curtis Dixon replaced Hill, he too considered Rosenwald school building "one of the most pressing and most important duties of the Supervisor of Negro Education," but in a new language of educational equity. In a 1932 speech to county superintendents prepared in part by assistant Negro school agent Robert L. Cousins, Dixon opined:

> When asked to discuss or comment on the education of Negro children in Georgia, one wonders just where to begin and where to stop; what to say and what not to say. It would be easy and soothingly soporific to beguile ourselves with a recount of what has been done in this field. We can refer with pride to the 269 Rosenwald school buildings which have been constructed in Georgia. We can point the inquirer to the better teaching equipment in the Rosenwald schools, but we prefer to hang a curtain of silence round about that in Negro school buildings in general. . . . We do not like to consider together, or even allow to be mentioned, agricultural economic factors which cause the operation of schools for Negroes during the winter months between the harvesting of the old and the planting of the new crops, the inclemency of the weather, and the physical conditions of school buildings for Negro children.

Reminding the superintendents that only 55 percent of the funds they received from the state for black children actually went to black schools, and that white schoolchildren enjoyed 91 percent of school funds even though they accounted for only 61 percent of the scholastic population, Dixon called for full funding of black public education and equal pay for black teachers. "I am fully aware of the rank heresy involved in a statement of this kind," he admitted.[37]

Dixon went further than most state agents for Negro schools, whose reports often documented the disparities in white and black public education and the efforts of outside agencies like the Julius Rosenwald Fund to redress some of the inequity but stopped short of demanding that their own white citizens take responsibility for ending the discrimination. More typical was the voluble staff led by Nathan C. Newbold at the North Carolina Division of Negro Education. They were members of the region's largest and most respected Negro education staff and boasted the greatest number of Rosenwald schools. Newbold, Moore, Attmore, Davis, and Credle had intensively mined the Rosenwald Fund to improve school facilities and programs for countless African American children. Their close cooperation allowed these officials to use the financial leverage provided by the Rosenwald Fund to make improvements in the black public education system that otherwise never would have occurred, demonstrating how Progressive black and white reformers who worked together could manipulate the Jim Crow system to the benefit of those whom it was meant to repress. Yet by the 1930s, key staff members had reached the limits of what the Rosenwald building program could do for educational equity.

The paternalism shared by North Carolina's agents fueled their energetic Rosenwald program while keeping it safely within the bounds of segregation. As Dr. George E. Davis wrote: "The more education white people and black people have the less do they fear the big-bear [*sic*] of social equality. . . . I believe in the aristocracy of brains."[38] Social equality could be managed, in Davis's view, by educated whites and blacks who would keep the rest of their respective groups in line. He himself voted and took great interest in politics at all levels, but agitation about rights and race repelled him: "We hear too much today from would-be race leaders, about race pride, race love, race superiority and race men," Davis warned. He urged cooperation with white paternalists instead, invoking "the blessings of liberty, I have so long enjoyed, and the many tender friendships I have made with the white race" that had "taught me the lessons of forgiveness and have awakened in me a patient, tolerant waiting for better days to come." Davis's color-blind "aristocracy of brains," combined with his personal beliefs and preferred strategies for change, led him to identify his own alliances with whites as the model for all progress for southern African Americans. At the same time, his paternalism buttressed his status as "double agent," to borrow historian Glenda Gilmore's usage, allowing him to turn a complaisant face toward North Carolina whites, while among African Americans he vouched for elite black commitment to advancing the interests of all black North Carolinians.[39]

In spite of efforts by agents like Davis, Credle, and Newbold to achieve parity between white and black education in North Carolina, others could see that educational equality remained elusive as long as whites hoarded most resources and left blacks to the philanthropists and reformers, secure in the knowledge that those groups posed no threat to white control. From within the state department of education, Charles H. Moore and W. A. Robinson had challenged the politics of black educational reform, Moore by discussing party politics and the unequal distribution of school funds, and Robinson by critiquing the Rosenwald Fund's vision of vocational education. Both state and Rosenwald program leaders took Moore and Robinson to task, yet even those North Carolina agents who espoused a less confrontational strategy pushed the boundaries of segregation as far as they could. In so doing, Newbold, Davis, and Credle exposed the limits of what could be done by "patient, tolerant waiting" and careful cultivation of white support.

Not even the state with the largest number of Rosenwald schools could avoid criticism for its discriminatory public education system or stave off alternate forms of African American educational activism. When the *Crisis* editor W.E.B. Du Bois contacted Newbold in 1926 about North Carolina schools, Newbold responded with a defensive challenge to Du Bois to come see the situation for himself: "Remember that up there in New York you are a long way from our problems which we are face to face with every day and you do not know the delicate mechanism with which progress advances in the South and how easily this may be thrown out of gear."[40] Newbold soon glimpsed the future as county superintendents began writing him about potential lawsuits charging discrimination in education. Newbold cautioned one superintendent that African Americans "know more about the law and they know more about the application of the law in general education in the general understanding of the affairs of life than many of us give them credit for knowing." He counseled black citizens to resolve equity issues with local authorities rather than seeking legal redress but warned superintendents that lawsuits were inevitable "unless there is a conscientious effort on the part of our school authorities to be fair and just in executing the school law as it applies to Negro children."[41]

By 1930, North Carolina's education department could no longer keep the NAACP at bay. Walter White offered to join black teachers in Lumberton in mounting a legal challenge to salary discrimination. State Superintendent A. T. Allen ordered Newbold to "find some way, if we possibly can, to keep him [White] out of North Carolina" and worried that "it would be almost suicidal for us if we should even tentatively agree for him to come into the State."[42] Thus, even though they agreed that pay equity was desirable, white state officials silenced themselves rather than enter a new arena of negotiation, the courtroom.

Rosenwald building agents and Negro school agents like Davis and Newbold sincerely believed in their own goals and methods, and they deserve credit for what they achieved in a twenty-year span. Yet despite its usefulness in demonstrating those achievements, the Rosenwald building program also delineated their limitations—the agents' enduring presumptions of paternalistic racial leadership, class privilege, and racial separation, and the persistence of racial discrimination within state departments of education. Edwin R. Embree acknowledged this ambivalence in his decree that the building program should cease so that the Rosenwald Fund could act as a stimulus to change rather than as a crutch for existing programs. He seemed to minimize the significance of the fund's major enterprise for southern public school systems and overlook its enduring appeal at the local level. Nevertheless, he grasped that the Rosenwald building program could only treat, not cure, one symptom of an inherently discriminatory system.

Consequently, when Embree acted on that analysis to close down the Rosenwald Fund's southern school program, he also terminated support for the African American men who held posts as Rosenwald building agents. Embree followed the precedent set by Julius Rosenwald, who had always argued that his grant programs offered only temporary incentives and had clearly instructed his philanthropic foundation to adapt to the changing needs of the present. In the spring of 1927, Rosenwald had sent word to Samuel L. Smith that he wanted to halve his contribution to the Rosenwald building agents' salaries and eliminate Virginia's salary grant entirely to encourage self-reliance by state departments of education. Samuel Smith convinced the Chicago office that states would simply drop the building agents altogether instead, so saving their jobs.[43]

Five years later, in the depths of the Great Depression, Rosenwald building agents lost their salary support for good. The General Education Board continued funding the white state agents for Negro schools, and the staffs of the other divisions at state education departments created with its sponsorship, such as the divisions of schoolhouse planning. But the black Rosenwald building agents found their careers less certain. Robert Russa Moton appealed to the General Education Board for a scholarship so that Alabama Rosenwald agent Marquis Griffin could attend Tuskegee until job prospects improved. Some succeeded in convincing white school officials that African Americans were essential members of the state education bureaucracy. Nolen Irby, Arkansas agent for Negro schools, fought hard for Rosenwald building agent Rufus C. Childress. Irby credited Childress and his predecessor, Percy Dorman, for ensuring that black schools were "modern and adequately equipped" and was appalled by the prospect of losing the Rosenwald Fund's salary support for a man with eleven years of field experience who was now sixty-five years old and with limited financial resources. Irby insisted that S. L. Smith scrounge up funding for July and August, after which Childress received a joint appointment as Arkansas' assistant supervisor for Negro elementary and county training schools, with salary support from the John F. Slater Fund, and as director of extension at the Pine Bluff AM&N College.[44]

State agents for Negro schools and Rosenwald building agents had their own reasons for embracing the school-building program. Their motivations joined personal commitment to black advancement through education with Progressive educational reforms and professional aspirations for themselves and black schools. Although only one aspect of their work, the Rosenwald school-building program's tangible results made it an especially effective vehicle for agents' personal and professional goals. Agents used the financial and professional leverage that the Rosenwald program afforded them to pressure other professionals, public officials, and citizens to support black public education. Consequently, the agents' success in building Rosenwald schools became a measure of their effectiveness, and a justification for expanding state support for black education. Although limited by agents' willingness to accept segregation, some agents used the Rosenwald program as a material strategy for achieving equity between black and white schools.

By the end of the Rosenwald building program in 1932, state agents for Negro schools and Rosenwald building agents had explored the possibilities and the limits of interracial cooperation between black and white professionals. White and black agents operated in overlapping but quite different worlds, within which they marshaled their professional and public constituencies behind the common goal of new school buildings. Their positions as the intermediaries between Rosenwald program administrators and Rosenwald school communities gave them great latitude and influence over the operation of the building program. For their statewide campaigns to succeed, however, they had relied on more than administrative directives or sympathetic readers of professional journals. Agents depended on the people of countless southern communities to take up the Rosenwald program as their own crusade.

PART III

Rosenwald Schools
in African American Communities

7

Local People and
School-Building Campaigns

Julius Rosenwald never intended that his name should represent African American public school buildings. His collaboration with Booker T. Washington caught the imagination of rural African Americans, their community leaders, and sympathetic white activists. The philanthropists and educational leaders who developed the Rosenwald school-building program intentionally involved a broad array of southerners, believing that the experience of the shared effort of building new schools for black children would make all of them better people. At the same time, they presumed, participants would transform their communities by adding a modern institution to the rural southern landscape that would stand as a beacon of hope for black children and the promise of racial harmony for all.

Local people, the subject of part 3, made their presence known at every step of the administrative evolution of the Rosenwald building program. They were not unwelcome, but their number and insistence both pleased and confounded Rosenwald program officials. Beginning with Booker T. Washington's original six-school experiment, Rosenwald school planners had assumed that their program would operate from the top down, through hierarchies of class, race, gender, and professional expertise. Julius Rosenwald and Tuskegee officials, and later the Rosenwald Fund's trustees and staff in Chicago, would set the policies and provide the money. Professional administrators at Tuskegee Institute and then the Rosenwald Fund's Southern Office in Nashville would implement those policies and distribute the money through state departments of education, relying heavily on state agents for Negro schools and the Rosenwald building agents. The Negro school agents and Rosenwald building agents in turn would run the building projects through the county school superintendents. These white and black men also expected that they could count on female African American educators and Jeanes industrial supervising teachers, as well as male educators and community leaders such as ministers and school trustees to take the Rosenwald message to rural African Americans.

A common thread of paternalism ran through these intersecting chains of command, one that began with Washington's 1914 request for promotional funds to pay local organizers, continued through the careers of Rosenwald building agents and state Negro school agents, and received emphatic attention with the building program's major reorganizations in 1920 and 1928. At every step, Rosenwald program planners and administrators assumed that rural black southerners required expert guidance from outside leaders to achieve a modern school. That paternalism persisted despite overwhelming evidence of local people's initiative and determination to build their own ideal.

Self-help was the key to local participation, embedded in the Rosenwald building program's demand that community members donate at least as much as their Rosenwald grant. Intended to elicit greater public funding for black school buildings, this requirement was often burdensome and sometimes punitive for rural black southerners. Even so, mandating the direct participation of southern African Americans in building Rosenwald schools reinforced a preexisting African American educational tradition and harnessed that tradition to the cause of modern public education. It also forced white southerners to acknowledge the material value of black southerners' contributions to their own public schools and to recognize black school-building campaigns as not unlike the school-improvement campaigns waged by some whites in their own communities. Uniting their local efforts with the power and prestige of state government and a northern philanthropy, rural black southerners buttressed their existing community institutions and identities, demanded public recognition and support from white authorities, and created modern symbols of black progress. Ultimately, black southerners proved the essential component of the coalition that built a Rosenwald school and gave it meaning within a local context.

African American Leadership and Initiative

The Rosenwald school-building program at one level was the product of a fortuitous meeting of minds between Booker T. Washington and Julius Rosenwald. But as James D. Anderson and other scholars have pointed out, the program gained its strength from grassroots supporters. Thus, at a deeper level, the Rosenwald school program represented the conjunction of a historic African American quest for the emancipatory power of learning with a newer group of allies. Historian Adam Fairclough locates Rosenwald schools within the broad sweep of African Americans' independent search for the "literacy and learning

... essential to their freedom."[1] The presence of that deep undercurrent of grass-roots activism and the development of its own leadership account for the welcome that southern African Americans gave to Washington and Rosenwald's program and for their persistence throughout the building program's changing policies and leadership and the vicissitudes of their own lives.

Local people did not wait for someone to offer them a Rosenwald school. They often started working on one before anyone at Tuskegee or Nashville received an application, acting on their cultural capital of "group consciousness and collective identity" to elicit local resources toward a shared goal of a new community institution.[2] This kind of local initiative burst forth in 1912 as soon as Julius Rosenwald announced his fiftieth-birthday gift to Tuskegee Institute, and it resumed vigorously in 1914 with the announcement that Booker T. Washington had convinced Julius Rosenwald to support new schools for black children across the American South. African American educators—principals, Jeanes supervisors, and teachers—were the local activists most likely to take the initiative, as well as two other leadership groups identified with education: school trustees and ministers.

Local educators embraced Rosenwald schools out of the same mixture of professional standards and personal commitment to "uplifting the race" as their counterparts at the state level. Their own experiences blended the concept of racial uplift promoted by African American professionals and activists with the Progressives' concern for raising professional standards.[3] Like Georgia's Beulah Rucker, who secured a Rosenwald grant for the school she founded in Gainesville, black educators had grown up in families that instilled them with a faith in education and sacrificed for their training; now they had a duty to the community's next wave of school patrons and children.[4] They labored in communities where school patrons expected teachers to act on that duty, and where teachers depended on patrons to fund their salaries for longer school terms, to maintain and supply schoolrooms, and if necessary to provide a home for themselves and the school. Black school teachers also provided key role models, for African American southerners also saw their schools as training grounds for the next generation of black leaders. As a writer in the *Louisiana Colored Teachers' Journal* had argued in opposition to white teachers in black schools, "under present conditions southern white teachers can never reach the hearts of Negro children and arouse therein a full conception of manhood and womanhood."[5]

Black principals, who typically were classroom teachers in addition to their administrative duties, were acutely aware of community needs and their own responsibilities. A few principals worked their requests up through the educational racial hierarchy, like the principal of Florida's Clearwater Colored School, E. L. Snyder, who prompted Pinellas County superintendent Dixie M. Hollins to send a letter of inquiry to Tuskegee Institute.[6] Most acted more directly, obtaining the needed information and beginning building campaigns before they brought white school authorities into the process. E. P. Simmons in 1918 started a five-year campaign for a Rosenwald building at Hollandale, Mississippi, where he served as principal of the black high school.[7] Another Mississippi principal, Eva L. Gordon, "began immediately working with the community people to raise money to qualify for a Rosenwald Fund Grant" after her election as principal of the Pike County Training School in 1919; the new building opened in 1921.[8] Similarly, I. E. Bryan secured a Rosenwald grant for a new school within two years of becoming principal of a school at Keysville, Georgia, in 1919.[9] Principal John L. Hairston organized a school-improvement league in East Martinsville, Virginia, in 1926, but it took six years before the new Rosenwald school opened in 1932.[10]

Jeanes industrial supervising teachers were ideal leaders for local Rosenwald building campaigns because of their expertise as community organizers of school-improvement projects. Jeanes supervisors were among the most prominent female community leaders in the rural South, holding their positions independently of any individual black school or principal, and reporting directly to the white county superintendent and state Negro school agent.[11] Alabama Negro school agent J. S. Lambert credited "the wholesome influence of supervising industrial teachers on the work of school building and improvement," claiming, "No phase of the work among negroes is commanding such enthusiastic interest on their part as that of promoting the building of Rosenwald schools."[12]

Booker T. Washington had tried from the start to involve Jeanes teachers in community campaigns for Rosenwald schools. Jeanes supervisors needed little direction and moved quickly to get Rosenwald aid for their counties. One of the first to act was the supervisor of Bullock County, Alabama, who convinced Clinton J. Calloway to add her county to the Rosenwald program in 1914.[13] C. D. Perry of Aiken, South Carolina, who attended the 1916 Jeanes supervisors' conference in North Carolina, was upset to discover that Rosenwald was giving money for schools in that state and not her own. With unconscious irony she appealed to the Jewish philanthropist to broaden his gifts to South Carolina: "We realize that you are a christian gentleman and as such you are interested in our people, in the attempt to make better citizens of them."[14] Louisiana's 1916 Wildsville School project was the brainchild of Jeanes supervisor Mary

N. Smith, who had begun the campaign over a year before Negro school agent Leo M. Favrot visited her community.[15]

Orchestrating Rosenwald school campaigns remained a Jeanes supervisor specialty for the next fifteen years. The Jeanes supervisor in Fluvanna County, Virginia, one of a small number of male Jeanes workers, wrote in 1929 that the completion of a two-teacher Rosenwald school "in the face of the strongest opposition," was "the most outstanding achievement of our entire career as Jeanes' supervisor in this county."[16] In 1929, the Rosenwald Fund paid homage to Virginia E. Randolph, whose example had inspired the entire Jeanes industrial supervising teacher program, and indirectly to all Jeanes teachers for their contributions to its building program. Randolph's five-room training school at Glen Ellen, Virginia, had burned early that year. While Henrico County's board of education deliberated on funding a new school, James Hardy Dillard directed Randolph to the Rosenwald Fund, which contributed a large grant of $5,000 for a two-story, ten-teacher brick building.[17]

"How can a teacher or community secure the $400 from the Rosenwald fund?" Memphis schoolteacher Helen Smith Casey asked Clinton J. Calloway in 1916.[18] For African American teachers, especially those in the rural South, school-improvement projects had been a necessary complement to classroom instruction since the end of the Civil War. Outside philanthropies offered ways to stretch patron contributions and meager public dollars. Teachers like Casey sought out Rosenwald grants, acting on their own when they worked at small schools without principals. Aurelia Pugh wanted copies of building plans to encourage her Grove Hill School patrons to raise money for a new school and consider consolidation with another school. A recent graduate of Tuskegee Institute, Inez O. Edwards was horrified by the "pitiful condition" of the community and school at Curry, Alabama. After just a few days on the job, she wrote to the state Negro school agent for help.[19] Schoolteacher F. H. Edwards informed North Carolina's state agent for Negro schools in 1916 that school patrons in Everetts already had cut 7,000 feet of timber and hauled it to their building site; now they needed some of the Rosenwald money that his wife had heard about at her Jeanes supervisors' conference.[20] Classroom teachers were not the only interested educators. In Georgia, Sumter County's African American agricultural extension agent took charge of a decade-long, countywide building program that produced five schools, two teachers' homes, and two shop buildings.[21]

In several instances, the educators who sparked successful Rosenwald school campaigns were actually continuing or reviving earlier local initiatives to obtain

Rosenwald money. Isaiah Whitley, principal of the African American school at Plateau in Mobile County, Alabama, inquired about Rosenwald funds for the first time in August 1912 after reading of Tuskegee Institute's role in distributing a portion of Julius Rosenwald's fiftieth-birthday gift. Like a number of other principals of schools with secondary and industrial programs, Whitley hoped to benefit from Rosenwald's gift for Tuskegee offshoots, only to be turned aside. Two years later, Whitley joined a second throng of correspondents seeking the dollar-for-dollar aid erroneously described in Tuskegee's initial announcement of the Rosenwald school-building program. Again Washington declined his request, sending a copy of the "Plan for Erection of Rural Schoolhouses" to show that Rosenwald money was meant for small rural schools only.[22] Whitley bided his time, enlisting the good offices of the state department of education in his campaign for a new and better building. At the end of 1916, he finally won a special appropriation of $600, rather than the plan's maximum $500, for the Mobile County Training School.[23]

African Americans living on the fringes of the South had a longer wait. Another of Tuskegee's 1914 correspondents was educator J. R. Coffey of Wewoka, Oklahoma, who asked for Rosenwald assistance to add classrooms, a music room, and a library to the school in the all-black town of Lima, which had just incorporated the previous year. Washington rejected Coffey's request as coming from a state and for purposes outside the current Rosenwald plan. Seven years later, following the 1920 reorganization and expansion of the school-building program, Lima citizens could watch the construction of Rosenwald Hall, a handsome brick four-teacher school (figure 43).[24] Under Oklahoma's separate school laws, African American school districts in all-black towns like Lima were the legally constituted majority school districts and received the full appropriation of state school funds; any white school in a majority black district was the "separate" school. Thus Lima's Rosenwald Hall was constructed with $1,200 from the Rosenwald Fund and $9,000 of public school funds.

Vocational agriculture teacher and Tuskegee alumnus Robert Taylor Gilmore of Marianna, Florida, grafted the Rosenwald program to his ongoing efforts at building schools. When Gilmore took a position as principal of black students at the Marianna Industrial School, a Florida state reform school, in 1909, not a single black public school stood in Jackson County. Gilmore claimed to have built three schools and inspired "many others to be built" over the next eight years.[25] Perhaps he prompted the Marianna Industrial School's secretary-treasurer to contact Booker T. Washington for help in 1914, having "just read an editorial on Mr. Rosenwald's generous offer to negro schools."[26]

Figure 43. Rosenwald Hall, Lima, Seminole County, Oklahoma, 1921. African Americans in Lima, one of Oklahoma's historic all-black towns incorporated in 1913, began petitioning Tuskegee Institute for a Rosenwald grant in 1914. Rosenwald Hall is a good example of a Rosenwald school that does not follow either a Tuskegee or a Rosenwald Fund plan. (Photograph by author)

Gilmore himself contacted Clinton Calloway in 1917 for assistance in raising funds to rebuild one of his schools that had been destroyed by a hurricane. The Rosenwald school that would bear his name was not constructed until 1922, after Gilmore moved to the county training school as its Smith-Hughes vocational teacher and principal. He set to work on the self-help requirement, donating three acres of land himself and securing the labor of local men to begin construction. Next he had the county superintendent submit an article to the local newspaper in which Gilmore pitched his venture to white residents' values as "good Christians" and their economic self-interest because they could not "successfully compete with other sections if in one the laborers are ignorant and degraded when in the other they are educated and elevated." The new two-story limestone building won a Rosenwald grant of $1,500 and, with "Gilmore Academy" carved above its entrance, appropriately memorialized a dogged campaigner for Jackson County's black schools.[27]

The prospect of a Rosenwald school inspired African American community leaders outside the classroom. Black school trustees, whether elected by school patrons or appointed by the white county superintendent or school board, eagerly grasped an opportunity to build upon their independent labors with a Rosenwald grant. D. P. Prater, chair of Piedmont, Alabama's black school trustee board, anxiously inquired about the Rosenwald program: "We did [not] know anything About the rosenwald before we Began Building therefore we went ahead and Done the Best we could we have gone as far as we can with out help our School need painting Black Bords Library water tank if there is any fon you help us pleas do so . . . we al are farmers own our Home."[28]

Far removed from Prater in class, location, and influence was Thomas Junius Calloway, brother of Tuskegee Extension Department director C. J. Calloway and a prominent member of Washington's "Bookerite" clique in the nation's capital, as well as an attorney, realtor, and a leader of the Maryland Inter-Racial Commission. T. J. Calloway was one of several trustees who conducted a survey of black school buildings in Prince George's County, Maryland, to assess and publicize the need for more Rosenwald campaigns.[29] Such trustee-led school drives provided the needed catalyst for new schools where local white authorities had not responded to materials circulated by the state agent for Negro schools. In 1928, African American trustees of the Springfield School in Tate County, Mississippi, instigated a campaign for "a three teachers school with the help of the Rosenwall Aid" by writing directly to Negro school agent Perry H. Easom, who offered them and the county superintendent a Rosenwald bonus for this "backward county" school.[30]

Ministers also could address state and county school officials with the authority of their calling and the support of congregations that had long taken responsibility for black schools when county boards of education would not. Rev. R. B. Angel began the long process of building a school with a May 1919 letter to Alabama Negro school agent J. S. Lambert: "dear Sir we ar try to bild a School on your plan here at Zin [Zion] Rest 3 ½ mils east of wedowee ala. . . . we have a little one room bilding cost us about $700 but we want to get on your plan."[31] The Rev. Amos H. Carnegie, armed with experience in six Rosenwald school campaigns in South Carolina, went to work on another school soon after he became pastor of the Methodist Episcopal Church in Marion, Virginia. He organized local masons and unskilled laborers to construct the $20,000 brick school, for which the Smyth County School Board purchased the site and materials and the Rosenwald Fund contributed $1,200.[32]

African American local initiative remained critical until the very end of the Rosenwald program. Persistent requests from black school supervisor B. A. Morse and community members of Montclair, Florida, finally paid off with a new Rosenwald building in 1929 that replaced an 1898 structure.[33] In 1929, teacher M. M. Leak wrote from his school in Tippo, Mississippi, to the state board of education because "we have been ask to built a consolidated Rosen Wall School at this place which is very much needed." When Vincent H. Harris began his travels as Georgia's Rosenwald building agent in 1930, he was surprised by the extent of local initiative he encountered. "I often find a small community raising money that there is no record on file for them," he reported, "but they understand about the Rosenwald school."[34]

White Leadership and Local Paternalism

Some white southerners took the initiative in Rosenwald campaigns as well, motivated by their own blend of professional aspirations, personal values, and business interests. Their actions demonstrated the power of white paternalism at the local level, where they controlled the flow of state funds into community schools. Paternalist—and maternalist—whites also recognized their economic dependence on black laborers, and the significance of educational opportunities for keeping that labor force on southern land. Rosenwald schools offered these individuals an opportunity to act on self-interest and to show good faith in interracial cooperation.

County school superintendents were the most likely white Rosenwald community activists. The state agents for Negro schools intensively recruited county school authorities, declaring that they had a professional and civic duty to improve the black public schools under their jurisdiction.[35] Rosenwald program staff, Negro school agents, and Rosenwald building agents courted county superintendents by sending them promotional materials, visiting their offices, proffering staff assistance and financial aid, and rewarding them with praise and more offers of aid. In response, superintendents wrote letters to Negro school agents, to C. J. Calloway at Tuskegee, to S. L. Smith in Nashville, to the Chicago office of the Julius Rosenwald Fund, and directly to Booker T. Washington and Julius Rosenwald, asking how they could get Rosenwald money.

Some county superintendents came to their positions already interested in educational reforms such as consolidation and transportation and eager to demonstrate their affinity with contemporary educational movements. In counties with Jeanes industrial supervising teachers, superintendents were already accustomed to school-improvement campaigns in black communities. The opportunity to boost limited local and state funds with outside contributions made the addition of black schools to the county's building program more acceptable to superintendents and their school boards. The Rosenwald building program also reaffirmed superintendents' role as paternalists who functioned as intermediaries between black citizens, the local school board, and the state department of education, and gave them positive publicity when local newspapers published their announcements about Rosenwald grants they had secured for new schools.[36]

County superintendents' letters document their newfound interest in black schools. W. R. Mills wrote to the North Carolina Negro school agent soon after accepting the superintendency of Craven County's schools, noting that a friend had just told him to look into the Rosenwald Fund but "Fran[k]ly I had never heard of this fund; please tell me something about it."[37] Escambia County, Alabama, superintendent W. S. Neal was better informed and realized that he could use the financial incentive to upgrade black schools to state-approved designs: "This is the first effort made in this county to build a state [plan] negro schoolhouse. . . . I have worked hard to do something for the negroes in this county and this is the first success I have had." B. H. Boyd wrote from Geneva County to demonstrate his sympathy with new ideas about rural education: "The thing I wish most to do is to build some decent colored school houses in this county."[38] Some clearly understood that, as state Negro school agents promised, they could demonstrate their professional caliber by endorsing black school initiatives like Rosenwald schools. Charl Ormond Williams, school superintendent of Shelby County, Tennessee, told Tennessee Negro school agent Samuel L. Smith that she felt "it [was] time to begin erecting some good colored schoolhouses." She asked him to petition the Tuskegee Extension Department for twelve Rosenwald buildings in 1917. Her work laid a foundation for Shelby County to amass the largest number of Rosenwald schools in Tennessee and, together with her consolidation and construction program for white schools, took Williams to the presidency of the National Education Association and a position at the organization's Washington, D.C., headquarters.[39]

County superintendents made common cause with elite whites who wanted Rosenwald schools for their own self-interest. Towel magnate James W. Cannon, for example, donated the land for a Rosenwald school planned at Kannapolis, North Carolina, by the Cabarrus County superintendent and local patrons.[40] Delta counties in Mississippi demonstrated the confluence of professional and economic interests that motivated white superintendent and planter initiative for Rosenwald campaigns. Peter F. Williams, superintendent of schools in Coahoma County, embarked on an ambitious Rosenwald school campaign after completing a consolidation and construction program for white schools. Williams planned to construct fifty Rosenwald-aided schools, grouping a three-teacher consolidated school, shop, and teachers' home in each district and locating the county training school near Clarksdale. His appeal to local planters emphasized the economic benefits of their tax investment: "I think I have convinced these plantation owners that many of the Negroes are moving away trying to find better educational opportunities for their children and that more will leave unless we provide for them decent schools and better homes."[41] Indeed, the Clarksdale Rotary Club adopted a lengthy set of resolutions congratulating themselves for "being at all times sensible of the obligation resting upon them to extend to the colored race help and symp[a]thy and kindness" and praising Julius Rosenwald and the Rosenwald Fund for "the most generous and timely donations" that had produced in their county "the finest system of vocational schools for the practical education of the colored race that now exists in the South."[42]

The Coahoma plan became a regional model. Following Coahoma County's success in retarding black out-migration with a Rosenwald construction program, Leflore County planters and business leaders publicly endorsed a one-mill tax to supplement Rosenwald aid and local contributions for ten groups of one and three-teacher schools.[43] Leflore's construction program then prompted Glendora merchant and planter J. S. Equen to seek funds for a two-teacher Rosenwald school in his own county: "These buildings are being put up in great number over Leflore County—and as [we] adjoin Leflore county, we are very anxious to build one here in Tallahatchee Co."[44]

Elite white women joined their men in viewing Rosenwald schools as an economic tool for attracting and retaining Mississippi's black labor force. Mrs. W. D. Hughes wrote from Coila to ask for information that her husband could present at a school meeting because "these schools are a success in Carroll [County] and we are deeply interested in these schools."[45] Letters written by elite white women evidence a maternalist ethos as well as an open recognition of the same economic self-interest that prompted white men to work for Rosenwald schools. These women expressed sympathetic concern for black schools in their requests for assistance and viewed their efforts as part of a Progressive reform campaign. Mrs. Julian B. Ennis wrote from her husband's "Lee Place" plantation, asking Alabama Negro school agent Lambert to "make clear to the negros just what the state will do for them and also advise them in regard to the Rosenwald Fund."[46] From Nitta Yuma, Mississippi, Mrs. Ellen B. Phelps Crump wrote to the Rosenwald Fund about obtaining a teachers' cottage to accompany the Rosenwald school already on her "place" that could be used as a community center by the county home demonstration agent and black women's clubs.[47] Other white Mississippians followed Ellen Crump's example: in Sunflower County, the Mayes Brothers Plantation donated the site for the Lombardy School, another group of planters gave $5,000 of the $8,400 needed for construction of the five-teacher Sunflower Plantation School on their property, and a Mrs. Baird sought aid for the school on her plantation.[48]

Sometimes whites acted as facilitators or patrons for African American applicants out of long-standing interest in and relationships with black educators, while others played the role of "white friend." In 1914, Principal T. J. Elder had written from Sandersville, Georgia, to Booker T. Washington: "I write you in reference to the offer of the Gentleman in Chicago of the Firm of Sears & Roebuck &c. Please send me details of the gift—and upon what plans or conditions." In return, he received only one of Washington's rejection letters.[49] Three years later, Elder successfully secured Rosenwald aid for the first time for a vocational building; after another nine years, G. S. Dickerman, a former agent of the John F. Slater Fund, took up Elder's case again. He published an appeal from his home in New Haven, Connecticut: "What if generous friends from the North should join with the local School Board, assisted by the Rosenwald Fund and what the people themselves could do, to replace the dingy old school-house that has done duty for thirty years with a commodious, substantial building that would be an ornament to the place?"[50] In Mount Dora, Florida, teachers remembered that white "winter visitor" Dr. Duncan C. Milner had been the ally who helped to secure a Rosenwald grant for a four-room school known as Milner-Rosenwald School.[51]

In other cases, county superintendents adapted their typical patronage practice of delegating all responsibility for black schools to a selected African American. T. B. Bonner wrote Alabama's Negro school agent James L. Sibley: "I have been informed by Superintendent Dowdle that you would aid our school to $300 if we would raise 300[.] I am ready to take up the work." Methodist minister M. C. Pulliam contacted Tuskegee Institute in 1918 after the county superintendent turned over Rosenwald materials to him for action. Two months later he wrote again for a set of plans because "I am sure it will help me greatly in raising the money. I appointed the building committee and they ask for the plan."[52]

Of course, local people of both races were not the only catalysts for Rosenwald schools. Inquiries from community members document the success of state agents for Negro schools, Rosenwald building agents, and Rosenwald program officials at Tuskegee and Nashville in publicizing the Rosenwald school-building program. The white state agents for Negro schools and assistant Negro school agents toured communities to organize construction projects as well, especially in the early years of the program.[53] Rosenwald building agents were especially influential outsiders and perceived themselves as leaders of school-building campaigns even when they had responded to local requests. Their efforts were appreciated and remembered: a 1947 local history recalled that the

Payne Rosenwald school building in Limestone County, Alabama, originated in a visit by Booker T. Washington Jr. that led to a two-year fund-raising drive and construction of the school in 1920.[54] Marquis Griffin attracted the notice of the Hale County superintendent, who credited Griffin with convincing African Americans to begin fund-raising for a new county training school. Decades later, L. M. Randolph remembered that Hurtsboro, Alabama, community members had decided to consolidate their two schools in 1927. "They raised money from every source they possibly could. There was a Mr. M. H. Griffin of Montgomery who was in charge of the Rosenwald Fund at that time.... And we raised enough money that we built the Rosenwald school."[55]

As all agents could testify, their own efforts meant little without local interest and commitment. African American and white community leaders who took the initiative for Rosenwald schools found that their campaigns succeeded if they found the necessary allies at local and state levels, and where their neighbors agreed that a Rosenwald school meshed with their needs and their desires.

ROSENWALD CAMPAIGNS AS STRATEGIES FOR LEVERAGING SOCIAL RIGHTS

Whether initiated by local people who "understand about the Rosenwald school," black community leaders, white citizens, or the county superintendent, and regardless of whether they conducted their campaigns in the Tuskegee era or by dealing with the Nashville office, Rosenwald school-building campaigns shared some common experiences—inspiration, sacrifice, inertia, dispute, celebration—yet defied uniformity. Examining the elements of a local Rosenwald building campaign can reveal how local people translated a reform movement led by outsiders into their own agenda for their community's future. As they did, black and white southerners worked with and against each other in unaccustomed ways, as when white county superintendents entered unfamiliar black communities to show support for a Rosenwald school, or when black church congregations overcame denominational rivalries to campaign jointly for a new schoolhouse. Consequently, the process of constructing a Rosenwald school was never as standardized as the paperwork trail that marked its progress. Many factors contributed to the success or failure of each local Rosenwald building campaign and shaped the way that it proceeded: the attitudes of the various black and white people involved at the state and local level, differences in state and local funding mechanisms for public education, and the intricacies of social, political, and economic conditions in any given community.

The seemingly straightforward process of qualifying for aid, constructing the school, and receiving a Rosenwald grant became a complex negotiation, largely because of the dual requirements for direct support by local black citizens and public ownership of the school. Furthermore, the public nature of the Rosenwald school-building program addressed the politics of race and school reform. As many participants in Rosenwald school campaigns knew and later scholars have documented, Progressive reform for black education had been predicated on the disfranchisement of black men. Far from rendering black schools a mechanism for silencing powerless black southerners, reforms like the Rosenwald school-building program offered an alternative route to citizenship rights. Rosenwald schools became tools that African Americans wielded to leverage social rights out of the Jim Crow South. Campaigns for Rosenwald schools, as recent sociological analyses demonstrate, "allowed southern blacks to partly achieve their educational policy objectives when they were completely excluded from formal politics and when state repression and the loss of civil rights made protest and insurgency prohibitively costly."[56]

Contacting Rosenwald and state officials for information about the building program was a first step to a new, modern public school building that met black aspirations. In most cases, the next step was a trip to the county superintendent's office or a meeting of the board of education. State agents for Negro schools and the Rosenwald program staff at Tuskegee and Nashville usually referred correspondents to their local school superintendents, who had to fill out and sign Rosenwald grant application forms. Before submitting an application for Rosenwald aid, the county superintendent had to select a building plan, ensure that a suitable site had been located, determine that black citizens had pledged enough of their own funds, and obtain approval and funding from the county board of education. State agents for Negro schools and Rosenwald building agents hoped that their promotional campaigns on behalf of black schools, and Rosenwald schools in particular, had prepared the superintendents for action.

When local black citizens and the white superintendent cooperated, they could present a united front to the county school board on the one hand and to state authorities on the other and establish an orderly chain of communication about the progress of the project. For example, having already discussed their interest in a new school and settled on a building plan with North Carolina Negro school agent N. C. Newbold, African American citizens appeared before the Hertford County Board of Education in September 1915 "and stated what they could pay on the house." Hertford County superintendent N. W. Britton then wrote Newbold to assure him that the county would pay in $400 and the patrons another $400 to secure $350 from the Rosenwald building program.[57] In communities like this, building a Rosenwald school brought local white school authorities into the process as the last link of the official chain of command. African American school patrons gave local school authorities an alternative interpretation to their role as white paternalists by casting them as the public servants of black community leaders and citizens.

Rosenwald school campaigns could help break through the indifference and hostility that black citizens usually encountered when they petitioned local white school authorities for increased school funding.[58] African American school patrons were harder to ignore or resist if they appeared in the superintendent's office or at school board meetings with news of Rosenwald financial assistance to combine with their own contributions or petitions from black school trustees. Black school patrons in Hawthorne, Florida, for example, persevered until both Rosenwald program administrators and local school authorities accepted their demands. A. D. Nelson of Hawthorne had inquired about the building program in 1914; perhaps another family member was the "Josh Nelson" who, with Chester Shell and seven other black men, repeatedly petitioned the Alachua County Board of Education for a school from 1922 to 1925. Shell finally won approval for a Rosenwald school in 1926 after raising $11,000 from his network of contacts with affluent whites that he had met in his career as railroad porter and sports guide.[59] According to Vincent H. Harris, as late as 1931, African Americans in Twiggs County, Georgia, had "never in their lives gone to the Local Board and asked for anything." One of the fifteen patrons whom he urged to attend a county board of education meeting made the attempt and, to the man's surprise, was invited to speak and to return with more patrons to a future meeting.[60]

Other African American southerners used the Rosenwald school-building program to invoke the power of state government over unwilling county school officials. Eddie Jeter of Carlisle, South Carolina, called upon state agent for Negro schools J. B. Felton to reprimand the local school board. "We as the colord trustees and patrons have went to work and got four acres of land, had it seveyed and deeds drawn and put in the Hands of the Supt. more then a year ago," Jeter wrote, being sure to tell Felton, "we plan to build a Rosenwall School." Community members had followed all the proper procedures and done more than the required amount of self-help, for according to Jeter they had "sawed cut and haul some where between 10 an 11 thousand feet of framing" in addition to contributing the land. After meeting every program requirement, "we can not Go any futher now. our white trustees and Supt. want [won't] do any for us. And we want some plan from you as what is best for us to do." Mentioning a Rosenwald campaign to the state agent for Negro schools was a sure-fire way to gain official attention to an otherwise routine example of discriminatory neglect. Felton forwarded Jeter's letter to county superintendent Frances Beaty with an offer of help, which finally brought county board action and the construction of the two-teacher Mount Rowell School in 1931.[61]

African American southerners like Jeter realized that they could leverage their direct connections with state officials and the monetary value of their contributions to force white support. If the Rosenwald program demanded African American self-help and public control of their schools, black southerners reasoned that Rosenwald officials were their natural allies against intransigent local school authorities. Rural African Americans made numerous complaints and requests for assistance from the Negro school agents. North Carolina's state agents for Negro schools, Nathan C. Newbold and William F. Credle, certainly found themselves continually responding to grievances lodged by black citizens who expected state action. Harvey Foster asked W. F. Credle to intervene in the stalled Rosenwald campaign for a new Tucker's Grove School:

> Remember we are crowded to death. 78 pupils of all grades from 1 to 7 reciting in the same room. A building about 18 by 24. Remember also that Prof. Beam the Co. Sup. had $280. turned over to him two years ago to put up a Rosenwald Bdg. The only thing he has done is to pile some lumber on the ground to warp and rot in the Sun. Mr. G. E. Davis [the Rosenwald building agent] can give you all the information you desire about conditions at Tuckers for he has been on the ground and know all about it. Sir, we need your help. Please come to our rescue.

Credle wrote to the offending Lincoln County superintendent and asked Foster to keep him informed if work did not get underway immediately, promising that "I shall in turn jog Mr. Beam's memory."[62]

Distance, white skin, and state authority allowed state agents for Negro schools to tell local authorities what their black constituents thought but might have not felt safe to say. The Brunswick County superintendent canceled his Rosenwald applications, saying board members and white voters opposed more taxes, and tried to blame the failed projects on black residents who "tax themselves to build churches and lodge rooms, and lose sight of the importance of schoolhouses," after N. C. Newbold took local school authorities to task. Newbold warned that their reluctance to spend money on black schools would not only halt a Rosenwald school project but would jeopardize all of their philanthropic grant opportunities: "Our friends, the General Education Board, the Smith-Hughes Fund and the Slater Board would not be willing to continue helping a proposition [the Brunswick County Training School at Southport] that is stagnant and where apparently no effort is being made to improve conditions.[63]

Like his African American constituents, Newbold called upon the power of the philanthropies to which he reported as financial leverage. But he also alluded to the power of African Americans as citizens and as voters for moral and political leverage. After complaints from local African Americans revealed that the Granville County school board had abandoned a proposed Rosenwald plan for a less expensive building at Stem, Newbold reminded the white school board members that they had a duty, as well as political self-interest, to respond to black voters' expectations:

> I am sure you can understand the disappointment suffered by the colored people in your community in the change of this plan. . . . You will agree with me I am sure that it is very much better to have a satisfied, contented group of people of whatever race they may be than it is to have a despondent group. The colored people are very jealous [zealous?] for the education of their children, and they are working very hard to do their part to get good schools. We have heard that the colored people helped as far as they could by their ballot to carry the bond election at Stem for better school buildings. They did this I am sure in the hope their own school would be improved.[64]

Unfortunately, Granville County African Americans and Newbold could never overcome the board's resistance to the model schools of the Rosenwald building program.

An acknowledgment from white school authorities that African Americans had a just claim to public school funds was important to Rosenwald campaign activists, who used Rosenwald money and the state officials who distributed it to pry those resources loose. A few could also assert themselves as voters even if, as at Stem, they could not guarantee any return on their votes. Southern disfranchisement laws eliminated the vast majority, but not all black voters from all elections. African Americans could vote in school bond elections in places where all taxpayers were eligible voters. In such referenda, black voters might in fact hold the balance of power. In North Carolina, state and county officials worried that Durham African Americans would not vote for a 1926 bond issue; black voters were also crucial to Raleigh's bond referenda in the 1920s.[65]

Variations in the methods that southern states used to eliminate black votes, the emergence of political machines that distributed poll tax receipts, and the expansion of the potential black electorate with ratification of the Nineteenth Amendment created or precluded political opportunities. In Tennessee, for example, which did not have a "grandfather clause" or an "understanding" test, black men—and then black women as well—who could pay the poll tax could and did vote. In Memphis and Shelby County, Robert R. Church Jr. led a black Republican political network that provided essential votes for the party and coexisted with Edward H. "Boss" Crump's emerging Democratic machine, which also mobilized black voters. But, as the state's Rosenwald building agent pointed out, the reverse was also true. Without access to the ballot box, African Americans in Haywood County, where extralegal repression did what state law could not, had no leverage with their white school board members.[66] Not surprisingly then, following the hidden agenda of their mentor Booker T. Washington, Rosenwald building agents like Clay and George E. Davis, as well as local school patrons, endorsed political activism, fighting an uphill battle against the white domination of partisan politics and all levels of government that made the Rosenwald building program necessary.

Self-Help and Community Fund-Raising

Black school patrons drew upon two related sources for their leverage with local authorities: established practices of educational self-help on the one hand, and the power and prestige that self-help elicited from the Rosenwald school-building program on the other. Local fund-raising could determine the outcome of a Rosenwald campaign and in the aggregate shaped the contours of the program's expansion across the South. From the beginning, Booker T. Washington had built self-help and community participation into the Rosenwald building program.[67] Since 1915, Julius Rosenwald and his building-program administrators had insisted that communities have their donations in hand before dispensing grant funds. Black school patrons risked censure if they did not live up to official expectations. William C. Graves, secretary to Julius Rosenwald, complained to Robert Russa Moton about the inadequate donation of land valued at $50 by patrons of the Longley school in Arkansas: "Mr. Rosenwald felt that, from appearances, it did not evidence a spirit of sacrifice or even of deep interest on the part of the residents, who relied chiefly on public funds and on his contribution for the school."[68] In North Carolina, state Negro school agent N. C. Newbold grumbled that the $30 in pledges and promises of two days hauling and six days labor for a Rosenwald school in Rockingham County were far too little: "If they really want a school, it seems to me that they ought to do more."[69] African American self-help not only demonstrated commitment to a school but was a tool of deference that pried open public school coffers. Maryland's state agent for Negro schools commented, "We can always more easily secure appropriations from the county levying body when the colored people have a sum to match the requested appropriation."[70]

Self-help at the community level meant repeated sacrifices from black school patrons. As historian James Anderson has pointed out, African Americans paid their taxes and then voluntarily taxed themselves a second time to build and maintain Rosenwald schools.[71] Many southern counties diverted state and local tax revenues for black schools to fund white schools and devoted school bond issues entirely to white school construction, increasing the burden of self-help beyond a "double tax." Nevertheless, black southerners organized themselves for yet another round of the educational fund-raising campaigns they had engaged in for more than half a century. Their activity proclaimed their own belief in the power of a school building as a transmitter of their own values and as a catalyst for economic and social change.[72] Rosenwald building agents, principals, Jeanes supervisors, and leading school patrons orchestrated the many individual donations necessary to demonstrate self-help.

Rosenwald campaign organizers almost invariably held rallies to which they invited community members and leaders and, on many occasions, "white friends" such as the county superintendent, school board members, and the state agent for Negro schools.[73] Their efforts echoed the rally days and special fund-raising events for school-improvement projects commonly used to energize the community and solicit contributions since at least the turn of the century. Clinton Calloway published accounts of some of the first Rosenwald school rallies in the *Messenger*: "Loachapoka, Lee County, Ala. $68.49 Raised in Last Rally. New Schoolhouse in Course of Erection"; "Little Zion Community, Montgomery County Fifty-nine Dollar Rally for Schoolhouse Building"; "One Hundred and One Dollars and Forty-seven Cents Raised for School House Building."[74] By the early 1920s, the rallies had become, in Horace Mann Bond's words, "highly conventionalized, yet peculiarly spontaneous." Likening the building program to "a high-pressure salesmanship campaign," Bond commented on the rally techniques developed by Alabama Rosenwald building agent Marquis H. Griffin, whose carefully planned events sometimes featured staged performances by a leading patron, timed for maximum audience response.[75]

Handbills that advertised the rallies made it clear that audience members should arrive with money in hand. A notice of the "Big Educational Rally" at an Alabama AME Zion Church in September 1918 announced: "Everybody is asked to come and bring a donation for the purpose of erecting a Rosenwald School House. We the undersigned have pledged to pay the amounts opposite our names." The list of names that followed, divided by gender, gave everyone a chance to observe which subscribers actually paid up the night of the rally (figure 44). At the "Big Barbecue" at the Antioch Baptist Church in Chambers County, its promotional handbill cautioned, "Each male patron is asked to pay $1.00 each; each lady is asked to pay 50 cents; each trustee is asked to pay $1.50." But the Friendship Baptist Church in that county had even higher goals. Its poster proclaimed: "EVERY MEMBER OF THE FINANCE COMMITTEE IS EXPECTED TO RAISE $100 EACH. Every one is expected to give all they can afford."[76] For those in the audience, signing their names to the pledge list or handing over money cemented their connection to the school, especially when the newspaper published a list naming each contributor and the amount.[77] Rallies that included white participants and observers bolstered those whites' perceptions of their own paternalistic goodwill while they allowed black patrons to make clear their own expectations of the whites in attendance, most commonly the state agent for Negro schools and county superintendent but also members of the school board and business leaders.

In addition to rallies, the leaders of Rosenwald building campaigns experimented with a variety of fund-raising techniques, including local committees or clubs and competitive money-making schemes. Clinton J. Calloway and William M. Rakestraw organized clubs named after themselves that competed to bring in the largest donations at each successive rally. Booker T. Washington Jr. organized Alabama school patrons into school-builders clubs; Charles H. Moore organized school-improvement leagues for North Carolina Rosenwald schools.[78] Thomas J. Calloway sought his brother Clinton's advice on—and a contribution to—the drive to raise $1,000 for a new Lincoln School building in Prince George's County, Maryland. Patrons there set up clubs named for their alma maters: Howard University, Morgan College, Hampton Institute, Tuskegee Institute, Maryland Normal School, the National Training School for Girls, and Prince George's County Schools.[79] George T. Rouson, pastor of the First Baptist Church in Murfreesboro, North Carolina, and the principal of its black school, handed out slips to community members that identified

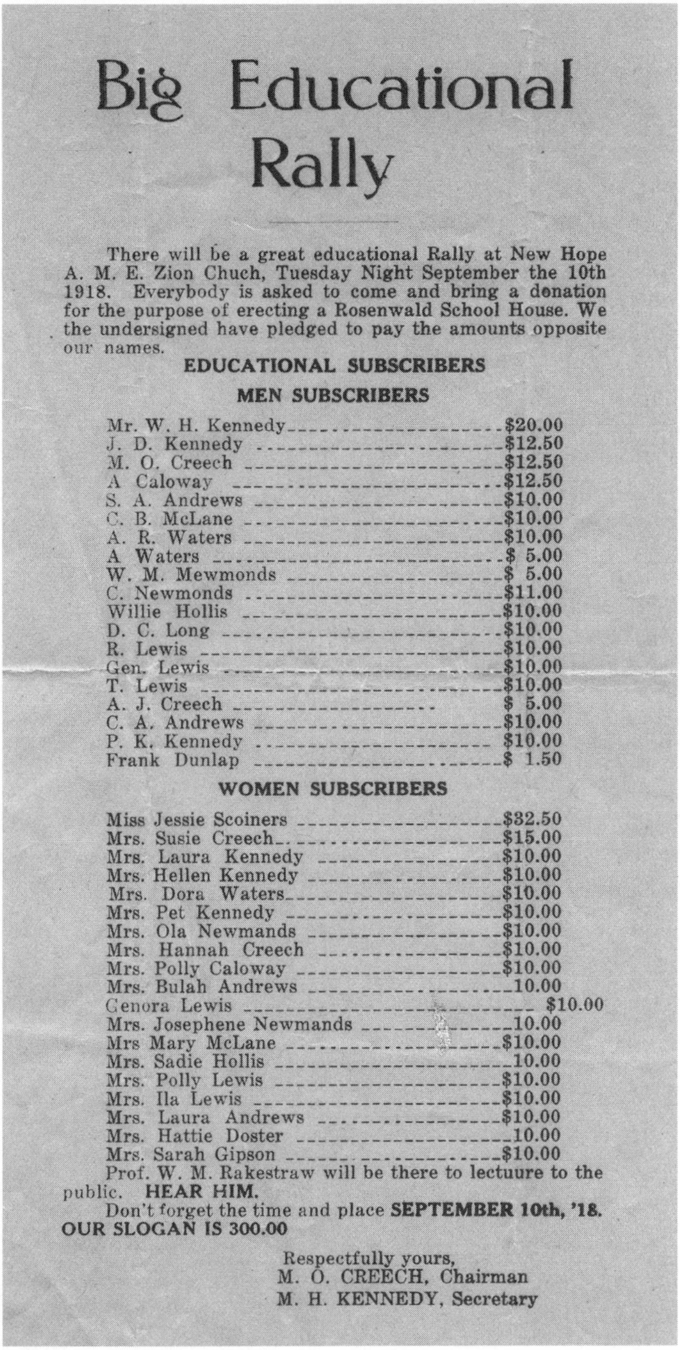

Big Educational Rally

There will be a great educational Rally at New Hope A. M. E. Zion Chuch, Tuesday Night September the 10th 1918. Everybody is asked to come and bring a donation for the purpose of erecting a Rosenwald School House. We the undersigned have pledged to pay the amounts opposite our names.

EDUCATIONAL SUBSCRIBERS

MEN SUBSCRIBERS

Mr. W. H. Kennedy	$20.00
J. D. Kennedy	$12.50
M. O. Creech	$12.50
A Caloway	$12.50
S. A. Andrews	$10.00
C. B. McLane	$10.00
A. R. Waters	$10.00
A Waters	$ 5.00
W. M. Mewmonds	$ 5.00
C. Newmonds	$11.00
Willie Hollis	$10.00
D. C. Long	$10.00
R. Lewis	$10.00
Gen. Lewis	$10.00
T. Lewis	$10.00
A. J. Creech	$ 5.00
C. A. Andrews	$10.00
P. K. Kennedy	$10.00
Frank Dunlap	$ 1.50

WOMEN SUBSCRIBERS

Miss Jessie Scoiners	$32.50
Mrs. Susie Creech	$15.00
Mrs. Laura Kennedy	$10.00
Mrs. Hellen Kennedy	$10.00
Mrs. Dora Waters	$10.00
Mrs. Pet Kennedy	$10.00
Mrs. Ola Newmands	$10.00
Mrs. Hannah Creech	$10.00
Mrs. Polly Caloway	$10.00
Mrs. Bulah Andrews	10.00
Cenora Lewis	$10.00
Mrs. Josephene Newmands	10.00
Mrs Mary McLane	$10.00
Mrs. Sadie Hollis	10.00
Mrs. Polly Lewis	$10.00
Mrs. Ila Lewis	$10.00
Mrs. Laura Andrews	$10.00
Mrs. Hattie Doster	10.00
Mrs. Sarah Gipson	$10.00

Prof. W. M. Rakestraw will be there to lectuure to the public. **HEAR HIM.**

Don't forget the time and place **SEPTEMBER 10th, '18.**
OUR SLOGAN IS 300.00

Respectfully yours,
M. O. CREECH, Chairman
M. H. KENNEDY, Secretary

Figure 44. Handbill for Rosenwald school rally, 1918. This handbill reflects several interesting features of school rallies: the division of labor and contributions between men and women, and the public rituals of giving. (Clinton J. Calloway Papers, University Archives and Museums, Tuskegee University)

them as members of the campaign for a Rosenwald teachers' home when they solicited money from individuals. Top money-getters earned prizes ranging from a white gold wristwatch to a gold $2.50 piece.[80]

Self-help for the sake of a Rosenwald school converted black men and women into activists who made short-term sacrifices for the promise of long-term improvements for their students and children. The "race leaders" of the late nineteenth and early twentieth centuries often spoke of "the masses" and sought or assumed their support, while white racists sneered at their alleged backwardness and white paternalists imposed their own guidelines for racial progress. Rosenwald self-help projects offer rare glimpses of those anonymous black southerners who gave back the fruits of their own success and performed the labor that brought forth a new school. Black landowners donated school sites, such as the African American farmers in Columbia County, Florida, who gave "a splendid ten-acre tract" for the King's Welcome School.[81] In Montgomery County, Virginia, an African American citizen donated the land for a Rosenwald school at Wake Forest, and the Shawsville and Elliston Parent-Teacher Associations purchased the sites for their new Rosenwald buildings.[82]

Local people brought their individual and community resources to Rosenwald campaigns, contributing in ways that expressed their own class, gender, and communal values. For most black southerners, donations to Rosenwald campaigns followed the patterns of daily labor. Although Georgia Rosenwald building agent Vincent Harris did not specify the genders of those who gave "a chicken, some a hog, some pine trees, while others give whatever they have and work on the building," it is not difficult to surmise that women and perhaps girls joined the hen clubs and men and boys the hog and tree clubs that he formed.[83] Men frequently cut the needed timber and hauled it from the forest to the sawmill and then to the school site; they hauled bricks, roofing materials, and equipment as well. Male patrons donated their labor to build and paint the school on their own, under the direction of the Rosenwald building agent, or for the contractor in charge of a construction project (figure 14). When cash was needed to supplement donated labor in a Burleson County, Texas, community, an elderly black man organized local boys to cut and sell cord wood, raising $90.[84] Male wage workers turned their daily labor into cash: laborers at the Hoover-Mason Phosphate Plant pledged one day's wages—between $2.25 and $5.00—to the Maury County Training School, and in East Baton Rouge Parish, Louisiana, "a local labor organization" made its own contribution to Burtville's building project.[85]

Observers credited women for the success of many Rosenwald campaigns.

Those women who managed campaigns as Jeanes supervisors certainly played key roles, and so did the women and girls with whom they worked. Some of the first Rosenwald schools were female-led enterprises, as published accounts attributed the success of the Loachapoka campaign to its "ladies" and that of the Notasulga School to schoolteacher Fannie Wheelis and the elderly Mary Johnson. Women like Wheelis used their status as members of the community's professional elite to call upon a broad range of citizens and organizations in vertical cross-class campaigns in which they led and others followed. Women like Mary Johnson, as respected female elders, challenged the men in their community horizontally across gender lines. At Cato, Arkansas, women prayed for help in getting their menfolk to finally cut the lumber for the planned school: "In answer to their prayers a storm came, blew down trees in every direction. The women drafted the men into service.... [They] followed the logs to and from the mill, served dinner for the school soldiers, each day." In Madison County, Tennessee, sixty women gave one dollar each as an incentive to both black men and the white men on the board of education for their community. South Carolina women offered a matching incentive of their own, contributing one-half of the community's required donation on the condition that men would give the other half.[86]

Women and girls prepared the food served at rallies, where food and entertainment were essential to draw a crowd. Female community members in Tennessee doubtless prepared the dishes sent in from all over McMinn County for a holiday banquet fund-raiser, or for the "old-time picnic" at Patton in Williamson County.[87] Women also sold their food at countless entertainments, picnics, suppers, cake walks, and pie struts, and donated the sales of butter, eggs, and chickens.[88] The quilt embroidered with the initials of community members and raffled off at a concert in Gallatin, Tennessee, no doubt was the product of female hands, and the concert one of the many "entertainments" that women organized for building campaigns.[89] Rosenwald building agents sometimes formed campaign clubs exclusively composed of women, such as the "thirteen clubs of ladies" that William Rakestraw organized during a rally at the Long Creek Baptist Church in Butler County, Alabama, and those that Louisiana Rosenwald building agent John S. Jones organized in Lincoln Parish for the Liberty Hill School.[90]

Women and children also joined Rosenwald campaigns indirectly, when the men of their households signed on to Rosenwald projects. Men could draw upon their gendered authority as the heads of their households to commit their families to a shared sacrifice for a common goal.[91] Especially in places where state school laws and local prejudice precluded significant public funds for Rosenwald school construction, the African American men who served as school trustees and male patrons assumed the financial burden by taking out loans from local banks. Their indebtedness allowed the building project to proceed and met the Rosenwald program's demand that all local contributions be deposited before disbursing a school grant, but it also put their households' assets at risk.[92]

Those with no credit at the bank used their labor as collateral for a Rosenwald school debt. When farmers in the Hopewell community in Neshoba County, Mississippi, organized for a new school building, they each promised the money from an acre of cotton every year to pay off their debt, taking seven years to pay off the building's mortgage and for "a farm shop, desks, sanitary water supply, insurance, and upkeep and repair work."[93] These were probably the African American tenants who, according to state Negro school agent Perry Easom, had arranged to have one of the officials of a local lumber company put up the cash for them, to be repaid by each tenant's annual acre of cotton. Easom was so taken by this plan that he urged white planters to copy the scheme.[94] In Wood County, Texas, the Rosenwald cotton patch was a communitywide project worked by "hands" and "pickers." Similarly, members of the Caledonia, Arkansas, community gave between fifty and one hundred pounds of cotton each to a community bale of seed cotton.[95] No doubt these "Rosenwald acres," "Rosenwald patches," and "Rosenwald bales" represented the work of entire black households. Although the men committed themselves as the heads of their families, women and children put in their labor as well.

Away from the fields, townspeople also came together as a community. "Men, women, and children gathered nights after their work and cleaned bricks by the thousands" in Jonesboro, Arkansas, salvaging the remains of a collapsed city auditorium "donated" by local officials for their new school.[96] Members of campaign committees like those in Murfreesboro, North Carolina, knocked on the doors of their neighbors and of the whites who employed them or with whom they traded in town.[97]

Communal bonds of faith and ritual overlapped with gender and family ties. Churches like the Israel CME Church in Jackson, Georgia, and the Wagram, North Carolina, Baptist Church provided meeting spaces for building committees and took up collections during services.[98] Richard S. Grossley, Mississippi's Rosenwald building agent, spoke to denominational assemblies and church congregations across the state: the Adams County Baptist Association; the National Convention of the Baptist Young People's Union and Sunday school; the Pearl Street AME Church in Jackson; the Conference of Presiding Elders of the AME Church; and the Meridian Conference of the Methodist Episcopal Church.[99] Tennessee Rosenwald building agent R. E. Clay repeatedly met with school patrons at their churches: the Methodist Episcopal Church at Lake Grove and the Colored Methodist Episcopal Church at Jones Chapel in Shelby County; the Baptist Church in Savannah in Decatur County; the St. Paul African Methodist Episcopal Church in Maury County; and the Methodist Episcopal Church in Clinton, Anderson County.[100] Members of fraternal organizations took up their own collections: Arkansas Rosenwald building agent Percy Dorman spoke at meetings of the Knights of Pythias and Court of Calanthe and the Masonic Grand Lodge to build support for educational projects and solicit funds.[101]

The sacrificial giving that whites praised and demanded could promise better educational facilities for children at the price of tightening the grip of debt and dependency on their parents' lives. Sharecroppers sacrificing their "Rosenwald acre" offer a noble, yet perilous example of the kinds of interactions with whites fostered by Rosenwald school-building campaigns, which tended to reinforce general assumptions that whites held ultimate power and that blacks could advance only within existing racial frameworks. Meanwhile, Julius Rosenwald, Booker T. Washington, and those who administered the building program always credited white southerners with support for Rosenwald schools and saw white donations to a building project as evidence of interracial cooperation and goodwill. Although their own records documented that donations from whites fell far behind other sources of funding, Rosenwald officials celebrated those instances and used the investment of public school funds as indirect evidence of white support. When Rosenwald Fund director Francis W. Shepardson argued, "The amount credited to the whites is not, strictly speaking, a fair showing, because in many communities, as we know, the whites have cooperated heartily through state or county funds under their control," he glossed over the contradiction between whites' "contribution" of tax funds that had been generated in part by levies on African Americans and the resulting double taxation of black southerners for their self-help contributions.[102]

Invitations to white school officials to attend Rosenwald school rallies and direct solicitation of their white neighbors by African American campaigners suggested the possibility of greater communication in communities divided by race and created opportunities for sympathetic white southerners to act on their paternalistic principles. Thus J. W. Cullors of Sand Flat, Texas, used the local newspaper to explain to Rains County whites what a Rosenwald building grant and Jeanes support for an industrial supervisor could mean if they would get behind the county superintendent and black school leaders. These interracial appeals used the language of black accommodation to reach white readers: "We are asking the white people, who wish our success to help us build such a school [with an industrial curriculum] here and I am sure we will feel grateful. . . . Our boys and girls will have the advantage of a training that will enable them to labor skillfully."[103] Bringing white officials into Rosenwald campaign meetings also forcibly reminded superintendents and school board members of black citizens' needs and determination. The Colored Citizens Progressive Club of Person County, North Carolina, announced that members had pledges of $1,300 and $400 cash in hand at a meeting attended by the school superintendent, who then assured the club of the county board of education's support.[104]

At countless Rosenwald rallies, suppers, and campaign meetings, African American southerners enacted the familiar rituals of deference to whites simultaneously with rituals of self-sacrifice that demonstrated their commitment as citizens to universal public education. In so doing, black Rosenwald activists created safe environments in which they could assert their right to public schools for their children and their expectations that they had legitimate claims upon public officials' attention and resources.

Obstacles within and outside African American Communities

The same factors that could promote a successful Rosenwald building campaign could turn negative and threaten a campaign's survival. Even community pride posed obstacles to Rosenwald school builders. State agents for Negro schools and Rosenwald building agents found some communities hesitant about building new schools, especially in the program's early years. The Rosenwald building program always required public ownership of any school it aided, which in many communities meant deeding privately owned black school property over to the county, or even the state. School trustees and patrons were understandably reluctant at first to give up land and buildings that they had labored to purchase and maintain, or to allow white outsiders—including local school authorities—control their schools.[105] Tuskegee's Clement Richardson reported that local people voiced the same doubts in every community he visited in the spring of 1918: "doubts as to the deeding of the land to the state, as to who is to teach in the school, as to what denomination is to take charge, etc. and so on."[106] Percy L. Dorman recalled: "My first experience as [Arkansas] Rosenwald Agent was difficult. I found a great deal of skepticism among the people and some school directors [trustees]. It was hard to convince some that there was a man on earth actually willing to give . . . so much money for their benefit, and to use the common expression, 'There was a bug under the chip' somewhere."[107] Former Louisiana Negro school agent Leo M. Favrot had similar memories of waiting for up to two hours while black southerners thought over the Rosenwald proposition and watched for an influential community member to signal the appropriate response. Some dismissed the offer of Rosenwald aid because the approved school plans showed unfamiliar building forms and window arrangements, and the idea of a one-teacher school as requiring not only a classroom but an industrial room and cloakrooms seemed excessive.[108] The whole process was new and unfamiliar; Charles H. Moore often found communities "not prepared to give anything but pledges" on his first visit but more willing on a second try.[109]

Even when Rosenwald school buildings were no longer novelties, Rosenwald campaigns could founder when the project challenged local leaders' authority. The arrival of black outsiders like Rosenwald building agents and the activism of Jeanes industrial supervising teachers complicated local power struggles with issues of class-based professional expertise and gender. Jeanes supervisor Agnes Wells Henderson persevered through such conflicts in Autauga County, Alabama. Jeanes supervisors were redoubtable women, and Henderson's example demonstrates both their capacity for leadership on school projects and their strong sense of their own stature as educators allied with powerful philanthropies. Their own sources of power and their own methods of community organization granted Jeanes supervisors dispensation to take charge and required men to acknowledge female authority, but they could also precipitate local conflict over the boundaries of gendered and professional power.

During the 1918 Jeanes supervisors conference at Tuskegee, Henderson pledged to build ten Rosenwald schools in her county, then increased her fundraising goal to sixteen schools, and next asked for a county training school.[110] Putting those plans into action brought Henderson into conflict with Rosenwald building agent Booker T. Washington Jr. and local minister Reverend W. D. Hargrove.[111] Booker T. Washington Jr. had bypassed Henderson and appointed Hargrove to chair the fund-raising drive for the Autaugaville Rosenwald school. After that campaign failed, Henderson infuriated them by conducting her own successful fund-raising drive. Hargrove had then tried to reinsert himself into the campaign, but when Henderson ignored him, "he sent for Mr. Washington and they got me in a private room and Mr. Washington told me that if I didnt make H[argrove] the chairman of that committee he would see to it that we received no Rosenwald money. He said if *he* said for us not to get any money we certainly would not get any and he told me that his father was the founder of the Jeanes Fund that paid me and that I was only in the work a few months and intimated that I was a parvenue."

The younger Washington had just met his match. Henderson "stripped him of his deceit and showed him that I did not belong to that class of limited workers that believed him the equal of his father. I told him his father was the founder of Tuskegee; but he evidently was not running it, neither would he run Autauga County." Henderson promised to "act in future as I had in the past, that is make my plans as though he (Washington) never lived." After Henderson's tongue-lashing, Booker T. Washington Jr. left her alone. Minister Hargrove tried to bring Henderson down with the same sorts of charges that were threatening North Carolina's Charles H. Moore during the First World War. After hearing Henderson call upon school patrons to give as generously to the school fund as they had to the stamp and bond drives for "the white man's war," Hargrove reported her to leading whites for lack of patriotism. After the controversy blew over, the two had cooperated on the Autaugaville project—or so she thought until Hargrove invited Robert Russa Moton to town "to give himself a little more prominence than I allow him." "These Methodist ministers have fought me to a finish in this county," she complained.[112]

Henderson's story offers a rare look into the intersection of personal ambition, professional status, gender, and religion in the power structure of a local school campaign. Her reference to "Methodist ministers" suggests that some of her problems lay in a local church. Rosenwald school campaigns often ran afoul of existing community institutions and neighborhood boundaries, including denominational rivalries. Competition between churches troubled a number of Rosenwald campaigns, especially if an existing school was identified with one congregation. Booker T. Washington Jr. found that Coppinsville, Alabama, Methodists sent their children to the public school while Baptists supported a private school, complicating his planned consolidation of the two schools, which stood within two hundred yards of each other. The same was true for schools housed in lodge halls. In Louisiana, Rosenwald building agent John S. Jones had problems with the Bernice School because "several secret orders have an interest in the building and each must be consulted before the title can be given to the Parish School Board."[113]

African Americans also rejected the program when its requirements threatened to remove a school from its place in their community landscape. Everyone wanted the new school close to their homes, so that Lineville, Alabama, patrons argued about on which side of town their Rosenwald school should stand.[114] Rural African Americans—like their white neighbors—at times opposed Rosenwald campaigns for consolidated schools that would displace an important public institution and take their children from their own community. As North Carolina's W. F. Credle noted about one community's deliberations about consolidation for a three-teacher Rosenwald school, "They want schoolhouses in their immediate communities for their little community gatherings and Sunday schools."[115] Black patrons also realized that their consolidated schools, unlike white ones, would likely have no public transportation and require their children to walk even longer distances to school. Thus while the proposed Rosenwald school might be a better building, parents sometimes preferred a substandard school building located nearby.[116]

Once a community had decided on a Rosenwald campaign, however, they still faced problems imposed by economic forces beyond their control. The plight of southern agriculture after the First World War trapped many rural African Americans in dire poverty and endless labor. Some families had to keep children in the fields to suit their employers, or for their own economic survival. In places where educational opportunities were virtually nonexistent and future prospects for economic or social advancement seemed dim, parents sometimes saw little point in schooling.[117] Adverse economic conditions sent local fund-raising campaigns into a tailspin. In the late 1910s and early 1920s, falling agricultural prices caused problems for tenants who had set aside some of their cotton crop to put toward a school and its equipment and now found themselves saddled with a school debt. As the cost of building Rosenwald schools spiraled because of rising prices during and after the First World War, and then because of the tighter standards enforced by Rosenwald Fund officials, community members and state officials watched some campaigns fall victim to "discouragement and failure." A Louisiana parish superintendent commented, "the Negroes seem to lose their nerve after raising $800.00 in addition to the sites," and Kentucky's Rosenwald building agent wryly noted that "$400 [is] not stimulating school building as it did when it covered about one third of the total cost" now that even a one-teacher building routinely cost over $2,000.[118]

Individuals and school organizations that took out loans in anticipation of a local campaign faced financial disaster if their community members could not make their pledges, or if white officials held up the promised Rosenwald assistance.[119] Rev. E. M. Williams of Morven, Georgia, asked Rosenwald building agent Vincent H. Harris for help when the Great Depression caught up with local contributors in 1932: "Now listen this is the facts in the case. We the Trustees of Morven Col. Pub. School have built a #1 Rosenwald two Teacher House at a cost of twenty five hundred dollars . . . we received $500.00 from the Rosenwald dept. The county only donated some equipment but havent helped on the [indebtedness?], and the town $100 and we have struggled and got it dow to about $1200.00 and a deal of us are on notes that are pass due the parties are threting to close us out and sell us out."[120] In this disastrous economic context, self-help contributed to the destruction of African American resources.

Other Rosenwald campaigns inevitably ran up against explicit racism in public school funding. In Roxboro, North Carolina, where the school board had just taken on the debt for a new white school building, one board member "seemed to have expressed the sentiment of all when she said they had 'racked and scraped' to get money for the white school and that they did not care to obligate themselves any further to provide for the colored people."[121] County school boards in Virginia's Northern Neck proved extraordinarily stingy. Public revenues appropriated for some Westmoreland County schools like Potomac and Templemans were less than their Rosenwald grants; African American contributions paid for half of these schools' costs. Black school patrons paid in $3,200 on the Kremlin School compared to $800 from the Rosenwald Fund and $1,000 from public revenue. Next door in Northumberland County, the training school represented an African American investment of $8,943 combined with $1,500 from the Rosenwald Fund and a mere $700 from public school authorities.[122]

More commonly, white school authorities made the same point through indifference, endless foot dragging, and repeated demands for additional African American donations. One reason that African Americans and Rosenwald building program staff paid so much attention to white county officials was that these people could facilitate or obstruct a Rosenwald building campaign. Overall, the bulk of funds expended on Rosenwald schools came from public sources, the state and local tax revenues set aside for education and expended at the local level. For all the talk about the importance of self-help, Rosenwald, Washington, and their allies saw it as temporary strategy that moved black and white southerners closer to their ultimate goal: a fully funded public school system for African Americans that would provide equal but separate resources and opportunities afforded to white children.

But the size and cost of model Rosenwald schools sometimes outstripped the combined local and Rosenwald contributions as well as local public school appropriations, bringing some local campaigns to a screeching halt. In Mississippi, county boards of education by law could not expend any state school funds on construction projects unless the county already had its own tax levy for building projects, and custom dictated that white schools take precedence for local funds as well. State Negro school agents Perry Easom and W. C. Strahan fought on a double front against local school authorities and unsympathetic Rosenwald Fund officials. To counteract white school officials' suspicions about the cost and purpose of Rosenwald schools, the Negro school agents stressed that "you may rest assured that there is positively no 'bug under the chip' in this matter. We give exactly the amount of aid promised, provided the building is constructed in accordance with plans, and there is no attempt to control the school in any way whatsoever." To the fund's Nashville staff, state Negro school agents tried to explain that local school boards both would not and could not provide the money necessary to build model schools, arguing that it was not the fault of the agents or the "poor negroes" if public funding was virtually nonexistent. As Easom protested, "I have no way in the world to force the public to pay more on these buildings." To remedy this situation, Mississippi's state agents successfully lobbied for a 1930 revision of state school law that allowed counties to impose local taxes specifically for African American construction projects.[123]

Self-help by African American school patrons, according to the Rosenwald program's white paternalists, would eventually inspire southern whites to accept their public responsibility for educating black children. In the meantime, it also became a major bone of contention between African American school patrons and white school authorities. Calculating the value of black contributions was problematic if the county superintendent did not fully support the project. J. M. Glenn, superintendent of schools in Gates County, North Carolina, complained that local African Americans had refused to move the bricks for their school and had raised only $200. Consequently, he had the lumber purchased by the school board for a Rosenwald school sent to other school construction sites. W. F. Credle and N. C. Newbold both reminded him that African Americans had donated the land on which their former church school had stood, valued at $1,500, yet Glenn still argued that the original agreement was that the county would appropriate $2,500 to match black contributions of $2,500 in cash in addition to the donated land.[124]

The influential white individuals and voters who put county superintendents into office also could delay a Rosenwald building campaign, even when African

Americans had met all of their requirements and Rosenwald administrators stood ready to release grant funds. Leo Favrot recalled that he had been impressed with the superintendent of Louisiana's Terrebonne Parish, who had proposed constructing a Rosenwald school in each ward, but three years later only one school had been built. "It must be, since the school board seemed so willing to go forward with Negro education, that the superintendent was deterred either by prominent sugar planters in his parish whose influence he feared, or by the influence of a neighboring superintendent who is distinctly hostile to Negro education and who seems to dominate school affairs to some extent in that section of the state," he speculated.[125] O. H. Bernard reported on counties where white public opinion circumscribed superintendents' support for Rosenwald campaigns to his superiors in the Tennessee Department of Education and the General Education Board.[126] The superintendent in Jones County, Georgia, told Rosenwald building agent Vincent Harris that he wanted to build a Rosenwald school, "but next year is election year and the least wrong step I make now, my opponents could easily spread a propaganda that would defeat me." Harris had to agree because, as he realized, "if he [the superintendent] is displaced . . . his successor would not make the same mistake."[127] Disfranchisement and racism thus muted the full potential of the Rosenwald school program for creating educational equity and forced black southerners to remain focused on self-help and alliances with outsiders like the Negro school agents and the Julius Rosenwald Fund.

The experiences of school patrons constructing the Springfield School near Senatobia, Mississippi, in 1929 echoed many of the themes that resounded through Rosenwald school campaigns in African American communities. Trustees Frank Jackson, Frank Allen, James Jones, Sam Hill, and John Hill took the initiative, writing Negro school agent Perry Easom for "a three teachers school with the help of the Rosenwall Aid." As they told Easom, they had a school site but no building and had outstayed their welcome in other lodgings: "we are without a house of any kind, only have a site, have been teaching for the past 4 or 5 yrs. in a church or private house but this time are barred from the privilege of either." The trustees apparently assumed that some demonstration of white support would benefit their appeal to state authorities, for they assured Easom that their school site was "surrounded by nothing but colored folk has but one white family 3 miles (Mr. T. Atkins) and they are very interested in the move as they have nothing but col[ored] labor."[128]

Despite evidence of white approval, "a nice lot of reliable subscriptions of both white and colored," and even a "backward county" bonus, Rosenwald school campaigners in Springfield watched their project wax and wane as they struggled to match local resources to a model school plan. After reviewing construction estimates, Tate County superintendent Winnie Clayton realized that the project had $1,000 less than the $3,600 needed for a three-teacher school. She met with the school trustees and told Easom that, "they are of the opinion that their people will be more interested in a two-teacher type of school and would contribute more liberally." With the county obviously unwilling or unable to do more, the trustees had to agree to scale back their request and cancel their application for the fund's 1928–29 budget year to raise more money. Easom's suggestion that Springfield patrons arrange to have the local planter put up the extra funds for the larger school and then charge it back to his tenants apparently fell on deaf ears. Springfield School was built in 1930 as a two-teacher school on Community School Plan 20–A.[129]

Springfield School's campaign suggests that, once local initiative and self-help had gained public recognition of African American school needs, a Rosenwald school-building campaign entered a second phase dominated by the construction process. Building a Rosenwald school created a new, modern place in a southern African American community. What that place might mean depended on the observer. A Rosenwald school expressed not only the architectural vision of its planners but the community vision of the people who used its spaces.

Building Schools, Contesting Meaning

Rosenwald Schools in the Southern Landscape

Local initiative and self-help campaigns tied the Rosenwald schools to their communities. Here the administrative process of building Rosenwald schools, intended to bring people together across the color line and nudge the South toward educational equity, intersected with a deeper local tradition shaped by class, gender, and faith as well as race. In successful Rosenwald school campaigns, the Rosenwald program's official hierarchy not only depended on but drew strength from the actions of local participants. Local leaders and citizens turned self-help into leverage for a better school and a stronger community.

Another key aspect of local campaigns was their tangible expression in a school building. Community members had little influence on school design, which Progressive educators and school architects claimed as their province. The Rosenwald program entrenched professional designers' authority in its own plan books, the Interstate School Building Service, and the enforcement of "approved" designs for Rosenwald schools. In everyday life, however, local people reinterpreted the Rosenwald school as a place of their own. Once again their efforts faced obstacles, most often from local whites who correctly interpreted the Rosenwald school's implicit visual challenge to white supremacy. Nevertheless, Rosenwald school supporters spread a blanket of over five thousand buildings across fifteen states that asserted black citizens' visions of a better future. The ways in which local people derived meaning from their older school buildings, inscribed meaning into new Rosenwald schools, and created a network of modern community schools produced the Rosenwald school-building program's distinctive contribution to the southern landscape.

SCHOOL BUILDINGS AS COMMUNITY INSTITUTIONS

Rosenwald school planners sometimes presumed that their structures would be the first schools constructed in rural African American communities. They shared a common Progressive disdain for older school buildings, which looked too much like churches, according to Fletcher B. Dresslar, or too accurately expressed community indifference. Reformers also pointed to public school statistics documenting the lack of publicly owned schools and the overcrowding of those that did exist to prove that African American schoolchildren had few opportunities for education. Historians have used reformers' descriptions and photographs to document how closely the material conditions in rural southern schools paralleled prevailing sentiments against tax-supported and state-controlled education.[1]

Certainly the school buildings of the late nineteenth century looked like familiar country homes and churches and quickly deteriorated without public funding, especially a problem for money-starved rural black schools. And the statistics that educational reformers eagerly collected amply document the ill effects of segregation and disfranchisement on the allocation of public school resources to black schoolchildren. The physical appearance of most black schools—and their seeming absence from much of the southern landscape—masked the significance of the school in African American community life.

Black southerners, however, viewed Rosenwald schools within a tradition of educational activism. They had developed that tradition against an equally long-standing practice of white opposition to their schools and teachers dating to the antebellum period. Decades of deliberate neglect created vast disparities between southern white schools and their black counterparts, especially in rural areas and despite the persistent underfunding of white public schools as well. African American school patrons, teachers, and principals had taken responsibility for school buildings when public authorities would not, incorporating schools into former houses, farm outbuildings, and any other available structures.[2] Thus, when a community leader took the initiative, or a crowd of school patrons gathered to meet a Rosenwald building agent, they had decided that a Rosenwald school would further that tradition by relocating it in a new modern structure built especially for teachers and students.

More often, the seemingly "new" Rosenwald schools replaced those that had found homes in the other key institutions of African American community life, churches and fraternal lodges. For example, the Mount Pleasant Church in Cotton Plant, Arkansas, sheltered a school until "the Rosenwald put in" a new building, according to former student Helen Howard.[3] At their best, churches and lodge halls tied schools tightly to their communities, but at their worst, such arrangements created friction among residents. From North Carolina, U. W. Lassiter reported that the school in his community had "been using the church property and they are grumbling about the children using the well and seats. The pastor is continually nagging the teacher about it, and she is almost ready to quit at times." Fred McDowell, another North Carolinian, complained that "the churches have shut their doors against us."[4] Conflicts between churches and schools were not common, but when church congregations complained about teachers and pupils using worship spaces, they revealed the underlying problem: that most black students and teachers were crowded into buildings never intended as formal learning environments, where they were hidden from public view and public responsibility.

Black southerners also used Rosenwald schools to update long-standing facilities that dated back to the Reconstruction era. Some Rosenwald structures replaced school buildings established in the 1860s and 1870s as Freedmen's Bureau and missionary schools, or as public schools established by Reconstruction state governments. The 1922 Rosenwald building in Chapel Hill, Maryland, continued an 1868 Freedmen's Bureau school, and the Clinton Colored School, another Maryland Rosenwald school constructed in 1926–27, stood on the location of the first African American school in the Surratts school district in 1869. In Florida, Tallahassee's Lincoln High School, which received a Rosenwald grant for a new building in 1929, had opened as Lincoln Academy in 1869 and in the 1870s was one of only three public schools in the state offering secondary education for African Americans. Others had grown up within church congregations, such as the 1926 Rosenwald building at Mars Bluff, South Carolina, which carried on a school founded by the Mount Zion Methodist Church in 1870.[5]

Schools with shorter histories still recorded local determination to have schools for African American children and demonstrate how rural citizens combined the benefits of philanthropic agencies like the Rosenwald building program to upgrade existing facilities. The Mecklenburg County Training School in Virginia began as a one-teacher school in 1915 when Robert A. Walker, Rev. J. H. Simmons, and Mary E. Simmons organized a patrons' league and raised enough money to rent a lodge hall. With the assistance of a white attorney, they convinced the school board to hire Mrs. Simmons as the teacher. Three years later, the patrons had enough money to build their own two-room frame school. After the arrival of Jeanes supervisor Matilda M. Booker in 1920, the school gained Slater Fund support as a county training school. The community then raised $3,250 and received a $1,500 Rosenwald grant for a new six-teacher building constructed in 1925, as well as a grant for a two-room industrial building in 1927.[6]

From the perspective of community activists, a Rosenwald building asserted that education was not only a personal and community value but was emerging as a public right of citizenship in the modern South. A Rosenwald school immediately moved schoolchildren and their teachers into a public space that offered a new focal point for the community. Raymond Spann recalled this transition from private to public within his own West Tennessee community. Construction of the Spann Rosenwald school "meant a whole lot to the community by being in the neighborhood. . . . [I]t really meant something for us to be able to stop meeting in little schools like 'Villey Ridge' which was close to nowhere and using the church at St. Paul as our school."[7] Schools like this looked inward to the community as new neighborhood institutions; they also looked outward to a broader network of modern public education that connected communities across the South.

CONSTRUCTING THE SCHOOL

Rosenwald school patrons, having gained official support for their applications and raised their self-help contribution, shifted their attention to the construction process. In the early years of the school-building program, Tuskegee officials encouraged black southerners to buy the land, turn over the deed to the county or state, and then build the school themselves. William Brown, chair of the building committee for the Brownville School, listed how his community paid for and built one of the original six Rosenwald schools in 1913. Over the past two years, they had raised funds from a trustees' rally, a Tom Thumb wedding, and a concert, as well as from solicitation envelopes, a mock farmers' conference, personal donations, and gifts from the school-improvement club and a separate women's improvement club. Those funds and the Rosenwald grant paid for lumber, shingles, bricks, stoves, and hardware, as well as for hauling the supplies and paying a carpenter. In-kind contributions included lumber salvaged from the former school building, the building site, and a credit of $88.70 for patrons' labor.[8]

When black patrons built the schools with their own labor, they made Booker T. Washington's ideal of self-help a visible process by pooling their skills to improve their own community. Nevertheless, the officials who implemented Washington's original plan soon came to see construction self-help as a liability, revealing the class-based paternalist and professional biases shared by African American Rosenwald building agents, the white state agents for Negro schools, and Rosenwald program officials. Alabama Negro school agent J. S. Lambert noted that "we have experienced considerable trouble" after giving out school building plans "in the hand of negroes prematurely."[9] Fletcher B. Dresslar's scathing indictment of the Tuskegee buildings' quality and white state agents' mistrust of black artisans made this sort of self-help increasingly rare after 1920.

As Rosenwald buildings took on larger and more complex appearances, and as state and county governments demanded greater accountability in return for their financial support, more school boards employed a standard bidding procedure and hired contractors to put up their new schools. Local black craftsmen remained on Rosenwald construction sites, as when the school board of Jefferson County, Tennessee, contracted with the Coleman Brothers firm to build the Nelson Merry School in 1932. Two generations of Coleman family men, brothers Ottis, Samuel, and William, and William's sons, Claude and Wallace, made the bricks from clay dug and burned on site.[10] Similarly, Almyra Wills recalled that her father contracted to build thirty-three Rosenwald schools for the Halifax County, North Carolina, board of education.[11] African American family businesses like these linked Rosenwald school construction to the local black community, but quite differently from the days when African American farmers and laborers donated workdays. The bidding process also shifted responsibility from private individuals, most often the African American school trustees, to public school authorities and, like the entire Rosenwald application and approval process, put some distance between the community and its school. In return, the community gained public recognition for its school as an integral part of the fabric of a county public school system, and an opportunity to attract positive public attention to its institutions.

Formalized construction procedures awakened the interest of white business operators who might benefit from the extension of government-sponsored school services into African American districts. Realtors tried to manipulate white officials in the interest of preserving and profiting from a community's segregated geography. They found county school authorities increasingly willing to purchase school sites as part of their regular bidding procedures for public works, or when donations of land were not forthcoming. In Florida, where land companies boomed and then busted in the 1920s, the Jefferson County Board of Public Instruction negotiated with the Wacissa Land Company to purchase the site of a proposed Rosenwald school with school bonds. The board then bid out the Wacissa Rosenwald school at the same time as a new white school at Aucilla, and with a similar notice to building contractors.[12] Attorney S. S. Mann exemplified North Carolina whites' recognition that the building program offered direct economic benefits. When he heard about the "Rosenthal endowment," he immediately wrote to the state department of education to offer nine acres of land at a low price. More than government contracts or private gain were involved in Rosenwald school property negotiations. In Benson, North Carolina, real estate dealers offered a site for the Rosenwald school that W. F. Credle interpreted as "an effort to segregate them in an undesirable section of the community." The Anson County, North Carolina, superintendent claimed that African Americans preferred sites on the fringes of town rather than a central location, perhaps out of self-defense, judging by his report that whites in Ansonville had dynamited a construction site they thought too close to town.[13]

Despite the threat of white backlash, Rosenwald school-building projects became noteworthy local stories in local media. Press releases and news reports published in African American and white-controlled newspapers announced new school buildings to a wider audience and invited them to follow the construction process. Headlines such as "Negroes Erecting Nice School House," "Negro School to Be Erected Soon/Board of Education Selects Site for New Four Oaks $1,500 Institution," or "Alamance County Training School for Negroes Will Be Located on Richmond Hill" let readers know where the building would go up, and from whom the county had obtained the land.[14] Other headlines identified local contractors—"Long Contractor for Negro School," "Board of Education Awards Contract for Colored School to M. B. Gregory,"—and reported the public's investment in new black schools: "Negro Schools in County Get New Buildings[.] Contracts Amounting to More Than $25,000 Awarded by County Board."[15] As construction progressed, articles like "Work on Colored School Nearing Completion[.] Contractors Expect to Finish in Two Weeks—Building a Handsome Structure" and "Work on Colored School Nears Completion[.] One of Best in State, Made Possible by Julius Rosenwald Fund" set the stage for later announcements of a building's dedication or opening ceremonies.[16]

In states like Mississippi, where county boards of education had limited legal authority to build schools, patrons and trustees like those at the Lee-Rosenwald Colored School in Marion County executed formal contracts with builders and bore most of the responsibility for building the new school. The Lee School patrons had already constructed one five-teacher school in 1925–26, contributing $2,600 of its $6,300 cost. Now they were planning another large building that the Rosenwald Fund would call the Marion-Lamar Consolidated School. School patrons would eventually invest $3,900, over one-third of the total cost of the new school, into this six-teacher building and its site.[17] Their 1931 building contract is an instructive example of the extraordinary measures undertaken by African American southerners for a "modern school building."[18]

Names alone suggest why they undertook this project. Ten male patrons of the Lee-Rosenwald Colored School signed the contract along with the three-man board of trustees. Two of the trustees shared surnames with four of the patrons (for a total of four Exposes and two Magees), and two pairs of patrons had the same last names as well (Lee and Caggan). The patrons had five acres of land "heretofore occupied by John Watts, and currently by Sophie Watts"; Owen Watts was another of the signatory patrons. Familial bonds as much as any tangible collateral backed these people's commitment to this community institution.

The size and value of the project required a careful listing of each party's responsibilities, revealing the multiple tasks necessary to meet the Rosenwald Fund's stipulations as well as the ways that local people combined self-help and construction shortcuts to keep a project within their means. Contractor Richard Kalil was to construct a Community School Plan 6–B structure, for which the plan and specifications were attached to the original contract. The contract also detailed how Kalil should interpret the fund's plan and specifications, dictating the sizes of joists and studs, the exterior and interior heights, and the number of coats of paint, and substituting transoms for windows over the front porch. Kalil would supervise the construction himself and provide all of the "properly manufactured concrete blocks" and most of the other building materials, as well as two skilled mechanics to handle the brick, concrete, and carpentry work. Although the contract did not specify who would make them, surely Kalil was intended to supervise the fashioning of one hundred desks "according to the Rosenwald desk plan" that still were taking the place of more expensive commercial patent desks as late as 1931. In return, the trustees and patrons agreed to an enormous amount of work, materials, and wages: to "haul at their own expense" all of the building materials; to "furnish at their own expense" all sand, gravel, and water needed; and to "furnish at their own expense" all skilled and unskilled labor as the contractor requested "from day to day," as well as to "erect or procure at their own expense a suitable house adjacent to said school" for the contractor's tools and equipment, provide a night watchman at the site, and take responsibility for any work-related injuries. Furthermore, although the contractor provided the "two skilled mechanics," the trustees agreed to pay one of these workers' wages up to $150.

Payment for Kalil's services was as complicated as the building specifications. Lee-Rosenwald trustees agreed to pay Kalil $5,600. That amount was immediately reduced by a $1,000 credit for the "considerable quantity of secondhand lumber, secondhand doors, secondhand windows, and some other miscellaneous material and some paint." The trustees bound themselves to solicit $2,600 from the Julius Rosenwald Fund through the county superintendent. Their own labor, or that of patrons or others they recruited, reduced their financial obligation by another $1,000. They signed two promissory notes for $575.00 each, due twelve and then twenty-four months later, to cover the remaining $1,000 due to Kalil and $150 to the skilled mechanic, guaranteed by a lien on the building and land.

The Marion-Lamar Consolidated School represented one of the larger, more complex buildings favored in later years of the Rosenwald building program, and the tremendous coordination and commitment required to build such schools. Other southern communities were not as hamstrung by state school laws and could more easily draw upon public funding; nevertheless, they often found themselves engaged in years of negotiation and fund-raising. Building the school was not enough for the Rosenwald building program; it had to be finished and equipped. Local campaigners often found that school officials stuck them with extra bills to pay for the required equipment and painting. Fred Drinkard explained to Clinton Calloway, "We has built a School with Some of the Rosen Wald funds and before the schoolhouse was Equip the County Supt paid all of the money out so that left us Blank thin I ask the county Supt About it and he said that he made the Ear [error] in the contract himself and he Would not ask the contracter to finish it. So you cand see We are still With a School house With out Equipped."[19] When teacher R. Irving Boone wrote to North Carolina assistant Negro school agent W. F. Credle to complain that the Wilkes County Training School still had not been painted three years after its construction, Credle's response was to suggest that black patrons raise money to pay for exterior paint themselves.[20] Repeated demands for more black contributions once again deflected the county school system's obligation to its black schools back onto the community. Every new payment was another voluntary tax on local school patrons, a discriminatory burden that would actually increase the cultural capital a community invested in its Rosenwald school.

THE ROSENWALD SCHOOL IN THE COMMUNITY: ASSERTING MEANING

Rosenwald schools had been designed to send implicit messages about black opportunity in the Progressive South, and they signaled a new stage of community life in the South's cultural landscape. Observers often singled them out as exemplary structures, in sharp contrast to the "shabbiest and shoddiest types of cabins, churches, and halls" endemic in black education.[21] The U.S. Bureau of Education labeled a photograph of a two-teacher Rosenwald school "A Colored School Unusually Well Constructed" in its 1919 survey of Alabama's public schools. Surveying Florida's black schools in the late 1920s, educational experts complained that "when one gets out into the county districts . . . one finds few, if any, buildings that would be rated as high or fair, with the exception of the schools that have been built with the assistance of the Rosenwald Fund." In East Texas, "the only Negro school buildings . . . that might be considered adequate for school purposes were the Rosenwald buildings."[22]

The exterior appearance of a Rosenwald school—product of the debates among Rosenwald building-program planners and designers and Progressive school architects—was only one clue to its meaning in the southern landscape. Local people brought their own traditions to the modern, standardized Rosenwald school and blended the two for the next generation of black students, parents, and patrons. They created places like the Jackson School in Smith County, Texas, described by Peggy B. Gill as "both a specific location that engenders a sense of community in terms of place and the symbolic representation of that community of place." Collectively, writes Adam Fairclough, "the Rosenwald schools were monuments to black achievement and symbols of black hopes for the future."[23] These monuments and symbols were not static, however, but places where children and adults walked and ran in and out in rhythms of school and play, celebration and ceremony. Their actions constructed the reformers' architectural schemes as public stages for community life.

Spaces for industrial education in Rosenwald facilities, which sparked continual debate, offer a clear example of the multiple meanings participants ascribed to Rosenwald schools. To many observers, an industrial room tempered a Rosenwald school's up-to-date appearance with a tangible reminder that this model black institution would conform to the prevailing racial order. Historians have documented the conflict between those who favored industrial education for African Americans and those who championed traditional academic training, a debate in which Booker T. Washington, Julius Rosenwald, and the white and black officials who operated the rural school-building program clearly sided with the vocational camp. State agents for Negro schools and Rosenwald building agents agreed in 1919 that "especially is it absolutely necessary that an Industrial Room be provided in every plan submitted before the plan is approved, and that in order to carry out the Rosenwald idea the school building including the Industrial Room be properly equipped."[24] They took that message directly to black communities. At the "Negro Day" during the 1926 West Tennessee Farmers Institute, Rosenwald building agent Robert

E. Clay "point[ed] out to these farmers that it was absolutely impossible for their children to succeed in their farming better than they had unless special training was given to the head, the hand, the heart and the health. And it was impossible to give this training without good Rosenwald Schoolhouses and efficient Negro teachers."[25]

In practice, however, teachers and patrons molded the industrial rooms to their own expectations. As state agents for Negro schools and Rosenwald building agents often complained, simply identifying an industrial room on a building plan did not guarantee an industrial curriculum. Demands for agricultural training precipitated conflict with teachers who espoused a different philosophy. Teacher Elias J. Murdock reportedly informed his black school trustees "if they expected him to go on the farm and plow and hoe they were craze, that he didn't come here for that purpose."[26] Where teachers and patrons preferred academic instruction to vocational subjects for their children, they simply ignored the industrial curriculum. Everyday realities limited industrial education just as effectively in many communities where local African American citizens had no sooner finished raising money to build a school and equip its regular classrooms than they had to start on a second long-term campaign to equip the industrial room. Oliver Williams, who attended the Cotton Plant, Arkansas, Rosenwald school in the 1930s, recalled a small, narrow room "supposed to have been a work shop" that served as a teachers' room because patrons had not been able to equip it properly, although a shop class did meet there at night.[27] The lack of trained vocational teachers hampered some schools; in others, the opening of a decent school building attracted so many new students that the industrial room had to be converted into a regular classroom. Cost-conscious superintendents acquiesced to local usage by eliminating the industrial rooms or enlarging them into classrooms because, as J. T. McKee observed, "from my experience the work rooms of the two teachers schools are being used very little."[28] On the other hand, some black school patrons saw industrial education as part of the modern educational system being provided to whites that should be extended to black schools, where it could support their own broader agenda for creating an independent institutional and community life.[29] Harris Oden, the person who complained about Elias Murdock, for example, was not a white official but the chair of the African American trustees board at Murdock's school.

Rosenwald planners and community members did share similar interpretations of the social aspect of their buildings. Just as their predecessor structures had been multipurpose buildings that served schoolchildren and teachers, church congregations, and fraternal lodge members, Rosenwald school buildings played multiple roles. Although their construction as purpose-built instructional rooms and school service spaces might have limited their usage, in fact the designers of Rosenwald schools anticipated that their structures would become community centers and designed them accordingly. Folding screens and sliding partitions between rooms could be pushed to the side or blackboards pushed up to open interior space for community gatherings, and stages set at the end of a classroom or in dedicated auditoriums supported musical and dramatic performances (figures 17, 19, 41, 42).[30] Mrs. Josephine Wheeler of Prosperity, South Carolina, recalled meeting her future husband at a magic show at the Shiloh School, where raised blackboards permitted a view of performers on a portable stage, as well as attending silent films and box supper socials with him in other Rosenwald facilities in the area. Mary Rogers explained that, when she was a student in the 1930s, community members in Eden Church, North Carolina, "used the school for everything": for church services, Sunday school classes, and entertainments.[31]

Whether or not an individual Rosenwald school emphasized industrial education, the building came to mean more to its community than an instructional environment for children. The response to a Rosenwald building was immediate and long-lasting. As construction got underway, cornerstone ceremonies announced local identity and pride, as when black masons laid the cornerstone of the Conecuh County Training School in Evergreen, Alabama, part of an impressive ceremony that included an address by Tuskegee principal Robert Russa Moton (figures 45–46).[32] Six hundred people gathered for the laying of a cornerstone for the training school in Warren County, Tennessee, where the white mayor of the county seat joined the black Rosenwald building agent on the speakers' platform.[33] Dedication events brought the Rosenwald campaign to a congratulatory finale. Over two thousand people attended the dedication of the Keith School in Dallas County, Alabama, in 1922.[34] The ceremony at the Vinegar Bend, Alabama, school marked yet another success for Mobile County Training School principal Isaiah J. Whitley and the other five members of the county campaign committee, who had kicked off a five-year, six-school construction program by inviting Booker T. Washington Jr. to the county in 1917.[35]

Black southerners integrated the completed building into the African American landscape by naming the school. The Rosenwald building program identified its schools by county, and then by a mixture of town names, given names, and the occasional school district number. A few simply bore the name "Rosenwald" or "county training school." Other schools honored such notables

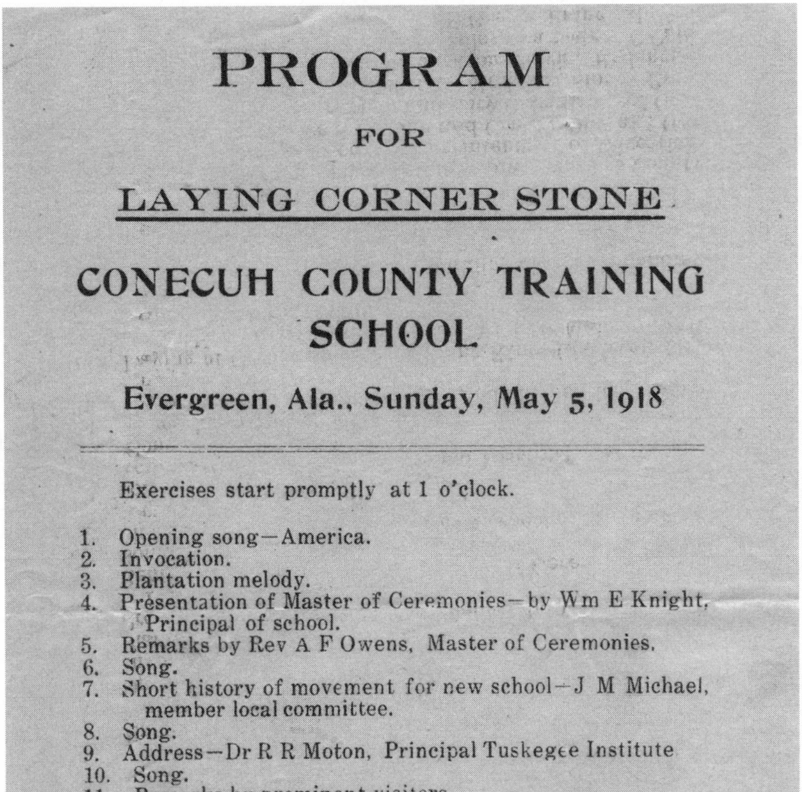

PROGRAM

FOR

LAYING CORNER STONE

CONECUH COUNTY TRAINING SCHOOL

Evergreen, Ala., Sunday, May 5, 1918

Exercises start promptly at 1 o'clock.

1. Opening song—America.
2. Invocation.
3. Plantation melody.
4. Presentation of Master of Ceremonies—by Wm E Knight, Principal of school.
5. Remarks by Rev A F Owens, Master of Ceremonies.
6. Song.
7. Short history of movement for new school—J M Michael, member local committee.
8. Song.
9. Address—Dr R R Moton, Principal Tuskegee Institute
10. Song.
11. Remarks by prominent visitors.
12. Reports of local committees on Funds Raised for "Dollar Rally."
13. Laying of Corner Stone by Coming King Lodge of Masons No. 70, Evergreen, Ala., Mr H C Malone, State Grand Master, presiding.
14. Song.
15. Closing remarks—Dr J A Franklin, chairman building committee.
16. Benediction.

Among the invited guests are the following: The County Board of Education; the County Superintendent of Education, Hon W R Bennett; Judge S P Dunn and County Officials; Hon W B Ivey, Mayor of Evergreen and City Officials; Prof Gordon Worley and Other School Officials; Mr Jas L Sibley, Rural School Agent, Montgomery; Mr Jackson Davis, Richmond, Va.; Dr James H Dillard, Charlottesvilles, Va.; Mr B C Caldwell, New Orleans, La.; Dr James E Gregg, Principal-Elect of Hampton Institute, Va.

Figure 45. Handbill for cornerstone-laying ceremony, Conecuh County Training School, Evergreen, Alabama, 1918. Events such as this, which featured important guests such as Tuskegee Institute principal Robert Russa Moton together with local leaders and the members of the Masonic lodge, celebrated a community's achievement. (Clinton J. Calloway Papers, University Archives and Museums, Tuskegee University)

Figure 46. Members of the Coming King Lodge of Masons No. 70 gather at the Conecuh County Training School, Evergreen, Alabama, 1918. (Rural School Photograph Collection, State Agent for Negro Rural Schools, Alabama Department of Education Records, Alabama Department of Archives and History, Montgomery, Alabama)

as Booker T. Washington, Paul Lawrence Dunbar, and the state Negro school agents and Rosenwald building agents. Much more common were church names—Mount Olive, Shiloh, Mount Zion—or familiar rural titles such as Shady Grove, Cedar Grove, Pleasant Grove that automatically located the new Rosenwald school within the preexisting landscape of black community life. Even when white authorities designated one name for the Rosenwald school, local people might prefer another: the Rosenwald school in South Carolina officially identified as Prosperity and later the Howard School, was the Shiloh School to those it served because it stood next to the Shiloh AME Church that had sponsored it.[36] Marianna, Florida, residents called the Jackson County Training School "Gilmore Academy" in honor of the man who led its building campaign. Names also provided continuity by tying the modern structure to a community's long-standing commitment to education, as with Tallahassee's Lincoln School, which dated to 1869.

The term "Rosenwald school" itself became an identifying label in which "Rosenwald" served as an adjective to distinguish it from other "colored" schools. No doubt some people mistakenly thought that the Rosenwald designation meant that Julius Rosenwald had paid for the building in its entirety. But once the confusion over the erroneous dollar-for-dollar grant announcement subsided, the reality that the Rosenwald grant was a match to local donations and that public funding was expected as well was widely publicized and understood. "Rosenwald school" became a descriptor for a building constructed specifically for African American children according to modern architectural and educational standards by forward-thinking community activists and leaders. Supporters invoked the Rosenwald school name to demonstrate their personal or professional success and community pride. Scholar James C. Carbaugh documented a Prosperity, South Carolina, man running for office in the African Methodist Episcopal Church on his record of establishing and teaching in Rosenwald schools. Virginia educators, like their peers across the South, sought recognition by reporting on successful Rosenwald building campaigns in the pages of their professional journal.[37]

Both participants and outsiders viewed Rosenwald schools as symbols of collective achievement. For some, that achievement was grounded in the family. Alfred Q. Jarrette, who wrote a biography of Julius Rosenwald, proudly recorded that his father, George W. Jarrette, had helped to build the Blakedale School in Anderson County, South Carolina, on land donated by Willis Sutton, his stepmother's father. Two uncles taught in the completed structure where Alfred Jarrette was a student, closing the family circle in the school.[38]

For others, the school expressed the spirit of the community. The Colored Public School Trustees Association of Prince George's County, Maryland, used Rosenwald schools as barometers of the communities they surveyed in 1923 and 1924, praising those that had completed Rosenwald projects and chiding school patrons and staff who had not yet taken action to replace their shabby facilities.[39] Jackson Davis of the General Education Board told another story of community pride and African American agency. He quoted the black minister who led a Virginia Rosenwald school campaign: "When the superintendent and our Jeanes teachers told us we could build this school, we did not think that we could do it. But here it is, nearly finished, and we are going to furnish it with new desks. Now we know that we can build schoolhouses and do any other good thing that we make up our minds to do." Davis certainly was hearing a narrative couched in the language of deference. Yet the minister also told a story of collective action in which the county's Jeanes teachers shared credit with the white superintendent for urging the project, and the minister himself was not only a spiritual leader but the president of the local school-improvement league.[40]

In all-black rural neighborhoods and towns, community identity included a strong sense of race pride and an independent black identity. Progressive whites active in reform causes in the South, including the Rosenwald building program, often proclaimed that new schools would build pride in a community. More likely, black southerners proudly included a Rosenwald school in their existing cultural landscapes and community identity. And in the everyday process of constructing community schools, black southerners asserted and white southerners acknowledged that identity and pride. Thus when D. P. Prater asked for Rosenwald money to support the building his community already had under construction, he made sure to tell the Alabama Negro school agent "we al are farmers own our Home."[41] In return, the white men who served as Negro school agents realized that their own goodwill and paternalism were not always sufficient to gain access to black communities. Georgia Negro school agent J. C. Dixon called upon Rosenwald building agent V. H. Harris to handle a consolidation proposal because "this, as you know, is an exceptional community, populated almost entirely by Negroes, almost all of whom are fairly well to do land owners. This means that they are men of good judgment and with minds of their own and must be handled very tactfully."[42] For black farmers in places like Betts Chapel, Texas, a Rosenwald school was simply a replacement building in an African American landscape populated by a school, stores, churches, and homes that had been evolving since emancipation.[43] Citizens of Oklahoma's all-black towns found the Rosenwald program a helpful ally as well; at least eleven of twenty-eight all-black towns boasted Rosenwald schools.[44]

This pattern of black agency, repeated thousands of times across fifteen states, broadened local African Americans' initiative and influence and put the burden on whites to recognize African Americans' educational needs and goals. Reflecting on the meaning of a Rosenwald school in 1923, Louisiana Negro school agent Leo Favrot judged, "there is no doubt that the building of Rosenwald schools has stimulated a greater interest in Negro education on the part of both white and colored people, has helped to make terms longer, to create a desire for better teachers, and a greater respect for the Negro school on the part of all concerned."[45] White observers like the state Negro school agents shaped their reports to emphasize interracial support by recognizing African American activism and the value of Rosenwald spaces.

THE ROSENWALD SCHOOL IN THE COMMUNITY: CONTESTING MEANING

Even with their modest facades and industrial rooms, and despite claims of interracial cooperation, some whites thought Rosenwald schools were too good for the black landscape. In 1918, Louisiana Negro school agent Leo Favrot lamented: "I have just lost my most interesting parish training school. It was burned down Saturday night by a low class of prejudiced whites. It was a school in Jackson Parish. We are doing all we can to try to run down the incendiaries, but we understand that the parish authorities are not with us, and it is going to be a hard job." Anticipating the legal strategies of later civil rights activists, Favrot considered pressing federal charges on the basis of the school's federally funded Smith-Hughes vocational program.[46]

The destruction of Rosenwald schools continued a pattern of white attempts to suppress black aspirations that extended back into the antebellum period and had become endemic in the post–Civil War South.[47] When Rosenwald schools burned, building program administrators pressed each other to determine what had happened. S. L. Smith followed up on reports of two school fires in North Carolina, asking "whether the fires were incendiary or accidental. If the former state whether they have been able to find out the guilty party and just what has been done by the legal authorities. . . . [I]s the feeling and relations between the races in these communities cordial?" Fires at frame buildings heated by wood-burning stoves were not uncommon, so white officials made a point of identifying accidental school fires to distinguish them from arson. They also claimed that many cases of arson resulted from factional divisions among black community members.[48] The reluctance of white Rosenwald building program staff and school officials to blame white incendiaries may stem in part from the Rosenwald Fund's policy of paying out a second grant for insured school buildings that had been destroyed and possibly from a reluctance to contradict their own propaganda about the positive effect that Rosenwald school projects had on relations between the races in southern communities. Furthermore, the Rosenwald Fund tried to avoid provoking racist vigilantes, realizing that the combination of Jewish philanthropy and African American education was tailor-made to trigger their wrath.

Thus, one of the favorite anecdotes told by Rosenwald program officials concerned the Mississippi county superintendent who arranged to build twenty-five schools in one month to forestall Ku Klux Klan opposition. As S. L. Smith recounted the story, Warren County school superintendent John H. Culkin wanted ten two-teacher and fifteen three-teacher buildings to replace forty of the "shacks" currently in use but realized that "there might be some individuals or an organization which would oppose building schools for Negroes, particularly because the superintendent was a Catholic and one of his board members was a Jew." Instead of the usual publicity that accompanied building campaigns, Culkin worked quietly through sympathetic whites and black supporters to have 160 mule-drawn wagons readied to meet a load of pre-cut lumber at the Vicksburg railroad depot on a specified day. When the wagons arrived at their designated building sites, local workmen had readied the foundations and began raising the walls. Meanwhile, the county's Jeanes supervisor had organized women's clubs to prepare lunches for the work crews, and club members and schoolchildren worked on the landscaping themselves. The superintendent, anticipating a court injunction against his plan, disappeared from public view for a week until all the buildings were framed and roofed. What Smith could only call "the group opposing the building of the schools" abandoned their legal challenge and threatened to defeat Superintendent Culkin, but, as Smith proudly pointed out, Culkin not only won at the county polls but went on to a state political career.[49]

Nevertheless, prepossessing structures like the two-story school at Wilson, Arkansas, made easy targets for antagonistic whites. The story of the Wilson School's construction, destruction, and resurrection became legendary among Rosenwald officials and the small Arkansas community's residents and suggests the economic causes of some antiblack violence. R. E. Lee Wilson had contributed most of the building's $55,000 cost, while school patrons had collected $1,000 for their self-help contribution, and the Rosenwald Fund awarded a grant of $1,500. Wilson "own[ed] every building in this town," as well as 30,000 acres of land that his black tenants planted in cotton. Thus the school was clearly part of his economic dominance, and any attack on it was anti-Wilson as well as antiblack. The new Wilson School building burned to the ground just hours before its dedication. A newspaper account of the school's burning described it as "a fire of unknown origin," but according to local black historians, the Wilson School "was so much like the white school that it is believed the community radicals burned it."[50] S. L. Smith came over from Nashville for the dedication ceremony, only to find "the building was in ashes. . . . Mr. Wilson looked on without discussing the probable cause, calmly smoking his cigarette."

Smith and the school's principal followed Wilson to his office, where he "really gave vent to his feelings" of paternalistic outrage. Wilson reportedly said: "I felt that these Negroes deserved this building. They have helped me to make what I have, and I wanted to do something to help them in a substantial way, while I am living." Wilson had no sympathy for the whites who challenged his authority over the local black labor force, and not much more for the distraught principal weeping over the community's loss. According to Smith, Wilson exclaimed: "Richards, for God's sake shut up. I will start to rebuilding it next Monday—an exact duplicate of the one that burned, except that I may build it of brick and hollow tile," obviously so that it could not burn down. That afternoon, Wilson repeated his offer to the crowd gathered at the Baptist Church, who pledged another $500 of their own. The new brick building surpassed its predecessor (figure 34). Accommodating fourteen teachers in its two-story rectangular block structure, the Wilson School cost $60,000, of which $1,000 came from the community and $58,454 from Robert Wilson, plus a second Rosenwald grant of $546.[51]

Most white opposition and direct action against Rosenwald schools reacted to African American success in adding a new, modern feature to the black landscape, which these whites interpreted as a clear signal that black people wanted equality. At times, the Rosenwald school came under attack for threatening the shifting boundaries between white and black neighborhoods and class aspirations. White "workmen" in Kingsport, Tennessee, who had built cottages on inexpensive land adjacent to a black settlement blocked construction of a Rosenwald school in that city for five years.[52] Kingsport, a new industrial planned city in northeastern Tennessee, attracted white workers seeking jobs, decent pay, and the opportunity to own their own homes. Black workers held the same ambitions for better lives for themselves and their families, expressed in part in their desire for a Rosenwald school. Those two landscapes of hope could not overlap without generating racial conflict within the city's working class.

Whites challenged the visible message of a Rosenwald school by invading its space and claiming its material advantages for themselves, hoping to bring the new school down to a level they believed more appropriate for African Americans or to reassert white power in black spaces. E. A. McGruder took the folding doors out of the Wedgeworth, Alabama, school and installed them in his new home. In Tensas Parish, Louisiana, David Miller confiscated the new patent desks at the Loam Land School for the school on his own plantation, using his power as the chair of the board of education and as a planter to retain control over the distribution of resources to black tenants.[53] J. L. Newman tried for years to take over the Parker's Chapel School, a three-teacher Rosenwald building in Seminole County, Oklahoma, for white students.[54] Yet the balance of power had slightly shifted. In these communities, black citizens had already forged alliances with officials at state departments of education and the Rosenwald building program, and they used the power of those allies to force the return or replacement of stolen items and to rebuild burned schools. Their Rosenwald schools strengthened African Americans' hold on the southern landscape.

ROSENWALD SCHOOLS IN AND ACROSS THE LANDSCAPE

A completed Rosenwald school stood as a symbol of community values and achievement, the visible result of local initiative and persistence. As a physical space where teachers, students, and patrons put a community's cultural capital—its resources, values, and aspirations—into action, each Rosenwald school fulfilled the goals of the school-building program's regional and state administrators as well as the local people who gave it meaning. Every Rosenwald school campaign followed its own unique path to achieve those goals. Local people also established a broader significance for their individual Rosenwald schools by forging partnerships with state and program authorities in a network that spanned fifteen states.

Rosenwald program planners expected that standardized designs would create that group identity, and the underlying consistency of Rosenwald school architecture did establish a common vocabulary of visual images and material culture for African American and white schools across the region. How that common vocabulary gained meaning and power becomes more clear when viewed from within the network of local people who sustained the Rosenwald school program rather than its plan books and official reports. One teacher's career provides a vantage point for tracing that development across time and space, that of Charles N. Hunter of North Carolina. Following Hunter from school to school illuminates the evolution of the building program at the local level between 1914 and 1932 and the interconnections between local people, state officials, and Rosenwald program administrators. The creation of a Rosenwald school network is perhaps most visible in North Carolina, the state with the largest number of Rosenwald buildings and an extensive documentary record, but such a network could be documented for many others.

Some background about Hunter himself can help explain why the downward spiral of his personal career created a valuable record of the dynamic expansion of the Rosenwald building program. Hunter had been born into slavery in 1852 and educated in a freedmen's school, at Shaw University, the University of South Carolina, and Hampton Institute, although he never earned an academic degree. He gained prominence as a founder of the North Carolina Industrial Association and as an active member of the National Association for the Advancement of Colored People and the North Carolina Negro Business League, as well as a Republican Party campaigner. A member of an activist elite of "race men" who had made the transition from enslavement to leadership and believed that they should now lead the African American masses, Hunter was an iconoclast who offered support to Democrats when the Republican Party turned to a lily-white strategy, organized a reunion of former slaves and masters, and supported a planned monument to "Mammy." To advance black North Carolinians in a white-dominated society, Hunter advocated self-help and industrial education and called for greater appreciation of black literary achievements as well as "the importance of race history."[55]

A major force among African American activists in his home state at the turn of the century, by the late 1910s Hunter had fallen out of step with a new generation of African American teachers, patrons, and students. Compounded by personal problems and conflicts with his former ally, the influential black businessman Berry O'Kelly, Hunter's professional prospects diminished. Hunter's unfortunately peripatetic career nevertheless provides a succession of snapshots of Rosenwald campaigns that reflect the program's runaway success across North Carolina. Like other principals and teachers, he initiated and implemented Rosenwald school-construction projects, inherited ongoing campaigns, raised local contributions, and ran afoul of both white superintendents and black school patrons when their school-building interests collided. He sought help from white state officials to gain access to Rosenwald money and to use their leverage over local authorities when he thought that African American schoolchildren were being shortchanged.

Charles Hunter's first experience with Rosenwald schools was a catalyst for North Carolina's entry into the building program. Hunter had been among those many African American educators who responded immediately to Booker T. Washington's announcement of Julius Rosenwald's new philanthropic agenda. In 1914, Hunter was principal of the Method Training School, of which Berry O'Kelly was the leading patron. He had already established relationships with Wake County superintendent Zebulon Judd, assistant superintendent Edith Royster, and state agent for Negro schools Nathan C. Newbold, with whom he was working to secure Slater Fund support for the Method school as a county training school and had already discussed the need for a new school facility. Fortuitously, Charles Hunter and Berry O'Kelly had arranged to meet with Zebulon Judd to talk about their building needs at the same time that the *New York Age* published Tuskegee Institute's press release.[56]

Coordinating their efforts with the state department of education, Hunter, O'Kelly, Newbold, and state superintendent J. Y. Joyner wrote simultaneously for information about Rosenwald grants on 2 and 3 July 1914. They had orchestrated their correspondence campaign by race. Joyner and Newbold wrote to Julius Rosenwald. Hunter and O'Kelly wrote to Booker T. Washington, who would have known O'Kelly and perhaps Hunter from his meetings with the state's black business leaders in 1910.[57] Claiming that he himself had been "preaching to our people here the Gospel of Self Help," Hunter informed Washington that he could expect a visit from Newbold, whom he described as "a man of rare excellence." Anticipating a positive response, Judd, Newbold, and Joyner prepared a letter of introduction for Berry O'Kelly to use in soliciting donations, assuring potential donors of a matching gift "from another source." But Booker T. Washington politely informed the North Carolinians that the Rosenwald plan was still being developed and warned Superintendent Judd that the Method school fell outside Rosenwald's concern for one-teacher schools in rural communities.[58]

Undeterred, Hunter, O'Kelly, and Method school patrons proceeded with their building project. Hunter, a leader within the North Carolina Teachers Association and editor of its journal, the *Progressive Educator*, saw his next chance when the association appointed Charles H. Moore as North Carolina's Rosenwald building agent. He asked Moore to "get Mr. Washington interested and have him join you in an appeal" for the Method school.[59] Although he was credited in 1914 with transforming the Method school into one of North Carolina's best African American schools, a few years later Hunter had fallen from grace. An ardent exponent of self-help, Hunter had greater difficulty in demonstrating his support for industrial education. A negative evaluation of the school by a visitor from Hampton Institute; Method church and lodge members' discomfort with Hunter's age and status as a former slave; growing tensions with teachers; and a falling out with Berry O'Kelly over Hunter's personal financial problems only added to his woes. Shortly after publishing an article in which he claimed that black North Carolinians would stay in the state if they could have decent wages and better schools, Hunter lost his job at Method in September 1917.[60]

Between 1914 and 1917, Hunter was part of an established network of African American activists and educators in North Carolina, which gave him standing to make his appeals to state authorities and Tuskegee Institute. Like many others who sought Rosenwald grants in the program's early years, he was unable to secure money for a large town school, but his campaign helped to put pressure on Tuskegee officials to broaden the program and to ally black educators and activists with state officials. By the time that Hunter returned to North Carolina schools, those precedents had borne fruit in an expanded building program, a growing staff of state bureaucrats attuned to philanthropic programs, and an upsurge of grassroots organizing. Everywhere he went,

Hunter found himself in a Rosenwald building or campaigning for one, reflecting black community activism and the growing strength of alliances between patrons, teachers, the Rosenwald building agent, and the state agent for Negro schools.

In the 1921–22 school year, Hunter taught at the Pleasant Hill School in Wake County, where a Rosenwald building was under construction, and was offered the principalship of the Wakefield-Zebulon School, a Rosenwald school built in 1919–20. Instead, Hunter took the principalship at the Haywood School in Chatham County, which had received a Rosenwald grant in 1918–19. At Haywood, Hunter initiated campaigns for county training school status and for Rosenwald assistance in either adding to the existing four-teacher Rosenwald school or for building a teachers' home. One of his fund-raising techniques borrowed on a strategy he had used previously at Method. Contributors to "The $5.00 Club" promised to give fifty cents cash and pay fifty cents a month into the Haywood School building fund at a local bank.[61] Next Hunter transferred to the Horton School (recorded in Rosenwald Fund files as the Pittsboro School), constructed in 1923–24. Hunter had suggested the name to commemorate George M. Horton, an African American writer who had been born in slavery nearby.[62] But unnamed "conditions . . . most unfortunate and unfair" arose simultaneously with the building's completion in the fall of 1923, and, after a brief stint at Johnston County's Booker T. Washington School, Hunter moved to Wilson's Mills and yet another Rosenwald building project.[63] This Rosenwald campaign had been underway at least since the spring of 1919, when Charles H. Moore reported that a rally had netted $157.50 for a new building. The project had foundered and almost wrecked in the winter of 1925–26, when a dispute erupted over the location of the new building. Hunter did not approve of the site, which he predicted to N. C. Newbold would prove "a bootleggers rendezvous and a crap shooters paradise." After the newly hired W. F. Credle and the state director of schoolhouse planning visited Wilson's Mills and approved the site, Hunter had to give in. But like other African American community leaders, once he had an official's attention, he attempted to leverage more support from the state and next inquired about additional funding for a teachers' home.[64]

Again Hunter came into an ongoing Rosenwald campaign and saw it to completion, only to lose his job. Parents complained that Hunter did not do enough for "advancement of the pupils there, in classroom work"; Hunter countered that older pupils and their parents had organized against him, and that other patrons did "not like to hear me speak kindly of the white people and do not like to hear the white people speak kindly of me," and denounced black school trustees as a "positive drawback to our schools."[65] By October 1926, Hunter had taken a teaching job at the Manchester School in Cumberland County, where once again he encountered a Rosenwald school under construction, which was dedicated in the spring of 1927. By now a familiar correspondent to the state's division of Negro education, Hunter kept W. F. Credle apprised of local school authorities' failure to live up to the Rosenwald Fund's standards: the blackboards were old and worn-out as well as too few, the desks and heating stoves likewise were broken cast-offs from other schools, and no toilets had been provided whatsoever. Credle pressured the county superintendent on building standards, but he could do nothing about a salary dispute that drove Hunter out of Manchester and to the already-completed Rosenwald school at Raeford in Hoke County in the fall of 1927.[66]

Despite his long and varied associations with the Rosenwald school-building program, Hunter could not bring himself to attend the elaborate dedication ceremonies for the 1928 building at the Berry O'Kelly Training School, the four-thousandth Rosenwald school building.[67] He could have testified not only to the sheer number of Rosenwald schools in the state but also to ways local people marshaled their resources to invest in modern school buildings and both cooperated and struggled with their local school authorities and each other. Stories from his experiences could have revealed how educators and school patrons used the Rosenwald building program to hold state and local governments accountable for the construction and operation of black public schools.

The Jones School in Martin County was probably Hunter's last encounter with a Rosenwald school before his death in 1932, and it offers a fitting example of the multiple meanings that Rosenwald program participants invested in their schools. As principal, Hunter presided over the Rosenwald School Day celebration. The materials he kept from that day offer not only a snapshot of a community's celebration of its Rosenwald building but an extended narrative of the local forces that brought the Rosenwald school into being. Hunter obtained a history of the Jones School prepared by its previous principal, who had also taught at the school for many years.[68] The 1925 Rosenwald facility had taken its place in a longer tradition of black education: "It is said that the Jones School had its origin as far back as the [eighteen] eighties. The first schools were taught in the church on the same plot of ground that present church and school now stand," until the community obtained a one-teacher building lit by six windows and equipped it with a small blackboard and about a dozen homemade desks. As the scholastic population grew, another teacher came to share the facility, and eventually one class moved to the lodge hall. Complaints about overcrowding mounted until a Jeanes supervisor arrived on the scene and, as happened in many southern communities, redirected local dissatisfaction into a Rosenwald campaign: "Mrs. Gray being Supervisor informed the Com[munity] of the Rosenwald Fund. Every body was interested and took hold at once." Families in the school district imposed a ten-dollar tax on themselves, held rallies, and printed up "begging cards" that they used to solicit individual contributions. With the required $500 local contribution in hand, the building went up in the summer and fall of 1925, although as was so often the case, the principal and teachers had to give several "socials" to raise another hundred dollars to furnish the building with the necessary window shades, as well as wastebaskets, wash basins, and curtains. The four-teacher school served over two hundred enrolled students, who, the writer proudly noted, won prizes each year at countywide competitions, demonstrated their needlework and cooking prowess in school exhibitions, and were still holding socials to raise funds for school equipment.

In contrast, Charles Hunter's account of the Rosenwald Day program, most of which followed the guidelines sent out by the Rosenwald Fund and the state division of Negro education, told a tale of a generous philanthropist, the white and black southerners who supported Martin County's black public schools, and the "neat, attractive" black churches in the midst of a transient African American tenant class. Both accounts are necessary to understand "what a change has been wrought," in Charles Hunter's words. The Jones School was a modern building far removed from the schools for black children commonly found in rural North Carolina when Hunter had begun his teaching career. When it opened in 1925, it joined over seven hundred other Rosenwald buildings across the state, each of which exemplified a community's enduring commitment to education and the philanthropy that gave them greater power to achieve their goals. Charles Hunter's journey from one Rosenwald school to another speaks volumes about him and the schools. An outspoken political and social commentator who found himself lacking the professional credentials and personal skills needed to maintain himself as an educational leader, Hunter could not adapt to the changing expectations of black school patrons. Yet those patrons had been following a path he blazed to Rosenwald grants in 1914, working on their own and with a receptive state education department to build the facilities that would advance their children.

Hunter's experiences within the network of Rosenwald schools record the schools' expansion across the landscape of one southern state; in combination with other accounts, his experiences also suggest the place of the Rosenwald school network within the history of black public education across time. Scholars such as Thomas W. Hanchett, David S. Cecelski, Vanessa Siddle Walker, and Betty J. Reed have placed North Carolina's Rosenwald schools in a historical continuum extending from Reconstruction through the late twentieth century. In particular, their accounts point up how the Rosenwald building program spoke to community values and benefited from the economic, social, and spiritual resources that local people contributed. They also help us to understand how specific Rosenwald schools came to embody something more than the institutionalized racism of segregation. The meanings and material resources that local people invested in these schools made them independent institutional alternatives to racism tightly bound to their communities through bonds of caring, professionalism, and community involvement. So strong was their hold that local people only reluctantly surrendered these schools and their successor buildings to school desegregation and integration plans. Today alumni associations celebrate these schools with reunions and monuments and commemorate them in a present-day grassroots network of activists forging their own alliances with state and national historical agencies.[69]

In *Cooperation in Southern Communities*, T. J. Woofter Jr. and Isaac Fisher commented on the goodwill fostered by the Commission on Interracial Cooperation: "the local community is the place in which permanent improvement in race relations must be made, and . . . the problem of race relations in its larger aspects is but the sum total of numerous local situations, and these can be satisfactorily adjusted only by conference and cooperation between the white and colored leaders within the local communities."[70] Woofter and Fisher were not blind to the realities of black life in the rural South even if they were overly optimistic about the effects of "conference and cooperation." But their words ring true in the experiences recorded by participants in the Rosenwald school-building program. Each Rosenwald school's story opens a small window into those "numerous local situations" that signal the critical significance of the local community. Products of a regional initiative that operated through state organizations to reach into local communities, Rosenwald schools stood in the past, and stand today, as physical reminders that "the local community is the place in which permanent improvement . . . must be made" and of the people who made that improvement possible.

Conclusion

From Model Schools to Historic Schools:
Rosenwald Schools after 1932

In his last official report, Georgia Rosenwald building agent Vincent H. Harris observed that he had fewer meetings to attend "because I could not give any encouragement as to the assistance a community would receive from the Rosenwald Fund." Even so, he had been campaigning in places where the board of education seemed favorable, and he reported that the Georgia Teachers and Educators Association would continue to work with school patrons and teachers to keep children in school and to increase public support.[1] Teachers and patrons would next join forces with the federal agencies created by Franklin Delano Roosevelt's New Deal. Meanwhile, the Julius Rosenwald Fund embarked on Edwin Embree's ambitious agenda for social change, and Samuel Smith monitored a new wave of professional school-design initiatives. Decades later, Rosenwald schools would reemerge from obscurity as historic places of community achievement and reminders of African Americans' historic struggle for educational justice.

For unknown numbers of African American southerners, as well as the Rosenwald building agents and the state agents for Negro schools, the demise of the Rosenwald school-building program had been a vast disappointment. Why should they have regretted the loss of the Rosenwald school-building program, which left thousands of black schoolchildren in dilapidated shacks and community churches untouched by any Rosenwald school campaign? Even though Rosenwald schools accounted for over half of the increased value of public school facilities between 1920 and 1930, investment in African American public schools still lagged behind the growing investment in white public schools, and segregation and discrimination would keep African American schools miserably underfunded for years to come.

Nevertheless, black southerners then and now, and succeeding generations of scholars and activists, have looked to Rosenwald schools as a significant step in the development of African American and universal public education in the modern United States. The Rosenwald school-building program instigated a public investment in black schools that otherwise would not have taken place

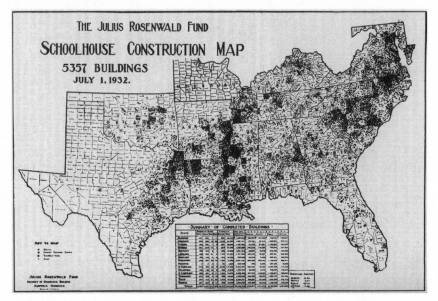

Figure 47. The Julius Rosenwald Fund School Construction Map, 1932. The Rosenwald Fund published these maps annually; this one, the last, shows the distribution of Rosenwald buildings in communities across fifteen states.

or would have been much smaller. Rosenwald schools housed one-third of the South's African American public school pupils and teachers and accounted for one-fifth of the South's black public schools and just under one-third of their property value (figure 47).[2] Significantly, that investment was now an integral part of the South's public school infrastructure. Black education did not depend on the Rosenwald building program, for clearly black southerners would continue their self-help or double taxation; a philanthropist or foundation could always give money. Instead, the Rosenwald building program sought to embed black schools in the South's public education systems, both by requiring public ownership and by using its grants and black self-help to leverage public funding. Working within the building program's guidelines, black southerners gained access to the growing power of southern educational bureaucracies and the public revenues. Furthermore, the Rosenwald program's emphasis on raising design and construction standards ensured increasing public investment in its schools. Tax revenues, as a result, eventually accounted for 63.73 percent of the cost of Rosenwald school construction, compared to 16.64 percent given by African Americans, 15.36 percent contributed by Julius Rosenwald and the Rosenwald Fund, and 4.27 percent by white donors. Furthermore, Rosenwald schools made it possible for more children to attend school for longer terms and to advance through higher grade levels, contributing to overall increases in African American school attendance and literacy, as well as to the decline in child labor.[3]

This study has argued that Rosenwald schools physically represented a better place for African Americans in the public landscape of the South. As Rosenwald schools became model schools, they also created potentially subversive physical statements about southern education by stripping away more and more of its racial identifiers. Those were the objectives of Rosenwald school program planners from Booker T. Washington and Julius Rosenwald to Edwin Embree and Samuel Smith and also of the state agents for Negro schools and Rosenwald building agents. They could celebrate real success in creating modern learning environments and advancing the cause of black education in their professions. The people who executed those plans in five thousand communities, especially African American southerners, not only made that success possible, but they also transformed Rosenwald schools into community institutions. The Rosenwald school-building program magnified the economic, social, and political leverage of their school campaigns.[4] Rosenwald schools became part of the cultural capital held by their communities, a productive investment in social change upon which community members could draw as they saw fit.

Community School Plans in the New Deal

As the national economic crisis worsened in 1932, the future of existing Rosenwald schools and opportunities for any other new investment in black public education seemed bleak. Some aspects of the Rosenwald Fund's programs related to school buildings would survive, at least for a few years, such as the library program and Rosenwald School Day. In addition, the fund's southern office in Nashville would continue its campaign for professional school design through the Interstate School Building Service and the National Council on Schoolhouse Construction, along with a new organization, the Committee on School Plant Rehabilitation. At the state and local levels, however, black public schools found their best ally in the federal government. New Deal agencies would temporarily pump some much-needed moneys back into school-improvement and school-construction projects, often using the Rosenwald Fund's plans and guidelines.

With the loss of its major project, the Rosenwald Fund's Southern Office cut Fred McCuistion and William F. Credle from the staff.[5] Most southern states' plans to construct new public schools for black children stopped just as abruptly. State agents for Negro schools like Georgia's J. Curtis Dixon hoped against hope for a change of heart in Chicago. "What do you really think, Mr. Smith?" Dixon asked the Nashville office director early in 1933. "Do you feel there may be more Rosenwald money available for school building purposes if and when the market conditions improve?"[6] He was not the only, or the last, public school official to ask this question. Florida Negro school agent Dewitt E. Williams received a 1936 petition from his state's Association of County Superintendents, who "respectfully urge[d] that the Rosenwald Fund resume the practice of encouraging by gifts the construction of suitable school buildings for negro children. . . . Many of us know from experience the good effect of a substantial contribution as an inducement to the Board to erect a building."[7]

State Negro school agents and the Rosenwald Fund's Southern Office began hunting for new funding sources from the federal government. North Carolina's Division of Negro Education applied for aid from the Reconstruction Finance Corporation, for example, and once President Franklin Delano Roosevelt began launching his New Deal agencies in 1933, state Negro school agents had more success with the Federal Emergency Relief Administration (FERA) and its Civilian Works Administration (CWA). By that fall, Samuel L. Smith was directing his correspondents to the CWA for assistance with schoolhouse renovation, toilet and privy construction, and building projects.[8] As President Roosevelt expanded the array of New Deal agencies, state agents for Negro schools asked Rosenwald Fund officers for help in lobbying federal program administrators to take up where the fund had left off, a task assigned to the Southern Office's new special field agent, Garth H. Akridge.[9]

The Julius Rosenwald Fund responded to the continuing demand for its services and the opportunity presented by federal initiatives with a new program for renovating existing Rosenwald schools in the mid-1930s. What became known as the school plant rehabilitation project had its roots in several different but related projects from the Rosenwald building program: the suggestions for repairing and repainting schools that Fred McCuistion prepared for Rosenwald School Day in the early 1930s; the General Education Board's support for state divisions of schoolhouse planning; and the Interstate School Building Service. In 1933 and 1934, Smith prepared two new pamphlets, *Suggestions for Repairing and Repainting School Plants* and *Suggestions for Improvement and Beautification, School Plants*, both issued jointly by the Rosenwald Fund and the Interstate School Building Service.[10] From 1934 until 1938, the Committee on School Plant Rehabilitation, led by S. L. Smith, met to set new standards and monitor the results. The committee's members were mostly former Fletcher B. Dresslar students and current directors of schoolhouse planning, and they continued the tradition of cooperation between the Julius Rosenwald Fund and the General Education Board.[11]

Members of the school plant rehabilitation committee began their work with a survey of the condition of all existing Rosenwald schools, from which they established priorities for their new improvement guidelines. The committee produced two bulletins that the Julius Rosenwald Fund published and circulated to state departments of education and state directors of the Works Progress Administration (WPA) and the National Youth Administration (NYA): *Improvement and Beautification of Rural Schools* and *Suggestions for Landscaping Rural Schools*. Smith also coordinated the efforts of three countywide demonstration projects for school plant rehabilitation in Coahoma County, Mississippi; Nash County, North Carolina; and Montgomery County, Tennessee; as well as a school landscaping demonstration for the State of Virginia. The Mississippi and Tennessee state departments of education and county superintendents cooperated with the FERA, WPA, and NYA to renovate and build schools; in all three locations, the Rosenwald Fund paid for a county school plant mechanic to direct the work, as well as for his truck and tools. The Montgomery County project, which covered all black and white public schools, employed between twenty-five and thirty men each from the FERA and WPA, and all available NYA laborers of both races.[12]

As Montgomery County's example suggests, the Rosenwald Fund's school plant rehabilitation project followed the same trajectory as Rosenwald School Day, from an initial focus on Rosenwald-aided schools to all black schools to schools for all children. School rehabilitation and landscaping bulletins helped to disseminate the project's goals and guidelines by using African American schools as examples of what could be done with any school building. They also dovetailed with the increasingly biracial celebrations of Rosenwald School Day. Leo M. Favrot, the General Education Board's representative on the school plant rehabilitation committee, had devised the plan for the contest, which state departments of education adopted and incorporated into Rosenwald School Day celebrations.[13] Printed programs for many Rosenwald School Day observances in the mid-1930s included portions of the Rosenwald Fund and ISBS pamphlets as well as instructions for the beautification contest, which in 1935 was limited to counties where either a Jeanes supervisor worked or at least one Rosenwald school stood. In succeeding years, the contest widened its potential audience to all black and any interested white public schools.

But some state agents for Negro schools had to admit that Rosenwald School Day was still less than a complete success, making the school plant contest even more problematic in the current economic crisis. J. Curtis Dixon of Georgia routinely exchanged copies of Rosenwald School Day bulletins with his peers in other state education departments. In 1935, he confessed to Mississippi state agent for Negro schools Perry H. Easom that he had not been especially diligent about distributing materials for the contests, commenting: "I am quite worried about both of these projects. I am wondering if the Rosenwald School Day Program has not served its purpose." Easom agreed and added, "I never have seen a great deal accomplished by Rosenwald Day." Dixon's assistant Negro school agent, Robert L. Cousins, complained two years later that "it is getting to be quite a problem to find interesting material for such a program."[14] Lacking widespread grassroots support and official state interest, school rehabilitation contests and Rosenwald School Day celebrations ceased soon after the closing of the Southern Office in Nashville.

The Julius Rosenwald Fund's school plant rehabilitation initiative, with or without Rosenwald School Day, never got past its emphasis on professional expertise to catch the imaginations of community members. The New Deal's investment in the nation's public school infrastructure did, and New Deal programs replaced the Rosenwald Fund in communities outside the school plant demonstration projects and contests.[15] For some community members, the New Deal revived an earlier Rosenwald school project, like that in New Hope, Alabama. Families there had begun raising their required contribution for a Rosenwald school in 1928. After several years, they purchased a school site only to discover that the Rosenwald building program had ended. "Not to be outdone, however," a teacher recalled, "the citizens of the community approached the County Board of Education for a school and the present structure, a two-room building, was built in 1936, with W.P.A. help."[16] In Rose Hill, Mississippi, newly appointed principal A. B. Hardy led what might have been a typical Rosenwald school campaign, but with the WPA. He had begun work in the Ticoh School in 1933, which met in a church because the school building had been torn down for salvage "with the hope of building a new one," perhaps an anticipated Rosenwald school. After contacting state agent for Negro schools Perry H. Easom, Hardy and a "conscientious group of followers" bought land and lumber and secured funding from the WPA. The new building followed a plan supplied by the Mississippi Department of Education—a Community School Plan 6–B.[17]

With New Deal agencies taking the place of the Julius Rosenwald Fund in school-building partnerships with African American communities, it was only fitting that the fund made one last grant for a Rosenwald school at the behest of President Franklin Delano Roosevelt. Samuel L. Smith had met briefly with Roosevelt when he was governor of New York during the 1929 meeting of the National Council on Schoolhouse Construction. A Rosenwald school near Warm Springs, Georgia, had impressed Roosevelt, and he wanted to see one built in his summer home community. Smith sent him one of the *Community School Plans* bulletins, but the county board of education used all of a $15,000 local building appropriation to build a seven-teacher Community School Plan structure for white children instead. Five years later, President Roosevelt informed Smith that Warm Springs was ready for the $2,500 Rosenwald grant Smith had "promised" for the black school. Edwin R. Embree reluctantly approved the project, as long as no one got the idea that the fund was renewing its interest in school construction and only if Roosevelt would take a public role.[18] The Eleanor Roosevelt School opened in March 1937 with a dedication speech by the president, the 5,358th and final Rosenwald building.[19]

Smith's final triumph has to be measured against the remaining desperate needs of African American public education in southern states. Carter G. Woodson had warned in 1927 that "only about one-half of the Negroes in most of the Southern states have actually been offered real facilities of education." In 1934, 1,428 of Mississippi's 3,737 public schools for African Americans still met in private buildings "such as barns, lodges, tenant cabins, churches," and surveys of black schools in other states found similar miserable conditions.[20] "Despite the good work done with the aid of the Rosenwald Fund," conceded Virginia's state Negro school agent, "there are still many buildings over the state that should be replaced with modern structures."[21]

That situation would remain unchanged for decades. In 1937, S. L. Smith and longtime secretary Bessie Carney closed the Southern Office of the Julius Rosenwald Fund.[22] State departments of education, meanwhile, continued to rely on *Community School Plans*. Smith transferred the plans to the Interstate School Building Service at George Peabody College for Teachers in 1937, along with the headache of replicating and distributing them. Georgia assistant Negro school agent R. L. Cousins asked Smith to reassure ISBS director Ray Hamon that his repeated requests for blueprints were for legitimate New Deal construction projects. "Without such plans," he reminded Smith, "it would be impossible for us to proceed with our building program since our help from the Division of Schoolhouse Construction is rather limited."[23] The Interstate School Building Service kept apace with the unceasing demand for these plans with

Figure 48. Rosenwald Middle School signs, Panama City, Bay County, Florida. This late twentieth-century school is a descendent of a four-teacher Rosenwald school constructed 1927–28. (Photograph by author)

Figure 49. Sign pointing to the Rosenwald softball fields, Osceola, Mississippi County, Arkansas. Citizens of Osceola constructed a six-teacher Rosenwald school here in 1925. A nearby stone tablet commemorates the school: "Dedicated to the Faculty and Students of Osceola Rosenwald High School, 1925–1971." (Photograph by author)

a 1941 supplement to the 1931 Rosenwald Fund plan book called *Community Units*, which featured designs for a freestanding meeting hall and a community center, and then its own version of *Community School Plans* with designs for specific classroom types and a homemaking cottage, cannery, and agricultural shop in 1944. Even in the midst of the Second World War, this publication still advertised the availability of the Rosenwald Fund's school plans at no cost.[24]

For at least a decade after the demise of the building program, the aura around Rosenwald schools remained strong. A 1939 article on southern schools for African Americans noted that "so strong is the tradition that good schools are Rosenwald schools," that some constructed after the program's demise appropriated the name for themselves.[25] In the years that followed, Rosenwald schools met varied fates, and while the Rosenwald name lingered on signs and in memories, in some places their history faded away even if pride in local schools did not.[26] Rosenwald schools had helped black public schools keep pace with, and even promoted, the improvements made to schools for white children.[27] In most states, that upward trend leveled off and public funding for black school buildings would decline until the late 1940s. Then the threat of desegregation inspired southern states to embark on massive building campaigns in a last-ditch effort to prove that separate could be equal. They were wrong, and desegregation cost even more Rosenwald schools their place on the landscape.

Many communities, however, held onto their Rosenwald schools as markers of communal spirit. Rosenwald schools had enlarged the black public landscape in southern states. The process of creating that new space had implications for social relationships in other public and private spaces as well. Building a Rosenwald school had required intense organization within African American communities, often with familiar male and female community leaders such as ministers and Jeanes supervisors at the forefront. They and the men, women, and children who supplied the community's contribution to the school could do so by relying on traditional divisions of labor by class, religious affiliation, gender, and age. But they also challenged and even fought each other over their school campaigns, risked financial ruin, and provoked white opposition. Furthermore, the Rosenwald building program required black and white people to cross over into each others' physical and social spaces, where they could find allies and build alternate networks of professional and local contacts. Even after control of the Rosenwald school program passed from African Americans at Tuskegee to all-white staff in Nashville and Chicago, the collaborative process of bringing a school to completion meant that black southerners played a public role in the Jim Crow South.

Rosenwald schools still remain standing in hundreds of communities across the fifteen states involved in the building program. Scores of newer school buildings still bear the name "Rosenwald" inherited from an earlier structure (figure 48). In some historic African American neighborhoods, a "Rosenwald Street" or "Rosenwald Softball Fields" sign still marks the place where community members walked to school and played (figure 49). Children still learn in Rosenwald buildings, and other people attend church and community gatherings in them, dwell inside their walls, or use them for storage. Churches and community-based social program agencies operate out of offices set up in former Rosenwald schools. Their survival—and their destruction—reflect the processes by which buildings gain and change meanings as people come together to build and use them.

Appendix 1

Agents in Rosenwald School States

State Agents for Negro Schools	Rosenwald Building Agents
Alabama	
James L. Sibley 1912–18	Cornelius B. Hosmer 1914–15
James S. Lambert 1918–42	Vernon W. Barnett 1915–20
Edward G. McGehee, Jr. 1931–?	Booker T. Washington Jr. 1915–19
	Marquis H. Griffin 1921–32
Arkansas	
Leo M. Favrot 1913–16	Percy L. Dorman 1918–22
John A. Presson 1917–24	Rufus C. Childress 1922–32
Fred McCuistion 1924–29	
F. T. Mitchell 1929–30	
Nolen M. Irby 1930–38	
Florida	
J. H. Brinson 1919–27	
Dewitt E. Williams 1927–1962(?)	
Georgia	
George D. Godard 1913–19	J. A. Martin 1919–21
Walter B. Hill Jr. 1920–30	Harrison C. Adams 1923–24
John Curtis Dixon 1930–37	S. H. Lee 1925–29
Robert L. Cousins (A) 1931–37	F. R Lampkin 1930
	Vincent H. Harris 1930–32
Kentucky	
Frank C. Button 1911–23	Francis M. Wood 1918–24
L. N. Taylor 1924–43	J. W. Bell 1922–24
Louisiana	
Leo M. Favrot 1916–23	O. W. Gray 1917–19
A. C. Lewis (A) 1919–22	John S. Jones 1919–32
A. C. Lewis 1922–40	
C. L. Barrow (A) 1930–39	
Maryland	
J. Walter Huffington 1917–45	
Mississippi	
John R. Ellis 1916–17	Richard S. Grossley 1918–23
Bura Hilbun 1917–28	B. B. Dansby 1923–26
W. C. Strahan (A) 1924–36	W. W. Blackburn 1926–32
Perry H. Easom 1928–?	

(continued)

State Agents for Negro Schools	Rosenwald Building Agents

Missouri
Charles G. Williams 1919–21
O. G. Sanford 1929–33

North Carolina
Nathan C. Newbold 1913–50   Charles H. Moore 1918–20
T. B. Attmore (A) 1919–21   George E. Davis 1920–32
William F. Credle (A) 1921–29

Oklahoma
E. A. Duke 1919–47

South Carolina
J. Herbert Brannon 1917–19
Joseph B. Felton 1919–47
W. A. Schiffley (A) 1925–45

Tennessee
Samuel L. Smith 1913–20   Robert E. Clay 1918–20
Ollie H. Bernard 1920–29   B. M. Young 1920
Dudley Tanner 1929–42   H. N. Robinson 1922–24
W. E. Turner (A) 1931–42   W. L. Porter 1924–25
     Robert E. Clay 1925–32

Texas
L. W. Rogers 1919–32
George T. Bludworth (A) 1923–33
Douglas B. Taylor (A) 1925–?

Virginia
Jackson Davis 1910–15   Thomas C. Walker 1920–32
Arthur D. Wright 1915–20
W. D. Gresham 1920–36
J. Blair Buck (A) 1930–32

Sources: Samuel L. Smith, *Builders of Goodwill: The Story of the State Agents of Negro Education in the South 1910–1950* (Nashville: Tennessee Book Co., 1950), 175–78; *The Negro Year Book: An Annual Encyclopedia of the Negro*, comp. Monroe N. Work (Tuskegee: Ala.: Negro Year Book Publishing Co., 1912–31/32); miscellaneous state department of education records.
(A) Assistant State Agent for Negro Schools

Appendix 2

Rosenwald Buildings, Capacity, and Funding

State	Buildings				Capacity		Funding				
	Schools	Homes	Shops	Total	Pupils	Teachers	Blacks	Whites	Tax Funds	Rosenwald	Total
Alabama	389	7	11	407	40,410	898	$452,968	137,746	445,526	248,526	1,285,060
Arkansas	338	19	32	389	46,980	1,044	172,134	53,714	1,420,852	305,741	1,952,441
Florida	120	1	4	125	22,545	501	54,758	67,021	1,186,602	124,325	1,432,705
Georgia	242	12	7	261	37,305	829	253,852	118,456	759,002	247,569	1,378,859
Kentucky	155	2	1	158	18,090	402	88,897	13,475	848,748	130,590	1,081,710
Louisiana	393	31	9	435	51,255	1,139	457,318	70,407	855,781	338,000	1,721,506
Maryland	149	2	2	153	15,435	343	84,973	5,224	699,761	109,700	899,658
Mississippi	557	58	18	633	77,850	1,730	859,688	323,143	1,128,673	539,917	2,851,421
Missouri	3		1	4	1,260	28	500	6,000	237,609	13,850	257,959
North Carolina	787	18	8	813	114,210	2,538	666,736	75,140	3,707,740	717,426	5,167,042
Oklahoma	176	16	6	198	19,575	435	28,865	5,475	948,054	145,055	1,127,449
South Carolina	481	8	11	500	74,070	1,646	507,994	224,525	1,706,241	435,600	2,892,360
Tennessee	354	9	10	373	44,460	988	296,388	28,027	1,354,157	291,250	1,969,822
Texas	464	31	32	527	57,330	1,274	392,851	60,495	1,623,800	419,376	2,496,521
Virginia	367	3	11	381	42,840	952	407,969	23,128	1,183,259	279,650	1,894,006
Total	4,977	217	163	5,357	663,615	14,747	4,725,891	1,211,975	18,105,805	4,364,869	28,408,520

Sources: James D. Anderson, *The Education of Blacks in the South, 1860–1935* (Chapel Hill: University of North Carolina Press, 1988), 155, and Edwin R. Embree, *Julius Rosenwald Fund: Review of Two Decades, 1917–1936* (Chicago: Julius Rosenwald Fund, 1936), 23.

Appendix 3

Annual Rosenwald School Construction
and Rosenwald Aid, 1913–32

Budget Year	Number of Schools	Rosenwald Aid
Tuskegee	640	263,515
1920–21*	429	356,335
1921–22	434	383,030
1922–23	464	386,836
1923–24	484	413,661
1924–25	486	414,106
1925–26	493	401,831
1926–27	479	410,697
1927–28	442	301,341
1928–29	373	323,600
1929–30	346	289,082
1930–31	225	329,893
1931–32	62	87,242

Source: "Rosenwald Schools Built by Years 1913–1932," folder 2, box 331, Julius Rosenwald Fund
Archives, Special Collections, John Hope and Aurelia E. Franklin Library, Fisk University.
*Includes 84 "cleanup" budget schools.

Appendix 4

Types of Rosenwald Schools and Their Cost

Type	Number	Total Cost	Rosenwald Aid
1T	968	1,822,750	385,557
2T	1,946	5,915,548	1,228,569
3T	763	3,270,166	634,616
4T	551	3,528,113	578,851
5T	226	1,778,586	253,280
6T	251	3,446,694	395,480
7T	61	864,025	85,750
8T	91	2,008,753	169,775
9T	31	516,064	40,475
10T	36	1,041,243	100,300
11T	11	284,885	15,350
12T	17	691,269	63,100
13T	1	74,000	2,600
14T	6	197,540	6,146
15T	4	105,614	8,600
16T	8	473,705	17,800
17T	2	179,256	5,200
(18T)*	(1)		
20T	2	162,000	6,000
22T	1	63,338	5,300

Sources: Lists in folder 2, box 331, Julius Rosenwald Fund Archives, Special Collections, John Hope and Aurelia E. Franklin Library, Fisk University.

*The 18-teacher school type does not appear on all lists.

Notes

INTRODUCTION

1. Hanchett, "Rosenwald Schools." My own initial work on Rosenwald schools within the context of rural reform can be found in *Rebuilding the Rural Southern Community*. Scores of preservation and historical documentation projects by community activists have been underway in recent years. Southern state historic preservation offices and historical agencies have joined forces with local groups to place Rosenwald schools on the National Register for Historic Places and conduct statewide surveys locating surviving buildings. The National Trust for Historic Preservation declared Rosenwald schools among the nation's most endangered historic buildings in 2002 and launched a preservation initiative headquartered at the trust's southern office in Charleston, South Carolina, and electronically at *Rosenwald Schools Initiative*, http://www.rosenwald-schools.org.

2. Recent analyses of African American education in the South that discuss the Rosenwald school-building program include J. Anderson, *Education of Blacks*; Leloudis, *Schooling the New South*; E. Anderson and Moss, *Dangerous Donations*.

3. Franklin, introduction to Franklin and Savage, eds., *Cultural Capital and Black Education*, xv.

CHAPTER 1. THE ROSENWALD-WASHINGTON PARTNERSHIP, 1912–15

1. L. Pearl Rouseau, "Loachapoka, Lee County, Ala.," *Tuskegee (Ala.) Messenger*, 10 January 1913, Tuskegee Clippings Files.

2. Louis R. Harlan's two-volume biography, *Making of a Black Leader* and *Wizard of Tuskegee*, dominates the scholarship on Washington and underpins my discussion of Washington's career in these pages. See also his "Washington in Biographical Perspective," in Harlan, *Washington in Perspective*, 3–24.

3. Washington, *Up from Slavery*, 1–33. Washington and ghostwriter Edgar Webber covered the same ground in *Story of My Life*, 13–33; Max Bennett Thrasher served as ghostwriter for *Up from Slavery*. On Washington's use of ghostwriters, see Harlan, *Making of a Black Leader*, 243–48. On Washington's early years, see Harlan's accounts in *Making of a Black Leader*, 3–51, and "Washington's West Virginia Boyhood" in Harlan, *Washington in Perspective*, 25–49.

4. On Armstrong, Hampton, and their influence on Washington, see Harlan, *Making of a Black Leader*, 52–77, 100–110, 201–3; Engs, *Educating the Disfranchised*; J. Anderson, *Education of Blacks*, 33–78. Donald Spivey offers an even more negative assessment in *Schooling for the New Slavery*, 7–70.

5. Engs, *Educating the Disfranchised*, 79–81; Hall, *Black Vocational, Technical, and Industrial Arts Education*, 5–15; Fleming, "Plight of Black Educators," 359–62; Kliebard, *Schooled to Work*, 1–25; E. Anderson and Moss, *Dangerous Donations*, 28–29; Nieves, "'We Gave Our Hearts,'" 14, 120–21, 278–91; J. Anderson, *Education of Blacks*, 34, 44–49, 66–72.

6. Washington, *Up from Slavery*, 157–71. Clearly this speech catapulted Washington to national prominence—a leap engineered by his white supporters, but one that Washington sustained through his own manipulations and by articulating a message that resonated with many rural black southerners. Harlan, *Making of a Black Leader*, 204–28.

7. Harlan, "Secret Life," and "Washington and the Politics of Accommodation," in Harlan, *Washington in Perspective*, 110–32, 164–79; Harlan, *Making of A Black Leader*, 229–71, 288–324; *Wizard of Tuskegee*, 3–31, 238–65, 295–358, 405–37.

8. Harlan, *Making of a Black Leader*, 202–5, 236; Harlan, "Washington and the Politics of Accommodation," 176–79.

9. Many of the educational programs targeting southern African Americans paralleled contemporary initiatives for American education in general. Donald Generals ties Washington to the educational philosophy of John Dewey in "Washington and Progressive Education." But as scholars such as James D. Anderson and Michael Dennis have shown, this linkage also provided white northern and southern reformers with an intellectual justification for limiting black public education programs to vocational training. J. Anderson, *Education of Blacks*, 78–109; Dennis, "Schooling along the Color Line."

10. Harlan, *Making of a Black Leader*, 78–156; Harlan, "Washington and the Kanawha Valley," in Harlan, *Washington in Perspective*, 50–67; Washington, *Up from Slavery*, 91.

11. Washington, *Story of My Life*, 83–86. Harlan also discusses this speech as a significant early statement of Washington's philosophy of accommodation and the role of industrial education within it in *Making of a Black Leader*, 161–62, and "Washington in Biographical Perspective," in Harlan, *Washington in Perspective*, 15.

12. Washington, *My Larger Education*, 145.

13. Woodson, *Education of the Negro*; Freedman, "African-American Schooling"; M. Mitchell, "'Good and Delicious Country.'"

14. Freedman, "African-American Schooling," 3; J. Anderson, "Ex-Slaves and the Rise of Universal Education"; J. Anderson, *Education of Blacks*, 4–32. Historical studies describing African American education in the Reconstruction years include Harlan, *Separate and Unequal*, 3–44; Bullock, *History of Negro Education*; Fleming, "Plight of Black Educators," 355–57; Wyatt-Brown, "Black Schooling during Reconstruction"; J. Anderson, *Education of Blacks*; Gilli, "History of Colored Schools"; Morgan, *Historical Perspectives*; Litwack, *Trouble in Mind*, 52–113; E. Anderson and Moss, *Dangerous*

Donations, 13–38; Granberry, "Black Community Leadership"; Span, "Alternative Pedagogy"; Span, "'I Must Learn Now.'"

15. Du Bois, *Negro Common School*; Fleming, "Plight of Black Educators," 356–57; Granberry, "Black Community Leadership," 255–56; Ayers, *Promise of the New South*, 45–54, 147–48, 211–13; Finnegan, "Lynching and Political Power," 191, 214–15; Hahn, *Nation under Our Feet*, 2–7, 276–80, 457–61; Nieves, "'We Gave Our Hearts.'"

16. Kirby, *Darkness at the Dawning*; Kousser, "Progressivism." Many studies have traced these developments at the regional and state levels, including Harlan's pioneering *Separate and Unequal*; Grantham, *Southern Progressivism*, 3–107, 246–74; Ayers, *Promise of the New South*, 412–21; Dittmer, *Black Georgia*, 90–162; Prather, *Resurgent Politics*; Margo, "Race Differences"; Link, *Hard Country*; McMillen, *Dark Journey*, 35–108; Leloudis, *Schooling the New South*; Walters, James, and McCammon, "Citizenship and Public Schools." See also Brundage, *Lynching in the New South*; McGerr, *Fierce Discontent*, 183–90, 215–17.

17. Bond, *Negro Education*, 88–192; Sherer, *Subordination or Liberation?* 9–18.

18. Davis, *Development and Present Status*, 11–93; Harlan, *Separate and Unequal*, 16–18; J. Anderson, *Education of Blacks*, 154–56.

19. J. Anderson, *Education of Blacks*, 3–44; G. Mitchell, "Growth of State Control," 103, 229; "Negro Common School, Mississippi"; *Child Welfare in Tennessee*, 149, 239–40; "Annual Report," 1917, in *Reports and Resolutions*, 16; *Biennial Report* [North Carolina], 1910/11–1911/12, 54–55. For an analysis of the ways that local control over school funding perpetuates discrimination, see Walters, "Educational Access."

20. "Division of Negro Education," *Biennial Report* [Kentucky], 1924–25, 33–34.

21. The separate school property tax was limited to one mill by the state constitution, effectively cutting off attempts to help most of the state's black schools and encouraging whites in separate school districts to create independent school districts or use intimidation to obtain more funding. *Biennial Report* [Oklahoma], 1917–18, 17; 1919–20, 39–41; 1927–28, 68–71.

22. *Annual Report* [Maryland], 1916, 7–37; Gilli, "History of Colored Schools."

23. "Annual Report," 1914, in *Reports and Resolutions*, 79; Cook, "Rejuvenation of the Rural Community," 76; *Report of the Arkansas Rural School Committee*; Alabama State Department of Education, *Annual Report*, 1913, 46–47.

24. Harris, "Introduction"; Favrot, "Negroes Not Receiving Benefits," in *Field Force Reports* (September 1917): 6–7, 62–63; Benner, "Strange Condition Indicated," in Alabama State Department of Education, *Annual Report*, 1920, 40–43.

25. Bond, *Negro Education*, 192.

26. "Report of W. F. Credle, Supervisor, Rosenwald Fund, May 1924," folder "Rosenwald Fund—W. F. Credle Reports," box 8, Special Subject File, Division of Negro Education, North Carolina Department of Public Instruction Records.

27. Eric Anderson and Alfred A. Moss Jr. argue that philanthropists and reformers like the General Education Board's Abraham Flexner grounded this argument in a

broader reconceptualization of the purpose and nature of schooling advocated by professional educators as much as their racial agenda in *Dangerous Donations*, 85–91. See also Engs, *Educating the Disfranchised*, 156; J. Anderson, *Education of Blacks*; Spivey, *Schooling for the New Slavery*, 71–108.

28. Washington, "Southern Negro Public Schools," *Norfolk Journal Guide* 10, no. 31 (5 December 1910), in folder 21, box 29, series 5, Southern Education Foundation Records.

29. For analyses of all of these philanthropies and their leadership, see Harlan, *Separate and Unequal*; J. Anderson, "Northern Foundations"; J. Anderson, *Education of Blacks*; E. Anderson and Moss, *Dangerous Donations*. Scholarly discussions placing Julius Rosenwald and the Julius Rosenwald Fund in the broader context of southern education began in the 1930s with works such as Leavell, *Philanthropy in Negro Education*, and McCormick, "Julius Rosenwald Fund." On the Peabody Fund, see Curry, *Brief Sketch*; Kasprzak, "George Peabody"; Dabney, *Universal Education*, 2:115–22; Dillingham, *Foundation of the Peabody Tradition*.

30. Fisher, *John F. Slater Fund*; Redcay, *County Training Schools*; Dabney, *Universal Education*, 2:433–39; J. Anderson, *Education of Blacks*, 66, 137–47.

31. Harlan, "Southern Education Board"; Harlan, *Separate and Unequal*, 75–101; Harlan, *Wizard of Tuskegee*, 186–93; Bullock, *History of Negro Education*, 89–116; E. Anderson and Moss, *Dangerous Donations*, 2–10, 42–53.

32. Dabney, *Universal Education*, 2:3–104, 219–33, 278–313; Harlan, "Southern Education Board"; Harlan, *Wizard of Tuskegee*, 186–93; Dennis, "Schooling along the Color Line."

33. *General Education Board: An Account of Its Activities*; Fosdick, *Adventure in Giving*; *General Education Board: Review and Final Report*, 1–42. For essential critical analyses of the General Education Board, see Harlan, *Separate and Unequal*; J. Anderson, *Education of Blacks*; Link, *Paradox of Southern Progressivism*; E. Anderson and Moss, *Dangerous Donations*.

34. Brawley, *Doctor Dillard*; Wright, *Negro Rural School Fund*; Dabney, *Universal Education*, 2:445–47; Harlan, *Wizard of Tuskegee*, 194–97; M. Williams et al., *Jeanes Story*.

35. Harlan, *Separate and Unequal*, 85–87; J. Anderson, *Education of Blacks*, 86.

36. Du Bois, *Souls of Black Folks*, chap. 3; D. Lewis, *Biography of a Race*.

37. On the class issues inherent in Progressive industrial education initiatives for elementary and secondary schools, see Cohen, "Industrial Education Movement"; Mitchell and Lowe, "To Sow Contentment." On gender, see Gilmore, *Gender and Jim Crow*; Walker, *All We Knew*; L. Jones, *Mama Learned Us*; Chirhart, *Torches of Light*.

38. On Washington's wider educational efforts, both in higher and public education, see Harlan, *Wizard of Tuskegee*, 174–201.

39. Washington, *My Larger Education*, 304.

40. Wadsworth, "Historical Perspective," 156–67.

41. Washington, *My Larger Education*, 150. For another account in which Washington placed the Macon County project in a historical context of independent African American economic and social life, see Washington, "Rural Negro Community."

42. Harlan, *Wizard of Tuskegee*, 131–32; Bond, *Negro Education*, 275; Stokes, *Tuskegee Institute*, 39; Washington, *My Larger Education*, 71–74, 304–6.

43. "Clinton J. Calloway, A.B."; Gray, Reed, and Walton, *History of the Alabama State Teachers Association*, 69; J. Anderson, *Education of Blacks*, 156–58.

44. Here Washington also instructed Calloway to use money from the Rogers account to begin recruiting new residents. Washington to Calloway, 3 January 1910, in Harlan et al., *Washington Papers*, 10:259.

45. Washington to Rogers Jr., 13 June 1909 and 4 December 1911, folder "Rogers, Henry Huttleston 1906–," box 75, Special Correspondence, Washington Papers, microfilm reel 68; Rogers Jr. to Washington, 10 February 1911, Washington to Rogers Jr., 20 February 1911, folder "Rogers Huddleston H. [*sic*], box 527, Supplemental Papers, Special Correspondence, Washington Papers, microfilm reel 396.

46. Washington to Rogers, 25 February 1907, folder "Rogers, Henry Huttleston, 1906–," box 75, Special Correspondence, Washington Papers, microfilm reel 68; Harlan, *Wizard of Tuskegee*, 140; Washington to Frissell, 5 July 1911, in Harlan et al., *Washington Papers*, 11:263–64.

47. Werner, *Julius Rosenwald*, 3–30. Peter M. Ascoli's forthcoming biography of his grandfather, *Julius Rosenwald: The Man Who Built Sears, Roebuck and Advanced the Cause of Black Education in the American South* (forthcoming, Indiana University Press, 2006), will offer many new insights relevant to this study. He illuminates Washington's skill in working with his financial benefactors and the combination of personal and business motivations shaping Rosenwald's approach to philanthropy. For more on Washington's fund-raising methods, see Enck, "Tuskegee Institute."

48. Sears then chaired the company's board but participated very little in board activities. Werner, *Julius Rosenwald*, 39–51, 66–67.

49. Ibid., 44, 357.

50. Ibid., 67–68; Emmet and Jeuck, *Catalogues and Counters*, 52–53, 128–36.

51. Werner, *Julius Rosenwald*, 80–106.

52. Woodson, "Story of the Fund," Chap. 2, 7–9, 14, folder 1, box 33, series I, and "Remarks Made by Mr. Rosenwald at Booker T. Washington luncheon," 18 May 1911, scrapbook 14, 36, series IV, Rosenwald Papers; Beilke, "'Partners in Distress,'" 28; Harlan, "Booker T. Washington's Discovery of Jews," in Harlan, *Washington in Perspective*, 152–63. For a comparison with Joel Spingarn, see D. Lewis, *Biography of a Race*, 486–90.

53. Werner, *Julius Rosenwald*, 107–26.

54. Ibid., 152–63.

55. "Julius Rosenwald and Booker T. Washington," *Tuskegee (Ala.) Messenger* 8 (February 1932), 4; Rosenwald to Villard, 2 July 1914, folder 13, box 26; typescript, dedica-

tion of Chicago YMCA for Colored Men, 15 June 1913, 8–9, folder 5, box 34, Series I, Rosenwald Papers.

56. Shepardson, "Rosenwald Rural Schools," 2, folder 1, box 331, Rosenwald Fund Archives; "Edited article by D. C. Vandercook for 'Association Men,' ca. 1920," folder 15, box 32, series I, Rosenwald Papers. Scholars have long pointed to the class basis for Progressive reform, which was fundamentally middle class in its value system even when sponsored by elites. For a recent interpretation, see McGerr, *A Fierce Discontent*.

57. Harlan, *Wizard of Tuskegee*, 128. Harlan discusses the Rosenwald-Washington partnership in *Wizard of Tuskegee*; James Anderson examines the origin and progress of the Rosenwald school-building program in his influential *Education of Blacks*, 156–85.

58. Washington to Rosenwald, 29 March 1912, folder "Rosenwald, Julius 1912 Jan.–June," box 75, Special Correspondence, Washington Papers, microfilm reel 68.

59. The ensuing paragraphs quote from this letter. Washington to Rosenwald, 21 June 1912, folder "Rosenwald, Julius 1912, Jan.–June," box 75, Special Correspondence, Washington Papers, microfilm reel 68; the same letter is in folder 8, box 336, Rosenwald Fund Archives, and is reprinted in Harlan et al., *Washington Papers*, 11:552–54. See also Bond, *Negro Education*, 275; Werner, *Julius Rosenwald*, 127–28; "Clinton J. Calloway, A.B."

60. "Clinton J. Calloway, A.B."

61. Washington to Rosenwald, 20 July 1912, folder "Rosenwald, Julius 1912 July–Oct.," box 76, Special Correspondence, Washington Papers, microfilm reel 69; the same letter is in folder 8, box 336, Rosenwald Fund Archives, and is reprinted in Harlan et al., *Washington Papers*, 11:562–63.

62. Rosenwald to Washington, 5 August 1912, folder "Rosenwald, Julius 1912 July–Oct.," box 76, Special Correspondence, Washington Papers, microfilm reel 69; the same letter is in folder 8, box 336, Rosenwald Fund Archives, and is reprinted in Harlan et al., *Washington Papers*, 11:576–77. Rosenwald and Washington also discussed training an accountant to help these institutions with their bookkeeping in this letter and in Washington to Rosenwald, 2 August 1912, 12 September 1912, folder "Rosenwald, Julius 1912 July–Oct.," box 76, Special Correspondence, Washington Papers, microfilm reel 69; the same letter is in folder 8, box 336, Rosenwald Fund Archives.

63. Wells-Barnett to Rosenwald, 13 August 1912, scrapbook 11, 154, series IV, Rosenwald Papers.

64. Washington to Rosenwald, 31 August and 12 September 1912, folder "Rosenwald, Julius 1912 July–Oct.," box 76, Special Correspondence, Washington Papers, microfilm reel 69; the same letter is in folder 8, box 336, Rosenwald Fund Archives.

65. For more on African American educators' vigilance in identifying potential donors, see Enck, "Black Self-Help," 87. A. M. Addison to Washington, 21 September 1912, and correspondence in folders "The Rosenwald Fund 1912 A-C," "The Rosen-

wald Fund 1912 D-H," "The Rosenwald Fund 1912 J-N," "The Rosenwald Fund 1912 P-R," and "The Rosenwald Fund 1912 S," box 77, Special Correspondence, Washington Papers, microfilm reel 70.

66. Rosenwald to Washington, 16 September 1912, folder "Rosenwald, Julius 1912 July–Oct.," box 76, Special Correspondence, Washington Papers, microfilm reel 69; Kushel to Washington, 17 September 1912, folder "Sears, Roebuck & Co., 1912–," Special Correspondence, box 85, Washington Papers, microfilm reel 77; the 16 September letter is also quoted in folder 11, box 53, series II, subseries 5, Rosenwald Papers.

67. Washington to Rosenwald, 30 September 1912, folder "Rosenwald, Julius 1912 July–Oct.," box 76, Special Correspondence, Washington Papers, microfilm reel 69; Washington to F. W. Kushel, 30 September 1912, folder "Sears, Roebuck & Co., 1912–," Special Correspondence, box 85, Washington Papers, microfilm reel 77.

68. Weiss, "Robert R. Taylor"; Weiss, "Tuskegee"; C. Williams, "From 'Tech' to Tuskegee." The Robert R. Taylor Homes in Chicago carry Taylor's name.

69. A handwritten note on Taylor's letter indicates that a copy was sent to Kushel. Taylor to Washington, 4 November 1912, folder "The Rosenwald Fund 1912 T-Y," box 77, Special Correspondence, Washington Papers, microfilm reel 69; Washington to Kushel, 2 November 1912?, folder "Sears, Roebuck & Co. 1912–," box 85, Special Correspondence, Washington Papers, microfilm reel 77.

70. Calloway to Washington, 5 November 1912, Washington to Calloway, 19 November 1912, folder 336, box 51, General Correspondence, Moton Papers. Tuskegee's famed agriculturalists George Washington Carver and Thomas M. Campbell and extension division staff ran these conferences, which Washington had inaugurated in 1892. A. Jones, "Role of Tuskegee."

71. Washington to Calloway, 15 October 1912, and Calloway to Washington, 26 November 1912, folder 336, box 51, General Correspondence, Moton Papers.

72. Estimates and order blanks from building material and mill work department, Sears, Roebuck and Co., 15 November 1912, [Kushel] to Washington, 16 November 1912, Taylor to Washington, [November 1912], Washington to Kushel, 29 November 1912, Coron to Washington, 7 December 1912, Calloway to Taylor, 14 December 1912 [notation by Taylor that he referred this to Washington], folder "Sears, Roebuck & Co., 1912–," box 85, Special Correspondence, Washington Papers, microfilm reel 77.

73. Washington to Rosenwald, 20 December 1912, Rosenwald to Washington, 26 December 1912, folder "Rosenwald, Julius 1912 Nov.–Dec.," box 77, Special Correspondence, Washington Papers, microfilm reel 69. Others continued to hope that Rosenwald's connection with Sears could benefit them, such as Mrs. Leila M. Daniel, who wrote to thank Rosenwald for his contribution to the new school in Spratt, Alabama, and then asked him to help her daughter attend Tuskegee Institute because "I have in the past ordered vehicles, organ and machine and house furnishings goods." Daniel to Rosenwald, 27 January 1916, folder 81, box 11, General Correspondence, Moton Papers.

74. "Information for Mr. Rosenwald" and "Memo: For Mr. Rosenwald" [January 1913], Washington to Rosenwald, 17 January 1913, folder "Rosenwald, Julius 1913 Jan.–Mar.," box 76, Special Correspondence, Washington Papers, microfilm reel 69; Washington to Rosenwald, 10 April 1913, 21 May 1913, and 6 December 1913, box 76, Special Correspondence, Washington Papers, microfilm reel 69; handwritten list of Rosenwald schools and costs [May 1913], Washington to Graves, 24 May 1913, Graves to Washington, 27 May 1913 and 15 September 1913, folder "Rosenwald, Julius 1913 Apr.–Dec.," Calloway to Washington, 3 April 1913 [copy sent to Rosenwald 10 April 1913], folder 8, box 336, Rosenwald Fund Archives; Rouseau, "Loachapoka, Lee County, Ala.," Fannie A. Wheelis, "Notasulga, Alabama," *Tuskegee (Ala.) Messenger*, 10 January 1913, Tuskegee Clippings Files.

75. Financial statement [July 1914], Graves to Washington, 27 July 1914, folder "Rosenwald, Julius 1914 Jan.–July," Washington to Graves, 5 August 1914, folder "Rosenwald, Julius 1914 Aug.–Dec.," box 76, Special Correspondence, Washington Papers, microfilm reel 69.

76. May 1913 correspondence between J. P. Slaton and Calloway, 8 May 1913, untitled folder [1], box 14, Calloway Papers; Washington to Rosenwald, 31 May 1913, and Rosenwald to Washington, 10 June 1913, folder "Rosenwald, Julius 1913 Apr.–Dec.," box 76, Special Correspondence, Washington Papers, microfilm reel 69; Rosenwald to Washington, 3 June 1913, folder "Sears, Roebuck & Co., 1912–," box 85, Special Correspondence, Washington Papers, microfilm reel 77.

77. "Negroes of Rural Districts of Alabama Building School Houses," *Montgomery (Ala.) Times*, 26 May 1913, Tuskegee Clippings Files; Wheelis, "Notasulga, Alabama"; "Making Over Negro Homes," *Boston Transcript*, 24 March 1915, reprinted in *Tuskegee Student* 27, no. 7 (3 April 1915), in scrapbook 14, 64, 69, series IV, Rosenwald Papers.

78. "Making Over Negro Homes"; Wheelis to Calloway, 15 April 1913 and 27 May 1913, untitled folder [2], box 14, Calloway Papers; "Negroes of Rural Districts."

79. "An Adventure in Education: The Rosenwald Schools," *Tuskegee (Ala.) Messenger*, February 1932, 2–3, 13–14, in folder 6, box 61, series III, Rosenwald Papers.

80. C. J. Calloway to J. L. Sibley, 13 April 1914 and 16 May 1914, folder "C," SG 15442, Rural School Agent Correspondence, Alabama Department of Education Records; Washington to Rosenwald, 25 January 1914 and 1 June 1914, folder "Rosenwald, Julius," box 527, Special Correspondence, Supplemental Papers, Washington Papers, microfilm reel 396; "To Educational Campaign . . . From February 1 to October 1, 1913," Washington to Graves, 2 October 1913, Washington to Rosenwald, 2 June 1914, Graves to Washington, 6 June 1914, folder "Rosenwald, Julius 1914 Jan.–July," box 76, Special Correspondence, Washington Papers, microfilm reel 69; Rosenwald to Washington, 3 June 1913, folder "Sears, Roebuck & Co., 1912–," box 85, Special Correspondence, Washington Papers, microfilm reel 77; "Urges Negroes to Remain in the South," *Montgomery (Ala.) Advertiser*, 1 June 1914, Tuskegee Clippings Files.

81. "Create Fund to Build Rural School Houses," *New York Age*, 25 June 1914, Tuskegee Clippings Files; "Press Release," Harlan et al., *Washington Papers*, 13:63–64.

82. Cook and Favrot to Rosenwald, 15 July 1914, and Favrot to Washington, 25 July 1914, folder "Rosenwald School Fund 1914 D-G," box 812, Donation File, Tuskegee Records, Washington Papers, microfilm reel 607.

83. Washington to Graves, 20 July 1914, folder "Rosenwald, Julius 1914 Jan.–July," box 76, Special Correspondence, Washington Papers, microfilm reel 69; Button to Washington, 26 October 1914, "Memorandum for Mr. Washington," Washington to Buxton [*sic*], 6 November 1914, folder "Rosenwald School Fund 1914 A-C," box 811, Donation File, Tuskegee Records, Washington Papers, microfilm reel 606; Smith to Rosenwald, 15 September 1914, folder "Rosenwald School Fund 1914 P-S," box 812, Donation File, Tuskegee Records, Washington Papers, microfilm reel 607.

84. Holloway to Washington, 9 July 1914, Washington to Holloway, 18 July 1914; Hendren to Washington, 18 September 1914, Hendren to Rosenwald, 29 October 1914, folder "Rosenwald School Fund 1914 H-K," box 812, Donation File, Tuskegee Records, Washington Papers, microfilm reel 607; J. Washington to B. T. Washington, 30 June 1914, B. T. Washington to J. Washington, 7 July 1914, Ramsey to Washington, 1 December 1914, folder "Rosenwald School Fund 1914 T-Z," box 812, Donation File, Tuskegee Records, Washington Papers, microfilm reel 607; "A Noble Gift," *Southern Letter* 30, no. 7 (July 1914): 106, in scrapbook 14, 106, series IV, Rosenwald Papers.

85. Washington to Beverly, 7 September 1914, Brown to Rosenwall [*sic*], 20 July 1914, Brown to Washington, 12 August 1912, folder "Rosenwald School Fund 1914 A-C," box 811, Donation File, Tuskegee Records, Washington Papers, microfilm reel 606; Randolph to Washington, 23 July 1914, folder "Rosenwald School Fund 1914 P-S," box 812, Donation File, Tuskegee Records, Washington Papers, microfilm reel 607.

86. Beard to Washington, 23 July 1914, folder "Rosenwald School Fund 1914 A-C," box 811, Donation File, Tuskegee Records, Washington Papers, microfilm reel 606.

87. Brown to Rosenwald, 13 April 1915, folder "Rosenwald, Julius 1915 Apr.–May," box 77, Special Correspondence, Washington Papers, microfilm reel 69.

88. Blackshear to Washington, 28 July 1914, folder "Rosenwald School Fund 1914 A-C," box 811, Donation File, Tuskegee Records, Washington Papers, microfilm reel 606.

89. Clark to Washington, 18 June 1914, folder "Rosenwald School Fund 1914 A-C," box 811, Donation File, Tuskegee Records, Washington Papers, microfilm reel 606.

90. Du Bois to Rosenwald, 25 June 1914, and Graves to Du Bois, 8 July 1914, folder "Rosenwald, Julius," box 527, Special Correspondence, Supplemental Papers, Washington Papers, microfilm reel 396; Graves to Washington, 8 July 1914, folder "Rosenwald, Julius 1914 Jan.–July," box 76, Special Correspondence, Washington Papers, microfilm reel 69.

91. "Education" [August 1914]; "Education" [September 1914].

92. "A Noble Gift," 106. Graves, Washington, and Scott periodically debated the merits of another press release specifically repudiating the broad dollar-for-dollar offer and exchanged frustrated letters about lingering public perceptions that such grants might be made. Graves to Scott, 14 September 1915, and Scott to Graves, 20 September 1915, folder "Rosenwald, Julius 1915 Aug.–Sept.," box 77, Special Correspondence, Washington Papers, microfilm reel 70; Graves to Washington, 9 October 1915 and 11 October 1915, and Washington to Graves, 15 October 1915, folder "Rosenwald, Julius 1915 Oct.–Nov.," box 77, Special Correspondence, Washington Papers, microfilm reel 70.

93. Washington to Sibley, 15 July 1914 and 21 July 1914, folder "W," SG 15443, Rural School Agent Correspondence, Alabama Department of Education Records; Washington to Dillard, 16 July 1914, folder 21, box 29, series 5, Southern Education Foundation Records; Washington to Graves, 16 July 1914, 17 July 1914, folder "Rosenwald, Julius 1914 Jan.–July," box 76, Special Correspondence, Washington Papers, microfilm reel 69; "Plan for Rosenwald Schoolhouses," folder "Rosenwald, Julius 1914 Aug.–Dec.," box 76, Special Correspondence, Washington Papers, microfilm reel 69.

94. Godard to Washington, 27 July 1914, and Favrot to Washington, 28 July 1914, folder "Rosenwald School Fund 1914 D-G," box 812, Donation File, Tuskegee Records, Washington Papers, microfilm reel 607; Cook to Washington, 12 August 1914, folder "Rosenwald School Fund A-C," box 811, Donation File, Tuskegee Records, Washington Papers, microfilm reel 606.

95. "Plan for Erection of Rural Schoolhouses," folder "Rosenwald, Julius 1914 Jan.–July," box 76, Special Correspondence, Washington Papers, microfilm reel 69; Graves to Washington, 22 September 1914, Washington to Graves, 2 October 1914, 9 October 1914, 30 November 1914, and "Plan for Erection of Rural Schoolhouses," folder "Rosenwald, Julius 1914 Aug.–Dec.," box 76, Special Correspondence, Washington Papers, microfilm reel 69; Graves to Washington, 27 July 1914, folder 8, box 336, Rosenwald Fund Archives.

96. Washington to Dillard, 3 August 1914, folder 21, box 29, series 5, Southern Education Foundation Records.

97. Washington to Dillard, 5 August 1914, folder 21, box 29, series 5, Southern Education Foundation Records.

98. Washington made the model school offer to Georgia on 6 August, according to Godard to Washington, 10 August 1914, folder "Rosenwald School Fund 1914 D-G," box 812, Donation File, Tuskegee Records, Washington Papers, microfilm reel 607; Washington to Calloway, 3 October 1914, Calloway to Washington, 19 October 1914, folder "Extension Dept. Calloway, Clinton J. 1914 Sept.–Oct.," box 715, Departmental File, Tuskegee Records, Washington Papers, microfilm reel 529; Washington to Calloway, 6 January 1915, folder "Extension Dept. Calloway, Clinton J. 1915 Jan.–Mar.," box 729, Departmental File, Tuskegee Records, Washington Papers, microfilm reel 543.

99. Washington repeated these sentiments to Kentucky and Virginia education

officers. Washington to J. H. Dillard, 5 August 1914, 14 August 1914, and Dillard to Washington, 5 September 1914, folder 21, box 29, series 5, Southern Education Foundation Records.

100. Calloway to Scott, 20 November 1914, folder "Extension Dept. Calloway, Clinton J. 1914 Nov.–Dec.," box 715, Departmental File, Tuskegee Records, Washington Papers, microfilm reel 529; Graves to Washington, 9 December 1914, folder "Rosenwald, Julius 1914 Aug.–Dec.," box 76, Special Correspondence, Washington Papers, microfilm reel 69; Washington to Rosenwald, 5 December 1914, folder 8, box 336, Rosenwald Fund Archives.

CHAPTER 2. NEW SCHOOLS: THE ROSENWALD RURAL SCHOOL-BUILDING PROGRAM AT TUSKEGEE, 1914–20

1. Graves to Washington, 15 January 1915, Washington to Graves, 16 January 1915, folder "Rosenwald, Julius 1915 Jan.–Feb.," box 76, Special Correspondence, Washington Papers, microfilm reel 69; Jones, "Editorial Wanderings," *Chicago Unity*, 4 March 1915, in scrapbook 14, 62, series IV, Rosenwald Papers; photograph album, "Tuskegee 1915," folder 24, box 39, series I, Rosenwald Papers.

2. Calloway to Washington, 11 February and 24 March 1914, folder "Extension Dept. Calloway, Clinton J. 1914 Jan.–May," box 714, Department File, Tuskegee Records, Washington Papers, microfilm reel 528.

3. *Negro Farmer* 2, no. 11 (19 June 1915), cover, in scrapbook 14, 68, series IV, Rosenwald Papers.

4. Floridians did not participate in the Rosenwald program for several years to come. Washington to Rosenwald, 17 March 1915, folder 8, box 336, Rosenwald Fund Archives; another copy of this letter is in folder "W," SG 15443, Rural School Agent Correspondence, Alabama Department of Education Records.

5. "Budget. Sept. 1914–Oct. 1915. Jeanes Fund," folder "Extension Dept. Calloway, Clinton J. 1914 Jan.–Mar.," box 714, Departmental File, Tuskegee Records, Washington Papers, microfilm reel 528; Calloway to Washington, 16 September 1914, folder "Extension Dept. Calloway, Clinton J. 1914 Nov.–Dec.," box 715, Departmental File, Tuskegee Records, Washington Papers, microfilm reel 529. Tuskegee officials at first proposed apportioning the assistant's salary and expenses between the Jeanes Fund and Julius Rosenwald but ultimately asked Rosenwald to fund the position entirely. Calloway, Gibson, and Palmer to Washington, 5 August 1914, folder "Committee Reports Aug.–Oct.," box 714, Departmental File, Tuskegee Records, Washington Papers, microfilm reel 528.

6. Once again Calloway asked for an allocation from the Jeanes Fund, but the money ultimately came from Rosenwald. Graves to Washington, 20 March 1915, folder "Rosenwald, Julius 1915 Mar.," box 77, Special Correspondence, Washington Papers, microfilm reel 69; Calloway to Washington, 5 December 1914, folder "Extension Dept. Calloway, Clinton J. 1914 Nov.–Dec.," box 715, Departmental File, Tuskegee Records,

Washington Papers, microfilm reel 529. See 1914 and 1915 correspondence between Calloway and Sibley in folder "C," SG 15442, Rural School Agent Correspondence, Alabama Department of Education Records. For a fuller discussion of these fieldworkers, see chapters 3 and 4.

7. "Plan for Erection of Rural Schoolhouses," folder "Rosenwald, Julius 1915 Oct.–Nov.," box 77, Special Correspondence, Washington Papers, microfilm reel 70; "Plan for Erection of Rural Schoolhouses," folder "Rosenwald School Fund 1914," box 811, Donation File, Tuskegee Records, Washington Papers, microfilm reel 606. Washington wanted to manage the out-of-state applications carefully, telling Calloway, "I do not care for you to make any more promises to do any schoolhouse building outside of Alabama without letting me know in advance." Washington to Calloway, 26 September 1915, folder "Extension Dept. Calloway, Clinton J. 1915 Sept.–Dec.," box 730, Departmental File, Tuskegee Records, Washington Papers, microfilm reel 544.

8. Calloway to Sibley, 25 May 1915, folder "C," SG 15442, Rural School Agent Correspondence, Alabama Department of Education Records; "Memoranda of a meeting," 23 May 1915, folder "Extension Dept. Calloway, Clinton J. 1915 Apr.–May," box 729, Tuskegee Records, Departmental File, Washington Papers, microfilm reel 543.

9. The State of Alabama distributed construction funds to county boards of education that would have gone entirely to white schools unless African American school patrons qualified for aid and convinced their school authorities to release the $200 state grants. Eligible schools had to be deeded over to the State of Alabama, and their construction had to follow approved state plans.

10. Washington to Sibley, 7 December 1914, 5 January 1915, 26 May 1915, Sibley to Washington, 16 December 1914, folder "W," SG 15443, Rural School Agent Correspondence, Alabama Department of Education Records. Studies addressing the widespread violence against African Americans and the targeting of black schools in particular include Dittmer, *Black Georgia*; McMillen, *Dark Journey*; Ayers, *Promise of the New South*; Brundage, *Lynching in the New South*; Litwack, *Trouble in Mind*; Hahn, *Nation under Our Feet*.

11. Southern states instituted similar requirements in the 1910s, and American educators in general sought state control over school buildings. See Barrett and Thomson, *Plans for Public Schoolhouses* (1914), 6; Alabama Department of Education, *Rural Schoolhouses*, 9; Chapman and Gilbert, *School Architecture*; "Education Is Chiefly a State Function."

12. Calloway to Sibley, 14 May 1913, untitled folder [1], box 14, Calloway Papers.

13. Washington to Calloway, 5 June 1913, and Sibley to Calloway, 6 June 1913, untitled folder [1], box 14, Calloway Papers.

14. Calloway to Washington, 12 June 1913, untitled folder [4], box 14, Calloway Papers.

15. Calloway to Washington, 31 May 1913, untitled folder [2], box 14, Calloway Papers.

16. Rather than using the Rosenwald gift, as Calloway had proposed, Washington quickly referred the project to James Hardy Dillard, head of the Anna T. Jeanes Fund. Calloway to Washington, 11 July 1913, and Calloway to Dillard, 14 August 1913, untitled folder [2], box 14, Calloway Papers; Sibley to Washington, 17 December 1913, folder "W," SG 15443, Rural School Agent Correspondence, Alabama Department of Education Records.

17. Calloway to Washington, 24 January 1914, folder "Extension Dept. Calloway, Clinton J. 1914 Jan.–May," and Carver to Washington, 30 November 1914, folder "Dept. of Research—Experiment Station 1914 Carver, George W.," box 714, Departmental File, Tuskegee Records, Washington Papers, microfilm reel 528; Calloway to Washington, 27 July 1914, folder "Extension Dept. Calloway, Clinton J. 1914 June–Aug.," box 715, Departmental File, Tuskegee Records, Washington Papers, microfilm reel 529; Calloway to Hazel, 24 November 1914, folder "Extension Dept. Calloway, Clinton J. 1914, Nov.–Dec.," box 715, Departmental File, Tuskegee Records, Washington Papers, microfilm reel 529; Taylor to Washington, 5 December 1914, 8 December 1914, Washington to Taylor, 7 December 1914, folder "Mechanical Industries, Taylor, Robert R., 1914 Nov.–Dec.," box 531, Departmental File, Tuskegee Records, Washington Papers, microfilm reel 717; correspondence between Taylor and Sibley for September, November, and December 1914, folder "T," SG 15443, Rural School Agent Correspondence, Alabama Department of Education Records.

18. Sibley to Taylor, 29 December 1914, Taylor to Sibley, 31 December 1914, folder "T," SG 15443, Rural School Agent Correspondence, Alabama Department of Education Records; Calloway to Sibley, 25 May 1915; Sibley to Graves, 8 May 1915, folder "Rosenwald, Julius 1915 Apr.–May," box 77, Special Correspondence, Washington Papers, microfilm reel 69; Taylor to Scott, 10 May 1915, folder "Mechanical Industries Taylor, Robert R. 1915 May–June," box 731, Departmental File, Tuskegee Records, Washington Papers, microfilm reel 545; Taylor to Washington, 19 July 1915, folder "Mechanical Industries, Taylor, Robert R. 1915, July–Aug.," box 732, Departmental File, Tuskegee Records, Washington Papers, microfilm reel 546; Sibley to Calloway, 11 August 1915, untitled folder [5], box 14, Calloway Papers; Calloway to Sibley, 23 August 1915, untitled folder [4], box 14, Calloway Papers; Newbold to Calloway, 11 August 1915, 1 September 1915, untitled folder [3], box 14, Calloway Papers; *Negro Rural School.*

19. Favrot to Sibley, 26 August 1915, folder "C," SG 15444, Rural School Agent Correspondence, Alabama Department of Education Records.

20. Newbold to Attmore, 11 April 1919, folder "A," box 4, General Correspondence of the Director, Division of Negro Education, North Carolina Department of Public Instruction Records; C. Dillard Jr. to Secretary, 1 October 1917, folder 164, box 24, General Correspondence, Moton Papers.

21. Chase, *Manual on School-houses*; Denton, "School-Houses," *Biennial Report* [Arkansas], 1879–80, 17. See also Gardner, *Town and Country School Buildings.*

22. Barrett and Thomson, *Plans for Public School Houses*; *Plans for Public School-houses*; Louisiana Department of Education, *Plans for Public School Buildings*; "School Yards and Schoolhouse Architecture," in *Reports and Resolutions*, 1906, 286–338; Adams and Alsup, *Plans and Specifications*; "Rural School Buildings in Arkansas," *Biennial Report* [Arkansas], 1907–8, 91–103; "Sketches Suggesting Plans," *Annual Report* [Georgia], 1911, 64–87; Texas Department of Education, *Consolidation of Rural Schools*, 24–67; Lynch, "Annual Report of the State Inspector of Elementary Rural Schools," *Biennial Report* [Florida], 1911–12, 221–26, and "School House Architecture," *Biennial Report* [Florida], 1915–16, 274–99; Lee, *Rural School Buildings*; "Rural Schools," *Biennial Report* [Oklahoma], 1915–16, 20–29; Duke, *Guide to Better Schools*; Chapman and Gilbert, *School Architecture*; "School Buildings," *Biennial Report* [Texas], 1916–18, 301–40. National publications making similar recommendations include Mills, *American School Building Standards*; Cubberley, *Rural Life*, 208–19.

23. "Rural School Buildings in Arkansas," 96; Barrett and Thomson, *Plans for Public Schoolhouses* (1914), 7; Adams and Alsup, *Plans and Specifications*, 3; Chapman and Gilbert, *School Architecture, Kentucky*, [7–8]. For examples of this developing aesthetic from general schoolhouse-design books, see Burrage and Bailey, *School Sanitation*; King, "School Architecture"; Willis, "Ideal Rural School Building."

24. *Negro Rural School*, 41–78. See also Glave, "'Garden So Brilliant,'" 405–6, for a discussion of school gardens and yards.

25. The two publications share plot plans, a design for an industrial building, and some of their illustrations and discussions of landscaping, classroom equipment, and sanitation. *Negro Rural School*, 9, 14–19, 33–37, 42–43, 83, 89–90; Alabama Department of Education, *Rural Schoolhouses*, 12, 14–15, 18–23, 40–43, 46, 76–77.

26. *Negro Rural School*, 9–10.

27. Calloway to Washington, 20 June 1913, untitled folder [4], box 14, Calloway Papers.

28. The social center function receives attention in the sources on school architecture cited previously; see also "Suggestion for a Rural Social Center."

29. *Negro Rural School*, 11–13. Washington sent a copy of the one-teacher plan to George Eastman with the assurance that he "should have left out a lot of the 'frills' that in my opinion make the matter more complicated" in his usual desire to appear conservative in his use of donors' funds. Washington to George Eastman, 2 June 1915, in Harlan et al., *Washington Papers*, 13:317.

30. *Negro Rural School*, 7, 82–88.

31. Ibid., 7–8.

32. Ibid., 127–28; Alabama Department of Education, *Rural Schoolhouses*, 70–71.

33. *Negro Rural School*, 89–90, 127–29; this booklet includes a plan that also appeared in Alabama Department of Education, *Rural Schoolhouses* as "Workshop Plan no. 1."

34. *Negro Rural School*, 14–19.

35. Ibid., 29–36.

36. Calloway to Madison, 17 June 1913, untitled folder [4], box 14, Calloway Papers; Madison to Calloway, 30 July 1913, untitled folder [2], box 14, Calloway Papers.

37. Washington to Calloway, 5 December 1914, folder "Extension Dept. Calloway, Clinton J. 1914 Nov.–Dec.," box 715, Departmental File, Tuskegee Records, Washington Papers, microfilm reel 529; Calloway to Washington, 13 January 1915, and undated "Form Letter" addressed to Newbold, folder "Extension Dept. Calloway, Clinton J., 1915, Jan.–Mar.," box 729, Departmental File, Tuskegee Records, Washington Papers, microfilm reel 543; Washington to Graves, 26 December 1914, Graves to Washington, 31 December 1914, folder "Rosenwald, Julius 1914 Aug.–Dec.," box 76, Special Correspondence, Washington Papers, microfilm reel 69; Anderson to Washington, 11 January 1915, folder "Sears, Roebuck & Co., 1912–," box 85, Special Correspondence, Washington Papers, microfilm reel 77; Washington to Williamson, 16 January 1915, in Harlan et al., *Washington Papers*, 13:224; Calloway to Sibley, 10 December 1914, folder "C," SG 15442, Rural School Agent Correspondence, Alabama Department of Education Records; Sibley to Washington, 16 December 1914, folder "W," SG 15443, Rural School Agent Correspondence, Alabama Department of Education Records.

38. Clayton to Sibley, 29 April 1915, and Sibley to Clayton, 4 May 1915, folder "C," SG 15442, Rural School Agent Correspondence, Alabama Department of Education Records.

39. Somerville to Calloway, 10 August 1915, and Calloway to J. Summerville [*sic*], 10 August 1915, untitled folder [5], box 14, Calloway Papers.

40. Washington to Calloway, 2 June 1915, Washington to Calloway, 4 June 1915, Calloway to Washington, 4 June 1915, folder "Extension Dept. Calloway, Clinton J. 1915 June–Aug.," box 730, Departmental File, Tuskegee Records, Washington Papers, microfilm reel 544.

41. Sibley to Calloway, 2 August 1917, folder "C," SG 15448, Rural School Agent Correspondence, Alabama Department of Education Records; Dresslar, *Report on the Rosenwald School Buildings*, 60, 63.

42. *Negro Rural School*, 122–23.

43. Scott to Graves, 6 November 1915, Graves to Scott, 6 November 1915, Scott to Rosenwald, 29 November 1915, folder "Rosenwald, Julius 1915 Oct.–Nov.," box 77, Special Correspondence, Washington Papers, microfilm reel 70; Washington to Calloway, 8 November 1915, in Harlan et al., *Washington Papers*, 13:426. For an account of the Chehaw school from the community perspective, consult the Beasley interview.

44. Scott to Rosenwald, 28 December 1915, folder "Rosenwald, Julius 1915 Dec.," box 77, Special Correspondence, Washington Papers, microfilm reel 70; Rosenwald to Low, 16 December 1915, in Harlan et al., *Washington Papers*, 13:482–84. Peter M. Ascoli's forthcoming biography of Julius Rosenwald explains the strained relationship between Rosenwald and Moton.

45. Calloway to Sibley, 11 October 1916, folder "C," SG 15448, Rural School Agent Correspondence, Alabama Department of Education Records; "Julius Rosenwald Fund Administrative Rulings," folder 1, box 331, Rosenwald Fund Archives; Bond, *Negro Education*, 275–76; Calloway, "Co-Operative School Building."

46. Graves to Moton, 20 June 1916, December 1916 correspondence between Sibley, Moton, and Graves, folder 79, box 11, General Correspondence, Moton Papers; 1916–17 correspondence between Sibley and Calloway in folder "C," SG 15448, Rural School Agent Correspondence, Alabama Department of Education Records.

47. Correspondence between Brannon and Calloway, May–June 1918, folder "General Correspondence, 1918," box 1, Calloway Papers. For examples of the forms he processed, see "Application for Rosenwald Aid" for the 1918 Brooklyn School in Conecuh County, Alabama, and "Statement, Rural Schoolhouse Building," for the 1918 Cut Off School, Orleans Parish, Louisiana, folder "Application and Reports for Rosenwald Fund 1916–1919," box 4, Calloway Papers. In 1916, Robert R. Taylor and William A. Hazel worked with Alabama Negro school agent James L. Sibley on revisions of plan 11. See correspondence between Sibley, Taylor, and Hazel, October 1916, folder "Correspondence Re: Teaching Applications and Rosenwald Fund Applications 1916," box 4, Calloway Papers.

48. "Quoted from Secretary's of Rosenwald Committee's Letter, Dated September 7th, 1916," signed Charles L. Coon, 19 September 1916, Newbold to C. J. Calloway, 26 November 1917, folder "General Correspondence, 1916–1917," box 1, Calloway Papers.

49. Calloway to Moton, 6 August 1917, folder "Rural School Correspondence 1917," box 3, Calloway Papers; "Monthly Report of Leo M. Favrot State Agent of Rural Schools for Negroes in Louisiana, July 1917 Narrative Report," 5–[6], file 775: "Supervisor of Rural Schools (Negro) Reports," series 1, subseries 1, *General Education Board Archives*, microfilm reel 69.

50. Calloway to Moton, 8 September 1917, folder "Rural School Correspondence, 1917," box 3, Calloway Papers.

51. Calloway to Smith, 29 June 1918, folder "Rosenwald Correspondence Tennessee 1918," box 10, Calloway Papers.

52. Calloway to Favrot, 11 October 1917, folder "Correspondence: Rosenwald Schools 1917," box 5, Calloway Papers; Calloway to Smith, 5 June 1918, folder "Rosenwald Correspondence Tennessee 1918," box 10, Calloway Papers; Graves to Scott, 21 November 1917, folder 79, box 11, General Correspondence, Moton Papers, Rosenwald to Moton, 23 May 1918, folder 250, box 36, General Correspondence, Moton Papers.

53. Smith to Rosenwald, 5 September 1917, folder 8, box 336, Rosenwald Fund Archives; Sibley, "Conference of Rural School Agents with Mr. Rosenwald," folder "Application and Reports for Rosenwald Fund 1916–1919," box 4, Calloway Papers; Sibley to

Rosenwald, 18 September 1917, folder "R," SG 15450, Rural School Agent Correspondence, Alabama Department of Education Records.

54. Sibley to Rosenwald, 18 September 1917; Graves also referred to Rosenwald's deliberations about "a permanent rural school department at Tuskegee" in a 27 September 1917 memorandum to Rosenwald, folder 8, box 336, Rosenwald Fund Archives.

55. Calloway to Scott, 13 September 1917, folder 80, box 11, General Correspondence, Moton Papers. Calloway had already complained to Moton that Jackson Davis had not followed up on General Education Board officer E. C. Sage's instructions to work closely with Calloway on the Rosenwald program. Calloway to Moton, 11 September 1917, folder "Correspondence Rosenwald Schools 1917," box 5, Calloway Papers.

56. The following paragraphs draw upon the "Plan for the Erection of Rural School Houses" dated 20 September 1917 in folder "Application and Reports for Rosenwald Fund 1916–1919," box 4, Calloway Papers, in folder 90, box 11, General Correspondence, Moton Papers, and in folder "C," SG 15450, Rural School Agent Correspondence, Alabama Department of Education Records.

57. Calloway to Sibley, 23 April 1918, folder "C," SG 15450, Rural School Agent Correspondence, Alabama Department of Education Records.

58. Scott had prepared the budget proposal, which included a full salary for Booker T. Washington Jr. as Alabama's "special rural school agent" and half salaries and expenses for building agents in Arkansas, Georgia, Louisiana, Mississippi, North Carolina, South Carolina, Tennessee, and Virginia. Scott to Executive Council, 28 September 1917, folder 1, box 331, Rosenwald Fund Archives; Scott, Robert, Calloway, Logan, and Mrs. [Margaret Murray] Washington to the Executive Council, 28 September 1917, folder 80, box 11, General Correspondence, Moton Papers. In practice, the existing Rosenwald committee continued to review applications and make policy recommendations. The Rosenwald committee usually consisted of Margaret Murray (Mrs. Booker T.) Washington, treasurer Warren Logan, secretary Emmett Scott and his successor Albion L. Holsey, registrar J. H. Palmer, director of industries Robert R. Taylor, and C. J. Calloway.

59. "Activities of the Fund," "Statement of Expenditures," 1918–22, folder 2, box 76, Rosenwald Fund Archives; "Sears Roebuck and Company Stock, October 30, 1917 to June 30, 1931," folder 2, box 331, Rosenwald Fund Archives; Woodson, "Story of the Fund," chap. 4, 17–19, folder 1, box 33, series I, Rosenwald Papers; Embree and Waxman, *Investment in People*, 28–29.

60. "Julius Rosenwald Fund Administrative Rulings"; Flexner to Rosenwald, 10 December 1917, Scott to Flexner, 17 December 1917, folder 1, box 331, Rosenwald Fund Archives.

61. Moton to Rosenwald, 26 February 1918, Graves to Moton, 5 March 1918, Moton to Graves, 27 March 1918, folder 250, box 36, General Correspondence, Moton Papers.

62. Wright to Calloway, 6 January 1918, folder "Correspondence Rosenwald Schools 1918," box 6, Calloway Papers. The lack of a General Education Board–funded state agent for Negro schools held back Florida's participation in the Rosenwald building program until 1920.

63. Wright asked about the building agent position in a separate letter to Calloway on 6 January 1918, folder "Correspondence Rosenwald Schools 1918," box 6, Calloway Papers.

64. Calloway to Phenix, 14 June 1917, and Phenix to Calloway, 22 June 1917, folder "Rural School Correspondence 1917," box 3, Calloway Papers; Wright to Calloway, 4 January 1918, Wright to Rosenwald, 5 January 1918, Calloway to Wright, 23 January 1918, folder "Correspondence Rosenwald Schools 1918," box 6, Calloway Papers.

65. For an example of the form letter about building agents, see Calloway to Hilbun, 6 December 1917; for an example of the responses, see Hilbun to Calloway, 22 December 1917, folder "Correspondence, Rosenwald Schools 1917," box 5, Calloway Papers.

66. Logan to Rosenwald, 28 April 1916, folder 8, box 336, Rosenwald Fund Archives; Dowdle to Sibley, 25 November, 12 December 1916, folder "D," SG 15448, Rural School Agent Correspondence, Alabama Department of Education Records; Sibley to Gray, 15 May 1915, folder "G," SG 15448, Rural School Agent Correspondence, Alabama Department of Education Records; "Some Reasons Why Conecuh County Needs a Training School," folder "K," SG 15449, Rural School Agent Correspondence, Alabama Department of Education Records. On the general context for these problems, see Tolnay, *Bottom Rung*, 124; Tindall, *Emergence of the New South*, 121–24.

67. "An Adventure in Education," 13; Moton to Graves, 5 November 1918, folder 250, box 36, General Correspondence, Moton Papers; Claxton to Moton, 24 September 1918, folder 251, box 36, General Correspondence, Moton Papers. The war affected not only Rosenwald schools; see Brinckloe, "Planning the Schoolhouse."

68. Dowell to Calloway, 5 October 1918, folder "General Correspondence," box 1, Calloway Papers; Smith to Calloway, 7 September 1918, folder "General Correspondence 1918," box 7, Calloway Papers; Smith to Calloway, 13 June 1918, folder "Rosenwald Correspondence Tennessee 1918," box 10, Calloway Papers.

69. "Julius Rosenwald Fund Administrative Rulings"; Moton to Graves, 9 December 1918, Rosenwald Committee to Executive Council, 6 February 1919, folder 8, box 336, Rosenwald Fund Archives.

70. Calloway to Lambert, 18 February 1919, folder "C," SG 15453, Rural School Agent Correspondence, Alabama Department of Education Records. For more on the postwar industrial boom and contrasting agricultural problems, see Tindall, *Emergence of the New South*, 70–142.

71. Werner, *Julius Rosenwald*, 178–218; Emmet and Jeuck, *Catalogues and Counters*, 197–98. A former Tuskegee Institute student wrote Calloway that he had just seen

Rosenwald at a YMCA canteen in France. Hill to Calloway, 4 September 1918, folder "C. J. Calloway Correspondence 1918," box 12, Calloway Papers.

72. Graves to Scott, 23 March 1917, folder 342, box 52, General Correspondence, Moton Papers; Graves to Moton, 29 March 1918, Moton to Graves, 10 July 1918, folder 250, box 36, General Correspondence, Moton Papers; Moton to Graves, 22 October 1918, folder 251, box 36, General Correspondence, Moton Papers; Rosenwald Committee to Executive Council, 23 December 1918, folder 335, box 50, General Correspondence, Moton Papers; Graves to Moton, 15 May 1919, 30 December 1919, folder 336, box 51, General Correspondence, Moton Papers; Graves to Moton, 29 March 1920, folder 340b, box 51, General Correspondence, Moton Papers; Graves to Moton, 7 November 1919, folder 8, box 336, Rosenwald Fund Archives. Rosenwald was a stickler about small expenses; for a similar complaint about waste in using telegrams instead of letters, see Rosenwald to Warburg, 20 May 1926, folder 8, box 33, series I, Rosenwald Papers. For another account of the troubled years 1917–20, see Stitely, "Bridging the Gap," 9–15.

73. Their complaints centered around Tuskegee's practice of allowing approved applications to collect before asking Rosenwald to send another installment of money, and a misplaced set of checks later found in a desk at the extension department. Sibley claimed that two county superintendents were so fed up with Tuskegee's delays and repeated demands for new reports that they might drop out of the program. Smith apologized to Calloway for getting him into trouble after Smith's inquiries to Sibley about payment procedures helped to inspire another complaint to Moton. But Sibley's leave of absence to study at Harvard did not help matters either. Sibley to Calloway, 23 August 1918, folder "General Correspondence 1918," box 7, Calloway Papers; Smith to Calloway, 18 July 1918, folder "Rosenwald Correspondence Tennessee 1918," box 10, Calloway Papers; Calloway to Sibley, 2 June 1916, folder "C," SG 15448, Rural School Agent Correspondence, Alabama Department of Education Records; Calloway to Lambert, 9 June 1919, 30 August 1919, folder "C," SG 15452, Rural School Agent Correspondence, Alabama Department of Education Records; August–September 1918 correspondence about Hayneville school in folder 251, box 36, General Correspondence, Moton Papers.

74. On the Great Migration and postwar violence, see Tindall, *Emergence of the New South*, 143–83.

75. Graves to Moton, 13 March 1919, folder 342, box 52, General Correspondence, Moton Papers; Dillard to Moton, 4 March 1919, folder 357, box 53, General Correspondence, Moton Papers; Dillard to Rosenwald, 11 March 1919, folder 8, box 336, Rosenwald Fund Archives. On the temporary shutdown of the program, see Calloway to Brannon, 29 March 1919, 8 April 1919, folder "Mary E. Foster Correspondence 1920," box 8, Calloway Papers.

76. Graves to Moton, 8 September 1919, folder 335, box 50, General Correspondence, Moton Papers; Graves to Moton, 24 September 1919, "Mr. Julius Rosenwald,

Aid for Colored Schools, Report on Audit of Accounts, January 1, 1915 to June 30, 1919," 23 August 1919, folder 336, box 51, General Correspondence, Moton Papers.

77. Agents also advised continuing aid for remodeling older buildings to Rosenwald standards; providing grants for additions to existing Rosenwald buildings and for teachers' homes; increasing grants to $600 for two-teacher buildings; and offering $800 or more for larger facilities. Additional resolutions called for continuing the matching grants to extend the school term and new application and inspection reporting procedures. Recommendations from the Conference of Rural School Agents for Negroes in the South and Rosenwald Schoolbuilding Agents, 17 July 1919, folder 336, box 51, General Correspondence, Moton Papers; excerpt from Rosenwald letter, folder "General Correspondence 1918," box 1, Calloway Papers.

78. For a discussion of the greater attention paid to urban school design, see Cutler, "Cathedral of Culture," 6–33.

79. General Education Board president Wallace Buttrick regularly played billiards with Dresslar during the afternoons of his business meetings at the college. Dresslar, *American Schoolhouses*; Dresslar, *Rural Schoolhouses*; S. Smith, *Builders of Goodwill*, 66–67; "In Memoriam"; "Brief of Features of Rural School Audit, Recommendations, and Correspondence on Method of Administering Rural School Construction," 4, folder 1, box 331, Rosenwald Fund Archives.

80. In late 1918, Newbold had unsuccessfully attempted to get Rosenwald money for a white Rosenwald building agent and was currently trying to bypass Calloway and Tuskegee to secure one hundred schools for his state; he had taken his request for another agent to the General Education Board. Newbold to Rosenwald, 1 December 1918, Graves to Newbold, 17 December 1918, Newbold to Graves, 21 December 1918, folder 8, box 336, Rosenwald Fund Archives; Newbold to Flexner, 17 May 1919, folder "E-F," and Newbold to Rosenwald, 19 May 1919, folder "R-T," box 4, General Correspondence of the Director, Division of Negro Education, North Carolina Department of Public Instruction Records; Newbold to Rosenwald, 19 May 1919 (the same letter asking for one hundred schools and Rosenwald's initial endorsement, followed by referral to Tuskegee for a final decision), Graves to Newbold, 27 May 1919, and June 1919 correspondence between Graves and Newbold, folder 336, box 51, General Correspondence, Moton Papers. On Newbold's own reordering of the racial hierarchy within North Carolina's black education staff, see chapter 5 below and Leloudis, *Schooling the New South*, 183–227.

81. Bachman to Flexner, 30 July 1919, Flexner to Rosenwald, 31 July 1919, folder 8, box 336, Rosenwald Fund Archives.

82. Dresslar, *Report on the Rosenwald School Buildings*, 6–12. For examples of other contemporary designs that allowed cross-lighting, see Adams and Alsup, *Plans and Specifications*, 30; Texas Department of Education, *Consolidation of Rural Schools*, 27, 30–31.

83. Dresslar, *Report on the Rosenwald School Buildings*, 29–42.

84. Ibid., 23. Many early twentieth-century school planners still included cupolas and belfries in their designs for public schools; for examples, see Barrett and Thomson, *Plans for Public Schoolhouses* (1903), frontispiece and 6; Adams and Alsup, *Plans and Specifications*, 22, 26, 34, 39; *Manual for Georgia Teachers*, [1912], 295; *Manual for Georgia Teachers* [1916]. Dresslar disliked them all; see *American Schoolhouses*, 123.

85. Dresslar, *Report on the Rosenwald School Buildings*, 7–9, 43–53.

86. Ibid., 18–20, 25–28, 34–35, 47–48.

87. Dillard to Rosenwald, 11 March 1919, folder 8, box 336, Rosenwald Fund Archives; "Brief of Features of Rural School Audit," Rosenwald Fund Archives; Calloway to Moton, 9 April 1919, folder 336, box 51, General Correspondence, Moton Papers; Moton to Dillard, 7 June 1919, folder 357, box 53, General Correspondence, Moton Papers.

88. Moton to Rosenwald, 21 July 1919, folder 336, box 51, General Correspondence, Moton Papers, "Suggestions Proposed on Change on Administration of Rosenwald Schoolhouse Building Movement," n.d., folder 342, box 52, General Correspondence, Moton Papers; Moton to Rosenwald, 21 July 1919, Moton to Flexner, 19 July 1919, folder 8, box 336, Rosenwald Fund Archives.

89. Rosenwald to Willcox, 3 September 1919, Willcox to Rosenwald, 16 September 1919, quoted in Subject Index Notebook, folder 7, "Rural Schools," box 53, series II, subseries 5, Rosenwald Papers. The subject index notebooks are Morris Werner's notes for his biography of Rosenwald and quote extensively from other records in the Rosenwald Papers.

90. Moton to Graves, 15 October 1919, 31 October 1919, folder 335, box 50, General Correspondence, Moton Papers; typescript draft "Introduction," folder 340a, box 51, General Correspondence, Moton Papers; correspondence between Moton and Dresslar and copies of Dresslar's report in folder 360, box 53, General Correspondence, Moton Papers.

91. Calloway to Moton, 8 September 1917. Calloway was still sending copies of *Negro Rural School* to potential applicants for Rosenwald aid in early 1918. Calloway to Davis, 23 January 1918, folder "General Correspondence 1918," box 1, Calloway Papers.

92. Calloway to Lambert, 3 July 1919, folder "C," SG 15452, Rural School Agent Correspondence, Alabama Department of Education Records; typescript recommendations, 17 July 1919, folder 336, box 51, General Correspondence, Moton Papers.

93. Moore, "Report, Rosenwald Schoolhouse Building for North Carolina," September 1919, folder 335, box 50, General Correspondence, Moton Papers; miscellaneous application and final report forms marked "used in all states," folder 340a, box 51, General Correspondence, Moton Papers; Calloway to Moton, 27 December 1919, Moton to Graves, 31 December 1919, folder 336, box 51, General Correspondence, Moton Papers; Newbold to Dresslar, 6 October 1919, folder "D," box 4, General Correspondence of

the Director, Division of Negro Education, North Carolina Department of Public Instruction Records; Calloway to Lambert, 9 March 1920 and attached form, SG 15464, Rural School Agent Correspondence, Alabama Department of Education Records.

94. Rosenwald may also have drawn upon his own precedents for dramatic business decisions. He had previously chosen to support Richard Warren Sears over his wife's brother, had rallied other Sears, Roebuck managers behind him in quashing Richard Sears's maverick financial schemes, and had direct experience with imposing order on Sears, Roebuck's wildly popular, but poorly executed, catalog sales operation.

95. The Tuskegee Rosenwald committee had decided to make out two new budget proposals for 1919–20, one for 300 more schools and another for the total of 645 schools actually requested by state Negro school agents, but Rosenwald had taken no action. Tuskegee committee members also may have written up the undated suggestions for handling the Rosenwald program that survive in Moton's files. Two of these documents expressed concern about the racial implications of a new administration. "Nothing should be done to lessen the confidence of the colored and white people in the South in the Negro's ability to direct movements for his own development," counseled one writer, and another: "There is a strong bond of sympathetic confidence between white and colored people so far as Tuskegee Institute is concerned; and too, the Institution is located almost in the center of the Negro population." "Minutes of Rosenwald Committee Nov. 8 [1919], folder 340c, box 51, General Correspondence, Moton Papers; "Helpful Suggestions in the Reorganization of the Rosenwald Fund for the Promotion of the Schoolhouse Building for Negroes in the Southern States," folder 340b, box 51, General Correspondence, Moton Papers; "Suggestions Proposed on Change on Administration of Rosenwald Schoolhouse Building Movement," folder 342, box 52, General Correspondence, Moton Papers.

96. Moton also reminded Graves that Rosenwald had twice asked him if Tuskegee could get one thousand schools built by the end of 1919 and alleged that the auditors had made a number of errors in their report. Graves to Moton, 6 October 1919, 11 October 1919, 29 October 1919, Moton to Graves, 15 October 1919, 25 October 1919, folder 335, box 51, General Correspondence, Moton Papers; "Minutes of Rosenwald Committee," 24 October [1919], folder 340c, box 51, General Correspondence, Moton Papers; Calloway to Moton, 27 December 1919, Graves to Moton, 30 December 1919, folder 336, box 51, General Correspondence, Moton Papers; Moton to Graves, 25 October 1919, 13 November 1919, Graves to Moton, 7 November 1919, Moton to Rosenwald, folder 8, box 336, Rosenwald Fund Archives; Taggart, *Private Philanthropy.*

97. Woodson, "Story of the Fund," chap. 4, 4–7; Moton to Rosenwald, 11 February 1920, folder 340a, box 51, General Correspondence, Moton Papers.

98. Moton to Rosenwald, 11 February 1920, folder 340a, box 51, General Correspondence, Moton Papers; Moton to Lambert, 24 February 1920, folder 341, box 52, General Correspondence, Moton Papers; Moton to Lambert, 24 February 1920,

folder "M," SG 15459, Rural School Agent Correspondence, Alabama Department of Education Records.

99. Smith to Moton, 28 February 1920, folder 340a, box 51, General Correspondence, Moton Papers.

100. Favrot sent copies of his letter to Rosenwald, Jackson Davis, and James Hardy Dillard and attached correspondence showing that he wanted greater flexibility in the size of schools aided and much larger grants. Favrot to Moton, 6 March 1920, Lunsford to Favrot, 1 March 1920, Favrot to Lunsford, 4 March 1920, folder 340a, box 51, General Correspondence, Moton Papers; see also copies of these letters in folder 8, box 336, Rosenwald Fund Archives; his earlier request for a model school at Southern University that Calloway rejected because it was not in a rural community is in Favrot to Rosenwald, 17 May 1918, folder 5, box 339, Rosenwald Fund Archives. He repeated his claims that the alleged construction problems resulted from the disparity between Tuskegee's plans and Dresslar's expectations and charged that Dresslar's standards were impossibly high even for many white schools in Favrot to Moton, 19 May 1920, folder 340b, box 51, General Correspondence, Moton Papers. Favrot was also smarting from a contretemps over his handling of school-term extension grants, which he had allocated according to his own perceptions of need and to provide higher salaries for some teachers rather than according to the specifics of the 1917 plan. But Moton still described him as "one of the finest of the group of supervisors." Favrot to Calloway, 5 April 1920, folder 342, box 52, General Correspondence, Moton Papers; Moton to Graves, 14 April 1920, "Department of Education Baton Rouge," folder 340a, box 51, General Correspondence, Moton Papers.

101. Biographer Morris Werner echoed Harris's comments, attributing the removal of the building program from Tuskegee in part to "white contractors in the South" who "resented the supervision of Tuskegee Negroes." Favrot to Rosenwald, 6 March 1920, folder 8, box 336, Rosenwald Fund Archives; Favrot to Calloway, 24 March 1920, folder 340a, box 51, General Correspondence, Moton Papers; Harris to Flexner, 30 March 1920, folder 2039, box 212, series 1, subseries 2, General Education Board Archives; Werner, *Julius Rosenwald*, 132.

102. Flexner to Rosenwald, 24 April 1920, folder 1, box 331, Rosenwald Fund Archives.

103. Rosenwald also wanted to limit the program to three hundred schools annually and move away from the term-extension grants but also to emphasize facilities for two or more teachers instead of one-teacher schools and add Texas to the program. "Some of Mr. Rosenwald's Thoughts about Rural School Building," folder 340b, box 51, General Correspondence, Moton Papers. The term-extension grants had proved problematic, as Rosenwald, Calloway, and Leo Favrot had just battled over Favrot's handling of Louisiana's term-extension appropriation; South Carolina Negro school agent J. B. Felton had also warned that state officials could not dictate term length or salaries to local school boards, and that Rosenwald likewise should not try "to impose from Chi-

cago restrictions on school activities in South Carolina." Felton to Calloway, 31 March 1920, folder 340a, box 51, General Correspondence, Moton Papers.

104. "Before Rosenwald Committee," 4–5 June 1920, folder 340c, box 51, General Correspondence, Moton Papers.

105. M. Washington to Buttrick, 24 May 1920, folder 2039, box 212, series 1, subseries 2, General Education Board Archives; Rosenwald to Moton, 11 June 1920, folder 342, box 52, General Correspondence, Moton Papers; Rosenwald to Mrs. Washington, 11 June 1920, folder 1231, box 153, General Correspondence, Moton Papers. Margaret Murray Washington kept the letter in one of her own stationery envelopes, which is inscribed "Mr. Holsey [illegible] to keep this MMW Personal."

CHAPTER 3. IDEAL SCHOOLS: THE JULIUS ROSENWALD FUND RURAL SCHOOL-BUILDING PROGRAM AT NASHVILLE, 1920–27

1. The following discussion of the 1920 plan refers to "Plan for Distribution of Aid from the Julius Rosenwald Fund for Building Rural Schoolhouses in the South," folder 340a, box 51, General Correspondence, Moton Papers; "Plan for Distribution of Aid from the Julius Rosenwald Fund for Building Rural Schoolhouses in the South" and "Julius Rosenwald Fund Administrative Rulings," folder 1, box 331, Rosenwald Fund Archives. Signers of the plan included Buttrick and Flexner of the General Education Board; Moton, Margaret Murray Washington, and Calloway of Tuskegee Institute; Dresslar of George Peabody College for Teachers; and state Negro school agents Smith (Tennessee), Favrot (Louisiana), and Lambert (Alabama).

2. Discussions of Rosenwald's changing approach to philanthropy, and the Rosenwald Fund's leadership strategies include Embree and Waxman, *Investment in People*; Leloudis, *Schooling the New South*, 213–23; E. Anderson and Moss, *Dangerous Donations*, 197–99.

3. "Activities of the Fund," "Statement of Expenditures," 1918–22, folder 2, box 76, Rosenwald Fund Archives.

4. Werner, *Julius Rosenwald*, 320-55; Ascoli, "Julius Rosenwald."

5. Rosenwald later authorized a special appropriation from the fund for the Penn School's campaigns to build more Rosenwald schools on the island. Smith to Moton, 8 August 1927, Smith to Moton, 19 September 1927, folder 5, box 336, and 1927–29 correspondence in folder 8, box 342, Rosenwald Fund Archives.

6. Shepardson is remembered today for his commitment to the Beta Theta Pi fraternity, which awards a Shepardson prize; a member of Phi Beta Kappa, he was a founder of the Association of College Honor Societies in 1925 and its president from 1925–33. Gilpin and Gasman, *Charles S. Johnson*, 11–12.

7. Stern, who was married to Marion Rosenwald, was also a housing reform activist in Chicago and later a contributor to and client of the Chicago Psychoanalytical Institute, founded in 1932. The leftist principles of Stern and his second wife, Martha Dodd Stern, attracted attention from the National Security Agency, whose operatives

in 1945 claimed he was a KGB contact. The couple moved to Prague after being indicted for espionage in 1957. Foster, "History of Fight for Housing Project"; Kirsner, *Unfree Associations*, 3; "Boris Morros."

8. "Brief Outline of Training and Experience of S. L. Smith," folder 2, box 76, Rosenwald Fund Archives; Dillard to Rosenwald, 11 March 1919, folder 8, box 336, Rosenwald Fund Archives; S. Smith, *Builders of Goodwill*, 22–26.

9. Smith later wrote that "the only reason that I can see for my being selected to take charge of the Southern schools program of the Fund in 1920 was the fact that I was the only one at the time who had specialized under Dr. Dresslar in schoolhouse planning and who had a complete set of plans from a one-teacher to a six-teacher type ready for use." Embree and Waxman, *Investment in People*, 41; Smith to Rosenwald, 10 June 1930, folder 6, box 128, Rosenwald Fund Archives; "In Memoriam," 8; Stitely, "Bridging the Gap," 16–27.

10. Handwritten note on Smith to Stern, 25 October 1930, folder 6, box 128, Rosenwald Fund Archives. Smith had written a glowing report of his visit to the Dunbar High School in Little Rock and the meeting of the National Council for Schoolhouse Planning described in chapter 4.

11. Clinton Calloway told his brother Thomas that his Rosenwald salary would be $3,000 annually; he spent his first month organizing all of the records to be sent to Nashville. Dillard to Rosenwald, 11 March 1919, folder 8, box 336, Rosenwald Fund Archives; C. J. Calloway to C. H. Calloway, 25 May 1920, C. J. Calloway to T. J. Calloway, 7 July 1920, C. J. Calloway to Ramsey, 6 September 1920, folder "Correspondence General 1920," box 8, Calloway Papers; "Report C. J. Calloway, Field Agent, The Julius Rosenwald Fund," September 1920, folder 636, box 88, General Correspondence, Moton Papers.

12. "Report C. J. Calloway, Field Agent, The Julius Rosenwald Fund," October, November, and December 1920, folder 636, box 88, General Correspondence, Moton Papers; Secretary to Shivery, 9 June 1921, folder "Correspondence General 1921," box 8, Calloway Papers.

13. For examples of Clinton Calloway's and state agents' efforts in reorganizing the paperwork on Tuskegee Rosenwald schools, see correspondence between Lambert and Smith in folder "B," SG 15456, Rural School Agent Correspondence, Alabama Department of Education Records; Lambert to Carney, 12 April 1921, folder "C," SG 15457, Rural School Agent Correspondence, Alabama Department of Education Records; Calloway to Lambert, 27 August 1920, folder "Macon County," SG 15459, Rural School Agent Correspondence, Alabama Department of Education Records. James Carbaugh discusses this issue in "Philanthropic Confluence," 83.

14. The Rosenwald Fund's record keepers thenceforth used two similar systems, one numerical and the other alphabetical, to track each budget year's projects. In the numerical system found on state lists of building projects, they lumped together all Tuskegee-era schools as year or budget number 1, the "cleanup" as year or budget number 2, and

the 1920–21 through 1930–31 years or budgets consecutively as numbers 3 through 13. Under the alphabetical system used to track Rosenwald Fund projects from the initial application through to the final grant payment, they assigned letters *A* through *K* to the 1920–21 through 1930–31 budgets, and numbered each project consecutively as applications came in. For example, the fifteenth project in 1920–21 was 15–A. They also maintained an index card file that they continuously updated with any changes in the building's status, such as an addition, cross-referenced to their collection of photographs documenting each building's completion. These cards and photographs are part of the Julius Rosenwald Fund Archives.

15. "Summary of Work Accomplished," "Completed Rosenwald Schools to June 30, 1921," Smith, "General Statement Concerning 1920–1921 Budgets," folder 1, and "Rosenwald Buildings Erected by Years Showing Number, Fund's Aid and Total Cost, 1913–1932," folder 2, box 331, Rosenwald Fund Archives.

16. Faucett to Lambert, 3 January 1920, Lambert to Faucett, 5 January 1920, folder "Autauga County," SG 15456, Rural School Agent Correspondence, Alabama Department of Education Records; Benson to Lambert, 13 August 1921, folder "Escambia County," SG 15457, Rural School Agent Correspondence, Alabama Department of Education Records.

17. Lambert to Calloway, 17 August 1920, Calloway to Lambert, 20 August 1920, Lambert to Calloway, 26 August 1920, folder "Macon County," SG 15459, Rural School Agent Correspondence, Alabama Department of Education Records; Smith to Lambert, 9 August 1921, folder "Baldwin County," SG 15456, Rural School Agent Correspondence, Alabama Department of Education Records.

18. Smith was involved in many other civic and reformist organizations, serving on the executive committee of the Tennessee Inter-racial Committee, as a director of the Tennessee Tuberculosis Association, the chair of school education for the Tennessee Parent-Teacher Association, a director of the National Education Association, life member and president of the National Council of Schoolhouse Construction, and the president of the Tennessee Association for the Relief and Rehabilitation of Ex-Convicts. He received an honorary doctorate in education from his alma mater, Southwestern Presbyterian University, in 1932. Clay, "A Brief Story of the Rosenwald Movement in Tennessee," typescript, 7 January 1927, folder 1, box 270, Tennessee Commissioner of Education Records; Clay, "Lifework of Dr. S. L. Smith."

19. Brundage, *Lynching in the New South*, 208–44; Tolnay and Beck, *Festival of Violence*, 202–38; Tindall, *Emergence of the New South*, 177–83, 187–96; Grantham, *Southern Progressivism*, 407–15; Link, *Paradox of Southern Progressivism*, 248–61.

20. Graves to Smith, 15 June 1921, Smith to Graves, 23 June 1921, Smith to Shepardson, 20 August 1921, Shepardson to Smith, 23 August 1921, folder 16, box 127, Rosenwald Fund Archives. All letters are marked personal and confidential. See also Brundage, *Lynching in the New South*, 188–89.

21. Scholars have noted this shift in many venues of southern reform, including

the Commission on Interracial Cooperation. See Grantham, *Southern Progressivism*, 406–8, 413–14.

22. Calloway to Moton, 16 December 1920, folder 636, box 88, General Correspondence, Moton Papers.

23. In addition to "a big year's work" he had planned with Smith that led to "better constructed schoolhouses," Calloway took on the presidency of the Alabama Teachers Association and asked sociologist Robert E. Park to suggest a reading list for a personal study of rural sociology. C. J. Calloway to Ferguson, 12 March 1921, 25 June 1921, Calloway to Park, 20 July 1921, C. J. Calloway to T. J. Calloway, 11 March 1921, 6 October 1921, folder "Correspondence General 1921," box 8, Calloway Papers; C. J. Calloway to T. J. Calloway, 8 July 1922, folder "Correspondence General 1922," box 9, Calloway Papers.

24. Shepardson wrote the official report on the meeting for the Rosenwald Fund and thus probably authored the notes containing the commentary about Calloway. C.J. Calloway to T.J. Calloway, 3 May 1923, folder "Correspondence General 1923," box 9, Calloway Papers; "Notes Made at Hampton, Virginia, Conference of State Agents," 6–9 May 1923, 6, folder 4, box 188, Rosenwald Fund Archives; Favrot to Smith, 10 November 1922, folder "Tennessee," box 25, Louisiana Department of Education Records.

25. Whatever his feelings about the building program, Calloway, or Moton, Rosenwald remained a faithful and generous member of the Tuskegee board of trustees until his death. C. J. Calloway to T. J. Calloway, 11 July 1923, folder "Correspondence General 1923," box 9, Calloway Papers; Davis to Credle, 3 July 1923, folder "D," box 86, General Correspondence, North Carolina Department of Public Instruction Records. Calloway's complaint should also be understood in the context of both Calloway brothers' close association with Booker T. Washington and Thomas Junius Calloway's role in the "Bookerite" faction in the nation's capital. For them, this was a rupture of a long-standing personal and professional relationship tied to the legacy of Booker T. Washington.

26. Stern to Smith, 26 July 1928, Smith to Stern, 28 July 1928, 1 August 1928, folder 12, box 187, Rosenwald Fund Archives.

27. "Report of S. L. Smith, State Rural School Supervisor for Tennessee," November 1919, folder 1469, and "Extract from letter of Mr. Jackson Davis to Dr. Flexner, dated January 24, 1916," folder 1472, box 158, series 1.1, General Education Board Archives; photographs of Fayette County Training School, negatives L1092, 1173, 2067, 2073, *Jackson Davis Collection*; S.L.S[mith], "A Story of the Julius Rosenwald Fund in Tenn. From the Beginning to July 1, 1920," folder 2, box 78, Rosenwald Fund Archives.

28. S[mith], "A Story of the Julius Rosenwald Fund in Tenn."; *Annual Report* [Tennessee], 1921–22: 26.

29. Smith to Moton, 13 September 1921, folder 636, box 88, Moton Papers; Smith to Credle, 22 December 1926, folder "S. L. Smith," box 3, Correspondence of the Supervi-

sor of the Rosenwald Fund, Division of Negro Education, North Carolina Department of Public Instruction Records. For an excellent discussion of the Rosenwald Fund's architectural designs, as well as an overview of the history of the building program and its implementation in North Carolina, see Hanchett, "Rosenwald Schools," 400–406. For the broader context of Progressive school architecture, see Cutler, "Cathedral of Culture," 6–33.

30. The following discussion considers "Community School Plans," pamphlet 1, folder 2046, pamphlets 2–8, folder 2047, box 213, series 1.11, General Education Board Archives; *Community School Plans*, 1927.

31. Dresslar, "Hygiene of Rural Schools;" Dresslar, *American Schoolhouses*, 124; Dresslar, *Report on the Rosenwald School Buildings*, 9–12, 16–19, 20–21; "General Specifications," *Community School Plans*, 1921.

32. His faith in the hygienic power of sunlight led Dresslar to prefer lighting from the east so that the sun's rays could act as a disinfectant on the classroom before students arrived. Dresslar, *Report on the Rosenwald School Buildings*, 9, 20–22; [Dresslar], "Proposed Plan for Six Negro Schools for New Hanover County," folder "Reports, Teacher list for Rosenwald Fund," box 5, Calloway Papers.

33. Dresslar, *American Schoolhouses*, 38–39; Dresslar, "Hygiene of Rural Schools," 1107–8; Dresslar, *Report on the Rosenwald School Buildings*, 12, 15, 36, 39; "General Specifications," *Community School Plans*, 1927.

34. Dresslar, *Report on the Rosenwald School Buildings*, 22.

35. Cutler, "Cathedral of Culture," 8.

36. "Paint Colors."

37. The original Tuskegee desk designs burned with the Boy's Trade Building at Tuskegee Institute, but homemade desks were still in use at new Rosenwald schools in the early 1930s. N[ewbold], "Discussion of Rosenwald Schools at Conference of State Agents Assembled at Nashville," January 1921, 4–6, and "Notes Made at the Conference of State Agents for Negro Rural Schools," November 1921, 14, folder 4, box 188, Rosenwald Fund Archives; Smith to Moton, 10 October 1921, Moton to Smith, 27 October 1921, folder 636, box 88, General Correspondence, Moton Papers.

38. For the connections between education, privies, and public health, see Link, "Privies, Progressivism, and Public Schools."

39. Dresslar, *Report on the Rosenwald School Buildings*, 30–31.

40. *Annual Report* [Georgia], 1920, 84; Blanton, *Handbook of Information*, 166; *Biennial Report* [Florida], 1923–24, 267, 268.

41. Embree, "How Negro Schools Have Advanced," 41; *Annual Report* [Georgia], 1921, 65; Marrs, Bludworth, and Taylor, *Negro Education in Texas* (1926), 17; *Biennial Report* [Florida], 1927–28, 221.

42. Hale, *Making Whiteness*, 136; McGerr, *Fierce Discontent*, 188–91.

43. Dresslar, *American School Buildings*.

44. For examples of Progressive educators seeking state control of school construc-

tion, see "School Buildings," *Biennial Report* [Kentucky], 1920–21, 35–36; "Education Is Chiefly a State Function." On standardization, see "Schoolhouse Plans," 22–23; "Uniformity in Schoolhouse Plans," 62; "Standardization of the Rural School Plant"; "Rural School Architecture"; Ittner, "School Building Policies"; "Standardized School House Design," pts. 1 and 2.

45. Standard treatments of the turn to social efficiency among southern Progressives include Tindall, *Emergence of the New South*, 224–41; Grantham, *Southern Progressivism*, 412–17; Link, *Paradox of Southern Progressivism*, 203–321. For a parallel discussion focusing on vocational education, see Kliebard, *Schooled to Work*, 44–54, 122–24.

46. Examples of these scorecards, standards, and school-building programs include the following works by Strayer and Engelhardt: "Score Card for Village and Rural School Buildings"; "Score Card for City School Buildings"; *Standards for Elementary School Buildings*; *Standards for High School Buildings*; *Report of the Survey*.

47. "School Architecture in 1917–18"; Cooper, "Standardization of Schoolhouses"; Cooper, "Economies Gained"; Cooper, "Hygienic Problems" (November and December 1919); Cooper, *Report of Committee*. Smith and Cooper served on this committee with some of the country's most famous school planners and architects, including S. A. Challman, Leonard P. Ayres, C. B. J. Snyder, Lewis M. Terman, James O. Betelle, John J. Donovan, William B. Ittner, and W. R. McCornack. The latter's work for the Rosenwald Fund at the end of the decade is discussed in chapter 4; Cutler discusses many of them in "Cathedral of Culture."

48. Smith, foreword to *Community School Plans*, 1924, 1927.

49. "The Julius Rosenwald Fund in the South, 1930–31," typescript attached to W. F. Credle to E. R. Embree, 18 July 1931, folder 2, box 331, Rosenwald Fund Archives.

50. J .T. Calhoun, rural white school supervisor in Mississippi, thanked both Dresslar and the Tennessee Department of Education in his introduction, noting also that several plans had been "drawn in the office of the General Agent of the Julius Rosenwald Fund." *Rural School Houses and Grounds* [Mississippi], 7, 39; Blanton and Borden, *School Grounds*, 20, 51, 55; Pruett, "Rural School Buildings," 57, 84.

51. Davis to Credle, 28 October 1924, folder "G. E. Davis, Building Agent, July 1924–February 1925," box 1, Correspondence of the Supervisor of the Rosenwald Fund, Division of Negro Education, North Carolina Department of Public Instruction Records; Hilbun to Shepardson, 23 January 1925, folder 3, box 340, Rosenwald Fund Archives. Pictures of new white school buildings published in state department of education annual reports and white state teachers' association periodicals offer visual evidence of the impact of Rosenwald plans. For examples, see "Stephens County Makes Rapid Strides"; "DeWitt County Schools"; "The Three R's."

52. Woodson, "The Story of the Fund," chap. 7, 1–10; Smith to Lambert, 26 March 1921, Lambert to Smith, 28 March 1921, SG 15459, Rural School Agent Correspondence, Alabama Department of Education Records.

53. Grants for four-, five-, and six-teacher schools originally were $1,200; $1,400;

and $1,600, respectively. All but one-teacher grants were scaled back by $100 in 1922. "Plan for Distribution of Aid," 1922–23, folder 1, box 331, Rosenwald Fund Archives.

54. "The Julius Rosenwald Fund Administrative Rulings."

55. *Community School Plans*, 1927.

56. Smith had been interested in teachers' homes since 1915, when he included them (with no outside funding) in county training-school projects. An undated set of recommendations for reorganizing the building program, probably generated by Tuskegee staff for one of Moton's meetings with Rosenwald in 1920, does include a proposal for teachers' homes. Smith to Flexner, 4 February 1915, folder 1472, box 158, series 1.1, General Education Board Archives; Sibley to Calloway, 9 March 1916, folder "C," SG 15448, Rural School Agent Correspondence, Alabama Department of Education Records; Smith to Rosenwald, 13 November 1919, folder 335, box 50, Graves to Moton, 30 December 1919, folder 336, and undated recommendations "In view of the splendid report by Dr. Dressler [*sic*]," folder 340a, box 51, General Correspondence, Moton Papers.

57. C. J. Calloway to T. J. Calloway, 20 March 1922, folder "Correspondence General 1923," box 9, Calloway Papers.

58. "Julius Rosenwald Fund Administrative Rulings"; "Plan for Distribution of Aid from the Julius Rosenwald Fund for Building Rural Schoolhouses in the South," 1920, 1922–23, 1923–24, 1924–25, folder 1, box 331, Rosenwald Fund Archives; "Julius Rosenwald Fund," 79, 81.

59. This discussion of teachers' homes draws upon *Community School Plans*, 1927.

60. Kliebard, *Schooled to Work*, 120–21, 129–42, 171–74; Kett, "Adolescence of Vocational Education"; Kantor, *Learning to Earn*; Hoffschwelle, *Rebuilding the Rural Southern Community*, 91–100.

61. [Smith], "Evolution of the Schoolhouse Construction Program by the Julius Rosenwald Fund," folder 1, box 331, Rosenwald Fund Archives; "Julius Rosenwald Fund Administrative Rulings," 6–7; Smith to Stern, 21 February 1927, folder 2, box 336, Rosenwald Fund Archives. See also Hall, *Black Vocational and Industrial Arts Education*, 173–200.

62. *Shop Plans*.

63. Robinson to Stern, 17 January 1927, folder 1, box 311, Rosenwald Fund Archives. Robinson was consistent in this position throughout his service in the North Carolina Division of Negro Education from 1921 to 1928; see Robinson to Newbold, 29 November 1923, folder "R," box 7, General Correspondence of the Director, Division of Negro Education, North Carolina Department of Public Instruction Records. For more on Robinson and his later career at the Atlanta University Laboratory School and as director of the Secondary School Study for the Association of Colleges and Secondary Schools for Negroes, see Goodenow, "Separate and Unequal."

64. Stern to Robinson, 25 January 1927, folder 1, box 311, Rosenwald Fund Archives. Robinson's publication of statistics showing the dismal number of accredited four-year

high schools for African Americans worried Stern, who privately hoped Robinson would not be reelected as president of the National Association of Teachers in Colored Schools. Stern to Smith, 19 July 1927, Smith to Stern, 21 July 1927, folder 1, box 311, Rosenwald Fund Archives.

65. Moton to Stern, 12 January 1928, folder 1060, box 136, Embree to Moton, 28 September 1928, folder 1231, box 153, General Correspondence, Moton Papers. Demonstration schools include the 1924 Felton Practice School and teachers' cottage at the Colored Normal, Industrial, Agricultural and Mechanical College of South Carolina, and the 1929 J. C. Corbin Laboratory School at the Arkansas Agricultural, Mechanical, and Normal College. "Felton Laboratory School" (Orangeburg: South Carolina State University, n.d.), Felton Training School Records; J. C. Corbin School photographs 5357.24–26.

66. Tuskegee's designers had included options for additions, but Dresslar did not think they were sufficient or properly carried out. Favrot had suggested that the fund offer aid for additions in 1921. [Dresslar], "Proposed Plan for Six Negro Schools for New Hanover County"; N[ewbold], "Discussion of Rosenwald Schools at Conference of State Agents Assembled at Nashville," 1921, 8–9; "Julius Rosenwald Fund Administrative Rulings."

67. 1927 Arkansas correspondence in folder 4, box 337, Rosenwald Fund Archives; "The Flood," *Biennial Report* [Mississippi], 1925–27, 11; Weathers to Julius Rosenwald, 2 October 1927, folder 3 "Rosenwald, Julius, Schools," box 34, series I, Rosenwald Papers. Florida received similar emergency funds in 1928 and Arkansas again in 1929.

68. "Notes Made at the Conference of State Agents for Negro Rural Schools," November 1921; "Libraries," folder 1, box 79, Rosenwald Fund Archives; Embree and Waxman, *Investment in People*, 60–63; Towne, "County Library Service"; Barker, *Rosenwald Library Demonstrations*; Wilson and Wight, *County Library Service in the South*; "How to Get Aid From the J.R.F.," 9; R. Jones, "Kentucky Negro Education Association (KNEA) Journal."

69. "Libraries in Teachers Colleges," folder 1, box 79, Rosenwald Fund Archives; R. Jones, "Kentucky Negro Education Association (KNEA) Journal," 63–64; "Annual Report of the Board of Trustees of the Colored Normal, Industrial, Agricultural and Mechanical College of South Carolina," 1928, in *Reports and Resolutions*, 1929, 34.

70. "Thousandths Rosenwald Schools," folder 8, box 343, Rosenwald Fund Archives.

71. See chapter 4 for O'Kelly's activism in 1914. Smith to Morton [*sic*], 19 November 1923, folder 636, box 88, General Correspondence, Moton Papers; "Thousandths Rosenwald Schools"; Smith to Stern, 9 June 1930, and "Five Thousandth Rosenwald School," *Southern Missioner*, n.d., 177–80, in folder 8, box 343, Rosenwald Fund Archives; Smith to Credle, 6 October 1927, 14 November 1927, folder "S.L. Smith—Field Agent," box 4, Correspondence of the Supervisor of the Rosenwald Fund, Division of Negro Education, North Carolina Department of Public Instruction Records.

72. Woodson's standing with and support from Julius Rosenwald and the Rosenwald Fund waxed and waned, although Rosenwald and especially Embree respected his work. For more on Woodson, Rosenwald, and the Rosenwald Fund, see Hine, "Carter G. Woodson"; Goggin, *Carter G. Woodson*, 72–73; Meier and Rudwick, *Black History*, 1–71.

73. Woodson published some of his research material from "The Story of the Fund" in his 1930 book, *The Rural Negro*. For an example of the commentaries sent in, see W.T.B. Williams, "The Rosenwald Fund in Negro Education," [1927], folder 2, box 76, Rosenwald Fund Archives. Moton to Stern, 6 August 1927, folder 1060, box 136, General Correspondence, Moton Papers.

74. "Negro Common School, Georgia," 260, 264; "Negro Common School, Mississippi"; "Negro Common School, North Carolina." Du Bois did print the Rosenwald Fund's maps and plans of aid for the building program and admired Julius Rosenwald, whose foundation helped to fund the NAACP and the *Crisis*, and Du Bois' *Black Reconstruction*. These articles, however, written by Horace Mann Bond and funded by a grant Du Bois secured from the American Fund for Public Research (Garland Fund), emphasized the systematic discrimination against African American education. Bond quoted extensively from a petition by African Americans in Jackson, Mississippi, that characterized Rosenwald schools as "the Negro's *second tax*" that facilitated white monopolization of public school funding in "Negro Common School, Mississippi," 102. See D. Lewis, *Fight for Equality*, 160, 189, 206, 281, 296, 350–78.

CHAPTER 4. SOUTHERN SCHOOLS AND RACE: NEW LEADERSHIP AND THE DEMISE OF THE BUILDING PROGRAM, 1927–32

1. Embree and Waxman, *Investment in People*, 29. Hanchett also notes the Carnegie library program as a possible model for Washington and Rosenwald in "The Rosenwald Schools," 396, 398; Van Slyck explains Carnegie's reform of American philanthropy and library architecture in *Free to All*.

2. Rosenwald's own health was declining, as he suffered suffered from Paget's disease and heart problems. To replace himself as president, Rosenwald first selected the executive vice president of the Illinois Central Railroad, Charles M. Kittle and then, after Kittle's death early in 1928, promoted Wood. Werner, *Julius Rosenwald*, 361; Emmet and Jeuck, *Catalogues and Counters*, 324–32.

3. Rosenwald had previously authorized use of both principal and income from his gifts and urged other philanthropists to do the same. Werner, *Julius Rosenwald*, 322–29; Embree and Waxman, *Investment in People*, 17; for Rosenwald's ideas about and philanthropic support for all varieties of black educational institutions in the 1920s, see Beilke, "'Partners in Distress.'"

4. Correspondence between Rosenwald, Embree, and Flexner, November–December 1927, folder 31, and Embree to Rosenwald, 1 March 1928, 16 March 1928, "Work of the Julius Rosenwald Fund Letter Number One, 6 March 1928, "Work of the Julius

Rosenwald Fund Letter Number Two," 8 March 1928, folder 31, box 104, Rosenwald Fund Archives; Embree, *Julius Rosenwald Fund*, 1928, [4], 6, 34.

5. Rosenwald to Trustees, 30 April 1928, quoted in Embree and Waxman, *Investment in People*, 31; Embree, *Julius Rosenwald Fund*, 1928, 7–11.

6. Stanfield, "Dollars for the Silent South," 120; see also Belles, "Julius Rosenwald Fund," 13–18; E. Anderson and Moss, *Dangerous Donations*, 199–200.

7. Embree's own published works during his tenure at the Rosenwald Fund include *Brown America*; with Johnson and Alexander, *Collapse of Cotton Tenancy*; with Simon and Mumford, *Island India*; *Every Tenth Pupil*; *Little Red Schoolhouse*; and *American Negroes*.

8. Gilpin and Gasman, *Charles S. Johnson*, 11–12, 33–34; Robbins, *Sidelines Activist*, 34–36. See also Gasman, "W.E.B. Du Bois and Charles S. Johnson."

9. Stanfield, "Dollars for the Silent South"; Belles, "Julius Rosenwald Fund"; Gasman and Gilpin, *Charles S. Johnson*; Robbins, *Sidelines Activist*; Dunne, "Next Steps," 3–6. For an excellent analysis of the racial paternalism that motivated many reformers like Embree, see J. Smith, *Managing White Supremacy*.

10. Embree to Rosenwald, 1 March 1928, folder 32, box 104, Rosenwald Fund Archives.

11. Embree, *Julius Rosenwald Fund*, 1928, [32]–33; Embree to Davis, 10 April 1928, folder 16, box 202, Rosenwald Fund Archives; "Conference of Trustees and Guests, Julius Rosenwald Fund," 29 April 1928, folder 1, and "Meeting of Trustees, Julius Rosenwald Fund," 30 April 1928," folder 2, box 57, series III, Julius Rosenwald Papers.

12. Studies of the Julius Rosenwald Fund's many new initiatives, which over the next twenty years moved toward a direct challenge to segregation, include Belles, "Julius Rosenwald Fund"; Perkins, "Welcome Consequences."

13. Smith to Felton, 8 October 1928, folder 4, box 342, Rosenwald Fund Archives.

14. "Docket, Meeting of the Executive Committee, Julius Rosenwald Fund," 13 June 1928, folder 4, box 56, series III, Rosenwald Papers; Smith to Felton, 11 July 1928, folder 4, box 342, Rosenwald Fund Archives; "Conference of State Agents of Rural Schools for Negroes," 4–5 June 1929, 11, folder 4, box 188, Rosenwald Fund Archives; Embree to Smith, Harrell to Smith, 4 April 1929, folder 12, box 331, Rosenwald Fund Archives.

15. "Meeting of Trustees, Julius Rosenwald Fund," 4 November 1928, 37–38, folder 3, box 57, series III, Rosenwald Papers; "Minutes of Julius Rosenwald Fund," 4 November 1928, 73–74, folder 1, box 341, Rosenwald Fund Archives; Smith to Felton, 8 November 1928, folder 4, box 342, Rosenwald Fund Archives; "Conference of State Agents of Rural Schools for Negroes," 4–5 June 1929, 15–16.

16. Embree and Waxman, *Investment in People*, 53; "Special Meeting of Trustees, Julius Rosenwald Fund," 11 May 1929, 5–6, folder 5, box 57, series III, Rosenwald Papers; "Conference of State Agents of Rural Schools for Negroes," 4–5 June 1929, Smith to Harrell, 17 August 1929, Felton to Smith, 23 September 1929, folder 1, box 336, Rosenwald Fund Archives.

17. In 1931, Alabama had 157 buses for white students and only 12 for black students. Smith to Stern, 11 October 1928, Smith to Harrell, 15 February 1929, 2 March 1929, 5 October 1929, Ledbetter to Smith, 5 October 1931, folder 1, Lambert to Smith, 15 March 1929, folder 5, box 336, Rosenwald Fund Archives; Johnson interview; Stewart interview.

18. Embree and Waxman, *Investment in People*, 65–67. The library programs outlasted the building program by a few years into the mid-1930s.

19. Williams, undated circular letter, "The Rosenwald Fund Aids Negro Schools as Follows," folder 2, box 331, Rosenwald Fund Archives; [Smith] to Dear Mr. [form letter for radio grants], 30 November 1929, folder 4, box 332, Rosenwald Fund Archives.

20. Poignard, "The Julius Rosenwald School" (sung to "My Old Kentucky Home"), 1936, folder 3, box 331, Rosenwald Fund Archives. For a discussion of radios in a white school, see Hamilton, "Radio in City Park School."

21. Newbold to Stern, 24 February 1927, folder 1, and Smith to Stern, 21 February 1927, folder 2, box 336, Rosenwald Fund Archives.

22. Hubert to Arthur, 25 November 1929, Evans to Stern, 4 June 1930, Smith to Stern, 12 June 1930, folder 3, box 342, Rosenwald Fund Archives.

23. Easom to Smith, 15 November 1929, Smith to Easom, 4 April 1931, folder 7, box 340, Rosenwald Fund Archives; Scott to Embree, 20 November 1929, folder 8, box 339, Rosenwald Fund Archives. Mississippi's vocational supervisor was J. H. Dean of Alcorn University. Georgia's vocational supervisor was L. S. Molette; South Carolina's was W. W. Watkins at CNIA&MC in Orangeburg. See material in folder "Jackson Davis," unit 1, series 62, Division of Negro Education, Georgia Department of Education Records; "Annual Report of the Board of Trustees of the Colored Normal, Industrial, Agricultural and Mechanical College of South Carolina," 1930, in *Reports and Resolutions*, 1931, 20.

24. Dillard was receptive to the idea and suggested beginning in Louisiana and North Carolina. Shepardson to Dillard, 3 February 1925, Dillard to Shepardson, 7 February 1925, folder 2, box 34, series 5, Southern Education Foundation Records.

25. J. Anderson offers a detailed analysis of the combination of class and race-specific agendas at work in the urban industrial high schools in *Education of Blacks*, 203–29.

26. For scholarly critiques of vocational education's flawed ideology and results, see Violas, "Reflections on Theories"; Kliebard, *Schooled to Work*.

27. Undated extract from minutes of the Julius Rosenwald Fund Board of Trustees, [4 November 1928], folder 2, box 253, Rosenwald Fund Archives.

28. "Item IV," [Julius Rosenwald Fund Executive Committee meeting, 14 August 1928], folder 2, box 253, Rosenwald Fund Archives.

29. Hall to Arthur, 2 October 1928, folder 8, box 294, Rosenwald Fund Archives.

30. Booker to Arthur, 10 December 1928, 30 September 1929, Arthur to Booker, 17

December 1928, Ogden to Embree, 11 February 1930, Embree to Ogden, 18 February 1930, folder 8, box 294, Rosenwald Fund Archives. Dunbar High School cost about $400,000, with the Rosenwald Fund contributing $67,000 for construction and $2,500 for the school library, and another $30,000 coming from the General Education Board to help with the vocational equipment.

31. Stern to Salmson, 16 May 1930, Altheimer to Stern, 6 June 1930, Julius Rosenwald to Salmson, 11 June 1930, folder 8, box 294, Rosenwald Fund Archives.

32. This was an interesting encounter, for Heller expressed himself as being more interested in helping African Americans in his city than in pleasing either Edgar Stern or white opponents to black education. A key controversy in New Orleans was the possible replacement of the African American principal with a white man. For this and additional correspondence between A. Stern, E. Stern, Heller, and Rosenwald, as well as discussions of Keller, McCornack, Johnson, and Byrd's studies, see Heller to A. Stern, 6 September 1930, and the materials in folder 3, box 310, Rosenwald Fund Archives.

33. Altheimer to Stern, 6 June 1930, folder 8, box 294, and Humphrey to Embree, 12 June 1928, folder 3, box 296, Rosenwald Fund Archives; "Rosenwald Fund to Give $25,000 to Col. School," *Maysville (Ky.) Ledger*, 16 July 1929, Tuskegee Clippings Files; "John G. Fee Industrial High School"; see also Turley-Adams, *Rosenwald Schools in Kentucky*.

34. Clerk and Keller, "Study of Paul Laurence Dunbar High School at Little Rock, Arkansas" and "Special Inquiry into the Industrial Status of the Negro and Statement of Attitudes of Negroes in Regard to the Dunbar High School in Little Rock," folder 9, box 294, Rosenwald Fund Archives.

35. Some of the industrial surveys utilized local expertise; for example, Forrester B. Washington of the Atlanta School of Social Work prepared the "Proposed Program of Industrial Training for Negroes of Columbus, Georgia," folder "Georgia," unit 1, series 14, Georgia Department of Education Records. On Johnson and Byrd, see Gilpin and Gasman, *Charles S. Johnson*, 93, 96–98; Lewis, *Fight for Equality*, 323, 328–29, 334; Beilke, "Changing Emphasis," 7–8; Gasman, "W.E.B. Du Bois and Charles S. Johnson."

36. Like many Rosenwald schools, Dunbar had a long tradition dating back to the first school for African Americans in Little Rock, the 1867 Union School. In 1931, it became the first African American high school to earn accreditation by the North Central Association; in 1935, its junior high, senior high, and junior college work earned accolades from the Arkansas Department of Education as one of the best high schools for black students in the United States. F. Jones, *Traditional Model*, 5, 12–15; "Dunbar Junior College and High School Commencement," *Bulletin of the Association of Teachers of Negro Youth of Arkansas* 4, no. 3 (July 1931), 12, in Sykes Collection; Hamilton to Arthur, 21 March 1931, folder 8, box 294, Rosenwald Fund Archives.

37. For details on other industrial high schools, see folder 1, box 171 (Atlanta), folder 10, box 174 (Birmingham), folder 2, box 208 (Greenville, South Carolina), folder 10,

box 299 (Montgomery and Mobile, Alabama), folder 8, box 344 (Salisbury, North Carolina, and Salisbury, Maryland), folder 15, box 369 (Wilmington, North Carolina), "Memorandum on Industrial High Schools and Trade Schools," 22 March 1930, "Industrial High Schools: Larger Projects," 25 April 1930, folder 2, box 253, Rosenwald Fund Archives; "Special Meeting of Trustees, Julius Rosenwald Fund," 26 April 1930, bound volume of minutes, box 58, and minutes of the executive committee and the board of trustees' meetings in boxes 56 and 57, series III, Rosenwald Papers. On the displacement of black workers by whites, see J. Anderson, *Education of Blacks*, 229–37.

38. "Conference of State Agents of Rural Schools for Negroes," 8–9 June 1928, 7, 14, folder 4, box 188, Rosenwald Fund Archives.

39. Lambert to Hill, 5 July 1927, Lambert to Smith, 3 February 1928, Lambert to Hill, 4 February 1928, folder "E. E. McGehee," unit 1, series 14, Georgia Department of Education Records. On the same issue in Arkansas, see Womack and McCuistion to Julius Rosenwald Fund, 26 March 1928 and [Smith?] to Womack, 3 May 1928, folder 2, box 337, Rosenwald Fund Archives.

40. "Conference of State Agents of Rural Schools for Negroes," 5–6 June 1930, folder 4, box 188, Rosenwald Fund Archives; "Division of Negro Education," *Annual Report* [Virginia], 1929–30, 70; Huffington to Smith, 15 March 1929, folder 9, box 339, Rosenwald Fund Archives.

41. Correspondence between Smith and Shepardson, 15–27 July 1925, folder 3, box 340, Rosenwald Fund Archives.

42. By 1930, its teachers and students also benefited from Rosenwald grants for term extension, transportation, and a library. D. Williams, *Rosenwald School Day*, 1930, cover, 4.

43. The first structure, known as the Junior High School, received aid from the General Education Board as well. It suffered fire damage in 1924 during a period of student unrest with the administration. The second building's ornamentation reflects the contemporary architectural trends that influenced the later *Community School Plans*, as discussed later in this chapter. The General Education Board also contributed toward its $56,000 cost. Lucy Ella Moten was the principal of Miner Normal School from 1883 to 1920. The Moten School is still used as a practice school by FAMU. Eaton, Dawson, Thompson, and Waldorf, *Historical and Architectural Survey*, 12, 44, 51, 54, 61, 76, and passim.

44. Agenda for "Annual Meeting of Trustees, Julius Rosenwald Fund," 16 November 1929, folder 6, and "Special Meeting of Trustees," 26 April 1930, folder 7, box 57, series III, Rosenwald Papers.

45. *Rosenwald School Day in Georgia*, 1930; Marrs, Bludworth, and Taylor, *Negro Education in Texas*, 1931, 10–11.

46. Missouri's department of education had recently created a department of Negro education with O. G. Sanford at its head, N. B. Young as Negro school inspector, and

state Jeanes supervisor Rebecca Davis. Davis had recently returned from Africa, where she had been the Jeanes supervisor for Liberia. Young's first tour of black schools had documented the same disparities in public education endemic in the southern states, and particular needs in central and southeastern Missouri, and the Rosenwald Fund expected to confine its aid to schools in these regions so similar to the traditional South. Young to Lee, 15 June 1928 and 22 June 1928, folder 1, box 341, Rosenwald Fund Archives.

47. Embree to Rosenwald, 26 May 1931, folder 9, box 33, series I, Rosenwald Papers. A proposal to hire a "younger man" (Sidney Frissell) to do field work for Smith languished for two years before McCuistion's arrival. The Chicago staff had grown as well, adding four members since 1928. McCuistion's publications include *Financing Schools*; *South's Negro Teaching Force*; "South's Negro Teaching Force"; *School Money*; *Graduate Instruction*.

48. Louisiana seems to have pioneered this concept in 1924 with "general public meetings held in all of the Rosenwald schools of the State." Lewis and Sisemore, *Special Report*, 1924, 38.

49. For an example of rally or patrons' day, see Virginia State Teachers Association and School Improvement League, *Program*. For Jeanes teachers' longtime efforts, see Lucretia T. Kennard, "Report of Supervisor of Colored Schools, Caroline County," *Annual Report* [Maryland], 1912, 95. Florida Jeanes supervisor Jenyethel Merritt's personal papers include copies of the 1930, 1932, and 1934 Rosenwald School Day programs, as well as copies of Rosenwald's biographical sketch and the "Suggestions for Beautifying School Grounds" distributed by the Fund for Rosenwald Day events in the Jenyethel Merritt Jeanes Teacher Collection. On the connection between field days and Rosenwald school day, see Krause, "Jeanes Supervisor," 134–35; on extension service community cleanup days and competitions for white and black women, see Hoffschwelle, *Rebuilding the Rural Southern Community*, 118–44.

50. Lewis and Bateman, *Rosenwald-Day Program*.

51. Some states held Rosenwald Day during April's National Negro Health Week instead. Smith to Credle, 6 March 1928, Credle to Smith, 8 March 1928, folder "S. L. Smith—Field Agent," box 4, Correspondence of the Supervisor of the Rosenwald Fund, Division of Negro Education, North Carolina Department of Public Instruction Records; Bludworth, "Rosenwald School Day Program."

52. "Report of Meeting—March 7, 1930," *Alabama Program of Julius Rosenwald Day Exercises* (n.p., [1930]), and "School Report and Guide for Scoring," folder "Alabama," unit 1, series 14, Georgia Department of Education Records. In 1931, Fred McCuistion updated the fund's boilerplate, adding specific instructions emphasizing repairing and repainting of the school buildings, inspections of all classrooms and their furnishings, and landscaping suggestions. Embree to Rosenwald, 20 May 1931, folder 9, box 33, series I, Rosenwald Papers; Duke, *Rosenwald School Day Program* in Oklahoma Department of Education Publications.

53. The Georgia Department of Education records hold a wide variety of Rosenwald School Day pamphlets from participating states from 1929 through the mid-1930s. *Rosenwald School Day Program* [Florida], [1930], and *Rosenwald School Day in Georgia*, 1931, in folder "J. C. Dixon," unit 1, series 62, Georgia Department of Education Records; *Rosenwald School Day Program* (North Carolina), 1929.

54. A. Lewis, *Rosenwald School Day Program*, 7.

55. "Kentucky School Building Day," 1930 (Frankfort: Kentucky State Department of Education, [1930]), folder "Kentucky," unit 1, series 14, Division of Negro Education, Georgia Department of Education Records; "Rosenwald School Day Issue."

56. Arkansas Division of Negro Education, *Rosenwald School Day*, cover. The pamphlet also illustrates the College Station bus and its passengers, the new Cross County Training School and shop, and the Wilson School shop.

57. The Boynton School also received coverage in the Florida Department of Education biennial report; in 1929, a tornado destroyed the Duncan School in Mississippi, but none of the more than one hundred children inside were killed, and only a few were hurt. In both cases, state education departments used the disasters to promote the use of Rosenwald building plans. D. Williams, *Rosenwald School Day Program*, 1929, cover, 4; *Biennial Report* [Florida], 1928–30, 155–57; "Report of W. G. Eckles, Director School Building Service," April 1929, and photograph with caption "Remains of School building for Negroes at Duncan," Reports of the Division of School Building Service, 1928–29, Mississippi Department of Education Records.

58. "Rosenwald Day Celebrated by Negro Students," *Moultrie (Ga.) Observer*, 7 March 1931, and "Rosenwald School Improvement Day," *Mocksville (N.C.) Record*, 4 March 1931, Tuskegee Clippings Files.

59. Circular letter from Smith, 29 November 1929, folder 5, box 332, Rosenwald Fund Archives; "Oklahoma, Number Schools Reporting Observance Rosenwald School Day, March 4, 1932," folder 2, box 342, Rosenwald Fund Archives; Duke, *Rosenwald School Day Program*, 1931, 1.

60. Williams to Hill, 20 March 1929, folder "Florida," unit 1, series 14, Division of Negro Eduacation, Georgia Department of Education Records; summary reports on Rosenwald School Days, folder 5, box 332, Rosenwald Fund Archives.

61. Of course, Julius Rosenwald would have known, or at least known of, Frank Lloyd Wright. Wright was the nephew of Jenkin Lloyd Jones, one of Julius Rosenwald's circle of reformers in Chicago in the 1910s. But the person behind this commission was Darwin D. Martin of the Larkin Soap Company. Martin's home in Buffalo, New York, is one of Wright's most notable Prairie School houses, and Martin had served with Rosenwald on the Council of National Defense committee on supplies during the First World War. Martin brought many commissions Wright's way and in the 1920s helped the architect with his difficult financial situation. Wright to Mumford, 7 January 1929, in Pfeiffer and Wojtowicz, *Frank Lloyd Wright*, 60; Quinan, *Frank Lloyd Wright's Mar-*

tin House, 215–16; 241; personal communication from Ms. Margo Stipe, Frank Lloyd Wright Archives, 13 April 2005.

62. "Project: Rosenwald Foundation School for Negro Children. 1929," in Drexler, *Drawings of Frank Lloyd Wright*, plate 94, 299. The Library of Congress holds another uninscribed copy of the design in the Donald D. Walker Collection, which is illustrated here.

63. *Annual Report* [Virginia], 1921–22, 29; *Annual Report* [Virginia], 1928, 28; "Report of W. G. Eckles, Director School Building Service," February–June 1929, Report of the Division of School Building Service 1928–29, Mississippi Department of Education Records; Smith to Easom, 25 May 1929, Rosenwald School Records, vol. 168, Mississippi Department of Education Records; *Annual Reports* [Georgia], 1929–30, 55; *Annual Report* [Tennessee], 1931–32, 302–3; Fosdick, *Adventure in Giving*, 122–23.

64. *Guide for Planning School Plants*, v; Alcorn, "Rosenwald Schools." The National Council on Schoolhouse Construction had its own subcommittee on standards. Today this organization is known as the Council of Educational Facility Planners, International. Yale Stenzler, executive director of public schools construction for the State of Maryland, kindly provided me with a copy of Alcorn's article from its journal.

65. Dresslar took great interest and pride in Haskell Pruett, with whom he developed a close personal as well as professional relationship. They collaborated on Dresslar's last publication: Dresslar and Pruett, *Rural School-Houses*. Dresslar recommended Pruett for General Education Board scholarships for his graduate studies at Peabody- and Rosenwald-funded fellowships with the ISBS, and introduced Pruett to S. L. Smith, who also promoted Pruett's candidacy for a General Education Board–funded position as schoolhouse construction agent for Oklahoma. Although both Dresslar and Smith hoped Pruett would join the Peabody faculty after completing his doctorate, he returned to Oklahoma and became a legendary faculty member at Oklahoma State University. The Haskell Pruett Collection of his papers and photographs are at the Oklahoma Historical Society.

66. Payne to Smith, 31 October 1928, Smith to Bachman, 31 October 1928, Smith to Stern, 10 November 1928 and 17 November 1928; Smith to Harrell, 9 January 1929, folder 2, box 314, Rosenwald Fund Archives; "The Julius Rosenwald Fund in the South 1930–31," folder 2, box 331, Rosenwald Fund Archives.

67. Hamon to Smith, 5 March 1936, folder 8, box 313, Rosenwald Fund Archives.

68. Payne to Embree, 17 June 1930, folder 8, box 318, Rosenwald Fund Archives.

69. Clipping, Fletcher B. Dresslar, "Organization of the Interstate School Building Service," *School Life* 15 (February 1930): 115–16, in Dresslar Papers; Interstate School Building Service, *For Better School Buildings*.

70. *Community School Plans*, 1928. The title-page illustration, a plot plan for a three-teacher school (Community School Plan 3-C) featuring a shop, school gardens, basketball court, and baseball diamond, became a favorite image for the Interstate School Building Service, despite the fund's growing distaste for small facilities.

71. *Building Plans for Rural School Houses*, 28; Arkansas 5-E plan in Pruett, *Rural School Buildings*.

72. Embree to Womack, 28 January 1929, folder 3, box 169, Rosenwald Fund Archives.

73. McCornack also wanted to require specific vocational equipment for the boys' and girls' trades and home economics classrooms. Stern to Rosenwald, 20 November 1930, Stern to Smith, 20 November 1930, folder 20, and "Minutes of Conferences to Discuss Revision of Community School Plans," 7–8 December 1930, folder 7, box 129, Rosenwald Fund Archives; "Minutes of Conference," 10 January 1931, folder 9, box 128, Rosenwald Fund Archives.

74. The perspective drawings for these designs are attached to Carney to Stern, 12 March 1931, folder 9, box 128, Rosenwald Fund Archives. The following discussion of these designs comments on these drawings and *Community School Plans*, 1931.

75. Docket items attached to Smith to Embree and Smith to Stern, 8 April 1931, folder 9, box 128, and "Community School Plans," folder 2, box 331, Rosenwald Fund Archives. Credle presented this material to the executive committee of the Interstate School Building Service, and the text later appeared in *Community School Plans*, 1931.

76. Handwritten notations on Carney to Stern, 12 March 1931.

77. Smith to Stern, 17 March 1931, and handwritten notes on same, folder 8, box 128, Rosenwald Fund Archives; Stern to Smith, 18 March 1931, 23 March 1931, folder 21, box 129, Rosenwald Fund Archives.

78. This building replaced the county training school constructed with Rosenwald aid under Tuskegee. "Webster County Training School and Rosenwald City High School"; list of Kentucky Rosenwald schools, folder 2, and "Report of School Building Day," 1931, folder 3, box 339, Rosenwald Fund Archives; Stern to Smith, 3 April 1931, folder 21, box 129, Rosenwald Fund Archives.

79. Rapeer, "One-Story Rural Consolidated Building"; miscellaneous school plans, some dated 1927–29, SG 13206, State Publications, Alabama Department of Education Records; *State Aid and Schoolhouse Planning*. For examples of white schools demonstrating similarly restrained styling on large structures to that seen in the 1931 *Community School Plans*, see Dawnville School, Whitfield County in *Annual Reports* [Georgia], 1927–28, and Ashton Junior High, Ben Hill County, and Plainfield Consolidated School, Dodge County, *Annual Reports* [Georgia], 1931–32. For an example of contemporary schoolhouse planning dedicated to Fletcher B. Dresslar that shows the repetitious floor plans needed for larger facilities, see Spain, Moehlman, and Frostic, *Public Elementary School Plant*.

80. In Chicago, Rosenwald pointedly returned to his office on the Thursday of the stock market crash in October 1929. He backed son Lessing Rosenwald's guarantee of all Sears, Roebuck employee stock holdings in the company and borrowed $7.7 million to cover all stock purchased on margin by Sears employees—despite losing $100 mil-

lion of his own personal fortune that day. Embree and Waxman, *Investment in People*, 9–10.

81. "Special Confidential Memorandum on the Kinds of Things That Should Be Supported by Foundations," 23 July 1930, folder 6, box 58, series III, Rosenwald Papers. Although no author is given, Embree is almost certainly the author as it was his job to make such recommendations to the board. Embree critiqued the General Education Board for not engaging in such efforts, writing Arthur Woods that "it does not seem to us that at present the Rockefeller boards are living up either to their brilliant history or to their present possibilities," and calling for "creative statesmanship" in education. Embree to Woods, 27 May 1930, folder 23, box 144, Rosenwald Fund Archives. Embree had publicized his expanding vision for the fund in *Julius Rosenwald Fund: A Review*, 1928, [32]–33, and *Julius Rosenwald Fund: A Review*, 1929, 3–20, 28–33.

82. "Conference of State Agents of Rural Schools for Negroes," 5–6 June 1930, 4, folder 4, box 188; "Conspectus of Present and Future Activities of the Julius Rosenwald Fund," 23 July 1930, 1–2, 4, folder 11, box 85, Rosenwald Fund Archives; *Addresses at the Conference on What White People Can Do*. On the significance of the fellowship program, see Beilke, "Changing Emphasis"; Perkins, "Welcome Consequences."

83. "Annual Meeting of Trustees," 16 November 1929, "Conspectus of Present and Future Activities," 10, 12, and "Continuing Projects," 1 May 1931, 1, folder 2, box 331, Rosenwald Fund Archives.

84. Bond served as a research associate in this project, which Foreman submitted as his doctoral dissertation in political science at Columbia University. Foreman, *Environmental Factors*, 38–41, table 3.

85. Embree to Rosenwald, 4 May 1931, folder 9, box 33, series I, Rosenwald Papers.

86. Docket items attached to Smith to Embree, and Smith to Stern, 8 April 1931, folder 9, box 128, Rosenwald Fund Archives.

87. The fund actually spent $34,527 on school buildings and related programs of the southern school program in 1932–33. "Tentative Recommendations of the Officers to the Special Trustees Committee Appointed to Consider Reorganization of the Southern School Program," n.d. [1931], folder 10, box 128, Rosenwald Fund Archives; Embree, *Julius Rosenwald Fund: Review*, 1931–33, 46.

88. Embree to Rosenwald, 22 June 1931, folder 9, box 33, series I, Rosenwald Papers.

89. On June 30, 1931, the fund held 184,524 shares of Sears, Roebuck and Company stock, mostly given by Julius Rosenwald and others donated by the Judge Julian W. Mack Trust and the Richard Hornberger Trust. The fund sold 41,350 shares between 1929 and 1931. "Sears Roebuck and Company Stock, October 30, 1917 to June 30, 1931," folder 2, box 331, Rosenwald Fund Archives.

90. "Continuing Projects," 1.

91. Newbold to Embree, 2 September 1931, Embree to Newbold, 9 September 1931, folder 5, box 341, Rosenwald Fund Archives. Embree used the phrase "crutch rather

than a stimulus" repeatedly in his explanations of the termination of the school-building program, including the 1930 "Special Confidential Memorandum," and Embree, *Julius Rosenwald Fund: Review*, 1931–33, 31.

92. "Meeting of Trustees, Julius Rosenwald Fund," 7 November 1931, folder 10, box 57, series III, Rosenwald Papers.

93. The clippings range from "Rosenwald's Gifts," *Lewisville (Ark.) Herald*, 25 February 1932, which is the oft-published short press release, to "Negro Education in This Section Greatly Aided by Late Rosenwald," *Shelby (N.C.) Star*, 20 January 1932, to "Rosenwald Gifts Put at over $70,000,000," *New York Times*, 23 January 1932, and are filed under "Educational Funds—1932, Rosenwald Fund," Tuskegee Clippings Files. On South Carolina media reaction, see Carbaugh, "Philanthropic Confluence," 97–98.

94. North Carolina's prominent eulogists included H. L. McCrorey, president of Johnson C. Smith University; C. C. Spaulding of the North Carolina Mutual Life Insurance Company; state supervisor of Negro elementary schools and field director of the state Congress of Colored Parents and Teachers Annie W. Holland; University of North Carolina president Frank Graham; Duke University president W. P. Few; Josephus Daniels, former navy secretary and editor of the *News and Observer*; and Governor O. Max Gardner. Some states had already had their Rosenwald School Day programs in press at the time of his death. All sent copies of their printed programs to the Rosenwald family, and they remain in folder 5, box 61, series III of the Rosenwald Papers. *Rosenwald School Day in Arkansas*, 1932, cover; *Program for Celebration*, 6; *In Memoriam: Julius Rosenwald*, 12.

95. Embree reported that the fund had used up two-thirds of its assets by 1936. Werner, *Julius Rosenwald*, 354; Smith to Felton, 8 June 1932, folder 4, box 342, Rosenwald Fund Archives; Embree, *Julius Rosenwald Fund: Review*, 1917–36, 4–6.

96. "Rosenwald Gifts Put at Over $70,000,000"; "Southern School Program," April 1932, folder 2, box 331, Rosenwald Fund Archives.

97. See the correspondence between Dixon, Smith, and Davis, July–November 1932, folder "JC Dixon," unit 1, series 62, Correspondence Relating to Funding Programs, Division of Negro Education, Georgia Department of Education Records.

98. Wright to Embree, 22 November 1932, Embree to Wright, 28 November 1932, folder 20, box 37, series 5, Southern Education Foundation Records.

99. By the mid-1940s, the Rosenwald Fund was supporting the NAACP's legal activism, and Charles H. Houston sat on its board of trustees and was deeply involved in what it called "Democracy through Church and Labor." Embree, *Julius Rosenwald Fund: Review*, 1931–33, 15–27; Embree, *Julius Rosenwald Fund: Review of Two Decades*, 1–21; Embree, *Julius Rosenwald Fund: Review*, 1944–46; Embree and Waxman, *Investment in People*.

100. "Serious Loss," *Durham (N.C.) Sun*, 29 July 1932, Tuskegee Clippings Files.

CHAPTER 5. ROSENWALD SCHOOLS AND THE PROFESSIONAL INFRASTRUC-
TURE FOR BLACK PUBLIC EDUCATION

1. In part 2, as elsewhere, I refer to the white men hired to supervise black public education by the General Education Board and southern states as "state agents for Negro
schools," "Negro school agents," "assistant state agents for Negro schools," or "assistant
Negro school agents." I refer to the African American men hired with Rosenwald support to conduct local campaigns and supervise building projects as "Rosenwald building agents" and "building agents." The term "agents" includes both groups. This work
does not discuss the other white state agents funded by the General Education Board.

2. Link, *Paradox of Southern Progressivism*, 203–321; Chirhart, *Torches of Light*.

3. Embree, "How Negro Schools Have Advanced," 41.

4. Fosdick, *Adventure in Giving*, 93–98; S. Smith, *Builders of Goodwill*, 7–62. The
General Education Board funded state Negro school agents and assistant Negro school
agents until 1952.

5. John R. E. Lee, a founder and first president of the National Association of Teachers in Colored Schools, had recently left Tuskegee to become principal of the Lincoln
School in Kansas City, Missouri. He would later become extension secretary of the
Urban League and president of Florida A&M College. Edwards, *Twenty-five Years in
the Black Belt*, 102; "Report of S. L. Smith, Rural School Supervisor for Tennessee, for
August 1914," folder 1468, box 158, series 1.1, General Education Board Archives; Watkins, *Alabama State University*, 95.

6. E. G. Grafton briefly held the appointment as Texas Negro school agent in 1918.
Memorandum from Jackson Davis, undated, Doughty to Sage, 13 May 1918, Grafton to
Sage, 13 May 1918, Blanton to Buttrick, 7 January 1919, Caldwell to Davis, 14 June 1919,
folder 1573, box 94, series 1, subseries 1, *General Education Board Archives*, microfilm
reel 138. The General Education Board handled the hiring of Joseph B. Felton for South
Carolina in similar fashion; see Gormon and Stickell, "Partners in Progress," 15–16.

7. S. Smith, *Builders of Goodwill*, 32–33, 176.

8. Report of "Committee appointed to co-operate with Supt. Dowell and State Authorities to secure the right kind of person to take Mr. Sibley's work," 10 September
1918, folder "General Correspondence 1918," box 1, Calloway Papers.

9. Fosdick, *Adventure in Giving*, 93; Jackson Davis, "James L. Sibley," in folder "Misc.
Masters (Tribute to James L. Sibley)," 1929, vol. 166, Rosenwald School Records, Mississippi Department of Education Records. Sibley resigned as Alabama's Negro school
agent to direct World War I veterans' rehabilitation, then the University of Georgia's
extension social work, and boys' agricultural club work at Auburn University. In 1925,
a consortium of philanthropies sent him and Jeanes supervisor Rebecca Davis to Liberia
as educational advisors, where Sibley died of yellow fever in 1929.

10. S. Smith, *Builders of Goodwill*, 15, 22–25.

11. Ibid., 26, 37–38, 177; S.L.S[mith], "A Story of the Julius Rosenwald Fund in

Tenn. from the Beginning to July 1, 1920," and Bernard, "The Julius Rosenwald Fund in Tennessee," folder 2, box 76, Julius Rosenwald Fund Archives; Duke, *Guide to Better Schools*; "New O.E.A. Officers."

12. The General Education Board speaker, probably Jackson Davis, went on to praise North Carolina's assistant Negro school agent, W. F. Credle, who devoted all of his time to the Rosenwald building program. "Special Report of Jas. L. Sibley, State Agent Colored Rural Schools for Alabama," December 1915, SG 15444, Rural School Agent Correspondence, Alabama Department of Education Records; [Shepardson?], "Notes Made at Hampton, Virginia, Conference of State Agents, May 6 to 9, 1923," 7, folder 4, box 188, Rosenwald Fund Archives.

13. Some states had multiple assistant agents for Negro schools, whose typical assignments included supervision of secondary schools and teacher training.

14. Felton, "W. A. Schiffley."

15. Davis to Marrs, 8 June 1923, Bachman to Rogers and Bludworth, 16 December 1925, folder 1574, box 94, series 1, subseries 1, *General Education Board Archives*, microfilm reel 138; Taylor, "Negro Education in Texas."

16. See, for example, the letters concerning Tennessee's annual allotments in folder 1, box 343, Rosenwald Fund Archives, and Dudley Tanner's 18 January 1930 letter announcing the plan of aid to Tennessee superintendents in folder 2, box 236, Tennessee Commissioner of Education Records. North Carolina Negro school agent letters to the Catawba County school superintendent asking for estimates of the number and types of next year's Rosenwald construction projects, and consequently notifying him of the state's appropriation and asking for project applications are in H. Thompson, "History of Negro Education," 65–66.

17. Calloway to Sibley, 20 May 1915, Sibley to Calloway, 22 May 1915, folder "C," SG 15442, Rural School Agent Correspondence, Alabama Department of Education Records; Smith to Lambert, 9 August 1921, Lambert to Smith, 15 August 1921, SG 15456, Rural School Agent Correspondence, Alabama Department of Education Records; Smith to Lambert 18 August 1921, SG 15462, Rural School Agent Correspondence, Alabama Department of Education Records.

18. See, for example, the September 1922 correspondence between Smith and Louisiana assistant Negro school agent Lewis on the architectural plans for the Bienville Parish School in box 25, Louisiana Department of Education Records.

19. Harrell, "The 1929 Conference of State Agents of Negro Schools, Atlantic City, June 4th and 5th," folder 4, box 188, Rosenwald Fund Archives.

20. S. Smith, *Builders of Goodwill*, 22–25; Smith to Buttrick, 11 May 1914, folder 1464, box 157, series 1.1, General Education Board Archives; folders "1911–1951 & n.d.," "1911–1912," and "1913–1951," in box 1, Correspondence, 1894–1910, Newbold Papers.

21. Sibley, miscellaneous writings in SG 15598, Rural School Agent Correspondence, Alabama Department of Education Records; Sibley, "Types of School Needed"

and "The Plantation School," *Annual Report* [Alabama], 1918, 98–99; "Negro Education," *Biennial Report* [Florida], 1918–20, 259–60.

22. Clarke and Brown, *History of the Black Public Schools*, 154; Leon Tyler interview, 8 December 1988, and Marie Brown interview, 12 December 1988, in Gilli, "History of Colored Schools in Maryland," 10–11, 20–21.

23. Wright spent the middle section of his career as a Dartmouth College professor of education. S. Smith, *Builders of Goodwill*, 38–39, 178.

24. Fosdick, *Adventure in Giving*, 301–2; S. Smith, *Builders of Goodwill*, 21–22, 175.

25. In *Builders of Goodwill*, Smith lists Rosenwald building agents among the assistant Negro school agents. However his account omits all but one of the building agents' service in the Tuskegee period, whose work is documented in their monthly reports contained in General Correspondence, Moton Papers, and in the annual volumes of *The Negro Year Book*.

26. Washington to Rosenwald, 12 September 1912, folder 8, box 336, Rosenwald Fund Archives.

27. Calloway to Washington, 3 April 1913, folder 8, box 336, Rosenwald Fund Archives; miscellaneous clippings from the *Tuskegee (Ala.) Messenger*, March–October 1913, Tuskegee Clippings Files.

28. Casby, "Warrior Stand Community," *Tuskegee (Ala.) Messenger*, 2 May 1913, Tuskegee Clippings Files. Rakestraw was the pastor of a church in Warrior Stand. "Warrior Stand Community," *Tuskegee (Ala.) Messenger*, 16 May 1913, Tuskegee Clippings Files; Calloway to Lambert, 11 April 1919, folder "C," SG 15453, Rural School Agent Correspondence, Alabama Department of Education Records.

29. Calloway had been asking for fieldworkers, initially to help communities qualify for state building grants, since March 1914. He also knew firsthand about the paperwork burden entailed in community organization and asked for both a "man whose entire time will be spent in schoolhouse building" and a stenographer. Calloway to Washington, 27 March 1914, folder "Extension Dept. Calloway, Clinton J. 1914 Jan.–May," box 714, Departmental File, Tuskegee Records, Washington Papers, microfilm reel 528; Calloway to Washington, 16 June 1914, folder "Extension Dept., Calloway, Clinton J., 1914 June–Aug.," box 715, Departmental File, Tuskegee Records, Washington Papers, microfilm reel 529; Calloway to Washington, 21 July 1914, folder "Committee Reports 1914 Mar.–July," box 714, Departmental File, Tuskegee Records, Washington Papers, microfilm reel 528.

30. Hosmer to Calloway, 10 October 1914, folder "Extension Dept., Calloway, Clinton J., 1914, Sept.–Oct.," box 715, Departmental File, Tuskegee Records, Washington Papers, microfilm reel 529; Hosmer's reports to Calloway for October and November 1914, Calloway to Washington, 19 December 1914, folder "Extension Dept., Calloway, Clinton J., 1914, Nov.–Dec.," box 715, Departmental File, Tuskegee Records, Washington Papers, microfilm reel 529; Calloway to Graves, 8 November 1915, folder 8, box 336, Rosenwald Fund Archives; Barnett to Sibley, 18 November 1914, folder "B," SG

15442, Rural School Agent Correspondence, Alabama Department of Education Records; Barnett to Sibley, 15 September 1915, folder "A," SG 15444, Rural School Agent Correspondence, Alabama Department of Education Records; Sibley to Calloway, 2 July 1917, folder "C," SG 15448, Rural School Agent Correspondence, Alabama Department of Education Records. Barnett is best remembered for his gospel quartet work. He taught R. C. Foster, whose Foster Singers became one of the most influential early quartets. Tuskegee Institute sent gospel quartets on fund-raising tours outside the South. "R. C. Foster"; Seroff, "Gospel Quartet Singing"; Enck, "Tuskegee Institute."

31. For examples of the joint selection and supervision of local building agents, see Sibley to Calloway, 31 August 1915, 15 September 1915, folder "C," SG 15444, Rural School Agent Correspondence, Alabama Department of Education Records; Sibley's correspondence with Scales, August–November 1915, folder "S," SG 15444, Rural School Agent Correspondence, Alabama Department of Education Records; Sibley's correspondence with Scales, January–February 1916, folder "S," SG 15449, Rural School Agent Correspondence, Alabama Department of Education Records; Sibley to Everett, 11 June 1917, 18 June 1917, Everett to Sibley, 4 July 1917, folder "E," SG 15448, Rural School Agent Correspondence, Alabama Department of Education Records.

32. Henry to Washington Jr., 26 July 1915, Calloway to Doggett, 3 September 1915, Doggett to Calloway, 6 September 1915, untitled folder [3], box 14, Calloway Papers; Lee to Calloway, 10 August 1915, "Rural Schoolhouse Building Summarized Report up to June 30, 1915," untitled folder [4], box 14, Calloway Papers.

33. Washington obviously wanted to control the building program, perhaps for the sake of greater accountability. But Washington's skillful use of patronage to maintain his Tuskegee machine suggests that he may have seen the building program as another tool of influence. The demand for access to the Rosenwald program from other sections of Alabama and the South soon made such close control impossible. Washington to Graves, 7 December 1914, folder 8, box 336, Rosenwald Fund Archives.

34. Washington to Rosenwald, 17 March 1915, folder 8, box 336, Rosenwald Fund Archives.

35. Washington to Calloway, 16 March 1915, folder "correspondence Re: Teaching Applications and Rosenwald Fund Applications, 1916," box 4, Calloway Papers; Washington to Logan, 8 June 1914; Calloway to Washington, 2 March 1915, Edwards, "Report of Supervising Industrial Teacher," February 1915, folder "Extension Dept. Calloway, Clinton J. 1915 Jan.–Mar.," box 729, Departmental File, Tuskegee Records, Washington Papers, microfilm reel 543; Calloway to Sibley, 24 March 1915, folder "C," SG 15442, Rural School Agent Correspondence, Alabama Department of Education Records; Lee to Sibley, 16 May 1917, folder "L," SG 15449, Rural School Agent Correspondence, Alabama Department of Education Records. Booker T. Washington Jr. was known familiarly as "Baker," although his schoolmates called him "Booker." He

had recently returned to Tuskegee Institute after his marriage. See Harlan, *Making of a Black Leader*, 153; Harlan, *Wizard of Tuskegee*, 113–16, 120–22.

36. Brannon to Calloway, 13 December 1917, Huffington to C. J. Calloway, 28 December 1917, folder "Correspondence Rosenwald Schools 1917," box 5, Calloway Papers.

37. Barnett had either switched jobs or received his salary from another source until he took over as official Rosenwald building agent. Lambert to Calloway, 12 April 1919, folder "W. M. Rakestraw Correspondence 1919," box 11, Calloway Papers; Lambert to Calloway, 13 May 1919, folder "C," SG 15453, Rural School Agent Correspondence, Alabama Department of Education Records; Barnett to Rennolds, 29 August 1919, folder 9, box 2, Rennolds Papers.

38. Calloway to Hilbun, 6 December 1917, Calloway to Hilbun, 20 December 1917, Hilbun to Calloway, 22 December 1917, folder "Correspondence Rosenwald Schools 1917," box 5, Calloway Papers; Hilbun to Calloway, 9 April 1918, 26 April 1918, folder "Rosenwald Correspondence Mississippi 1918–1919," box 9, Calloway Papers; Howard to Calloway, 2 January 1918, folder "C. J. Calloway Correspondence 1918," box 11, Calloway Papers.

39. Posey, *Against Great Odds*, 171; C. Thompson, *History of the Mississippi Teachers Association*, 122; Siddle Walker, "Organized Resistance," 378–79.

40. "Rosenwald Buildings," *Biennial Report* [Arkansas], 1919–20, 33–34, microfilm reel 5; Hicks, *History of Louisiana Negro Baptists*, 195–96, 203–4.

41. "Francis Marion Wood"; Hardin, *Onward and Upward*, 25.

42. Vincent, *Centennial History*, 227; "Mr. John Sebastian Jones," *Louisiana Colored Teachers Journal* 23 (May 1947): 2, 13, and "Funeral Services of John Sebastian Jones, 28 December 1959," "Dreams and Reality: A Tribute," 20 February 1986, in J. S. Jones vertical file, University Archives, John C. Cade Library, Southern University, Scotlandville, Louisiana. Edna Jordan Smith brought Jones's work with Rosenwald schools back into public view in the 1980s; see Durusau, "Pioneers in Black Education."

43. In Georgia, Clark University and the Georgia State Teachers and Education Association, the state Commission on Interracial Cooperation, and even the white Georgia Education Association provided funds for various Rosenwald building agents between 1923 and 1931. Patterson, *History of the Arkansas State Teachers Association*, 12, 21, 30–32; "Biographical Sketch of R. C. Childress"; *Yearbook on Negro Education*, 71; C. Thompson, *History of the Mississippi Teachers Association*, 123; S. Smith, *Builders of Goodwill*, 46–47; *Annual Report* [Georgia], 1923–24, 4; *Annual Report* [Georgia], 1925–26, 39; *Annual Report* [Georgia], 1931–32, 33.

44. Rhodes, *Jackson State University*, 75; C. Thompson, *History of the Mississippi Teachers Association*, 122–23.

45. Dansby and Blackburn both participated in "flying squadrons" of educators who addressed public meetings about the pitiable condition of Mississippi's black public

schools, organized in the mid-1920s by the Mississippi Association of Teachers in Colored Schools. Blackburn joined the Jackson State College board of trustees in 1932, when his position as Rosenwald building agent ended. Dansby, *Brief History of Jackson College*, 94; C. Thompson, *History of the Mississippi Teachers Association*, 66.

46. "Rosenwald to Aid Kentucky Schools," *Cleveland Advocate*, 10 August 1918; "Report of F. C. Button," *Biennial Report* [Kentucky], 1918–19, 234.

47. "Discussion of Rosenwald Schools at Conference of State Agents Assembled at Nashville, January 5 and 6, 1921," 15–16, "Notes Made at Hampton, Virginia, Conference of State Agents May 6 to 9, 1923," 6, folder 4, box 188, Rosenwald Fund Archives.

48. Notes of meeting of state and building agents, 16–17 July 1919, box 50, folder 335, General Correspondence, Moton Papers; S. L. Smith to A. K. Stern, 26 July 1928, multiple telegrams, December 1928 and November 1929, folder 12, box 187, Rosenwald Fund Archives; notes and minutes of conferences of state agents, 1921, 1923, 1928–31, folder 12, box 188, Rosenwald Fund Archives.

49. Apparently O. W. Gray was not the preferred candidate for the job, for Favrot had asked Calloway's approval for the hire, citing Gray's fund-raising experience as the Coleman College field agent and location in the midst of cotton country. Calloway to Moton, 6 August 1917, folder "Rural School Correspondence 1917," [2], box 3, and Favrot to Calloway, 6 November 1917 and 26 December 1917, folder "Correspondence: Rosenwald Schools 1917," [4], box 5, Calloway Papers; "Report of State Agent of Rural Schools for Negroes," *Field Force Reports*, November 1917, 92; "Report of O. W. Gray, State Rural School Building Agent," November 1917, folder 164, box 24, General Correspondence, Moton Papers.

50. Gray, "Report, Rural Schoolhouse Building for Louisiana," May 1918, folder 251, box 36, General Correspondence, Moton Papers.

51. Gray, "Report, Rural Schoolhouse Building, Louisiana," June 1918, folder 251, box 36, General Correspondence, Moton Papers; Gray, "Report, Rural Schoolhouse Building, Louisiana," July 1918, folder 255, box 36, General Correspondence, Moton Papers.

52. Favrot did ask Calloway to increase Gray's salary so that he would not have to ask local people to pay for the car he rented to get to their community. He apparently never secured state funding for Gray's salary, for in 1937 Gray tried unsuccessfully to document his state employment for the new state teachers' retirement program. Gray to Calloway, 5 March 1918, 19 September 1918, 15 October 1918, folder "C. J. Calloway Correspondence 1918," box 12, Calloway Papers; Favrot to Calloway, 21 October 1918, folder "Rosenwald Correspondence Louisiana 1918–19," box 9, Calloway Papers; March 1937 correspondence between Gray, Favrot, and Smith, and Smith to Gray, 4 May 1937, folder 3, box 331, Rosenwald Fund Archives.

53. Perkins to Calloway, 3 April 1919, folder "C. J Calloway Correspondence 1919," box 12, Calloway Papers.

54. Gray to Morten [*sic*], 30 July 1919, Calloway to Holsey, 5 August 1919, folder 342, box 52, General Correspondence, Moton Papers.

55. Barnett to Lambert, 9 February, 17 September, 16 October 1920, Lambert to Barnett, 14 February, 13 September 1920, folder "B," SG 15464, Rural School Agent Correspondence, Alabama Department of Education Records.

56. Jones, "Report, Rosenwald Schoolhouse Building for Louisiana," May 1919, July 1919, August 1919, folder 335, box 50, General Correspondence, Moton Papers.

57. Bond, *Negro Education*, 281; "Report of M. H. Griffin, State Supervisor Teacher-Training and Rosenwald Fund Agent for Alabama," June 1921–July 1922, SG 15466, Rural School Agent Correspondence, Alabama Department of Education Records.

58. Former Negro school agent George Godard temporarily handled black school matters. "Walter B. Hill Defends Work for Rural Schools," *Atlanta Constitution*, 31 May 1924, and "Whose Pig Is Hit?" *Macon (Ga.) Daily Telegraph*, 28 June 1924, Tuskegee Clippings File; "Report of Walter B. Hill, Special Supervisor July 1, 1925, to December 31, 1926," *Annual Reports* [Georgia], 1923–24, 4–6, and *Annual Reports* [Georgia], 1925–26, 38. On Walter B. Hill Sr., see Dennis, "Schooling along the Color Line," 147–49; Dennis, *Lessons in Progress*, 117–60. Chirhart also discusses the Hill family's reform careers in *Torches of Light*, 80–85, 100–103; see also Dittmer, *Black Georgia*, 141–62.

59. S. Smith, *Builders of Goodwill*, 28–29.

60. Calloway to Moton, 11 December 1919, folder 336, box 51, General Correspondence, Moton Papers.

61. General Education Board officials had overruled the state superintendent on Hilbun's replacement, hiring Easom over assistant agent W. C. Strahan, whom they deemed "too unyielding in his attitude toward both whites and Negroes, but particularly toward Negroes." Favrot to Dillard, 18 June 1928, 16 August 1928, 22 August 1928, folder 19, box 27, series 5, Southern Education Foundation Records. Easom soon earned the respect of Mississippi's African American educators; see Bowman, "P. H. Easom," 26–27.

62. Easom to Smith, 29 August 1929, Wooten to Smith, 1 September 1929, Smith to Wooten, 4 September 1929, Wooten to Smith, 6 September 1929, Anderson to Smith, 19 October 1929, Smith to Harrell, 9 September 1929, folder 4, box 340, Rosenwald Fund Archives.

63. Easom to Irvine, 29 August 1929, Rosenwald School Records, General Correspondence, vol. 141, Mississippi Department of Education Records; Smith to Wooten, 9 September 1929, 17 September 1929, Wooten to Smith, 14 September 1929, folder 2, box 340, Rosenwald Fund Archives; Bond to Smith, 9 October 1929, Smith to Harrell, 11 October 1929, Harrell to Smith, 14 October 1929, Smith to Embree, 19 December 1929, Bond to Smith, 30 May 1930, Smith to Bond, 30 May 1930, McLendon to General Manager, Sears, Roebuck & Co., 1 August 1930, McLendon to Rosenwald, 1 August 1930, McLendon, letter to the editor, *Memphis Commercial Appeal*, n.d., Mitchell to Smith, 14 November 1930, Bond to Smith, 25 November 1930, Smith to Bond, 25

November 1930, Smith to Stern, 2 December 1930, 3 December 1930, Smith to Embree, 2 January 1931, folder 4, box 340, Rosenwald Fund Archives.

64. "Ex-School Head Again on Trial," *Memphis Evening Appeal*, 3 December 1930, "Rosenwald Fund Fraud Argued in Jackson Court," *Montgomery (Ala.) Advertiser*, 5 December 1931, "Nordic Charged in Negro School Case Hangs Jury," *Houston Informer*, 26 December 1931, "Embezzler of Negro Funds Seeks Delay," *Norfolk (Va.) Journal and Guide*, "White Supervisor of Negro Schools Asks Delay in Theft Trial," *Kansas City (Mo.) Call*, 3 June 1932, "School Embezzler Suspect Trial Near," *Pittsburgh Courier*, 11 June 1932, Tuskegee Clippings Files; Smith to Bond, 4 April 1932, folder 4, box 340, Rosenwald Fund Archives; S. Smith, *Builders of Goodwill*, 30–31.

65. As Tangipahoa Parish superintendent, Lewis had established one of the state's earliest training schools, which received positive publicity for its industrial program. "Helpful Work Being Done for Negroes in Tangipahoa," *New Orleans Picayune*, 12 November 1922, Tuskegee Clippings Files.

66. Lewis to Smith, 30 April 1930, Credle to Lewis, 6 May 1930, Lewis to Smith, 16 April 1931, folder 5, box 339, Rosenwald Fund Archives.

67. Favrot to Smith, 14 April 1931, folder 5, box 339, Rosenwald Fund Archives.

68. Favrot to Smith, 20 April 1931, Harris to Smith, 27 April 1931, Lewis to Smith, 1 May 1931, Smith to Edwin R. Embree, 29 June 1931, folder 5, box 339, Rosenwald Fund Archives. Lewis returned nine Rosenwald grants, with interest.

69. Embree to Smith, 5 May 1931; Smith to Stern, 6 May 1931, Stern to Smith, 11 May 1931, Embree to Smith, 19 May 1931, folder 5, box 339, Rosenwald Fund Archives. Lewis applied to Smith for a new grant to build a new school on a new site in Armant later in 1931. Perhaps ironically, ensuing correspondence among fund staff shows that they misfiled Louisiana's refund check, and it was not deposited. Ultimately the Rosenwald Fund did support a school there. Lewis to Smith, 16 November 1931, folder 5, box 339, Rosenwald Fund Archives.

70. Bludworth to Smith, 21 October 1930, folder 4, box 343, Rosenwald Fund Archives; Favrot to Embree, 30 October 1931, Embree to Favrot, 2 November 1931, folder 4, box 188, Rosenwald Fund Archives.

71. Several studies explore reforms in North Carolina public education, including the Rosenwald building program. My own assessment of the Rosenwald building program in North Carolina parallels Hanchett, "Rosenwald Schools," 408–9, and Leloudis, *Schooling the New South*, 213–28. See also Prather, *Resurgent Politics*.

72. Newbold's early interest in African American education can be seen in his personal papers, which include resolutions of thanks from black teachers. See folders "1911–1951 & n.d.," "1911–1912," and "1913–1951," box 1, Correspondence, 1894–1910, Newbold Papers. On Newbold, state Jeanes agent Annie Holland, and the work of the county Jeanes supervisors, see Leloudis, *Schooling the New South*, 185–92, 201–11, 227–28; Gilmore, *Gender and Jim Crow*, 161–65, 197–99.

73. S. Smith, *Builders of Goodwill*, 12–13, 48–49; H. Brown, *E-qual-ity Education*, 93–122; Hanchett, "Rosenwald Schools," 408–9.

74. Circulars from the North Carolina State Teachers Association, 10 August 1915, 7 June 1916, folder "1915," box 4, and folder "1916," box 5, Correspondence, Hunter Papers; Murray, *History of the North Carolina Teachers Association*, 32; Hanchett, "Rosenwald Schools," 409–11.

75. For example, see Moore, "Report for March, 1918, to the Department Public Instruction, Raleigh, N.C., Members of Executive Committee, Rural School Department, State Teachers' Asso'n [*sic*]," retyped as Moore, "Report Rural Schoolhouse Building, North Carolina," March 1918, folder "North Carolina 1918 Rosenwald Reports," box 10, Calloway Papers. The North Carolina Mutual Life Insurance Company remains the oldest and largest African American business in the United States. My thanks to Nyoni Collins for pointing out the connections with Booker T. Washington.

76. For examples, see "Report for March, 1918," and "Report, Rosenwald Schoolhouse Building" May 1919, August 1919, September 1919, November 1919, December 1919, March 1920, folder 251, box 36, folder 335, box 50, and folders 336, 340b in box 51, General Correspondence, Moton Papers.

77. See correspondence between Moore and Newbold, December 1918–February 1919, folder "M," box 4, General Correspondence of the Director, Division of Negro Education, North Carolina Department of Public Instruction Records.

78. Newbold to Attmore, 3 September 1915, Newbold to Akers, 10 April 1916, folder "A," box 2, General Correspondence of the Director, Division of Negro Education, North Carolina Department of Public Instruction Records.

79. April 1917 correspondence between Best and Newbold, Barker to Newbold, 7 March 1918, folder "B," box 3, General Correspondence of the Director, Division of Negro Education, North Carolina Department of Public Instruction Records.

80. Moore to Calloway, 23 July 1918, folder "C. J. Calloway Correspondence 1918," box 11, Calloway Papers; Moore, "Report Schoolhouse Building for North Carolina," November 1919, folder 336, box 51, General Correspondence, Moton Papers.

81. Moore, "As to Negro Education," *Greensboro (N.C.) Daily News*, 2 February 1919, Tuskegee Clippings Files; Newbold to Flexner, 17 May 1919, folder "E-F," box 4, General Correspondence of the Director, Division of Negro Education, North Carolina Department of Public Instruction Records; Moore, "The Negro at the Front and at Home," in folder "M," box 4, General Correspondence of the Director, Division of Negro Education, North Carolina Department of Public Instruction Records; Newbold to Rosenwald, 1 December 1918, folder 8, box 336, Rosenwald Fund Archives; "To County Superintendents and County Boards of Education," 15 April 1919, folder 335, box 50, General Correspondence, Moton Papers.

82. Coon was formerly associated with the Southern Education Board and had revealed the discriminatory financing of public education. Newspaper articles about the

conflict with Moore mention that Coon had already been in the news for slapping a female teacher in the face. Moore had visited Wilson County in August 1918 and reported a positive meeting with Coon. He did not mention the September 1919 incident in his monthly report and returned to Wilson County later that year to raise funds from the Conference of the Cape Fear AME Zion Church. His successor, Dr. George E. Davis, visited Wilson in 1922 and found "conditions at the present time are far from favorable for Negro Education. . . . The psychological moment will come. It pays to wait and watch." "Report, Rosenwald Schoolhouse Building, North Carolina," August 1918, 2, folder 251, box 36, General Correspondence, Moton Papers; "Report, Rosenwald Schoolhouse Building, North Carolina," September 1919, folder 335, box 50, General Correspondence, Moton Papers; "Report, Rosenwald Schoolhouse Building, North Carolina," December 1919, folder 340b, box 51, General Correspondence, Moton Papers; "Supt. Coon Refuses to See Supervisor Moore," *Raleigh (N.C.) Independent*, 20 September 1919, "Insult to State Agent," *New York Age*, 20 September 1919, Tuskegee Clippings Files; "Report of G. E. Davis, Supervisor of Rosenwald Buildings for North Carolina," October 1922, detail 5, folder "Rosenwald Fund—G. E. Davis Reports," box 8, Special Subjects File, Division of Negro Education, North Carolina Department of Public Instruction Records; Gilmore, *Gender and Jim Crow*, 159–60.

83. Haley, *Charles N. Hunter*, 219–22.

84. A. M. Moore to Newbold, 11 August 1920, folder "M," box 4, General Correspondence of the Director, Division of Negro Education, North Carolina Department of Public Instruction Records. Percy Murray states that Charles Moore retired as NCTA extension director two years later because of ill health in his *History of the North Carolina Teachers Association*, 32. The NCTA continued to pay the expenses of the Rosenwald building agent at least until 1923. Davis to Credle, 26 September 1923, folder "1922–23 Reports," box 87, General Correspondence of the Superintendent, North Carolina Department of Public Instruction Records.

85. Hanchett, "Rosenwald Schools," 410.

86. "Report of G. E. Davis, Supervisor, Rosenwald Buildings," January 1927, folder "Rosenwald Fund—G. E. Davis Reports," box 8, Special Subject File, Division of Negro Education, North Carolina Department of Public Instruction.

87. Davis to Newbold, 3 August 1922, folder "D," box 5, General Correspondence of Supervisor of the Rosenwald Fund, North Carolina Department of Public Instruction Records; Davis to Newbold, 5 March 1923, folder "1922–23 Reports," box 87, General Correspondence, Office of the Superintendent, North Carolina Department of Public Instruction Records.

88. Davis to Credle, undated, folder "D," box 2, Correspondence of the Supervisor of the Rosenwald Fund, Division of Negro Education, North Carolina Department of Public Instruction Records.

89. Credle identified Davis to other whites as "Dr. Davis" as well; he also used prop-

er titles when corresponding with black citizens. See folder "G," box 4, Correspondence of the Supervisor of the Rosenwald Fund, Division of Negro Education, North Carolina Department of Public Instruction Records.

90. Davis to Credle, 15 September 1922, Credle to Davis, 18 September 1922, folder "1922–23 Reports"; Credle to Smith, 18 August 1922, folder "1922 General Field Agent for Rural Schools S. L. Smith"; Smith to Credle, 9 April 1923, folder "1923 General Field Agent for Rural Schools S.L. Smith," all in box 87, General Correspondence, Office of the Superintendent, North Carolina Department of Public Instruction Records.

91. Credle to Smith, 10 September 1923, Smith to Credle, 12 September 1923, folder "S. L. Smith—Rosenwald Field Agent, June 1923–June 1924"; Credle to Davis, 14 September 1923, G. E. Davis to Credle, 17 September 1923, folder "G. E. Davis Building Agent August 1923–June 1924," all in box 1, Correspondence of the Supervisor of the Rosenwald Fund, Division of Negro Education, North Carolina Department of Public Instruction Records.

92. Davis to W. F. Credle, 12 September 1924, 28 October 1924, folder "G. E. Davis, Building Agent July 1924–February 1925," box 1, Correspondence of the Supervisor of the Rosenwald Fund, Division of Negro Education, North Carolina Department of Public Instruction Records; Davis to Credle, 3 November 1925, folder "D," box 2, Correspondence of the Supervisor of the Rosenwald Fund, Division of Negro Education, North Carolina Department of Public Instruction Records.

93. Davis to Credle, n.d., folder "D," box 3, Correspondence of the Supervisor of the Rosenwald Fund, Division of Negro Education, North Carolina Department of Public Instruction Records.

94. Davis to Credle, 6 April 1922, Credle to Davis, 29 April 1922, folder "1922–23 Reports," box 87, General Correspondence, Office of the Superintendent, North Carolina Department of Public Instruction Records.

95. Drawing city boundaries to exclude African Americans from urban services was not uncommon; the Moore County superintendent explained a similar situation at Aberdeen in 1916. McLeod to Newbold, 5 February 1916, folder "Ma-Mc," box 2, General Correspondence of the Director, Division of Negro Education, North Carolina Department of Public Instruction Records; Davis to Credle, 16 January 1926, folder "D," box 2, Correspondence of the Supervisor of the Rosenwald Fund, Division of Negro Education, North Carolina Department of Public Instruction Records.

96. On the other hand, Calloway reported favorably on Davis to the state superintendent E. C. Brooks, noting that both whites and blacks were positive about Davis, and congratulated Brooks on "your policy in using Negroes to *help* make and execute plans for Negro uplift." Calloway to Brooks, 6 June 1922, folder "B"; Davis to Credle, 3 July 1923, folder "D," box 86, General Correspondence, Office of the Superintendent, North Carolina Department of Public Instruction Records; Davis to Credle, 3 April 1922, folder "1922–23 Reports," box 87, General Correspondence, Office of the Superinten-

dent, North Carolina Department of Public Instruction Records; Davis to Credle, 28 April 1927, folder "D," box 3, Correspondence of Supervisor of the Rosenwald Fund; "Negro Common School in North Carolina," 117–18, 133–35.

Chapter 6. Spreading the Rosenwald Message in Southern Education

1. "Results of the Rosenwald Fund in the South," n.d., folder 2, box 76, Rosenwald Fund Archives.

2. E. Anderson and Moss, *Dangerous Donations*, 9, 62.

3. For recent discussions of school reform and state power, and the connections between race and schooling, see Link, *Hard Country*; Link, *Paradox of Southern Progressivism*; Keith, *Country People*; Leloudis, *Schooling the New South*; Hoffschwelle, *Rebuilding the Rural Southern Community*.

4. J. H. Brinson, "Report of State Agent for Negro Education," *Biennial Report* [Florida], 1923–24, 267–70.

5. See also P. Smith, "Distribution of Rosenwald Schools."

6. Favrot, "Narrative Report, Parish Industrial Work," *Field Force Reports*, November 1916, 6–7; Favrot, "Rosenwald Fund Projects," *Field Force Reports*, December 1916, 87; Favrot, "Report of State Agent of Rural Schools for Negroes," *Field Force Reports*, April 1917, 104; Favrot, "Report of State Agent of Rural Schools for Negroes," *Field Force Reports*, October 1917, 92.

7. Favrot also listed Gray among the speakers at a regional Jeanes conference in March 1918. Favrot, "Report of State Agent of Rural Schools for Negroes," *Field Force Reports*, October 1917, 92; Favrot, "Negro Rural Schoolhouse Building," *Field Force Reports*, December 1917, 76–77; Favrot, "Report of State Agent of Rural Schools for Negroes," *Field Force Reports*, January 1918, 30–31; Favrot, "Report of State Agent of Rural Schools for Negroes," *Field Force Reports*, March 1918, 25.

8. Harris's "Negro Public Education," 131–34 reprints the circular letter he sent to accompany Favrot's bulletin. For examples of such publications from other states, see [McCuistion], *"Me Too"*; Marrs, Bludworth, and Taylor, *Negro Education in Texas*, 1926; Marrs, Bludworth, and Taylor, *Negro Education in Texas*, 1931.

9. Favrot, *Aims and Needs*, 6–14, 17.

10. [Favrot], *Rosenwald Negro Rural Schools*, 3–4.

11. Ibid. Examples of the contemporary prescriptive literature on rural education include Carney, *Country Life*; Cubberley, *Rural Life*; scholarly treatments of the topic include Leloudis, *Schooling the New South*, 143–76; Link, *Hard Country*, 73–172; Hoffschwelle, *Rebuilding the Rural Southern Community*, 13–60.

12. Favrot, *Aims and Needs*, 24; Favrot, *Report on Special Activities, 1919–20*; Favrot and Lewis, *Report on Special Activities, 1920–21*; Favrot and Lewis, *Report on Special Activities, 1921–22*; Lewis and Sisemore, *Special Report*, 5, 37.

13. Other state agents for Negro schools used the white teachers' associations' publications sporadically, probably reflecting individual choices about promotional strategy and association editors' policies. See, for example, Felton, "Conference of State Agents"; Felton, "Rosenwald School Building Program"; "Progress in Bowie County"; Bludworth, "Rosenwald Fund in Texas"; "A Worthy Example"; D. Taylor, "Limestone County Training School"; Bludworth, "Rosenwald School Day Program"; Bludworth, "Negro Training Schools"; Lambert, "Negro Education in Alabama"; Lambert, "Some Agencies."

14. Favrot, "Negro Public Education," 248.

15. Favrot, "Needs of Negro Schools," 250; see also Harris, "Negro Public Education"; "Louisiana Colored State Teachers Association," 272–73. Favrot falls squarely in the pattern Grantham describes for southern white reformers after the First World War in *Southern Progressivism*, 406–7.

16. Reagan to Favrot, 8 September 1920, Superintendent's Records, 1904–23, Louisiana Department of Education Records. The white Louisiana Teachers' Association and the state board of education jointly sponsored *Louisiana School Work* and its successor, *Southern School Work*. In 1925, *Southern School Work* became the *Journal of the Louisiana Teachers' Association* and dropped the department of Negro education.

17. Clark, "Colored Education"; Clark, "New Normal School"; J. Jones, "Rosenwald Schools"; J. Jones, "Rosenwald School Work"; J. Jones, "Educational Value."

18. J. Jones, "Rosenwald School Work."

19. J. Jones, "Educational Value"; Such pictures still hang in some surviving Rosenwald schools, the legacy of African American teachers in Rosenwald schools who received financial assistance to attend Tuskegee Institute summer programs. In 1918, these teachers asked for pictures of Booker T. Washington, Robert Russa Moton, and Julius Rosenwald for their schools. Clinton Calloway offered these at a modest price through Tuskegee, and the Rosenwald Fund continued the practice. Resolutions of Rosenwald teachers attending Tuskegee Summer School, 15 July 1918, folder "Application and Reports for Rosenwald Fund 1916–1919," box 4, Calloway Papers; Calloway to "Dear Teacher," 4 March 1919, folder "Mary E. Foster Correspondence 1920," box 8, Calloway Papers.

20. Trousdale, "Schools of DeSoto Parish."

21. Other examples of the activities discussed below for Kentucky include Player, "To The Colored Teachers of Louisiana," 8 March 1918, Superintendent's Records, 1904–23, Louisiana Department of Education Records; Easom to Brown, 22 July 1929, Rosenwald School Records, General Correspondence, vol. 141, Mississippi Department of Education Records; *The Thirtieth Annual Meeting of the Florida State Teachers Association*, 28–30 December 1920, and *Minutes of the Thirty-fourth Annual Convention of the Florida State Teachers Association*, December 29–31, 1924, folder 1, box 1, Gilbert Porter Florida State Teachers Association Collection; Nelum, "Study of the First Seventy Years."

22. Russell, *Kentucky Negro Education Association*; *Proceedings of the Kentucky Negro Educational Association*, 1917, 1919, 1923, 1924, 1926, 1928.

23. "Resolutions Reported by the Legislative Committee of the K.N.E.A. at the 47th Annual Session," *Proceedings of the Kentucky Negro Educational Association*, 1923, 25–26.

24. "Special Resolutions Adopted at K.N.E.A. Meeting, Louisville, KY., April 24, 1924," *Proceedings of the Kentucky Negro Educational Association*, 1924, 37; "Resolutions Adopted at the 1925 Session of the K.N.E.A.," *Proceedings of the Kentucky Negro Educational Association*, 1925, 23; "Declaration of Principles," *Proceedings of the Kentucky Negro Educational Association*, 1929, 31; Financial Records of Philanthropic Funds, 1924–34, 16–17, Kentucky Department of Education Records.

25. "John G. Fee Industrial High School"; "The Mayo-Underwood School," "Rosenwald Schools," "Funds Aiding Our Colored Schools," "Rosenwald School Day Issue," "How to Get Aid From the J.R.F.," *KNEA Journal* 1, no. 3 (February 1931): cover, 3, 6–7, 9; "One of Our New Rural Buildings"; "One of Our New City Schools," 1931; "One of Our New City Schools," 1932.

26. Perry, *History of the American Teachers Association*, 15–23, 45–52; Fultz, "African American Teachers"; Fairclough, *Teaching Equality*, 1–19.

27. Jackson, *History of the Virginia State Teachers' Association*, 42–94; Jordan, "Impact of the Negro Organization Society"; 9–69; Link, *Hard Country*, 192–93; "Resolutions of Negro State Teachers' Association."

28. Walker had been state customs collector in the 1890s, an appointment from President William McKinley. My thanks to Phyllis McClure of Washington, D.C., for information about and photographs of Walker's home. Jordan, "Impact of the Negro Organization Society," 41–42; "Report of the Executive Committee"; "Kenbridge Graded School." An example of the surging number of articles discussing Rosenwald school projects include five in *Virginia Teachers' Bulletin* 6, no. 2 (March 1929): 15–18. W. D. Gresham apparently published only one article in this journal other than summaries of two addresses he delivered at VSTA meetings: "Working Together."

29. "Conference of State Agents of Rural Schools for Negroes June 4 and 5, 1929," folder 4, box 188, Rosenwald Fund Archives.

30. "Report of W. F. Credle Supervisor Rosenwald Fund, May 1924," folder "Rosenwald Fund, WF Credle Reports," box 8, Special Subject File, and correspondence between Credle and Sentelle in folder "Sentelle, Shepardson Feb. 1924–January 1925," box 1, Correspondence of the Supervisor of the Rosenwald Fund, Division of Negro Education, North Carolina Department of Public Instruction Records. For insight into the superintendents' attitudes and limited interest in their black schools, see Cooke, *White Superintendent*.

31. Davis to Credle, 3 November 1925.

32. Sibley to Archibald, 8 April 1915, folder "A," SG 15442, Rural School Agent Correspondence, Alabama Department of Education Records; Brinson to Scruggs, 1

September 1925, folder "Correspondence, 1925," box 2, Jefferson County School Board Records. For an example from another state, see Dudley Tanner to "Dear Superintendent," 18 January 1930, folder 2, box 236, Tennessee Commissioner of Education Records; for the correspondence involved in constructing Rosenwald schools in a single county, see H. Thompson, "History of Negro Education," 66–71.

33. J. Smith discusses Rennolds's correspondence concerning the racial identity of various Essex County residents in *Managing White Supremacy*, 225–26. Wright to Rennolds, 25 June 1915, folder 3, box 1; Wright to Rennolds, 3 May 1917, 3 October 1917, folder 3, Ball to Rennolds, 19 November 1918, folder 7, Calloway to Rennolds, 30 January 1919, folder 8, Ball to Rennolds, 18 August 1919, folder 9, Wright to Rennolds, 2 September 1920, 4 September 1920, and Hart to Division Superintendents, 19 October 1920, folder 10, all in box 2, Rennolds Papers; 1923–1929 correspondence between Gresham and Rennolds, in folders 4, 7, 9 in box 3; folders 2, 5, 6, 7, 9 in box 4; folder 6, box 5, Rennolds Papers.

34. "George D. Godard, Special Supervisor," *Annual Report* [Georgia], 1913, 56, 58; *Annual Report* [Georgia], 1915, 41; *Annual Report* [Georgia], 1917, 44.

35. Calloway to Moton, 7 June 1917, folder "Rural School Correspondence 1917," box 3, Calloway Papers. For the context in which Calloway made this assessment, see Harlan, *Separate and Unequal*, 210–47; for another discussion of Godard and his successor Walter B. Hill Jr., see Chirhart, *Torches of Light*, 73–103.

36. "Report of Walter B. Hill, Supervisor," *Annual Report* [Georgia], 1920, 84, 86–87; *Annual Report* [Georgia], 1921, 65–68, 73–74; *Annual Report* [Georgia], 1922, 90–93, 98–99.

37. "Buildings," *Annual Reports* [Georgia], 1929–30, 30; *Jeanes Supervision*, 37–42. Arkansas state agent for Negro schools Nolen Irby voiced similar opinions in *Program for the Equalization of Educational Opportunities*, 46–48, 135–37; African American educators reported in 1938 that Mississippi's state agent for Negro schools had realized that "the evils of the system exist fundamentally with the system itself" in "P. H. Easom," 27.

38. "Report of Dr. G. E. Davis, Supervisor Rosenwald Building for North Carolina," March 1929, folder "Rosenwald Fund—G. E. Davis Reports," box 8, Special Subject File, Division of Negro Education, North Carolina Department of Public Instruction Records.

39. "Report of G. E. Davis, Supervisor Rosenwald Buildings," May and June 1931, folder "Rosenwald Fund—G. E. Davis Reports," box 8, Special Subject File, Division of Negro Education, North Carolina Department of Public Instruction Records. For more on Davis's philosophy, as well as that of Newbold and Credle, see Leloudis, *Schooling the New South*, 211–27; Hanchett, "The Rosenwald Schools"; Gilmore, *Gender and Jim Crow*, 186; see also Fairclough, *Teaching Equality*, 16.

40. Newbold to Du Bois, 28 April 1926, folder "N-R," box 8, General Correspon-

dence of the Director, Division of Negro Education, North Carolina Department of Public Instruction Records.

41. Newbold to Siske, 6 April 1927, folder "Speeches, Reports, Misc.," box 8, General Correspondence of the Director, Division of Negro Education, North Carolina Department of Public Instruction Records. For a similar assessment of Newbold, see Gilmore, *Gender and Jim Crow*, 226.

42. Newbold to Allen, 24 September 1930, Allen to Newbold, 25 September 1930, folder "A," box 10, General Correspondence of the Director, Division of Negro Education, North Carolina Department of Public Instruction Records.

43. "Minutes of Julius Rosenwald Fund," 4 November 1928, "Special Meeting of Trustees, Julius Rosenwald Fund," 11 May 1929, Stern to Smith, 6 September 1928, folder 4, and [Stern?] to Smith, 5 May 1927, Smith to Stern, 13 April 1928 and 17 April 1928, folder 5, box 331, Rosenwald Fund Archives; "Annual Meeting of Trustees, Julius Rosenwald Fund," 16 November 1929.

44. Embree to Stern, 14 November 1931, folder 33, box 105, Rosenwald Fund Archives; Moton to Favrot, 16 December 1932, folder 1385, box 167, General Correspondence, Moton Papers; *Biennial Report* [Arkansas], 1930–32, 60; Hirst to Smith, 2 May 1932 and Smith to Hirst, 28 July 1932, folder 2, box 337, Rosenwald Fund Archives; Patterson, *History of the Arkansas State Teachers Association*, 33; "Biographical Sketch of R. C. Childress," in *Arkansas Rosenwald Day*.

CHAPTER 7. LOCAL PEOPLE AND SCHOOL-BUILDING CAMPAIGNS

1. J. Anderson, *Education of Blacks*; Fairclough, "'Being in the Field,'" 66–67.

2. Franklin, introduction to Franklin and Savage, eds., *Cultural Capital and Black Education*, xiv.

3. Gaines, *Uplifting the Race*; Shaw, *What a Woman*; Chirhart, *Torches of Light*. See also Fultz, "'Morning Cometh'"; Siddle Walker, *Their Highest Potential*.

4. Chirhart, "'Better for Us'"; Pitts, "Three Who Cared."

5. "White Teachers in Negro Schools"; Fairclough, "'Being in the Field,'" 65–91; Fairclough, *Teaching Equality*; Sherer, *Subordination or Liberation?*, 18; J. Anderson, *Education of Blacks*, 31; Hahn, *Nation under Our Feet*, 276–80.

6. Hollins to Scott, 24 October 1916, folder 81, box 11, General Correspondence, Moton Papers.

7. "$15,000 High School Planned for Negroes," *Memphis Commercial Appeal*, 9 October 1923, Tuskegee Clippings Files.

8. Gordon, "Fifty-two Years of Public Service," in Mississippi Retired Teachers Association, *Bells Are Ringing*, 127.

9. I. S. Caldwell, "Colored School at Keysville Directed by I. E. Bryan Has Attracted National Attention," *Augusta (Ga.) Herald*, 21 November 1926, Tuskegee Clippings Files.

10. "Henry County."

11. Williams et al., *Jeanes Story*; Leloudis, *Schooling the New South*; Gilmore, *Gender and Jim Crow*, 161–65; Krause, "Jeanes Supervisor"; Krause, "'We Did Move Mountains!'"

12. Washington Jr., "Report, Rural Schoolhouse Building," April 1918, SG 15451, Rural School Agent Correspondence, Alabama Department of Education Records; "Rosenwald Schools," in *Annual Report* [Alabama], 1919, 123. J. S. Lambert probably wrote the short overview of black public education in Alabama since 1900 that claimed Jeanes supervisors had impressed the need for school buildings on Booker T. Washington, at least partially inspiring the Rosenwald program. "Division of Negro Education," in *Annual Report* [Alabama], 1931, 79.

13. Calloway to Sibley, 28 October 1914, folder "C," SG 15442, Rural School Agent Correspondence, Alabama Department of Education Records.

14. Perry to Rosenwald, 29 March 1916, folder 81, box 11, General Correspondence, Moton Papers.

15. Smith to Calloway, 25 August 1916, Calloway to Smith, 29 August 1916, Stricklen to Calloway, 6 December 1916, folder "Correspondence Re: Teaching Applications and Rosenwald Fund Applications 1916," box 4, Calloway Papers.

16. "Mr. Abrams Writes."

17. Randolph to Dillard, 18 February 1929 and 11 April 1929, Dillard to Randolph, 12 April 1929, folder 7, box 29, series 5, Southern Education Foundation Records.

18. Casey to Calloway, 7 June 1918, folder "General Correspondence, 1918," box 1, Calloway Papers; Fairclough, "'Being in the Field,'" 77.

19. Edwards to Sibley, 15 October 1915, folder "E," and Pugh to Sibley, 21 August 1915, folder "P," SG 15444, Rural School Agent Correspondence, Alabama Department of Education Records.

20. Edwards to Newbold, 14 February 1916, folder "E," box 2, General Correspondence of the Director, Division of Negro Education, North Carolina Department of Public Instruction Records.

21. "Rosenwald Schools Built in Last 10 Years in Sumter County Cost $28,240," *Americus (Ga.) Recorder*, 22 November 1931, Tuskegee Clippings Files.

22. August and November 1912 correspondence between Whitley and Washington, and Schwartz to Washington, 25 August 1912, folder "The Rosenwald Fund 1912 P-R," box 77, Special Correspondence, Washington Papers, microfilm reel 70; Whitley to Washington, 16 July 1914 and Washington to Whitley, 20 July 1914, folder "Ro Rosenwald School Fund 1914 T-Z," box 812, Donation File, Tuskegee Records, Washington Papers, microfilm reel 607; 1914 list of names of those sent the "Plan for Erection of Rural Schoolhouses," folder "Ro Rosenwald School Fund A-C, 1914," box 811, Donation File, Tuskegee Records, Washington Papers, microfilm reel 606.

23. December 1916 correspondence between Sibley, Moton, and Graves, folder 79, box 11, General Correspondence, Moton Papers; December 1916 correspondence between Sibley, Moton, and Graves, folder "M," SG 15449, Rural School Agent Cor-

respondence, Alabama Department of Education Records; Calloway to Sibley, 30 December 1916, folder "Correspondence Re: Teaching Applications and Rosenwald Fund Applications, 1916," box 4, Calloway Papers.

24. Coffey to Washington, 7 October 1914, 26 October 1914, Washington to Coffey, 12 October 1914, folder "Ro Rosenwald School Fund A-C 1914," box 811, Donation File, Tuskegee Records, Washington Papers, microfilm reel 606. My thanks to Mayor Tammy Hill and her family, who are working to save Lima's Rosenwald Hall.

25. Gilmore to Calloway, 22 October 1917, folder "Correspondence: Rosenwald Schools 1917," box 5, Calloway Papers.

26. Cowart to Washington, 17 August 1914, folder "Ro Rosenwald School Fund A-C, 1914," box 811, Donation File, Tuskegee Records, Washington Papers, microfilm reel 606.

27. The school remained known as Gilmore Academy until 1952. A monument erected by the school's alumni association now marks the site. Westbrook, "Struggle for Educational Equity," 75–84, 95–97.

28. Prater to Lambert, 29 April 1919, folder "P," SG 15454, Rural School Agent Correspondence, Alabama Department of Education Records.

29. Calloway et al., *Survey of Colored Public Schools*. My thanks to Susan G. Pearl for providing me with a copy of this publication.

30. Jackson, Allen, Jones, S. Hill, and J. Hill to P. H. Easom, 13 November 1928, and Jones to W. C. Strahan, 14 January 1929, Cancelled Applications, Rosenwald School Records, vol. 161, Mississippi Department of Education Records. The application was renewed and completed the following year.

31. Angel to Lambert, 24 May 1919, folder "A," SG 15452, Rural School Agent Correspondence, Alabama Department of Education Records.

32. "Rosenwald School at Marion, Virginia, Tribute to Founder," *Pittsburgh Courier*, [6?] December 1931, Tuskegee Clippings Files.

33. Parthenia Jones Williams, "Montclair Schools," in *Through Schoolhouse Doors*, 156–57.

34. Leak to State Board of Education, 26 February 1929, vol. 141, Mississippi Department of Education Records; Harris, "Monthly Report of Rosenwald Building Agent," March 1931, folder "Vincent H. Harris," unit 1, series 62, Division of Negro Education, Georgia Department of Education Records; on Harris and Georgia Rosenwald schools, see Siddle Walker, "Organized Resistance," 378–79.

35. Davis to Smith, 24 March 1927, box 331, folder 1, Rosenwald Fund Archives.

36. Tidwell to Lambert, 15 May 1919, folder "T," SG 15454, Rural School Agent Correspondence, Alabama Department of Education Records; "Negro School Gets Gift From Smith-Rosenwald Fund," *Columbus (Miss.) Dispatch*, 8 October 1926, Tuskegee Clippings Files.

37. Mills to Newbold, 11 April 1919, folder "M," box 4, General Correspondence

of the Director, Division of Negro Education, North Carolina Department of Public Instruction Records.

38. Neal to Sibley, 24 September 1915, folder "N," SG 15444, Rural School Agent Correspondence, Alabama Department of Education Records; Boyd to Lambert, 17 September 1919, folder "B," SG 15452, Rural School Agent Correspondence, Alabama Department of Education Records.

39. Charl Ormond Williams, who also campaigned for Tennessee's woman suffrage movement, was part of an influential female circle of white educators in Shelby County. Together with her predecessor and sister Mabel Williams Hughes and successor Sue M. Powers, Williams cooperated with outside philanthropies and African American educators to construct the state's most complex system of suburban and rural schools for black children. Smith to Calloway, 25 September 1917, folder 80, box 11, General Correspondence, Moton Papers; Hoffschwelle, *Rebuilding the Rural Southern Community*, 43, 81–83; Rogers, *Light from Many Candles*, 123–26, 178–80, 231–33.

40. "Report of G. E. Davis, Rosenwald Building Agent for North Carolina," October 1922, detail 3, folder "Rosenwald Fund—G. E. Davis Reports," box 8, Special Subjects File, Division of Negro Education, North Carolina Department of Public Instruction Records.

41. S. Smith, *Builders of Goodwill*, 126–32. Williams and Favrot tried to interest the Jeanes Fund in a multifaceted study of and program for Coahoma County's black homes as well as its schools. A fire destroyed the county training-school complex in 1930; by the mid-1930s Coahoma's surviving Rosenwald schools were dilapidated and targeted by the Rosenwald Fund's school plant rehabilitation program, as discussed in the conclusion. Dillard to Favrot, 4 June 1925, Favrot to Dillard, 15 June 1925, folder 19, box 27, series 5, Southern Education Foundation Records; Easom to Smith, 12 February 1930, folder 4, and 1934–39 correspondence in folder 5, box 340, Rosenwald Fund Archives.

42. Resolutions of the Clarksdale Rotary Club, n.d., folder 1, box 299, Rosenwald Fund Archives.

43. "Negro High Site Chosen" and "Work on Negro School," *Memphis Commercial Appeal*, 12 and 26 September 1924; "Coahoma County Takes Big Stride in Negro Schools," *Vicksburg (Miss.) Herald*, 17 March 1925, "Group System Negro Schools" and "Coahoma Leads with Schools for Negroes," *Greenwood (Miss.) Commonwealth*, 27 June and 4 August 1925, "Plan Negro Schools," *Memphis Commercial Appeal*, 11 July 1925, "Mississippi County Sets Pace in Negro Education," *Columbus (Ga.) Enquirer*, 15 February 1926, Tuskegee Clippings Files.

44. Equen to Morgan, 14 October 1929, Strahan to Equen, 18 October 1929, folder "Rosenwald Pending Matters 1928–1929," vol. 142, Rosenwald School Records, General Correspondence, Mississippi Department of Education Records.

45. Hughes to Strahan, 14 March 1930, vol. 141, Rosenwald School Records, General Correspondence, Mississippi Department of Education Records.

46. Ennis to Lambert, 11 December 1918, folder "E," SG 15453, Rural School Agent Correspondence, Alabama Department of Education Records.

47. Crump also chaired the Sharkey County Better Homes committee. Ford to Rosenwald, 4 February 1928, Crump to Stern, 22 February 1928; Smith to Crump, 6 March 1928, folder 3, box 340, Rosenwald Fund Archives. For the interconnections between the Better Homes movement, home demonstration clubs, and rural schools for black and whites, see Hoffschwelle, *Rebuilding the Rural Southern Community*, chaps. 4–6.

48. Grossley, "Report, Rosenwald Schoolhouse Building for Mississippi," September 1919, folder 335, box 50, General Correspondence, Moton Papers; Hilbun to Carney, 8 July 1922, folder 2, box 340, Rosenwald Fund Archives; Mississippi Rosenwald School list, folder 4, box 339, Rosenwald Fund Archives; Easom to Yarbrough, 5 March 1929, folder "Rosenwald Pending Matters 1928–1929," vol. 142, Rosenwald School Records, General Correspondence, Mississippi Department of Education Records.

49. Elder to Washington, 29 July 1914, Washington to Elder, 5 August 1914, folder "Ro Rosenwald School Fund 1914 D-G," box 812, Donation File, Tuskegee Records, Washington Papers, microfilm reel 607.

50. A new wood shop at the Sandersville Colored Industrial School was illustrated in the Georgia Department of Education's *Annual Report*, 1917, 42. Dickerman had been the field director of the Slater Fund from 1907 to 1910; his appeal was reprinted as Dickerman, "Rural Negro Education." Principal Elder was a graduate of Atlanta University and Mrs. Sanders an alumna of Spelman College. They are buried in front of their Rosenwald-aided school.

51. *Through Schoolhouse Doors*, 186.

52. Pulliam to Scott, 16 April 1918, folder 251, box 36, General Correspondence, Moton Papers; Pulliam to Calloway, 15 June 1918, folder "C. J. Calloway Correspondence 1918," box 11, Calloway Papers; Bonner to Sibley, 26 April 1915, SG 15442, Rural School Agent Correspondence, Alabama Department of Education Records. On the practice of "political farming out of patronage" to a selected African American by a county superintendent, see Godard to Dillard, 28 September 1914, folder 3, box 28, series 5, Southern Education Foundation Records.

53. Favrot documented his tours of Louisiana communities in *Field Force Reports*; Huffington reported on his speaking appearances in Maryland Rosenwald rallies in *Annual Report*, 1919, 121–22. Georgia Jeanes supervisors noted that Godard and Hill had traveled the state to encourage black school improvement in *Jeanes Supervision*, 33–35.

54. "Payne," in *Retrospective Glances*; Washington Jr., "Report, Rural Schoolhouse Building," April 1918, SG 15451, Rural School Agent Correspondence, Alabama Department of Education Records.

55. Colebeck to Lambert, 20 July 1922, SG 15461, Rural School Agent Correspondence, Alabama Department of Education Records; Randolph interview.

56. Strong et al., "Leveraging the State," 658–60, 662, 672–77.

57. Britton to Newbold, 13 September 1915, folder "B," box 2, General Correspondence of the Director, Division of Negro Education, North Carolina Department of Public Instruction Records.

58. For an example from Elizabeth City, North Carolina, see Drew to Board of Education, 2 October 1928, folder "A. T. Allen—State Superintendent," box 5, Correspondence of the Supervisor of the Rosenwald Fund, Division of Negro Education, North Carolina Department of Public Instruction Records.

59. Nelson is on the 1914 list of names of those sent the "Plan for Erection of Rural Schoolhouses"; "Chester Shell," "Chester Shell Elementary: A History," and Bill Shields, "500 Pupils Attend School Dedication," *Gainesville (Fla.) Sun*, 18 March 1976, in *Chester Shell Elementary School*.

60. Harris, "Georgia Monthly Report of Rosenwald Building Agent," July and August 1931, folder "Vincent Harris, Reports," unit 1, series 62, Division of Negro Education, Georgia Department of Education Records.

61. Jeter to Fulton, 21 April 1930, Beaty to Adams, 21 April 1930, Felton to Beaty, 23 April 1930, folder "Union County Assorted Papers, Pamphlets and Correspondence Concerning Negro Schools and Rosenwald Fund ca. 1928," box 2, Union County Board of Education Papers. Frances Beaty's letter to district trustees' chair B. F. Adams asking for the deed and application forms for the Mount Rowell school suggests that she knew of Jeter's attempt to bring state officials into the situation.

62. Davis described Beam as "everything but sympathetic and just in dealing with his Negro schools," and as bordering on hostility to black schools in 1925. Foster to Credle, 5 July 1925, Credle to Foster, 7 July 1925, Foster to Credle, 22 July 1925, folder "F," box 2, Correspondence of the Supervisor of the Rosenwald Fund, Division of Negro Education, North Carolina Department of Public Instruction Records.

63. Guthrie to Newbold, 17 September 1920, Newbold to Guthrie, 13 September 1920, folder "G," box 5, General Correspondence of the Director, Division of Negro Education, North Carolina Department of Public Instruction Records.

64. Newbold to Webb, 11 January 1923, Webb to Newbold, 17 January 1923, folder "W"; Newbold to Bragg, 20 February 1923, folder "B," box 6, General Correspondence of the Director, Division of Negro Education, North Carolina Department of Public Instruction Records.

65. Crow, "Some Effects of Farm Tenancy," 14; Newbold to Martin, 22 April 1926, folder "M," box 8, General Correspondence of the Director, Division of Negro Education, North Carolina Department of Public Instruction Records.

66. Clay to Bernard, 1 September 1925, folder 1, box 270, Tennessee Commissioner of Education Records; Miller, *Mr. Crump of Memphis*; Church and Walter, "Robert Reed Church, Jr.;" Couto, *Lifting the Veil*.

67. Washington to Rosenwald, 12 September 1912, folder 8, box 336, Julius Rosenwald Fund Archives.

68. Graves to Moton, 5 December 1917, folder 342, box 52, General Correspondence, Moton Papers.

69. Crawford to Hickerson, 12 October 1915, Newbold to Hickerson, 14 October 1915, folder "H," box 2, General Correspondence of the Director, Division of Negro Education, North Carolina Department of Public Instruction Records.

70. "Supervision of Colored Schools," in *Annual Report* [Maryland], 1921, 109.

71. J. Anderson, *Education of Blacks*, 171–73, 176–79. Arthur D. Wright made the same observation in 1914, noting that African Americans "not only pay willingly according to the value of their property, but that many go beyond this with personal contributions to their schools. . . . This is in reality a voluntary school tax, and often means a sacrifice." "Negro Schools," *Annual Report* [Virginia], 1913–14, 113.

72. See, for example, Turner, "'Getting It Straight,'" 217–23; E. Anderson and Moss, *Dangerous Donations*, 37.

73. For descriptions of rallies, see Favrot, "Report of State Agent of Rural Schools for Negroes," *Field Force Reports*, April 1917, 104, as well as reports by the Rosenwald building agents in General Correspondence, Moton Papers.

74. "Loachapoka, Lee County, Ala." and "Notasulga, Alabama," 10 January 1913, "Little Zion Community, Montgomery County" and "Big Zion Community, Montgomery County," 21 March 1913, "One Hundred and One Dollars and Forty-seven Cents Raised for School House Building" and "Shorters, Ala.," 2 May 1913, *Tuskegee (Ala.) Messenger*, Tuskegee Clippings Files.

75. Bond, *Negro Education in Alabama*, 281–85, 347.

76. "Big Educational Rally," [two copies, one with notations]; "Big Barbecue"; "Big Barbecue and Picnic," folder "Programs Etc.," box 11, Calloway Papers.

77. "Loachapoka, Lee County, Ala. $68.49 Raised in Last Rally. New Schoolhouse in Course of Erection" set the precedent for publishing individual contributions collected at a rally for one of the South's first Rosenwald building campaigns; see also "Money Is Raised for Negro School," *Yazoo (Miss.) Herald*, 23 January 1925, Tuskegee Clippings Files, and the unidentified newspaper clipping included in Henderson to Lambert, 4 January 1919, SG 15453, Rural School Agent Correspondence, Alabama Department of Education Records. An unpublished list of donors can be found attached to Hickerson to Newbold, 28 March 1916, folder "H," box 2, General Correspondence of the Director, Division of Negro Education, North Carolina Department of Public Instruction Records.

78. Washington Jr., "Report, Rural Schoolhouse Building, Alabama," July 1918, 1, SG 15454, Rural School Agent Correspondence, Alabama Department of Education Records; Moore, "Report, Rural Schoolhouse Building, North Carolina," April 1918, 2, folder 251, box 36, General Correspondence, Moton Papers.

79. T. J. Calloway to C. J. Calloway, 7 May 1919, 18 October 1919, C. J. Calloway to T. J. Calloway, 5 November 1919, "Building Fund, School 2, District 13," folder "Correspondence General 1919," box 8, Calloway Papers.

80. Rouson to Credle, 22 December 1925, folder "R," box 2, Correspondence of the Supervisor of the Rosenwald Fund, Division of Negro Education, North Carolina Department of Education Records.

81. *Biennial Report* [Florida], 1921–22, 332. The ten acres supported an extensive vocational agriculture program.

82. "Progress of Negro Education." Rosenwald building agents and state Negro school agents constantly reported that black community members had paid for the school site, such as F. M. Wood's notations that patrons at Adairville bought 3 1/2 acres of land valued at about $800 and those at Mayslick had expended $1,450 for their 3 acres. "Report, Rosenwald Schoolhouse Building for Kentucky," February 1920, folder 340c, March 1920, folder 340b, box 51, General Correspondence, Moton Papers.

83. Harris was a vocational teacher, and not surprisingly his club formulations follow the girls' poultry clubs and boy's hog clubs initiated by the cooperative extension service. Harris, "Georgia Monthly Report of Rosenwald Building Agent," February 1932, narrative 1, folder "Vincent Harris, Reports," unit 1, series 62, Division of Negro Education, Georgia Department of Education Records.

84. Woodson, "Story of the Fund," chap. 7, 12–13, 14, 15–16.

85. A benevolent association made a contribution to the East Baton Rouge school as well, although whether that group was all-male, all-female, or gender integrated is unknown. R. E. Clay to O. H. Bernard, 1 March 1926, folder 1, box 270, Tennessee Commissioner of Education Records; Jones, "Report, Rosenwald Schoolhouse Building for Louisiana," July 1919, folder 335, box 50, General Correspondence, Moton Papers.

86. Woodson, "Story of the Fund," chap. 7, 5–6, 7, 9.

87. R. E. Clay to O. H. Bernard, 31 December 1925, 31 May 1926, folder 1, box 270, Tennessee Commissioner of Education Records, microfilm reel 89.

88. S. Smith, "A Story of the Julius Rosenwald Fund in Tenn. from the Beginning to July 1, 1920," folder 2, box 76, Julius Rosenwald Fund Archives; Washington Jr., "Report, Rural Schoolhouse Building, Alabama," June 1918, SG 15453, Rural School Agent Correspondence, Alabama Department of Education Records.

89. Woodson, "Story of the Fund," chap. 5, 7.

90. "Monthly Report of Wm. Rakestraw," July 1919, SG 15452, Rural School Agent Correspondence, Alabama Department of Education Records; Jones, "Report, Rosenwald Schoolhouse Building in Louisiana," April 1920, folder 340b, box 51, General Correspondence, Moton Papers.

91. Tolnay, *Bottom Rung*, 32–41.

92. Shepardson to Smith, 25 January 1925; Smith to Shepardson, 30 January 1925, folder 5, box 339, Rosenwald Fund Archives.

93. The Hopewell School was a three-teacher structure for which local African Americans contributed $1,400 of the $3,000 cost; whites gave another $900 and the fund $700; no public funds were used. The debt was finally paid off in 1935. C. Thompson,

History of the Mississippi Teachers Association, 45; list of Mississippi Rosenwald schools, folder 4, box 339, Rosenwald Fund Archives.

94. Easom to Henderson, 5 November 1929, folder "Rosenwald Pending Matters 1928–1929," vol. 142, Rosenwald School Records, General Correspondence, Mississippi Department of Education Records; Easom to McAlilly, 12 January 1929, Easom to Blount, 12 January 1929, folder "Cancelled Applications," vol. 161, Rosenwald School Records, Mississippi Department of Education Records.

95. Woodson, "Story of the Fund," chap. 7, 11–12; Dorman, "Report, Rosenwald Schoolhouse Building for Arkansas," October 1919, folder 336, box 51, General Correspondence, Moton Papers.

96. Woodson, "Story of the Fund," chap. 7, 15; "Negroes of Jonesboro Took Brick of Auditorium and Built a School," *Memphis Commercial Appeal*, 20 January 1924, Tuskegee Clippings Files.

97. Rouson to W. F. Credle; R. E. Clay to O. H. Bernard, 30 January 1926, folder 1, box 270, Tennessee Commissioner of Education Records.

98. "Move to Obtain a Model School," *Jackson (Ga.) Progress-Argus*, 24 December 1926, and "Jackson Negroes Start Movement to Obtain Industrial School," *Atlanta Constitution*, 25 December 1926, Tuskegee Clippings Files; Moore, "Report, Rosenwald Schoolhouse Building for North Carolina," June 1919, folder 335, box 50, General Correspondence, Moton Papers.

99. Grossley, "Report, Rosenwald Schoolhouse Building, Mississippi," June 1918, folder 251, box 36, General Correspondence, Moton Papers; June 1919, folder 335, box 50, General Correspondence, Moton Papers; October 1919, folder 336, December 1919, March 1920, April 1920, folder 340b, January 1920, folder 340c, box 51, General Correspondence, Moton Papers.

100. R. E. Clay to O. H. Bernard, 30 January 1926, folder 1, box 270, 1 January 1928, 30 September 1929, 30 November 1929, folder 3, box 269, Tennessee Commissioner of Education Records.

101. Dorman may have used the money to supplement the portion of his salary and expenses paid by Julius Rosenwald; his appearances also disseminated information and garnered fraternal orders' approval that would be helpful in rural communities. Dorman, "Report, Rural Schoolhouse Building, Arkansas," July 1918, folder 255, and Dorman, "Report, Rural Schoolhouse Building—Arkansas," August 1918, folder 251, box 36, General Correspondence, Moton Papers. Charles Moore made similar appeals to denominational assemblies and Masonic grand lodges; see "Report, Rosenwald Schoolhouse Building for North Carolina," November 1919, folder 336, and December 1919, folder 340b, box 51, General Correspondence, Moton Papers.

102. Shepardson to Smith, 17 March 1922, folder 2, box 340, Rosenwald Fund Archives.

103. J. W. Cullors, letter to the editor, *Rains County (Tex.) Leader*, 14 April 1922, in Bay, *Sand Flat School*.

104. "Roxboro Negroes Are Raising Sum," *Durham (N.C.) Herald*, 26 April 1928, Tuskegee Clippings Files.

105. Washington Jr., "Report, Rural Schoolhouse Building for Alabama," May 1918, folder 251, box 36, General Correspondence, Moton Papers.

106. Richardson to Calloway, 23 April 1918, folder "General Correspondence 1918," box 7, Calloway Papers.

107. "Rosenwald Agent Lauds This Philanthropist," *Tuskegee Student*, 31 May 1919, scrapbook 14, 110, series IV, Rosenwald Papers.

108. Favrot, "The First Rosenwald Buildings in Arkansas and Louisiana," folder 2, box 76, Rosenwald Fund Archives.

109. Moore, "Report, Rosenwald Schoolhouse Building, North Carolina," August 1918, 2, folder 251, box 36, General Correspondence, Moton Papers.

110. The following paragraphs draw from Henderson to Lambert, 4 January 1919, and attached clipping, "Rosenwald Schools for County of Autauga," SG 15453, Rural School Agent Correspondence, Alabama Department of Education Records.

111. Moton to Calloway and Rakestraw, 26 May 1919, Calloway to Rakestraw, 3 June 1919, folder "W. M. Rakestraw Correspondence 1919," box 11, Calloway Papers; Henderson to Calloway, 4 June [1919], folder "Correspondence General No Date," box 10, Calloway Papers; W. D. Hargrove to Calloway, 8 June 1919, folder "C. J. Calloway Correspondence 1918," box 12, Calloway Papers.

112. Henderson to Calloway, 4 June [1919], folder "Correspondence General No Date," box 10, Calloway Papers.

113. Washington Jr., "Report, Rural Schoolhouse Building," April 1918, SG 15451, Rural School Agent Correspondence, Alabama Department of Education Records; Jones, "Report, Rosenwald Schoolhouse Building for Louisiana," February 1920, folder 340c, box 51, General Correspondence, Moton Papers.

114. Washington Jr., "Report, Rural Schoolhouse Building," April 1918, SG 15451, Rural School Agent Correspondence, Alabama Department of Education Records.

115. "Report of W. F. Credle, Supervisor Rosenwald Fund, May 1925," folder "Rosenwald Fund—W. F. Credle Reports," box 8, Special Subject File, Division of Negro Education, North Carolina Department of Public Instruction Records.

116. For examples from Arkansas, see Dorman, "Report, Rural Schoolhouse Building for Arkansas," May 1918, folder 251, box 36, General Correspondence, Moton Papers; Dorman, "Report, Rosenwald Schoolhouse Building for Arkansas," February 1919, folder 339, box 51, General Correspondence, Moton Papers.

117. Tolnay, *Bottom Rung*, 25–44; Scarborough interview.

118. Lunsford to Favrot, 1 March 1920, folder 8, box 336, Rosenwald Fund Archives; Wood, "Report, Rosenwald Schoolhouse Building for Kentucky," May 1920, 2, folder 340c, box 51, General Correspondence, Moton Papers.

119. Johnson to Favrot, 10 January 1921, Favrot to Johnson, 13 January 1921, Johnson

to Favrot, 2 May 1921, Superintendent's Records, Louisiana Department of Education Records.

120. Williams to Harris, 12 March 1932, folder "Vincent H. Harris," unit 1, series 62, Georgia Department of Education Records.

121. "Report of W. F. Credle, Supervisor Rosenwald Fund, May 1925," folder "Rosenwald Fund—W. F. Credle Reports," box 8, Special Subject File, Division of Negro Education, North Carolina Department of Public Instruction Records.

122. List of Virginia Rosenwald schools, folder 7, box 343, Rosenwald Fund Archives; Morris, "Julius Rosenwald High School"; McClure, "Rosenwald Schools in Virginia." My thanks to Phyllis McClure for sharing her Northern Neck research with me.

123. Littleton to Easom, 21 December 1928, Easom to Littleton, 31 January 1929, and Everett to Strahan, 13 April 1929, Rosenwald Pending Matters 1928–29, vol. 142, Rosenwald School Records, General Correspondence, Mississippi State Department of Education Records; Strahan to Smith, 22 September 1930 and Easom to Credle, 15 October 1930, folder 4, box 340, and Easom to Embree and Smith, 1 October 1940, folder 2, box 299, Rosenwald Fund Archives.

124. Credle to Glenn, 16 October 1922, Glenn to Newbold, 7 November 1922, Newbold to Glenn, 13 November 1922, and Glenn to Newbold, 15 November 1922, folder "G," box 6, General Correspondence of the Director, Division of Negro Education, North Carolina Department of Public Instruction Records.

125. [Shepardson] to Favrot, 25 May 1923, Favrot to Shepardson, 27 May 1923, folder 5, box 339, Rosenwald Fund Archives.

126. Credle to Smith, 16 April 1926, folder "SL Smith," box 2, Correspondence of the Supervisor of the Rosenwald Fund, Division of Negro Education, North Carolina Department of Public Instruction Records; "Report of O. H. Bernard, State Rural School Agent for Tennessee," October 1925, folder 1, box 14, Tennessee Commissioner of Education Records, microfilm reel 4.

127. Harris, "Georgia Monthly Report of Rosenwald Building Agent," folder "Vincent H. Harris," December 1931, unit 1, series 62, Georgia Department of Education Records.

128. Springfield School correspondence, November 1928–February 1929, Cancelled Applications Rosenwald School Records, vol. 161; Springfield School correspondence, October–November 1929, Cancelled Applications, Rosenwald School Records, vol. 162, Mississippi Department of Education Records.

129. Ibid.

CHAPTER 8. BUILDING SCHOOLS, CONTESTING MEANING: ROSENWALD SCHOOLS IN THE SOUTHERN LANDSCAPE

1. Harlan, *Separate and Unequal*, 20; Link, *Hard Country*, 49–52; Keith, *Country People*, 126–42; Hoffschwelle, *Rebuilding the Rural Southern Community*, 36–37.

2. Walters, James, and McCammon, "Citizenship and Public Schools."

3. Howard interview; Siddle Walker describes the origins of the 1925 Yanceyville, North Carolina, Rosenwald school in the Stephens House, a residence purchased by school patrons in 1906 in *Their Highest Potential,* 15–18.

4. Lassiter to Credle, 20 January 1927, folder "L," and McDowell to Allen, 7 October 1926, folder "R," box 3, Correspondence of the Supervisor of the Rosenwald Fund, Division of Negro Education, North Carolina Department of Public Instruction Records.

5. Pearl, *African-American Heritage Survey,* 94–95, 134; Herman and Barnes, *African-American Education in Leon County,* 105–7; Randle, "Mt. Zion Rosenwald School," 16–17.

6. Richardson, *Development of Negro Education,* 29–32; Virginia Rosenwald school list, folder 7, box 343, Rosenwald Fund Archives.

7. Raymond Spann quoted in Woods, "Julius Rosenwald Fund School Building Program," 141–42.

8. Brown, "We the Building Committee of Brownsville School Number Two," 1913, untitled folder [1], box 14, Calloway Papers.

9. Lambert to Gillis, 18 October 1919, SG 15457, Rural School Agent Correspondence, Alabama Department of Education Records.

10. "Long Contractor for Negro School," *Trenton (Tenn.) Democrat,* 7 December 1927, Tuskegee Clippings Files; "Notice to Building Contractors," folder "Correspondence, 1928," box 2, Jefferson County School Board Records; Crippens, "School History." My thanks to both the late Mr. Crippens and Kathy Bennett, then of the Nashville Public Library, for this reference.

11. Wills interview.

12. The 1927 bond election failed, leaving Jefferson County school authorities in dire financial straits; nevertheless, the two-teacher Wacissa Rosenwald School was constructed in 1927–28. Wacissa Land Company to Board of Public Instruction of Jefferson County, 7 May 1927, F. H. Beach to [school board], 30 May 1927, folder "Correspondence, 1917–1928," "Notice to Building Contractors" for Aucilla and Wacissa schools, 1928, folder "Correspondence, 1928," box 2, Jefferson County School Board Records.

13. S. S. Mann to W. F. Credle, 7 November 1925, folder "M," and Credle to Smith, 16 April 1926, folder "SL Smith," box 2, Allen to Credle, 7 February 1929, folder "A," box 5, in Correspondence of the Supervisor of the Rosenwald Fund, and "Report of W. F. Credle, Supervisor Rosenwald Fund," March 1929, folder "Rosenwald Fund—WF Credle Reports," box 8, Special Subject File, all in Division of Negro Education, North Carolina Department of Public Instruction Records.

14. "Negroes Erecting Nice School House," *Sparta (Ga.) Ishmaelite,* 6 March 1930, "Negro School to Be Erected Soon/Board of Education Selects Site for New Four Oaks $1,500 Institution," *Selma (N.C.) Johnstonian,* 1 March 1928, "Work to Begin Soon/

Negro School Here: Alamance County Training School For Negroes Will Be Located on Richmond Hill," *Burlington (N.C.) News*, 19 June 1928, Tuskegee Clippings Files.

15. "Long Contractor for Negro School"; "New School/Board of Education Awards Contract for Colored School to M. B. Gregory," *Harrodsburg (Ky.) Herald*, 27 March 1931; "Negro Schools in County Get New Buildings," *Lake Worth (Fla.) Herald*, 5 April 1929, Tuskegee Clippings Files.

16. "Work on Colored School Nearing Completion," *Madison (Fla.) Recorder*, 8 March 1929; "Work on Colored School Building Nears Completion," *West Point (Ga.) News*, 29 January 1931, Tuskegee Clippings Files.

17. Although the 1931 school does not appear on the Rosenwald Fund's Mississippi typescript list, which ends in 1929–30, both the Lee and Marion-Lamar Consolidated schools are documented in the Rosenwald Fund's card file for Marion County, Mississippi, Rosenwald Fund Archives.

18. Agreement and Memorandum of Understanding between the Lee-Rosenwald Colored School Board of Trustees and Richard Kalil, 22 July 1931, folder 4, box 340, Rosenwald Fund Archives.

19. Drinkard began the school campaign in 1917. Fred Drinkard to E. J. Scott, 10 January 1917, folder "Rural School Correspondence 1917," box 3, Calloway Papers; Drinkard to C. J. Calloway, 28 January 1919, folder "General Correspondence 1919," box 1, Calloway Papers.

20. After Boone raised $150 in cash and labor for exterior painting, he had Credle's attention and support, and the two men tried, apparently unsuccessfully, to get more resources for the school. Credle offered to find more money for the Wilkes County Training School and suggested a Rosenwald appropriation for adding six rooms to the building. Boone then asked for a teachers' home as well. Neither was built, at least with Rosenwald aid. Correspondence between R. I. Boone and W. F. Credle, September 1927–March 1928, folder "B," box 4, Correspondence of the Supervisor of the Rosenwald Fund, Division of Negro Education, North Carolina Department of Public Instruction Records.

21. Favrot, "The Service of a Rosenwald Building Agent Is Greatly Needed in Several States," 1928, folder 16, box 202, Rosenwald Fund Archives.

22. *Educational Study of Alabama*, plate 4; *Official Report of Educational Survey*, 7; Davis, *Development and Present Status*, 59–60.

23. Gill, "Community, Commitment," 88; Fairclough, "'Being in the Field'"; Siddle Walker, *Their Highest Potential*; Reed, *Brevard Rosenwald School*.

24. Recommendations from the Conference of Rural School Agents for Negroes in the South and Rosenwald Schoolbuilding Agents, July 14–17, 1919, folder 336, box 51, General Correspondence, Moton Papers.

25. R. E. Clay to O. H. Bernard, 2 August 1926, folder 1, box 270, Tennessee Commissioner of Education Records.

26. This dispute was only one episode in a troubled career for Murdock, as docu-

mented by correspondence to Alabama's agents for Negro schools. Murdock to Sibley, 23 December 1913, Oden to Sibley, 8 May 1914, SG 15443, Rural School Agent Correspondence, Alabama Department of Education Records.

27. Attmore to Newbold, 7 May 1919, folder "A," box 4, General Correspondence of the Director, Division of Negro Education, North Carolina Department of Public Instruction Records; Williams interview.

28. McKee to Lambert, 31 January 1920, SG 15457, Rural School Agent Correspondence, Alabama Department of Education Records.

29. Nieves, "'We Gave Our Hearts.'"

30. Parthenia Jones Williams, "Montclair Schools," in *Through Schoolhouse Doors*, 159.

31. Hawkins, "Rosenwald Schools: The Chicago Connection," 20; Rogers interview. My thanks to Erin Shaw, then of the South Carolina Department of Archives and History, for sharing the Hawkins article with me.

32. Photographs of the cornerstone ceremony at the Conecuh County Training School, box 1, Rural School Photograph Collection, State Agent for Negro Rural Schools, 1915–17, Alabama Department of Education Records.

33. Woodson, "Story of the Fund," folder 2, box 76, series I, Rosenwald Papers, chap. 5, 8.

34. "Report of M. H. Griffin, State Supervisor Teacher-Training and Rosenwald Fund Agent for Alabama," July 1922, folder "M. H. Griffin," SG 15466, Rural School Agent Correspondence, Alabama Department of Education Records.

35. "Vinegar Bend Dedicated Rosenwald School," *Mobile (Ala.) Forum*, 13 October 1922, Tuskegee Clippings Files; see also "Program of the Dedication of Eastern Shore Industrial School, Daphne, Alabama," SG 15450, Rural School Agent Correspondence, Alabama Department of Education Records.

36. Hawkins, "Rosenwald Schools: The Chicago Connection," 20–21. I am grateful to Rev. Dr. Bruce Jackson and the members of the Shiloh AME congregation for allowing me to visit with them and see the Shiloh School.

37. Carbaugh, "Philanthropic Confluence," 96; "Progress of Negro Education"; "Report of Mrs. Mary F. Mitchell"; "Henry County Shows Commendable Progress"; Gordon, "Fifty-two Years of Public Service," in Mississippi Retired Teachers Association, *Bells Are Ringing*, 127.

38. Jarrette, *Julius Rosenwald*, 22–24.

39. T. Calloway et al., *Survey of Colored Public Schools*.

40. Davis to Smith, 24 March 1927, folder 1, box 331, Rosenwald Fund Archives.

41. Prater to Lambert, 29 April 1919, folder "P," SG 15454, Rural School Agent Correspondence, Alabama Department of Education Records.

42. Dixon to Harris, 2 March 1931, folder "Vincent H. Harris," unit 1, series 62, Correspondence Relating to Funding Programs, Division of Negro Education, Georgia Department of Education Records.

43. "Betts Chapel, Texas."

44. Savage, "Julius Rosenwald Fund," 18.

45. Favrot to Jones, 19 March 1923, Superintendent's Records, 1904–23, Louisiana Department of Education Records; see also Bernard, "The Julius Rosenwald Fund in Tennessee," folder 2, box 76, Julius Rosenwald Fund Archives; "Annual Report of the State Superintendent of the State of South Carolina," 1922, *Reports and Resolutions*, 176; "Annual Report of the State Superintendent of the State of South Carolina," 1930, *Reports and Resolutions*, 3; Leake, "Survey of the Negro Public Schools," 67; "Negro Education," *Biennial Report* [Florida], 1925–26, 224; Dixon to Credle, 13 October 1931, folder "WF Credle," unit 1, series 62, Correspondence Relating to Funding Programs, Division of Negro Education, Georgia Department of Education Records.

46. Favrot to Sibley, 23 April 1918, SG 15450, Rural School Agent Correspondence, Alabama Department of Education Records.

47. Bullock, *History of Negro Education*; McMillen, *Dark Journey*; Litwack, *Trouble in Mind*; Hahn, *Nation under Our Feet*, 278–80.

48. Smith to Credle, 10 December 1921, Credle to Smith, 13 December 1921, folder "1921 General Field Agent for Rural Schools S. L. Smith," box 86, General Correspondence, Office of the Superintendent, North Carolina Department of Public Instruction Records; Credle to Smith, 3 February 1923, folder "1923 General Field Agent for Rural Schools S. L. Smith," box 87, General Correspondence, Office of the Superintendent, North Carolina Department of Public Instruction Records.

49. S. Smith, *Builders of Goodwill*, 122–25.

50. Tolnay and Beck argue that competition over economic resources was also a fundamental cause of lynching in the New South in *Festival of Violence*. "Negro School Burns," *Montgomery (Ala.) Advertiser*, 22 September 1924, Tuskegee Clippings Files; Alena E. Wiley, Willie M. Robinson, Helen Nunn, and Sara Patton, *Blytheville/Mississippi County Black Culture Sesquicentennial Scrapbook* (n.p., 1986), 57, folder 34, box 2, Sykes Collection; list of Arkansas Rosenwald schools, folder 3, box 337, Rosenwald Fund Archives.

51. S. Smith quoted in Woodson, "The Story of the Fund," chap. 5, 10–12. Smith published a rather different account of the Wilson School in 1950, attributing the fire to workmen who dropped lighted cigarettes. However, this description of the Wilson School comes in a summary of the presentation he gave to white civic clubs and educators in Helena, Arkansas, calling for the construction of a new African American school at Elaine, the site of a violent racial clash in 1919. He had been cautioned "not to rekindle the flame of unrest which had been smothered temporarily by a realization that the children were being denied of a proper education," which may have tempered his account. S. Smith, *Builders of Goodwill*, 132–38.

52. "Report of O. H. Bernard, State Rural Agent for Tennessee," March 1924, folder 7, box 270, Tennessee Commissioner of Education Records.

53. Smith to Foreman, 18 May 1931, folder 5, box 339, Rosenwald Fund Archives;

see also C. J. Calloway to J. S. Lambert, 3 September 1919, Wilburn to Lambert, 6 September 1919, SG 15452, Rural School Agent Correspondence, Alabama Department of Education Records.

54. Brown to Rosenwald, 20 February 1926, folder 3, box 34, series I, Rosenwald Papers.

55. For additional biographical information and analysis, see Haley, *Charles N. Hunter*; E. Lewis, "Invoking Concepts." Rumors of alcoholism, for which there is no documentation, may have dogged Hunter's educational career.

56. Hunter to O'Kelly, 6 December 1913, Royster to Hunter, 17 December 1913, Newbold to Hunter, 31 March 1914, Judd to Hunter, 23 June 1914, folder "1913–1914," box 4, Correspondence, Hunter Papers.

57. My thanks to Nyoni Collins, executive director of the Sankofa Center for Black Family and Community History, Durham, North Carolina, for pointing out the connection to Washington's earlier contact with O'Kelly.

58. Hunter to Washington, 2 July 1914; Newbold to Hunter, 4 July 1914; Washington to Hunter, 7 July 1914; Washington to Berry O'Kelly, 7 July 1914; Washington to Judd, 17 July 1914; Judd to Hunter, 20 July 1914; Washington to Hunter, 23 October 1914; multiple copies of solicitation letters, responses, and thank-you letters, 1914, all in folder "1913–1914," box 4, Correspondence, Hunter Papers; Hunter to Washington, 2 July 1914, Washington to Hunter, 7 July 1914, folder "Rosenwald School Fund 1914 H-K"; Newbold to Julius Rosenwald, 3 July 1914; Joyner to Rosenwald, 3 July 1914; Graves to Newbald [*sic*], 6 July 1914; Berry O'Kelly to Washington, 2 July 1914; Judd, Joyner, and Newbold, "To Whom It May Concern," 7 July 1914; O'Kelly to "My Dear Sir," 15 July 1914, all in folder "Rosenwald School Fund 1914, L-O," box 812, Donation File, Tuskegee Records, Washington Papers, microfilm reel 607. Newbold's 4 July letter to Hunter indicates that he had seen an advance copy of Hunter's letter, suggesting that Hunter was the unnamed person who, Newbold had told Rosenwald on 3 July, had brought the *New York Age* article to his attention.

59. Hunter to Moore, 10 August 1915, folder "1915," box 4, Correspondence, Hunter Papers.

60. Giles to Haywood, 26 June 1916, Hunter to Giles, 7 July 1916, Hunter to Dillard, 9 December 1916, Newbold to Hunter, 20 December 1916, Hunter to Giles, 25 December 1916, folder "1916," O'Kelly to Hunter, 7 August 1917, folder "1917," box 5, Correspondence, Hunter Papers. Hunter spent the war years working variously as a newspaper editor, an agent of the Food Administration, and a workman at the Norfolk naval yard.

61. Correspondence between Hunter, Newbold, and Robinson, Merrit to Hunter, 7 June 1922, folder "1921, Oct.–1922, June"; Newbold to Hunter, 19 February 1923, Thompson to Hunter, 26 February 1923, folder "1922, July–1923, June," "The Haywood School Building Fund" attached to Dudley to Hunter, 26 January 1923, folder "1922,

July–1923, June," box 7, and form for the Berry O'Kelly School, undated folders, box 11, Correspondence, Hunter Papers.

62. Hunter to School Committee, 12 September 1923; undated essays "Self help," "Dedication of Our School Building," and "A County Teacher Training and Industrial School," folder "1923, July–Dec.," box 7, Correspondence, Hunter Papers.

63. Newbold to Hunter, 8 October 1923, folder "1923, July–Dec.," box 7, Correspondence, Hunter Papers; King to Hunter, 14 September 1925, folder "1925," box 8, Correspondence, Hunter Papers.

64. Moore, "Report, Rosenwald Schoolhouse Building for North Carolina," March 1919, folder 335, box 50, General Correspondence, Moton Papers; December 1925 and January 1926 correspondence between Hunter, Newbold, and Credle, folder "H," box 2, Correspondence of the Supervisor of the Rosenwald Fund, North Carolina Department of Public Instruction Records.

65. King to Hunter, 4 June 1926, Hunter to Marrow, 5 June 1926 and 22 June 1926; Marrow to Hunter, 1 September 1926, "Negroes to Have New School Building," *Smithfield (N.C.) Herald*, 29 December 1925, Tuskegee Clippings Files.

66. Chesnutt to Hunter, 12 October 1926, Frobins to Hunter, 20 December 1926, folder "1926," box 8, Correspondence, Hunter Papers; correspondence between Hunter, Newbold, and Allen, Hunter to Bowley, 25 March 1927, folder "1927," box 9, Correspondence, Hunter Papers; October and November 1926 correspondence between Hunter and Credle, folder "H," box 3, Correspondence of the Supervisor of the Rosenwald Fund, Division of Negro Education, North Carolina Department of Public Instruction Records. Both Moore and Davis had participated in rallies for the Raeford School in 1920. Moore, "Report, Rosenwald Schoolhouse Building for North Carolina," January 1920, folder 340c, box 51, General Correspondence, Moton Papers; "Report of G. E. Davis, Rosenwald Building Agent for North Carolina," October 1920, detail 2, folder "Rosenwald Fund—G. E. Davis Reports," box 8, Special Subject File, Division of Negro Education, North Carolina Department of Public Instruction Records.

67. O'Kelly to Hunter, 9 April 1928, folder "1928," box 9, Correspondence, Hunter Papers.

68. The undated materials probably were from 1930 or 1931. North Carolina's Rosenwald School Day booklet included "A Short Story of Our Local School," and the Jones School history probably was prepared for use at that point of the day's events. Unidentified teacher, "Jones School," and C. N. Hunter, "Rosenwald Day at Jones' School," undated folders, box 12, Hunter Papers; *Rosenwald School Day Program*, N.C., 1929, 22.

69. Comparable discussions for other states can be found in Franklin and Savage, *Cultural Capital*. Hanchett, "Rosenwald Schools"; Cecelski, *Along Freedom Road*; Siddle Walker, *Their Highest Potential*; Reed, *Brevard Rosenwald School*. The Fairmont Chapter of Rosenwald Alumni meets monthly in Fairmont, North Carolina. My

thanks to member Robert Delane Shaw for the chapter's 2002 calendar. The Rosenwald Schools Community Project spearheaded by Nyoni Collins has been underway for several years; for its partnership with the North Carolina State Historic Preservation Office, see Brown, *Survey of North Carolina's Rosenwald Schools*, and with the National Trust for Historic Preservation, see [Collins], "Remembering the Rosenwalds in Robeson County: An Oral History," in Hoffschwelle, *Preserving Rosenwald Schools*.

70. Woofter and Fisher, *Cooperation in Southern Communities*, 7; Stitely, "Bridging the Gap," 21.

Conclusion. From Model Schools to Historic Schools: Rosenwald Schools after 1932

1. Harris, "Monthly Report of Rosenwald Building Agent," June 1932, folder "Vincent Harris, Reports," unit 1, series 62, Division of Negro Education, Georgia Department of Education Records.

2. J. Anderson, *Education of Blacks*, 179–84.

3. Tolnay, *Bottom Rung*, 44–46; Fairclough, *Race and Democracy*, 11–12; Fairclough, "'Being in the Field,'" 73.

4. Strong et al., "Leveraging the State"; Donohue, Heckman, and Todd, "Schooling of Southern Blacks."

5. McCuistion joined the staff of the Southern Association of Colleges and Secondary Schools as the executive officer of the Committee on Approval of Negro Schools, and Credle returned to the North Carolina Department of Public Instruction in its schoolhouse planning division.

6. Dixon to Smith, 24 February 1933, folder "JC Dixon," unit 1, series 62, Division of Negro Education, Georgia Department of Education Records.

7. The superintendents neglected to mention the matching contributions from black school patrons that made the Rosenwald grants "substantial." Resolutions attached to Williams to Dixon, 4 September 1936, folder "Florida," unit 1, series 14, Division of Negro Education, Georgia Department of Education Records. For more requests, see below and other letters dated 1933–38 in folder 3, box 331, Rosenwald Fund Archives.

8. Newbold to Smith, 11 February 1933, folder "S," box 11, General Correspondence of the Director, Division of Negro Education, North Carolina Department of Public Instruction Records; Smith to Simmons, 27 November 1933, folder "JC Dixon," unit 1, series 62, Division of Negro Education, Georgia Department of Education Records; see also Williams, *Improvement of School Houses*, 8–9, 11–13,15–19; *Rosenwald School Day Program*, Mississippi, 1935, 14, folder "Rosenwald Fund (Julius Rosenwald)," Subject Files, Rosenwald School Records, Mississippi Department of Education Records; *Rosenwald School Day Program*, Oklahoma, 1934, 14.

9. Easom to Embree, Smith, and Alexander, 2 February 1935, Embree to Easom, 5 February 1935, folder 3, box 331, Rosenwald Fund Archives. Akridge was also working on a Ph.D. from Teachers College, Columbia University.

10. Smith to Cousins, 9 December 1933, folder "JC Dixon," unit 1, series 62, Division of Negro Education, Georgia Department of Education Records; *Suggestions for Repairing*; *Suggestions for Improvement*; "Annual Report of the State Superintendent of the State of South Carolina," in *Reports and Resolutions*, 1933, 30.

11. See the materials in folder 2, box 332, and folders 6 and 7, box 336, Rosenwald Fund Archives. Two of the rehabilitated schools were the Loachapoka and Notasulga schools in Alabama, which had been among the original six experimental Tuskegee Rosenwald schools. The Notasulga School still stands.

12. *Improvement and Beautification*; *Suggestions for Landscaping*; S. Smith, *Stimulation and Demonstration*; S. Smith, "Progress in Schoolhouse Construction." Edwin R. Embree explained that school plant improvement was an integral part of the countywide demonstrations of the Rosenwald Fund's Council on Rural Education in the late 1930s, although he was much more upset about rote learning than the school environment in *Little Red Schoolhouse Southern Style*, 2–4, 23; see also Embree, *Every Tenth Pupil*.

13. S. Smith, *Stimulation and Demonstration*; Smith to Dixon, 8 November 1934, folder "Loose Papers Found Together," unit 1, and multiple folders on school plant contests in unit 3, series 62, Division of Negro Education, Georgia Department of Education Records; photographs, "Stevens High School before spring beautification program" and "N.Y.A. Agricultural Trainee project," folder 7, box 2, Leffall Memorial Collection; "School Buildings—Improvement"; *School Plant Improvement, Public Forums*.

14. Dixon to Easom, 18 February 1935, Easom to Dixon, 26 February 1935, folder "P. H. Easom, Jackson, Miss.," R. L. Cousins to E. A. Duke, 23 March 1937, folder "Oklahoma," unit 1, series 14, Division of Negro Education, Georgia Department of Education Records.

15. Cousins to Smith, 10 September 1938, folder "JC Dixon," unit 1, series 62, Division of Negro Education, Georgia Department of Education Records.

16. "New Hope," in *Retrospective Glances*.

17. A. B. Hardy, "Jasper County Agricultural High School."

18. Embree to Smith, 24 November 1934, folder 32, box 105, Rosenwald Fund Archives.

19. Smith's claim that Roosevelt's experiences with the Eleanor Roosevelt School in Warm Springs influenced his decision to include school buildings in the WPA's mandate seems exaggerated. S. Smith, *Builders of Goodwill*, 72–84. Additional material on the Warm Springs school project, including Smith's landscaping plan, can be found in folder "Loose Papers Found Together," unit 1, series 62, Division of Negro Education, Georgia Department of Education Records. See also [Cyriaque], "Last Rosenwald School."

20. Woodson, "Story of the Fund," chap. 10, 1; Mississippi Education Association, "Report of the Committee on Improvement of Negro Education," 28 March 1940,

3, folder 12, box 146, Rosenwald Fund Archives; Meece, "Negro Education in Kentucky."

21. "Negro Education," *Annual Report* [Virginia], 1932–33, 72–73.

22. Smith became provost in charge of public relations at George Peabody College for Teachers. Alfred K. Stern had already left the Chicago office in 1935, and he remained on the board of trustees until 1937.

23. Smith to Cousins, 28 December 1937, Cousins to Smith, 10 September 1938, folder "JC Dixon," unit 1, and materials in folder "Hamon, Ray L.," unit 2, series 62, Division of Negro Education, Georgia Department of Education Records.

24. *Community Units*; *Community School Plans*, 1944. Funding for the 1944 plan book came from the General Education Board through a grant by the American Council on Education.

25. Beech, "Schools for a Minority."

26. Carbaugh, "Philanthropic Confluence," 103–4.

27. Donohue, Heckman, and Todd, "Schooling of Southern Blacks," 11.

Bibliography

UNPUBLISHED PRIMARY SOURCES

Alabama Department of Education Records. Alabama Department of Archives and History, Montgomery.

Beasley, David. Interview by Paul Ortiz. Tuskegee, Alabama. 12 July 1994. From "Behind the Veil: Documenting African-American Life in the Jim Crow South." Center for Documentary Studies at Duke University. Rare Book, Manuscript, and Special Collections Library, Duke University, Durham, North Carolina.

Calloway, Clinton J. Papers. University Archives and Museums, Tuskegee University, Tuskegee, Alabama.

Dresslar, Fletcher B. Papers. Special Collections and University Archives, Jean and Alexander Heard Library, Vanderbilt University, Nashville.

Felton Training School Records. South Carolina State University Historical Collection, Orangeburg.

General Education Board Archives. Rockefeller Archive Center, Sleepy Hollow, New York.

Georgia Department of Education Records. Georgia Department of Archives and History, Atlanta.

Howard, Helen. Interview by Doris G. Dixon. Cotton Plant, Arkansas. 19 July 1995. From "Behind the Veil: Documenting African-American Life in the Jim Crow South." Center for Documentary Studies at Duke University. Rare Book, Manuscript, and Special Collections Library, Duke University, Durham, North Carolina.

Hunter, Charles N. Papers. Rare Book, Manuscript, and Special Collections Library, Duke University, Durham, North Carolina.

J. C. Corbin School, Photographs 5357.24–26. Arkansas History Commission, Little Rock.

Jefferson County School Board Records, 1914–64. Florida State Archives, Tallahassee.

Johnson, Ruth. Interview by Rhonda Mawhood. Tillery, North Carolina. 25 June 1993. From "Behind the Veil: Documenting African-American Life in the Jim Crow South." Center for Documentary Studies at Duke University. Rare Book, Manuscript, and Special Collections Library, Duke University, Durham, North Carolina.

Jones, J. S. Vertical file. University Archives, John C. Cade Library, Southern University, Scotlandville, Louisiana.

Julius Rosenwald Fund Archives. Special Collections, John Hope and Aurelia E. Franklin Library, Fisk University, Nashville.

Kentucky Department of Education Records. Kentucky Department for Libraries and Archives, Frankfort.

Lefall, Martha Jordan. Memorial Collection. Southeastern Regional Black Archives Research Center and Museum, Florida Agricultural & Mechanical University, Tallahassee.

Louisiana Department of Education Records. Louisiana State Archives, Baton Rouge.

Merritt, Jenyethel. Jeanes Teacher Collection. Southeastern Regional Black Archives Research Center and Museum, Florida Agricultural & Mechanical University, Tallahassee.

Mississippi Department of Education Records. Mississippi Department of Archives and History, Jackson.

Moton, Robert Russa. Papers. University Archives and Museums, Tuskegee University, Tuskegee, Alabama.

Newbold, Nathan Carter. Papers. Rare Book, Manuscript, and Special Collections Library, Duke University, Durham, North Carolina.

North Carolina Department of Public Instruction Records. North Carolina State Archives, Raleigh.

Oklahoma Department of Education Publications. Oklahoma State Archives, Oklahoma City.

Porter, Gilbert. Florida State Teachers Association Collection. Southeastern Regional Black Archives Research Center and Museum, Florida Agricultural & Mechanical University, Tallahassee.

Randolph, L. M. Interview by Paul Ortiz. Tuskegee, Alabama. 12 July 1994. From "Behind the Veil: Documenting African-American Life in the Jim Crow South." Center for Documentary Studies at Duke University. Rare Book, Manuscript, and Special Collections Library, Duke University, Durham, North Carolina.

Rennolds, William Gregory. Papers, 1906–47. Personal Papers Collection, Library of Virginia, Richmond.

Rogers, Mary. Interview by Karen Ferguson. Enfield, North Carolina. 1 July 1993. From "Behind the Veil: Documenting African-American Life in the Jim Crow South." Center for Documentary Studies at Duke University. Rare Book, Manuscript, and Special Collections Library, Duke University, Durham, North Carolina.

Rosenwald, Julius. Papers. Special Collections Research Center, Joseph Regenstein Library, University of Chicago, Chicago, Illinois.

Scarborough, George, Jr. Interview by Chris Stewart and Kara Miles. Durham, North Carolina. 27 May 1993. From "Behind the Veil: Documenting African-American Life in the Jim Crow South." Center for Documentary Studies at Duke University. Rare Book, Manuscript, and Special Collections Library, Duke University, Durham, North Carolina.

Southern Education Foundation Records. Atlanta University Center Archives, Atlanta, Georgia.

Stewart, Ada Mae. Interview by Tunga White. Moultrie, Georgia. 6 July 1994. From "Behind the Veil: Documenting African-American Life in the Jim Crow South." Center for Documentary Studies at Duke University. Rare Book, Manuscript, and Special Collections Library, Duke University, Durham, North Carolina.

Sykes, Curtis. Collection of Black History Materials, 1931–68. Arkansas History Commission, Little Rock. Microfilm.

Tennessee Commissioner of Education Records. Tennessee State Library and Archives, Nashville. Microfilm.

Union County Board of Education. Papers, 1907–39. South Carolina Archives, Columbia.

Washington, Booker T. Papers. Manuscript Division, Library of Congress, Washington, D.C. Microfilm.

Williams, Oliver. Interview by Doris Dixon. Cotton Plant, Arkansas. 21 July 1994. From "Behind the Veil: Documenting African-American Life in the Jim Crow South." Center for Documentary Studies at Duke University. Rare Book, Manuscript, and Special Collections Library, Duke University, Durham, North Carolina.

Wills, Almyra. Interview by Rhonda Mawhood. Whitakers, North Carolina. 30 June 1993. From "Behind the Veil: Documenting African-American Life in the Jim Crow South." Center for Documentary Studies at Duke University. Rare Book, Manuscript, and Special Collections Library, Duke University, Durham, North Carolina.

PUBLISHED PRIMARY SOURCES

Adams and Alsup, Architects. *Plans and Specifications for Public School Buildings.* Prepared for the Tennessee Superintendent of Public Instruction. [Nashville: 1907].

"Addresses at the Conference on What White People Can Do to Promote Negro Education." *George Peabody College for Teachers Bulletin* 19, no. 8 (October 1930).

Alabama State Department of Education. *Annual Report for Scholastic Year.* 1913–20.

———. *Rural Schoolhouses and Grounds.* Bulletin 52. Montgomery: Brown Printing, 1916.

Annual Report of the Department of Education to the General Assembly of the State of Georgia. 1911–24.

Annual Report of the State Board of Education Showing Condition of the Public Schools of Maryland. 1912–21.

Annual Report of the State Superintendent of Public Instruction of Tennessee. 1921–22.

Annual Report of the Superintendent of Public Instruction for the Commonwealth of Virginia. 1913/14–1932/33.

Annual Reports of the Department of Education to the General Assembly of the State of Georgia for the Biennium. 1923/24–1931/32.

Arkansas Division of Negro Education. *Rosenwald School Day in Arkansas.* Little Rock: Central Printing, [1930].

Arkansas Rosenwald Day and School Improvement Day. [Little Rock: Arkansas Department of Education, 1937].

Barker, Tommie Dora. *Rosenwald Library Demonstrations in the South*. American Library Association, 1932.

Barrett and Thomson, Architects. *Plans for Public School Houses*. Prepared for the State Superintendent of Public Instruction. Raleigh, N.C.: Edwards and Broughton, 1903, 1914.

Beech, Gould. "Schools for a Minority." *Survey Graphic* 28, no. 10 (October 1939): 615. *The New Deal Network*. http://www.newdeal/feri.org/survey/39b15.htm.

Biennial Report of the State Superintendent of Public Instruction. 1879/80–1919/20. State Records, Arkansas History Commission, Little Rock. Microfilm.

Biennial Report of the State Superintendent of Public Instruction. Oklahoma City: Oklahoma State Board of Education, 1917/18–1927/28.

Biennial Report of the Superintendent of Public Instruction of Kentucky. Frankfort: State Journal Company, 1924–25.

Biennial Report of the Superintendent of Public Instruction of North Carolina. Raleigh: Edwards and Broughton Printing, [1912].

Biennial Report of the Superintendent of Public Instruction of the State of Florida. Tallahassee: T. J. Appleyard, State Printer, 1911/12–1928/30.

Biennial Report of the State Superintendent of Public Instruction, State of Texas, 1916–18. Austin: State Board of Education, [1918].

Blanton, Annie Webb. *A Handbook of Information as to Education in Texas, 1918–1922*. Bulletin 157. Austin: Texas Department of Education, 1923.

Blanton, Annie Webb, and L. D. Borden. *School Grounds, School Buildings, and Their Equipment*. Bulletin 148. [Austin]: Texas Department of Education, 1922.

Bludworth, G. T. "Negro Training Schools." *Texas Outlook* 15, no. 4 (April 1931): 22.

———. "The Rosenwald Fund in Texas." *Texas Outlook* 12, no. 2 (February 1928): 52.

———. "Rosenwald School Day Program." *Texas Outlook* 12, no. 6 (June 1929): 36–37.

"Boris Morros and Alfred K. Stern Connections to other KGB Personnel." 4 January 1945. *The VENONA Documents*. http://www.nsa.gov/dos/venona/docs/Jan45/04_Jan_1945_R3_m1_p1.gif.

Brinckloe, William Draper. "Planning the Schoolhouse in War-Time." *American School Board Journal* 56, no. 2 (February 1918): 27–28.

Burrage, Severance, and Henry Turner Bailey. *School Sanitation and Decoration*. Boston: D. C. Heath, 1899.

Calloway, Clinton J. "Co-Operative School Building." In *National Cyclopedia of the Colored Race*, edited by Clement Richardson, 569–70. Montgomery, Ala.: National Publishing, 1919.

Calloway, Thomas J., George D. Brown, Ignatius Mitchell, and Isaiah Gray. *A Survey of Colored Public Schools of Prince George's County, Maryland.* Trustees' Association, [1924].

Carney, Mabel. *Country Life and the Country School: A Study of the Agencies of Rural Progress and of the Social Relationship of the School to the Country Community.* Chicago: Row, Peterson, 1912.

Chapman, J. Virgil, and Mrs. V. O. Gilbert. *School Architecture, Kentucky.* Bulletin 10, no. 2. Frankfort: Kentucky Department of Education, [1917].

Chase, C. Thurston. *A Manual on School-houses and Cottages for the People of the South.* Washington, D.C.: Government Printing Office, 1868.

Child Welfare in Tennessee. [Nashville]: National Child Labor Committee for the Tennessee Child Welfare Commission, 1920.

Clark, J. S. "Colored Education." *Southern School Work* 7 (April 1919): 424–25.

———. "The New Normal School." *Southern School Work* 7 (December 1919): 160.

Community School Plans. Nashville: Julius Rosenwald Fund, 1921.

———. Bulletin 3. Rev. ed. Nashville: Julius Rosenwald Fund, 1927.

———. Rev. ed. Nashville: Julius Rosenwald Fund, 1928.

———. Rev. ed. Nashville: Julius Rosenwald Fund Southern Office, 1931.

———. Nashville: Interstate School Building Service, George Peabody College for Teachers, 1944.

Community Units. Supplement no. 2 to Julius Rosenwald Fund *Community School Plans* (1931). Nashville: Interstate School Building Service, George Peabody College for Teachers, 1941.

Cook, George B. "The Rejuvenation of the Rural Community." *Proceedings of the Forty-fifth Annual Session of the Arkansas State Teachers' Association.* Little Rock: H. G. Pugh Printing, 1912.

Cooper, Frank Irving. "Economies Gained in Standardizing Schoolhouse Plans." *American School Board Journal* 59, no. 8 (August 1919): 34–36, 89–90.

———. "Hygienic Problems in Schoolhouse Construction." Pts. 1 and 2. *American School Board Journal* 59, no. 11 (November 1919): 37–38, 101, 103; 59, no. 12 (December 1919): 40, 99.

———. *Report of Committee on School House Planning.* Washington, D.C.: National Education Association, 1925.

———. "The Standardization of Schoolhouses." *American School Board Journal* 56, no. 6 (June 1918): 28–30.

Cubberley, Ellwood P. *Rural Life and Education: A Study of the Rural-School Problem as a Phase of the Rural-Life Problem.* Boston: Houghton Mifflin, 1914.

"DeWitt County Schools." *Texas Outlook* 11, no. 3 (March 1927): 52.

Dickerman, G. S. "Rural Negro Education: Thirty-seven Years in One Georgia School." *Atlanta University Bulletin*, 2nd ser., no. 66 (December 1926): 4–14.

Dresslar, Fletcher B. *American Schoolhouses.* U.S. Bureau of Education Bulletin 5. Washington, D.C.: Government Printing Office, 1911.

———. "The Hygiene of Rural Schools." In *Journal of Proceedings and Addresses of the Fiftieth Annual Meeting of the National Education Association,* 1106–10. Chicago: University of Chicago Press, 1912.

———. *Report on the Rosenwald School Buildings.* Bulletin 1. Nashville: Julius Rosenwald Fund, 1920.

———. *Rural Schoolhouses and Grounds.* U.S. Bureau of Education Bulletin 12. Washington, D.C.: Government Printing Office, 1914.

Dresslar, Fletcher B., and Haskell Pruett. *Rural School-Houses, School Grounds, and Their Equipment.* Bulletin 12. Washington, D.C.: Government Printing Office, 1930.

Duke, E. A. *A Guide to Better Schools.* Oklahoma City: Oklahoma Superintendent of Public Instruction, 1916.

———. *Rosenwald School Day Program, March 6, 1931.* Bulletin 121–B. Oklahoma City: Oklahoma State Department of Education, 1931.

———. *Rosenwald School Day Program, March 2, 1934.* Bulletin 121-E. Oklahoma City: Oklahoma State Department of Education, 1934.

"Education." *Crisis* (August 1914): 176; (September 1914): 216–17.

An Educational Study of Alabama. U.S. Bureau of Education Bulletin no. 41. Washington, D.C.: Government Printing Office, 1919.

"Education Is Chiefly a State Function. Therefore, Schoolhouse Construction Should Be Controlled by the State!" *American School Board Journal* 52, no. 4 (April 1916): cover illustration.

Edwards, William J. *Twenty-five Years in the Black Belt.* Boston: Cornhill Company, 1918. Reprint, Tuscaloosa: University of Alabama Press, 1993.

Embree, Edwin R. *Every Tenth Pupil: The Story of Negro Schools in the South* [Chicago]: Julius Rosenwald Fund, [1934]. Reprinted from *Survey Graphic* 23 (November 1934): 538–41.

———. "How Negro Schools Have Advanced under the Rosenwald Fund." *Nation's Schools* 1, no. 5 (May 1928): 37–44.

———. *Julius Rosenwald Fund: A Review to June 30, 1928.* Chicago: [Julius Rosenwald Fund], 1928.

———. *Julius Rosenwald Fund: A Review to June 30, 1929.* Chicago: [Julius Rosenwald Fund], 1929.

———. *Julius Rosenwald Fund: Review for the Two-Year Period 1931–1933.* [Chicago: Julius Rosenwald Fund], 1933.

———. *Julius Rosenwald Fund: Review for the Two-Year Period 1944–1946.* [Chicago: Julius Rosenwald Fund], 1946.

———. *Julius Rosenwald Fund: Review of Two Decades, 1917–1936.* Chicago: Julius Rosenwald Fund, 1936.

————. *Little Red Schoolhouse, Southern Style*. [Chicago]: Julius Rosenwald Fund, 1938. Reprinted from *Atlantic Monthly* 160 (November 1937): 636–43.

Favrot, Leo M. *Aims and Needs in Negro Public Education in Louisiana*. Bulletin 2. Baton Rouge: Louisiana State Department of Education, 1918.

————. "Needs of Negro Schools and How to Attain Them." *Southern School Work* 7 (January 1918): 248–50.

————. "Negro Public Education." *Louisiana School Work* 5 (February 1917): 247–48.

————. *Report of Special Activities in Negro Education in Louisiana, Session 1919–20*. Bulletin 14. Baton Rouge: Louisiana Department of Education, 1920.

[Favrot]. *Rosenwald Negro Rural Schools in Louisiana 1917 and 1918*. [Baton Rouge: Louisiana Department of Education, 1919?].

Favrot, Leo M., and A. C. Lewis. *Report on Special Activities in Negro Education in Louisiana, Session 1920–21*. Bulletin 18. Baton Rouge: Louisiana Department of Education, 1921.

————. *Report on Special Activities in Negro Education in Louisiana, Session 1921–22*. Bulletin 100. Baton Rouge: Louisiana Department of Education, 1922.

Felton, J. B. "Conference of State Agents for Negro Rural Schools, Nashville, Tenn., January 5–6, 1921." *South Carolina Education* 2, no. 5 (15 February 1921): 19–20.

————. "Rosenwald School Building Program in South Carolina." *South Carolina Education* 7, no. 7 (April 1926): 274.

————. "W. A. Schiffley." *South Carolina Education* 7, no. 1 (October 1925): 24.

Field Force Reports. Educational Bulletin vols. 1–3. Baton Rouge: Louisiana Department of Education, 1914–18.

Gardner, E. C. *Town and Country School Buildings*. New York: E. L. Kellogg, 1888.

The General Education Board: An Account of Its Activities, 1902–1914. New York: General Education Board, 1915.

The General Education Board Archives: The Early Southern Program. New York: Rockefeller University, 1993; distributed by Scholarly Resources. Microfilm.

Gresham, W. D. "Working Together for the Negro Children of Virginia." *Virginia Teachers' Bulletin* 7, no. 1 (February 1931): 7.

Hamilton, W. A. "Radio in City Park School." *Texas Outlook* 14, no. 5 (May 1930): 56.

Hardy, A. B. "Jasper County Agricultural High School." *Mississippi Educational Journal* 14 (February 1938): 95.

Harlan, Louis R., Raymond W. Smock, Geraldine McTigue, Susan Valenza, Sadie M. Harlan, and Nan E. Woodruff, eds. *The Booker T. Washington Papers*, vols. 10–13. Urbana: University of Illinois Press, 1981–84.

Harris, T. H. "Negro Public Education." *Southern School Work* 7 (November 1918): 131–34.

"Henry County Shows Commendable Progress." *Virginia Teachers' Bulletin* 9, no. 3 (May 1932): 13.

"How to Get Aid from the J.R.F." *KNEA Journal* 1, no. 3 (February 1931): 9.

Improvement and Beautification of Rural Schools: Report of Committee on School Plan Rehabilitation. Nashville: Julius Rosenwald Fund Southern Office, 1936.

In Memoriam: Julius Rosenwald, 1862–1932. Raleigh, N.C.: State Superintendent of Public Instruction, [1932].

Interstate School Building Service. *For Better School Buildings.* Nashville: Interstate School Building Service, 1929.

Ittner, William B. "School Building Policies and the War, and Standardization of School Buildings." *American School Board Journal* 55, no. 9 (September 1917): 23–24.

The Jackson Davis Collection of African American Educational Photographs. Albert and Shirley Small Special Collections Library, University of Virginia, Charlottesville, Virginia. http://www.lib.virginia.edu/small/collections/jdavis/.

"The John G. Fee Industrial High School." *KNEA Journal* 1, no. 2 (December 1930): 10–11.

Jones, J. S. "Educational Value of the Rosenwald School." *Southern School Work* 8 (April 1920): 335–36.

———. "Rosenwald Schools in Louisiana." *Southern School Work* 7 (May 1919): 450–51.

———. "Rosenwald School Work in Louisiana." *Southern School Work* 7 (December 1919): 160–61.

"Julius Rosenwald Fund." *Crisis* 33, no. 2 (December 1926): 79–81.

"Kenbridge Graded School." *Virginia Teachers' Bulletin* 5, no. 4 (November 1928): 13.

King, Beverly S. "School Architecture as an Influence." *American School Board Journal* 46, no. 1 (January 1913): 17–21.

Lambert, J. S. "Negro Education in Alabama." *Alabama School Journal* 46 (December 1928): 17, 19, 22.

———. "Some Agencies That Have Aided Negro Education in Alabama." *Alabama School Journal* 49 (December 1931): 19–20.

Lee, R. E. *Rural School Buildings.* Clemson Agricultural College Extension Work Bulletins 10, no. 2 (April 1914).

Lewis, A. C. *Rosenwald School Day Program.* Bulletin 147. Baton Rouge: Louisiana State Department of Education, 1929.

Lewis, A. C., and J. W. Bateman. *Rosenwald-Day Program.* Bulletin 102. Baton Rouge: Louisiana State Department of Education, 1927.

Lewis, A. C., and W. A. Sisemore. *Special Report on Negro Education in Louisiana Session 1923–1924.* Bulletin 104. Baton Rouge: Louisiana State Department of Education, 1924.

"Louisiana Colored Teachers' Association." *Southern School Work* 7 (January 1918): 272–73.

Louisiana Department of Education. *Plans for Public School Buildings.* Baton Rouge: Times Publishing, 1906.

Manual for Georgia Teachers. Atlanta: Georgia State Department of Education, [1912].

———. Atlanta: Georgia State Department of Education, [1916].

Marrs, S.M.N., G. T. Bludworth, and D. B. Taylor. *Negro Education in Texas*. Bulletin 294. Austin: Texas State Department of Education, 1931.

———. *Negro Education in Texas: Special Activities and Industrial Aid*. Bulletin 212. Austin: Texas Department of Education, 1926.

[McCuiston, Fred]. *Financing Schools in the South: Some Data Regarding Sources, Amounts, and Distribution of Public School Revenue in the Southern States*. [Nashville?]: Conference of Directors of Educational Research for Southern States, 1930.

———. *"Me Too": Four Years with the Public Schools in Arkansas*. Little Rock: Arkansas Department of Education, [1927?].

———. *School Money in Black and White*. Chicago: Julius Rosenwald Fund, 1935.

———. *The South's Negro Teaching Force*. Nashville: Julius Rosenwald Fund, 1931.

———. "The South's Negro Teaching Force." *Journal of Negro Education* 1, no. 1 (April 1932): 16–24.

Mills, Wilbur T. *American School Building Standards*. Columbus, Ohio: Franklin Educational Publishing, 1915.

Mississippi Department of Education. *Biennial Report and Recommendations of the State Superintendent of Public Education*. 1925–27.

"Mr. Abrams Writes from Fluvanna County." *Virginia Teachers' Bulletin* 6, no. 2 (March 1929): 16.

"The Negro Common School, Georgia." *Crisis* 32, no. 5 (September 1926): 248–64.

"The Negro Common School, Mississippi." *Crisis* 33, no. 2 (December 1926): 90–102.

"The Negro Common School, North Carolina." *Crisis* 34, no. 3 (May 1927): 79–80, 96–97; no. 4 (June 1927): 117–18, 133–35.

The Negro Rural School and Its Relation to the Community. Tuskegee, Ala.: Tuskegee Normal and Industrial Institute Extension Department, 1915.

"New O.E.A. Officers." *Oklahoma Teacher* 9, no. 1 (September 1927): 13.

Official Report of Educational Survey Commission on the Education of Negroes in Florida. Tallahassee: Florida State Department of Education, [1929?].

"One of Our New City Schools." *KNEA Journal* 2, no. 1 (October-November 1931): cover, 6.

———. *KNEA Journal* 3, no. 1 (October-November 1932): cover.

"One of Our New Rural Buildings." *KNEA Journal* 1, no. 4 (April 1931): cover.

"Paint Colors and Directions for Painting." *Community Schools*. Pamphlet no. 14. Nashville: Julius Rosenwald Fund, 1922.

Plans for Public Schoolhouses. Raleigh, N.C.: E. M. Uzzell, 1914.

Proceedings of the Kentucky Negro Educational Association. 1917–29.

Program for Celebration of Julius Rosenwald Day in Alabama. Montgomery: Division of Education for Negroes, State Department of Education, 1932.

"Progress in Bowie County." *Texas Outlook* 11, no. 12 (December 1927): 27–28.

"Progress of Negro Education in Montgomery County." *Virginia Teachers' Bulletin* 6, no. 2 (March 1929): 18.

Pruett, Haskell. *Rural School Buildings.* [Oklahoma City]: Oklahoma Department of Public Instruction, 1928.

———. "Rural School Buildings for Oklahoma." Master's thesis, University of Oklahoma, 1928.

Rapeer, Louis W. "The One-Story Rural Consolidated Building." *American School Board Journal* 59, no. 9 (September 1919): 3–39, 105.

Report of the Arkansas Rural School Committee. [1916?].

"Report of the Executive Committee." *Virginia Teachers' Bulletin* 3, no. 1 (March 1926): 2–3.

"Report of Mrs. Mary F. Mitchell, Jeanes Agent of Halifax County, South Boston, Virginia." *Virginia Teachers' Bulletin* 7, no. 1 (February 1931): 8.

Reports and Resolutions of the General Assembly of the State of South Carolina. Columbia, S.C.: Gonzales and Bryan, 1906–31.

"Resolutions of Negro State Teachers' Association." *Virginia Teachers' Bulletin* 2, no. 1 (March 1925): 7.

Rosenwald School Day in Arkansas. 1932.

Rosenwald School Day in Georgia. [Atlanta]: State Department of Education and State Teachers and Educational Association, 1930.

———. 1931.

"Rosenwald School Day Issue." *KNEA Journal* 1, no. 3 (February 1931).

Rosenwald School Day Program. Raleigh, N.C.: State Superintendent of Public Instruction, 1929.

———. Bulletin 121–E. Oklahoma City: Oklahoma Department of Education, 1934.

Rosenwald School Day Program, March 7, 1930. Tallahassee, Fla.: T. J. Appleyard, Inc., 1930.

"Rosenwald to Aid Kentucky Schools." *Cleveland Advocate,* 10 August 1918. Ohio Historical Society. *The African-American Experience in Ohio, 1850–1920.* http://dbs.ohiohistory.org/africanam/page1.cfm?ItemID=7428.

"Rural School Architecture." *American School Board Journal* 54, no. 4 (April 1917): 33.

Rural School Houses and Grounds. Bulletin 26. Jackson: Department of Education, State of Mississippi, 1921.

"School Architecture in 1917–18." *American School Board Journal* 56, no. 4 (April 1918): 40.

"School Buildings—Improvement and Beautification Contest." *Tennessee Teacher* 4 (September 1936): 31–32.

"Schoolhouse Plans." *American School Board Journal* 47, no. 10 (October 1913): 22–23.

School Plant Improvement, Public Forums, Negro Education. Bulletin 371. Austin: Texas Department of Education, 1937.

Shop Plans. Bulletin 17. Nashville: Julius Rosenwald Fund, 1927.

Smith, S. L. "Progress in Schoolhouse Construction and Rehabilitation." *Proceedings of the Eighteenth Annual Meeting,* National Council on Schoolhouse Construction, 1940 [1941?], 60–63.

———. *Stimulation and Demonstration in School Plant Rehabilitation.* Nashville: Interstate School Building Service. Reprinted from *American School and University* 11 (1938): 202–8.

Spain, Charles L., Arthur B. Moehlman, and Fred W. Frostic. *The Public Elementary School Plant.* New York: Rand McNally, 1930.

"Standardization of the Rural School Plant." *School and Society* 1, no. 7 (13 February 1915): 217–26.

"Standardized School House Design." Pts. 1 and 2. *American Architect* 114 (6 November 1918): 559–64; 114 (13 November 1918): 589–91.

State Aid and Schoolhouse Planning. Montgomery: Alabama Department of Education, Division of Schoolhouse Planning, 1930.

"Stephens County Makes Rapid Strides." *Texas Outlook* 9, no. 9 (September 1925): 14.

Strayer, G. D., and N. L. Engelhardt. *Report of the Survey of the Schools of Watertown, Massachusetts.* New York: Teachers College, Columbia University Bureau of Publications, 1931.

———. "Score Card for City School Buildings." *Teachers College Bulletin,* 11th ser., no. 10 (17 January 1920).

———. "Score Card for Village and Rural School Buildings of Four Teachers or Less." *Teachers College Bulletin,* 11th ser., no. 9 (3 January 1920).

———. *Standards for Elementary School Buildings.* New York: Teachers College, Columbia University, 1923.

———. *Standards for High School Buildings.* New York: Teachers College, Columbia University, 1924.

"Suggestion for a Rural Social Center Schoolhouse." *American School Board Journal* 54, no. 1 (January 1917): 26.

Suggestions for Improvement and Beautification, School Plants. Nashville: Julius Rosenwald Fund and the Interstate School Building Service, 1934–35.

Suggestions for Landscaping Rural Schools. Nashville: Julius Rosenwald Fund Southern Office, 1936.

Suggestions for Repairing and Repainting School Plants. Nashville: Julius Rosenwald Fund and the Interstate School Building Service, 1933.

Taylor, D. B. "Limestone County Training School." *Texas Outlook* 12, no. 7 (July 1928): 23.

Texas Department of Education. *Consolidation of Rural Schools, School Buildings and Plans, and Local Taxation.* Bulletin 15. Austin: Austin Printing, 1912.

"The Three R's Being Improved in the First Honor Rural School of Cooke County." *Texas Outlook* 11, no. 8 (August 1927): 13–14.

Towne, J. E. "County Library Service of the Julius Rosenwald Fund." In *School and County Library Cooperation*, pamphlet no. 11, edited by Edith A. Lathrop. Washington, D.C.: U.S. Office of Education, 1930.

Trousdale, Fannie Mae. "The Schools of DeSoto Parish." *Southern School Work* 7 (February 1919): 290.

Tuskegee Clippings Files. University Archives and Museums, Tuskegee University, Tuskegee, Alabama.

"Uniformity in Schoolhouse Plans." *American School Board Journal* 48, no. 1 (January 1914): 62.

Virginia State Teachers Association and School Improvement League. *Program and Circular of Information for Rally Day in Colored Schools*. [Richmond: 1914?].

Virginia Teachers' Bulletin 6, no. 2 (March 1929): 15–18.

Washington, Booker T. *My Larger Education: Being Chapters from My Experience*. Garden City, N.Y.: Doubleday, Page, 1911.

———. "The Rural Negro Community." *Annals of the American Academy of Political and Social Science* 40 (March 1912): 81–89.

———. *The Story of My Life and Work: An Autobiography*. Toronto: J. L. Nichols, 1901.

———. *Up from Slavery: An Autobiography*. New York: Doubleday Page, 1901. Reprint, Garden City, N.Y.: Doubleday, 1963.

"Webster County Training School and Rosenwald City High School." *KNEA Journal* 1, no. 3 (February 1931): 16.

Williams, D. E. *March 1, 1929 Rosenwald School Day Program*. Tallahassee, Fla.: T. J. Appleyard, Inc., [1929].

———. *Improvement of School Houses and Beautification of School Grounds for Negroes, 1935 Rosenwald Program*. Tallahassee: Florida Department of Public Instruction, 1935.

———. *Rosenwald School Day Program, March 7, 1930*. Tallahassee, Fla.: T. J. Appleyard, Inc., [1930].

Willis, B. F. "The Ideal Rural School Building." *American School Board Journal* 52, no. 6 (June 1916): 22–26.

Woofter, T. J., Jr., and Isaac Fisher, eds. *Cooperation in Southern Communities: Suggested Activities for County and City Inter-Racial Committees*. Atlanta: Commission on Inter-Racial Cooperation, [1921].

"A Worthy Example." *Texas Outlook* 12, no. 6 (June 1928): 35–36.

A Yearbook on Negro Education in Alabama in 1930–31. Montgomery: Alabama State Teachers Association with cooperation of the Division of Negro Education in the State Department of Education, [1931].

Secondary Sources

Alcorn, Virgie. "Rosenwald Schools." *CEFP Journal* (July-August 1986).

Anderson, Eric, and Alfred A. Moss Jr. *Dangerous Donations: Northern Philanthropy and Southern Black Education, 1902–1930.* Columbia: University of Missouri Press, 1999.

Anderson, James D. *The Education of Blacks in the South, 1860–1935.* Chapel Hill: University of North Carolina Press, 1988.

———. "Ex-Slaves and the Rise of Universal Education in the New South, 1860–1880." In *Education and the Rise of the New South,* edited by Ronald K. Goodenow and Arthur O. White, 1–25. Boston: G. K. Hall, 1981.

———. "Northern Foundations and the Shaping of Southern Black Rural Education, 1902–1935." In *The Social History of American Education,* edited by B. Edward McClellan and William J. Reese, 287–312. Urbana: University of Illinois Press, 1988.

Ascoli, Peter M. "Julius Rosenwald and the Founding of the Museum of Science and Industry." *Journal of Illinois History* 2, no. 3 (Winter 1999): 162–82.

Ayers, Edward L. *The Promise of the New South: Life after Reconstruction.* New York: Oxford University Press, 1992.

Bay, Elaine Nall. *Sand Flat School.* http://txgenes.com/txrains/sandf/htm.

Beadie, Nancy, and Kim Tolley, eds. *Chartered Schools: Two Hundred Years of Independent Academies in the United States, 1727–1925.* New York: RoutledgeFalmer, 2002.

Beilke, Jayne R. "The Changing Emphasis of the Rosenwald Fellowship Program, 1928–1948." *Journal of Negro Education* 66, no. 1 (Winter 1997): 3–15.

———. "'Partners in Distress': Jewish Philanthropy and Black Education during the Progressive Era." *American Educational History Journal* 29, no. 1 (2002): 26–34.

Belles, A. Gilbert. "The Julius Rosenwald Fund: Efforts in Race Relations, 1928–1948." Ph.D. diss., Vanderbilt University, 1972.

"Betts Chapel, Texas." Texas State Historical Association and General Libraries, University of Texas. *The Handbook of Texas Online.* http://www.tsha.utexas.edu/handbook/online/articles/view/BB/hvbbr.html.

"Biographical Sketch of R. C. Childress." *Arkansas Rosenwald Day and School Improvement Day.* [Little Rock: Arkansas Department of Education, 1937].

Bond, Horace Mann. *Negro Education in Alabama: A Study in Cotton and Steel.* Associated Publishers, 1939. Reprint, New York: Octagon Books, 1969.

Bowman, J.G.H. "P. H. Easom and Negro Education in Mississippi." *Mississippi Education Journal* 15 (November 1938): 26–27.

Brawley, Benjamin. *Doctor Dillard of the Jeanes Fund.* 1930. Reprint, Freeport, N.Y.: Books for Libraries Press, 1971.

Brown, Claudia R. *A Survey of North Carolina's Rosenwald Schools: A Public-Private Partnership for Historic Preservation.* North Carolina State Historic Preservation Office. http://www.hpo.dcr.state.nc.us/rosenwald/rosenwald.htm.

Brown, Hugh Victor. *E-qual-ity Education in North Carolina among Negroes.* Raleigh, N.C.: Irving-Swain Press, 1964.

Brundage, W. Fitzhugh. *Lynching in the New South: Georgia and Virginia, 1880–1930.* Urbana: University of Illinois Press, 1993.

Bullock, Henry Allen. *A History of Negro Education in the South: From 1619 to the Present.* Cambridge: Harvard University Press, 1967.

Carbaugh, James C. "The Philanthropic Confluence of the General Education Board and the Jeanes, Slater, and Rosenwald Funds: African-American Education in South Carolina, 1900–1930." Ph.D. diss., Clemson University, 1997.

Cecelski, David S. *Along Freedom Road: Hyde County, North Carolina, and the Fate of Black Schools in the South.* Chapel Hill: University of North Carolina Press, 1994.

Chester Shell Elementary School. http://www.sbac.edu/~shell/.

Chirhart, Ann Short. "'Better for Us Than It Was for Her': African American Families, Communities, and Reform in Modern Georgia." *Journal of Family History* 28, no. 4 (October 2003): 578–602.

———. *Torches of Light: Georgia Teachers and the Coming of the Modern South.* Athens: University of Georgia Press, 2005.

Church, Roberta, and Ronald Walter. "Robert Reed Church, Jr., 1885–1952." In *Profiles of African Americans in Tennessee,* edited by Bobby L. Lovett and Linda T. Wynn, 32–34. Nashville: Annual Local Conference on Afro-American Culture and History, 1996.

Clarke, Nina H., and Lillian B. Brown. *History of the Black Public Schools of Montgomery County, Maryland 1872–1961.* New York: Vantage Press, 1978.

Clay, Robert E. "The Lifework of Dr. S. L. Smith in the Dual Educational System." *Tennessee Teacher* 5 (December 1937): 11–12.

"Clinton J. Calloway, A.B." In *The National Cyclopedia of the Colored Race,* edited by Clement Richardson, 1:25. Montgomery: National Publishing, 1919.

Cohen, Sol. "The Industrial Education Movement, 1906–17." *American Quarterly* 20, no. 1 (Spring 1968): 95–110.

Cooke, Dennis Hargrove. *The White Superintendent and the Negro Schools in North Carolina.* Peabody Contributions to Education no. 73. Nashville: George Peabody College for Teachers, 1930.

Couto, Richard A. *Lifting the Veil: A Political History of Struggles for Emancipation.* Knoxville: University of Tennessee Press, 1993.

Crippens, Nathaniel. "School History." *The Nelsenior.* Yearbook of the Nelson Merry High School, Jefferson County, Tenn. 1943.

Crow, Eugene Ryan. "Some Effects of Farm Tenancy on Public Education in South Carolina." Master's thesis, University of South Carolina, 1924.

Curry, J.L.M. *A Brief Sketch of George Peabody, and a History of the Peabody Education Fund through Thirty Years.* Cambridge: Cambridge University Press, 1898. Reprint, New York: Negro Universities Press, 1969.

Cutler, William W., III. "Cathedral of Culture: The Schoolhouse in American Educational Thought and Practice since 1820." *History of Education Quarterly* 29, no. 1 (Spring 1989): 1–40.

[Cyriaque, Jeanne]. "The Last Rosenwald School." *Reflections* (newsletter of the Georgia African American Historic Preservation Network, Historic Preservation Division) 4, no. 2 (April 2004): 1–2.

Dabney, Charles William. *Universal Education in the South.* Vol. 2, *The Southern Education Movement.* Chapel Hill: University of North Carolina Press, 1936.

Dansby, B. Baldwin. *A Brief History of Jackson College: A Typical Story of the Survival of Education among Negroes in the South.* Jackson: Miss.: Jackson State College, 1953.

Davis, William R. *The Development and Present Status of Negro Education in East Texas.* Teachers College, Columbia University, Contributions to Education no. 626. New York: Teachers College, Columbia University Bureau of Publications, 1934. Reprint, New York: AMS Press, 1972.

Dennis, Michael. *Lessons in Progress: State Universities and Progressivism in the New South, 1880–1920.* Urbana: University of Illinois Press, 2001.

———. "Schooling along the Color Line: Progressives and the Education of Blacks in the New South." *Journal of Negro Education* 67, no. 2 (Spring 1998): 142–56.

Dillingham, George A. *The Foundation of the Peabody Tradition.* Lanham, Md.: University Press of America, 1989.

Dittmer, John. *Black Georgia in the Progressive Era, 1900–1920.* Urbana: University of Illinois Press, 1977.

Donohue, John J., III, James J. Heckman, and Petra E. Todd. "The Schooling of Southern Blacks: The Roles of Legal Activism and Private Philanthropy, 1910–1960." Stanford Law School Public Law and Legal Theory Working Paper no. 11 and John M. Olin Program in Law and Economics Working Paper no. 198. http://lawschool.stanford. edu/olin/workingpapers/WP198DONOHUE.pdf.

Drexler, Arthur. *The Drawings of Frank Lloyd Wright.* New York: Horizon Press for the Museum of Modern Art, 1962.

Du Bois, W.E.B. *The Negro Common School.* Atlanta University Publications no. 6. Atlanta: Atlanta University Press, 1901.

———. *The Souls of Black Folks: Essays and Sketches.* Chicago: A. C. McClurg, 1903. Reprint, New York: Signet/Penguin Books, 1995.

Dunne, Matthew William. "Next Steps: Charles S. Johnson and Southern Liberalism." *Journal of Negro History* 83, no. 1 (Winter 1998): 1–34.

Durusau, Mary. "Pioneers in Black Education Finally Noted." *Sunday Advocate*, 16 February 1986. Reprinted in http://www.alhgs.com/pub-pioneers.html.

Eaton, James N., Murell Dawson, Sharyn Thompson, and Gwendolyn Waldorf. *Historical and Architectural Survey of the Florida Agricultural and Mechanical University.* Vol. 1. Tallahassee: 1995.

Embree, Edwin R. *American Negroes: A Handbook.* New York: John Day, [1942].

———. *Brown America: The Story of a New Race.* New York: Viking Press, 1931.

———. *Island India Goes to School.* With Margaret Sargent Simon and W. Bryant Mumford. Chicago: University of Chicago Press, [1934].

Embree, Edwin R., and Julia Waxman. *Investment in People: The Story of the Julius Rosenwald Fund.* New York: Harper and Brothers, 1949.

Emmet, Boris, and John E. Jeuck. *Catalogues and Counters: A History of Sears, Roebuck and Company.* Chicago: University of Chicago Press, 1950.

Enck, Henry S. "Black Self-Help in the Progressive Era: The 'Northern Campaigns' of Smaller Southern Black Industrial Schools, 1900–1915." *Journal of Negro History* 61, no. 1 (January 1976): 73–87.

———. "Tuskegee Institute and Northern White Philanthropy: A Case Study in Fund Raising, 1900–1915." *Journal of Negro History* 65, no. 4 (Fall 1980): 336–48.

Engs, Robert F. *Educating the Disfranchised and Disinherited: Samuel Chapman Armstrong and Hampton Institute, 1839–1893.* Knoxville: University of Tennessee Press, 1999.

Fairclough, Adam. "'Being in the Field of Education and Also Being a Negro . . . Seems . . . Tragic': Black Teachers in the Jim Crow South." *Journal of American History* 87, no. 1 (June 2000): 66.

———. *Race and Democracy: The Civil Rights Struggle in Louisiana, 1915–1972.* Athens: University of Georgia Press, 1995.

———. *Teaching Equality: Black Schools in the Age of Jim Crow.* Athens: University of Georgia Press, 2001.

Finnegan, Terence. "Lynching and Political Power in Mississippi and South Carolina." In *Under Sentence of Death: Lynching in the South,* edited by W. Fitzhugh Brundage, 189–218. Chapel Hill: University of North Carolina Press, 1997.

Fisher, John E. *The John F. Slater Fund: A Nineteenth Century Affirmative Action for Negro Education.* Lanham, Md.: University Press of America, 1986.

Fleming, Cynthia Griggs. "The Plight of Black Educators in Postwar Tennessee, 1865–1920." *Journal of Negro History* 64, no. 4 (Fall 1979): 355–64.

Foreman, Clark. *Environmental Factors in Negro Elementary Education.* New York: W. W. Norton for the Julius Rosenwald Fund, 1932.

Fosdick, Raymond B. *Adventure in Giving: The Story of the General Education Board.* New York: Harper and Row, 1962.

Foster, A. L. "History of Fight for Housing Project Told." *Chicago Defender,* 26 October 1940, 16. In *Racial and Religious Covenants in the U.S. and Canada,* by Wendy Plotkin. http://www.public.asu.edu/~wplotkin/DeedsWeb/wells.html.

"Francis Marion Wood." *Archives of Maryland Online* 509, 1. http://www.mdarchives.state.md.us/megafile/msa/speccol/sc2900/sc2908/000001/000509/html.

Franklin, V. P., and Carter Julian Savage, eds. *Cultural Capital and Black Education: African American Communities and the Funding of Black Schooling, 1865 to the Present.* Greenwich, Conn.: Information Age, 2004.

Freedman, David. "African-American Schooling in the South Prior to 1861." *Journal of Negro History* 84, no. 1 (Winter 1999): 1–47.

Fultz, Michael. "African American Teachers in the South, 1890–1940: Powerlessness and the Ironies of Expectations and Protest." *History of Education Quarterly* 35, no. 4 (Winter 1995): 400–422.

———. "'The Morning Cometh': African-American Periodicals, Education, and the Black Middle Class, 1900–1930." *Journal of Negro History* 80, no. 3 (Summer 1995): 97–112.

Gaines, Kevin K. *Uplifting the Race: Black Leadership, Politics, and Culture in the Twentieth Century.* Chapel Hill: University of North Carolina Press, 1996.

Gasman, Marybeth. "W.E.B. Du Bois and Charles S. Johnson: Differing Views on the Role of Philanthropy in Higher Education." *History of Education Quarterly* 42, no.4 (Winter 2002): 493–516.

General Education Board: Review and Final Report, 1902–1964. New York: General Education Board, 1964.

Generals, Donald. "Booker T. Washington and Progressive Education: An Experimentalist Approach to Curriculum Development and Reform." *Journal of Negro Education* 69, no. 3 (Summer 2000): 215–34.

Gill, Peggy B. "Community, Commitment, and African American Education: The Jackson School of Smith County, Texas, 1925–1954." In *Cultural Capital and Black Education: African American Communities and the Funding of Black Schooling, 1865 to the Present,* edited by V. P. Franklin and Carter Julian Savage, 81–96. Greenwich, Conn.: Information Age, 2004.

Gilli, Angelo C., Sr. "History of Colored Schools in Maryland." Typescript. Maryland State Archives, Annapolis, Maryland, [1992?].

Gilmore, Glenda Elizabeth. *Gender and Jim Crow: Women and the Politics of White Supremacy in North Carolina, 1896–1920.* Chapel Hill: University of North Carolina Press, 1996.

Gilpin, Patrick J., and Marybeth Gasman. *Charles S. Johnson: Leadership beyond the Veil in the Age of Jim Crow.* Albany: State University of New York Press, 2003.

Glave, Dianne D. "'A Garden So Brilliant with Colors, So Original in Its Design': Rural African American Women, Gardening, Progressive Reform, and the Foundation of an African American Environmental Perspective." *Environmental History* 8, no. 3 (July 2003): 395–411.

Goggin, Jacqueline. *Carter G. Woodson: A Life in Black History.* Baton Rouge: Louisiana State University Press, 1993.

Goodenow, Ronald K. "Separate and Unequal Progressive Education: A Southern Case Study." In *Education and the Rise of the New South,* edited by Ronald K. Goodenow and Arthur O. White, 196–214. Boston: G. K. Hall, 1981.

Gormon, Bob, and Lois Stickell. "Partners in Progress: Joseph B. Felton, the African-American Community, and the Rosenwald School Program." *Carologue* 18 (Fall 2002): 14–20.

Granberry, Dorothy. "Black Community Leadership in a Rural Tennessee County, 1865–1903." *Journal of Negro History* 83, no. 4 (Fall 1998): 249–57.

Grantham, Dewey W. *Southern Progressivism: The Reconciliation of Progress and Tradition*. Knoxville: University of Tennessee Press, 1983.

Gray, Jerome A., Joe L. Reed, and Norman W. Walton. *History of the Alabama State Teachers Association*. Washington, D.C.: National Education Association, 1987.

Guide for Planning School Plants. National Council on Schoolhouse Construction, 1949.

Hahn, Steven. *A Nation under Our Feet: Black Political Struggles in the Rural South from Slavery to the Great Migration*. Cambridge: Harvard University Press, 2003.

Hale, Grace Elizabeth. *Making Whiteness: The Culture of Segregation in the South, 1890–1940*. New York: Vintage Books, 1999.

Haley, John. *Charles N. Hunter and Race Relations in North Carolina*. James Sprunt Studies in History and Political Science, vol. 60. Chapel Hill: University of North Carolina Press, 1987.

Hall, Clyde W. *Black Vocational, Technical, and Industrial Arts Education: Development and History*. Chicago: American Technical Society, 1973.

Hanchett, Thomas W. "The Rosenwald Schools and Black Education in North Carolina." *North Carolina Historical Review* 65, no. 4 (October 1988): 387–427.

Hardin, John A. *Onward and Upward: A Centennial History of Kentucky State University, 1886–1986*. Frankfort: Kentucky State University, 1987.

Harlan, Louis R. *Booker T. Washington in Perspective: Essays of Louis R. Harlan*. Edited by Raymond W. Smock. Jackson: University Press of Mississippi, 1988.

———. *Booker T. Washington: The Making of a Black Leader, 1856–1901*. New York: Oxford University Press, 1972.

———. *Booker T. Washington: The Wizard of Tuskegee, 1901–1915*. New York: Oxford University Press, 1983.

———. *Separate and Unequal: Public School Campaigns and Racism in the Southern Seaboard States, 1901–1915*. Chapel Hill: University of North Carolina Press, 1958.

———. "The Southern Education Board and the Race Issue in Public Education." *Journal of Southern History* 23, no. 2 (May 1957): 189–202.

Hawkins, Andy. "The Rosenwald Schools: The Chicago Connection." *Mid-Carolina Journal* 1, no. 1 (Winter 1988–1989): 20.

Herman, Debra, and Althemese Barnes, *African-American Education in Leon County, Florida: Emancipation through Desegregation, 1863–1968*. Tallahassee, Fla.: John G. Riley Research Center and Museum of African-American History, 1997.

Hicks, William. *History of Louisiana Negro Baptists from 1804 to 1914*. Nashville: National Baptist Publishing Board, [1915]. University of North Carolina Library, *Documenting the American South*. http://docsouth.unc.edu/church/hicks/menu/html.

Hine, Darlene Clark. "Carter G. Woodson, White Philanthropy and Negro Historiography." *History Teacher* 19, no. 3 (May 1986): 405–25.

Hoffschwelle, Mary S. *Preserving Rosenwald Schools*. Washington, D.C.: National Trust for Historic Preservation, 2003.

—————. *Rebuilding the Rural Southern Community: Reformers, Schools, and Homes in Tennessee, 1900–1930.* Knoxville: University of Tennessee Press, 1998.

"In Memoriam" [Fletcher B. Dresslar]. *Peabody Reflector* 3 (March 1930): 5–8, 19.

Irby, Nolen Meaders. *A Program for the Equalization of Educational Opportunities in the State of Arkansas.* George Peabody College for Teachers Contribution to Education no. 83. Nashville: George Peabody College for Teachers, 1930.

Jackson, Luther P. *A History of the Virginia State Teachers Association.* Norfolk, Va.: Guide Publishing, 1937.

Jarrette, Alfred Q. *Julius Rosenwald: Son of a Jewish Immigrant, A Builder of Sears, Roebuck and Company, Benefactor of Mankind.* Greenville, S.C.: Southeastern University Press, 1975.

Jeanes Supervision in Georgia Schools, A Guiding Light for Education: A History of the Program from 1908–1975. [Atlanta?]: Georgia Association of Jeanes Curriculum Directors and Southern Education Foundation, 1975.

Johnson, Charles S. *The Collapse of Cotton Tenancy: Summary of Field Studies and Statistical Surveys, 1933–35.* With Edwin R. Embree and Will W. Alexander. Chapel Hill: University of North Carolina Press, 1935.

Jones, Allen W. "The Role of Tuskegee Institute in the Education of Black Farmers." *Journal of Negro History* 60, no. 2 (April 1975): 252–67.

Jones, Faustine Childress. *A Traditional Model of Educational Excellence: Dunbar High School of Little Rock, Arkansas.* Washington, D.C.: Howard University Press, 1981.

Jones, Lu Ann. *Mama Learned Us to Work: Farm Women in the New South.* Chapel Hill: University of North Carolina Press, 2002.

Jones, Reinette F. "Kentucky Negro Education Association (KNEA) Journal: Accounting of Librarians and Libraries." *Kentucky Libraries.* http://www.uky.edu/Subject/knea.html.

Jordan, Elizabeth Cobb. "The Impact of the Negro Organization Society on Public Support for Education in Virginia, 1912–1950." Ed.D. diss., University of Virginia, 1978.

Kantor, Harvey A. *Learning to Earn: School, Work, and Vocational Reform in California, 1880–1930.* Madison: University of Wisconsin Press, 1988.

Kasprzak, John F. "George Peabody and the Peabody Education Fund: A Study in Reconciliation." Master's thesis, American University, 1966.

Keith, Jeanette. *Country People in the New South: Tennessee's Upper Cumberland.* Chapel Hill: University of North Carolina Press, 1995.

Kett, Joseph F. "The Adolescence of Vocational Education." In *Work, Youth, and Schooling: Historical Perspectives on Vocationalism in American Education,* edited by Harvey Kantor and David B. Tyack, 79–109. Stanford, Calif.: Stanford University Press, 1982.

Kirby, Jack Temple. *Darkness at the Dawning: Race and Reform in the Progressive South.* Philadelphia: J. B. Lippincott, 1972.

Kirsner, Douglas. *Unfree Associations inside Psychoanalytic Institutes.* http://human-nature.com/kirsner/chap3.html.

Kliebard, Herbert M. *Schooled to Work: Vocationalism and the American Curriculum, 1876–1946.* New York: Teachers College Press, 1999.

Kousser, J. Morgan. "Progressivism—For Middle-Class Whites Only: North Carolina Education, 1880–1910." *Journal of Southern History* 46, no. 2 (May 1980): 169–94.

Krause, Bonnie. "The Jeanes Supervisor: Agent of Change in Mississippi's African American Education." *Journal of Mississippi History* 65, no. 2 (Summer 2003): 127–45.

———. "'We Did Move Mountains!': Lucy Saunders Herring, North Carolina Jeanes Supervisor and African American Educator, 1916–1968," *North Carolina Historical Review* 80, no. 2 (April 2003): 188–212.

Leake, Janet Scott. "Survey of the Negro Public Schools of Columbia, South Carolina." Master's thesis, University of South Carolina, 1932.

Leavell, Ullin Whitney. *Philanthropy in Negro Education.* George Peabody College for Teachers Contributions to Education no. 100. Nashville: George Peabody College for Teachers, 1930.

Leloudis, James L. *Schooling the New South: Pedagogy, Self, and Society in North Carolina, 1880–1920.* Chapel Hill: University of North Carolina Press, 1996.

———. "School Reform in the New South: The Woman's Association for the Betterment of Public School Houses in North Carolina, 1902–1919." *Journal of American History* 69, no. 4 (March 1983): 886–909.

Lewis, David Levering. *W.E.B. Du Bois: Biography of a Race, 1868–1919.* New York: Henry Holt, 1993.

———. *W.E.B. Du Bois: The Fight for Equality and the American Century, 1919–1963.* New York: Henry Holt, 2000.

Lewis, Earl. "Invoking Concepts, Problematizing Identities: The Life of Charles N. Hunter and the Implications for the Study of Gender and Labor." *Labor History* 34, nos. 2–3 (Spring-Summer 1993): 292–308.

Link, William A. *A Hard Country and a Lonely Place: Schooling, Society, and Reform in Rural Virginia, 1870–1920.* Chapel Hill: University of North Carolina Press, 1986.

———. *The Paradox of Southern Progressivism, 1880–1930.* Chapel Hill: University of North Carolina Press, 1992.

———. "Privies, Progressivism, and Public Schools: Health Reform and Education in the Rural South, 1909–1920." *Journal of Southern History* 54, no. 4 (November 1988): 623–42.

Litwack, Leon. *Trouble in Mind: Black Southerners in the Age of Jim Crow.* New York: Alfred A. Knopf, 1998.

Margo, Robert A. "Race Differences in Public School Expenditures: Disfranchisement and School Finance in Louisiana, 1890–1910." *Social Science History* 6, no. 1 (Winter 1982): 9–33.

McClure, Phyllis. "Rosenwald Schools in the Northern Neck." *Virginia Magazine of History and Biography* 113, no. 2 (2005): 114–45.

McCormick, J. Scott. "The Julius Rosenwald Fund." *Journal of Negro Education* 3, no. 4 (October 1934): 605–26.

McCuistion, Fred. *Graduate Instruction for Negroes in the United States.* George Peabody College for Teachers Contribution to Education no. 255. Nashville: George Peabody College for Teachers, 1939.

McGerr, Michael. *A Fierce Discontent: The Rise and Fall of the Progressive Movement in America, 1870–1920.* New York: Free Press, 2003.

McMillen, Neil R. *Dark Journey: Black Mississippians in the Age of Jim Crow.* Urbana: University of Illinois Press, 1989.

Meece, Leonard Ephraim. "Negro Education in Kentucky." *Bulletin of the Bureau of School Service* 10, no. 3 (March 1938): 67–76.

Meier, August, and Elliott Rudwick. *Black History and the Historical Profession, 1915–1980.* Urbana: University of Illinois Press, 1986.

Miller, William D. *Mr. Crump of Memphis.* Baton Rouge: Louisiana State University Press, 1964.

Mississippi Retired Teachers Association. *Bells Are Ringing.* Jackson, Miss.: Jackson Public Schools Print Shop, 1976.

Mitchell, Guy Clifford. "Growth of State Control of Public Education in Louisiana." Ph.D. diss., University of Michigan, 1942.

Mitchell, Mary Niall. "'A Good and Delicious Country': Free Children of Color and How They Learned to Imagine the Atlantic World in Nineteenth-Century Louisiana." In *Chartered Schools: Two Hundred Years of Independent Academies in the United States, 1727–1925,* edited by Nancy Beadie and Kim Tolley, 137–57. New York: Routledge-Falmer, 2002.

Mitchell, Theodore R., and Robert Lowe. "To Sow Contentment: Philanthropy, Scientific Agriculture, and the Making of the New South: 1906–1920." *Journal of Social History* 24, no. 2 (Winter 1990): 317–40.

Morgan, Harry. *Historical Perspectives on the Education of Black Children.* Westport, Conn.: Praeger, 1995.

Morris, Eleanor Robinson. "The Julius Rosenwald High School of Northumberland County, Virginia." *Bulletin of the Northumberland County Historical Society* 29 (1992): 61–68.

Murray, Percy. *History of the North Carolina Teachers Association.* [Washington, D.C.]: National Education Association, [1984].

The Negro Year Book: An Annual Encyclopedia of the Negro. Compiled by Monroe N. Work. Tuskegee, Ala.: Negro Year Book Publishing Company, 1912–31/32.

Nelum, Junior Nathaniel. "A Study of the First Seventy Years of the Colored Teachers State Association of Texas." Ed.D. diss., University of Texas, 1955.

Nieves, Angel David. "'We Gave Our Hearts and Lives to It': African-American Women Reformers, Industrial Education, and the Monuments of Nation-Building in the Post-Reconstruction South, 1877–1938." Ph.D. diss., Cornell University, 2001.

Patterson, Thomas E. *History of the Arkansas State Teachers Association.* Washington, D.C.: National Education Association, 1981.

Pearl, Susan G. *African-American Heritage Survey, 1996.* Upper Marlboro: Maryland-National Capital Park and Planning Commission, Prince George's County Planning Department, 1996.

Perkins, Alfred. "Welcome Consequences and Fulfilled Promise: Julius Rosenwald Fellows and *Brown v. Board of Education.*" *Journal of Negro Education* 72, no. 3 (Summer 2003): 344–56.

Perry, Thelma D. *History of the American Teachers Association.* Washington, D.C.: National Education Association, 1975.

Pfeiffer, Bruce Brooks, and Robert Wojtowicz, eds. *Frank Lloyd Wright and Lewis Mumford: Thirty Years of Correspondence.* New York: Princeton Architectural Press, 2001.

Pitts, Winfred E. "Three Who Cared: Beulah Rucker, E. E. Butler, and Ulysses Byas—Twentieth-Century Trailblazers in Education for African Americans in Gainesville, Georgia." *Georgia Historical Quarterly* 87, no. 2 (Summer 2003): 245–74.

Posey, Josephine McCann. *Against Great Odds: The History of Alcorn State University.* Jackson: University Press of Mississippi, 1994.

Prather, H. Leon, Sr. *Resurgent Politics and Educational Progressivism in the New South: North Carolina, 1890–1913.* Rutherford, N.J.: Fairleigh Dickinson University Press, 1979.

Quinan, Jack. *Frank Lloyd Wright's Martin House: Architecture as Portraiture.* New York: Princeton Architectural Press, 2004.

Randle, Lisa B. "Mt. Zion Rosenwald School." National Register of Historic Places Nomination Form. Washington, D.C.: U.S. Department of the Interior, 2001.

"R. C. Foster." *Alabama's Music Hall of Fame.* http://www.alamhof.org/fosterrc.htm.

Redcay, Edward E. *County Training Schools and Public Secondary Education for Negroes in the South.* Washington, D.C.: John F. Slater Fund, 1935.

Reed, Betty J. *The Brevard Rosenwald School: Black Education and Community Building in a Southern Appalachian Town, 1920–1966.* Jefferson, N.C.: McFarland, 2004.

Retrospective Glances of Limestone County Negro Education. Limestone County Negro Teachers Association, 1947.

Rhodes, Lelia G. *Jackson State University: The First Hundred Years, 1877–1977.* Jackson: University Press of Mississippi, 1979.

Richardson, Archie G. *The Development of Negro Education in Virginia, 1831–1970.* [Richmond?]: Richmond, Virginia, chapter, Phi Delta Kappa, 1976.

Robbins, Richard. *Sidelines Activist: Charles S. Johnson and the Struggle for Civil Rights.* Jackson: University Press of Mississippi, 1996.

Rogers, Lucille. *Light from Many Candles: A History of Pioneer Women in Education in Tennessee.* Nashville: Xi State, Delta Kappa Gamma, 1960.

Russell, Harvey C. *The Kentucky Negro Education Association.* Norfolk, Va.: Guide Quality Press, 1946.

Savage, Cynthia J. "The Julius Rosenwald Fund: Northern Philanthropy in Oklahoma's Separate Schools." *Chronicles of Oklahoma* 77, no. 1 (Spring 1999): 4–21.

Scardaville, Michael et al. *A Brief History of South Carolina Schools from 1895 to 1945.* Columbia: South Carolina Department of Archives and History, 1989.

Seroff, Doug. "Gospel Quartet Singing in Jefferson County, Alabama." *The Database of Recorded American Music.* http://dlib.home.nyu.edu/dram/Objid/2588.

Shaw, Stephanie J. *What a Woman Ought to Be and to Do: Black Professional Women Workers during the Jim Crow Era.* Chicago: University of Chicago Press, 1996.

Sherer, Robert G. *Subordination or Liberation?: The Development and Conflicting Theories of Black Education in Nineteenth-Century Alabama.* University: University of Alabama Press, 1977.

Siddle Walker, Vanessa. "Organized Resistance and Black Educators' Quest For School Equality, 1878–1938." *Teachers College Record* 107, no. 3 (2005): 355–88.

———. *Their Highest Potential: An African American School Community in the Segregated South.* Chapel Hill: University of North Carolina Press, 1996.

Smith, J. Douglas. *Managing White Supremacy: Race, Politics, and Citizenship in Jim Crow Virginia.* Chapel Hill: University of North Carolina Press, 2002.

Smith, Patti Elizabeth. "The Distribution of Rosenwald Schools in Louisiana and Their Suggested Impact on Black Education." Master's thesis, Louisiana State University, 1992.

Smith, Samuel L. *Builders of Goodwill: The Story of the State Agents of Negro Education in the South, 1910 to 1950.* Nashville: Tennessee Book, 1950.

Span, Christopher M. "Alternative Pedagogy: The Rise of the Private Black Academy in Early Postbellum Mississippi, 1862–1870." In *Chartered Schools: Two Hundred Years of Independent Academies in the United States, 1727–1925,* edited by Nancy Beadie and Kim Tolley, 211–27. New York: RoutledgeFalmer, 2002.

———. "'I Must Learn Now or Not At All': Social and Cultural Capital in the Educational Initiatives of Formerly Enslaved African Americans in Mississippi." In *Cultural Capital and Black Education: African American Communities and the Funding of Black Schooling, 1865 to the Present,* edited by V. P. Franklin and Carter Julian Savage, 1–13. Greenwich, Conn.: Information Age, 2004.

Spivey, Donald. *Schooling for the New Slavery: Black Industrial Education, 1868–1915.* Westport, Conn.: Greenwood Press, 1978.

Stanfield, John H. "Dollars for the Silent South: Southern White Liberalism and the Julius Rosenwald Fund, 1928–1948." In *Perspectives on the American South: An Annual Review of Society, Politics and Culture,* edited by Merle Black and John Shelton Reed, 117–38. New York: Gordon and Breach Science Publishers, 1984.

Stitely, Thomas Beane. "Bridging the Gap: A History of the Rosenwald Fund in the Development of Rural Negro Schools in Tennessee, 1912–1932." Ph.D. diss, George Peabody College for Teachers, 1975.

Stokes, Anson Phelps. *Tuskegee Institute: The First Fifty Years*. Tuskegee, Ala.: Tuskegee Institute Press, 1931.

Strong, David, Pamela Barnhouse Walters, Brian Driscoll, and Scott Rosenberg. "Leveraging the State: Private Money and the Development of Public Education for Blacks." *American Sociological Review* 65, no. 5 (October 2000): 658–81.

Taggart, Robert J. *Private Philanthropy and Public Education: Pierre S. du Pont and the Delaware Schools, 1890–1940*. Newark: University of Delaware Press, 1988.

Taylor, Douglas Barnes. "Negro Education in Texas." Master's thesis, University of Texas, 1927.

Thompson, Cleopatra D. *The History of the Mississippi Teachers Association*. Washington, D.C.: NEA Teachers' Rights; Jackson: Mississippi Teachers Association, 1973.

Thompson, Herbert W. "A History of Negro Education in the Catawba School System from 1865 to 1960." Ed.D. diss., Pennsylvania State University, 1964.

Through Schoolhouse Doors: A History of Lake County Schools. Lake County [Florida] Retired Teachers Association, 1982.

Tindall, George B. *The Emergence of the New South, 1913–1945*. Baton Rouge: Louisiana State University Press, 1967.

Tolnay, Stewart E. *The Bottom Rung: African American Family Life on Southern Farms*. Urbana: University of Illinois Press, 1999.

Tolnay, Stewart E., and E. M. Beck. *A Festival of Violence: An Analysis of Southern Lynchings, 1882–1930*. Urbana: University of Illinois Press, 1995.

Turley-Adams, Alicestyne. *Rosenwald Schools in Kentucky, 1917–1932*. Prepared for the Kentucky Heritage Council and the Kentucky African American Heritage Commission, 1997.

Turner, Kara Miles. "'Getting It Straight': Southern Black School Patrons and the Struggle for Equal Rights in the Pre- and Post-Civil Rights Eras." *Journal of Negro Education* 72, no. 2 (Spring 2003): 217–29.

Van Slyck, Abigail A. *Free to All: Carnegie Libraries and American Culture, 1890–1920*. Chicago: University of Chicago Press, 1995.

Vincent, Charles. *A Centennial History of Southern University and A&M College, 1880–1980*. Baton Rouge: Southern University, 1981.

Violas, Paul Constantine. "Reflections on Theories of Human Capital, Skills Training and Vocational Education." *Educational Theory* 31, no. 2 (Spring 1981): 137–51.

Wadsworth, Erwin Winningham. "A Historical Perspective of Education in Macon County, Alabama, 1836–1967." Ed.D. diss., Auburn University, 1968.

Walker, Melissa. *All We Knew Was to Farm: Rural Women in the Upcountry South, 1919–1941*. Baltimore: Johns Hopkins University Press, 2000.

Walters, Pamela Barnhouse. "Educational Access and the State: Historical Continuities and Discontinuities in Racial Inequality in American Education." *Sociology of Education*, extra issue (2001): 35–49.

Walters, Pamela Barnhouse, David R. James, and Holly J. McCammon. "Citizenship and Public Schools: Accounting for Racial Inequality in Education in the Pre- and Post-Disfranchisement South." *American Sociological Review* 62, no. 1 (February 1997): 34–52.

Watkins, Levi. *Alabama State University: A History of the First One Hundred and Fourteen Years, 1867–1981.* Montgomery: Alabama State University, 1994.

Weiss, Ellen. "Robert R. Taylor of Tuskegee: An Early Black American Architect." *ARRIS: Journal of the Southeast Chapter of the Society of Architectural Historians* 2 (1991): 3–19.

———. "Tuskegee: Landscape in Black and White." *Winterthur Portfolio* 36, no. 1 (Spring 2001): 19–37.

Werner, Morris R. *Julius Rosenwald: The Life of a Practical Humanitarian.* New York: Harper and Brothers, 1939.

Westbrook, Gayle Williams. "The Struggle for Educational Equity and Access: The Role of the Rosenwald Philanthropy in the Establishment of Gilmore Academy in Marianna, Florida." Ph.D. diss., Florida Agricultural and Mechanical University, 2000.

Williams, Clarence G. "From 'Tech' to Tuskegee: The Life of Robert Robinson Taylor, 1868–1942." *MIT Archives and Special Collections.* http://libraries.mit.edu/archives/mithistory/blacks-at-mit/taylor.html.

Williams, Mildred M., Kara Vaughn Jackson, Madie A. Kincy, Susie W. Wheeler, Rebecca Davis, Rebecca A. Crawford, Maggie Forte, and Ethel Bell. *The Jeanes Story: A Chapter in the History of American Education, 1908–1968.* Jackson, Miss.: Southern Education Foundation, 1979.

Wilson, Louis R., and Edward A. Wight. *County Library Service in the South: A Study of the Rosenwald County Library Demonstration.* Chicago: University of Chicago Press, [1935].

Woods, Jerry Wayne. "The Julius Rosenwald Fund School Building Program: A Saga in the Growth and Development of African-American Education in Selected West Tennessee Communities." Ed.D. diss., University of Mississippi, 1995.

Woodson, Carter G. *The Education of the Negro Prior to 1861.* New York: G. P. Putnam's Sons, 1915. Reprint, New York: Arno Press, 1968.

———. *The Rural Negro.* Washington, D.C.: Association Publishers, 1930. Reprint, New York: Russell and Russell, [1969].

Wright, Arthur D. *The Negro Rural School Fund, Inc. (Anna T. Jeanes Foundation), 1917–1933.* With Edward E. Redcay. Washington, D.C.: Negro Rural School Fund, 1933.

Wyatt-Brown, Bertram. "Black Schooling during Reconstruction." In *The Web of Southern Social Relations: Women, Family, and Education,* edited by Walter J. Fraser Jr., R. Frank Saunders Jr., and Jon L. Wakelyn, 145–65. Athens: University of Georgia Press, 1985.

Mary S. Hoffschwelle is professor of history at Middle Tennessee State University. She is the author of *Rebuilding the Rural Southern Community: Reformers, Schools, and Homes in Tennessee, 1900–1930* (1998) and *Preserving Rosenwald Schools* (2003).

Index

Mary S. Hoffschwelle is professor of history at Middle Tennessee State University. She is the author of *Rebuilding the Rural Southern Community: Reformers, Schools, and Homes in Tennessee, 1900–1930* (1998) and *Preserving Rosenwald Schools* (2003).